TAKING
ACTION

A Handbook for RTI at Work™

SECOND EDITION

Mike **Mattos** ◆ Austin **Buffum** ◆ Janet **Malone**

Luis F. **Cruz** ◆ Nicole **Dimich** ◆ Sarah **Schuhl**

Solution Tree | Press

a division of
Solution Tree

555 North Morton Street
Bloomington, IN 47404
800.733.6786 (toll free) / 812.336.7700
FAX: 812.336.7790

email: info@SolutionTree.com
SolutionTree.com

Visit **go.SolutionTree.com/RTIatWork** to download the free reproducibles in this book.

Printed in the United States of America

Library of Congress Cataloging-in-Publication Data

Names: Mattos, Mike (Mike William) author. | Buffum, Austin G. author. | Malone, Janet, author. | Cruz, Luis F., author. | Dimich, Nicole, author. | Schuhl, Sarah, author.
Title: Taking action : a handbook for RTI at work / Mike Mattos, Austin Buffum, Janet Malone, Luis F. Cruz, Nicole Dimich, Sarah Schuhl.
Other titles: Handbook for response to intervention at work
Description: Second edition. | Bloomington, IN : Solution Tree Press, [2025] | First edition published in 2018. | Includes bibliographical references and index.
Identifiers: LCCN 2024014817 (print) | LCCN 2024014818 (ebook) | ISBN 9781958590430 (paperback) | ISBN 9781958590447 (ebook)
Subjects: LCSH: Response to intervention (Learning disabled children)--United States. | Learning disabled children--Education--United States. | Individualized instruction--United States.
Classification: LCC LC4705 .B85 2025 (print) | LCC LC4705 (ebook) | DDC 371.9--dc23/eng/20240609
LC record available at https://lccn.loc.gov/2024014817
LC ebook record available at https://lccn.loc.gov/2024014818

Solution Tree
Jeffrey C. Jones, CEO
Edmund M. Ackerman, President

Solution Tree Press
President and Publisher: Douglas M. Rife
Associate Publishers: Todd Brakke and Kendra Slayton
Editorial Director: Laurel Hecker
Art Director: Rian Anderson
Copy Chief: Jessi Finn
Senior Production Editor: Christine Hood
Copyeditor: Jessi Finn
Proofreader: Mark Hain
Text and Cover Designer: Abigail Bowen
Acquisitions Editors: Carol Collins and Hilary Goff
Content Development Specialist: Amy Rubenstein
Associate Editors: Sarah Ludwig and Elijah Oates
Editorial Assistant: Anne Marie Watkins

With love and gratitude to my sisters and brothers: Marc Galliher, Jacquie Mix, Dawn Petersen, John Taylor, and Karen Coyne.

—MIKE MATTOS

When I was young, my father told me you're lucky if you have two friends in your lifetime; if you have one good friend, you are extremely lucky. Now that I am seventy-six years old, I have found his words to be accurate. I dedicate this book to my dear, true friend, Mike Mattos.

—AUSTIN BUFFUM

I dedicate this book to my grandchildren and the educators who serve them. Finn, Bailey, Parker, and Tahoe, the future is yours!

—JANET MALONE

I dedicate this book to Mike Mattos, Anthony Muhammad, and Pamela Cruz, three of the most influential and highly effective educators I know. Thank you for your support and continuous influence in both my professional and personal lives.

—LUIS F. CRUZ

To all children, who deserve schools that see them for their possibilities, and the countless educators who are pivotal in the relentless pursuit to ensure learning at high levels for all students. And to the amazing people who lift me up and inspire me to be better: Mike Mattos and the RTI team, Linnea Dimich, and Rob and Lorna Anderson.

—NICOLE DIMICH

To those who challenge and inspire me to work toward every student learning: Mike Mattos, Timothy Kanold, Sharon Kramer, Mona Toncheff, my sister Anna Tapley, and the many educators I have had the privilege to work with in school districts across the United States.

—SARAH SCHUHL

ACKNOWLEDGMENTS

We are so grateful for our association and collaboration with Jeffrey Jones, Douglas Rife, and the exceptional professionals at Solution Tree. We know this collaboration has been so successful because we share a common vision: *to transform education worldwide to ensure learning for all*! The publications team, starting with our outstanding editor, has edited and improved every sentence of all our books. Renee Marshall and the events team have made this content available through RTI at Work™ institutes and workshops, while Shannon Ritz and the professional development department have extended our work to schools and districts around the world. Most important, Solution Tree's efforts to promote our work have demonstrated the highest level of professionalism. We look forward to our continued collaboration for years to come.

We call our intervention recommendations RTI *at Work* because we built them on the Professional Learning Community at Work® (PLC at Work) process. We believe it is impossible to develop an effective system of interventions unless the system builds on a school functioning as a PLC. The leading authors of this process—Richard DuFour, Rebecca DuFour, and Robert Eaker—have generously shared their knowledge, expertise, and friendship. We hope this book leads others to the power of the PLC at Work process and honors the work of Rick, Becky, and Bob.

We are also blessed to work with an exceptional team of RTI at Work associates from around the world. They are all outstanding educators. Serving as practitioners, they have gained the depth of knowledge and understanding only achieved through doing the work at the highest levels. They graciously share their expertise with us and with educators from St. Louis to Singapore and beyond.

And like virtually all educators, we view our work as a labor of love. We have a singular focus—to help every student have the kind of future we would want for our own children. When your career requires you to give to others, it is essential to have people in your life who fill your heart and soul with their love. We are so blessed to have these people in our lives. Each of us would like to thank them.

- Mike Mattos: Anita and Laurel Mattos
- Austin Buffum: Lesley Buffum
- Janet Malone: My professional colleague and longtime friend, Diane Cantelli
- Luis F. Cruz: Three very special ladies in my life—Marina, Anali, and Mayita (Your dad loves you always and forever.)
- Nicole Dimich: Maya, Rhys, and Chase Vagle
- Sarah Schuhl: Jon, Jacob, and Sam Schuhl

This book is an extension of the inspiration you fill us with every day.

Visit **go.SolutionTree.com/RTIatWork** to download the
free reproducibles in this book.

TABLE OF CONTENTS

Reproducible pages are in italics.

PART TWO

ABOUT THE AUTHORS

 **Mike Mattos** is an internationally recognized author, presenter, and practitioner. He co-created the RTI at Work™ approach to systematic interventions. Mike is also a thought leader in professional learning communities (PLCs) and the PLC at Work® process, advancing the work of his mentors Richard DuFour and Robert Eaker. In 2024, the Global Gurus organization recognized him as one of the thirty most influential educational thought leaders in the world.

Mike is proud of the twenty-three years he served on-site as a history teacher and, later, an administrator. He is the former principal of Marjorie Veeh Elementary School and Pioneer Middle School in Tustin, California. At both schools, he helped create Model PLCs, improving learning for all students. In 2004, Marjorie Veeh, an elementary school with a large population of youth at risk, won the California Distinguished School and National Title I Achieving School awards.

A National Blue Ribbon School, Pioneer is among only thirteen schools in the United States that the GE Foundation selected as a Best-Practice Partner and is one of eight schools that Richard DuFour chose to feature in the video series *The Power of Professional Learning Communities at Work: Bringing the Big Ideas to Life*. Based on standardized test scores, Pioneer ranked among the top 1 percent of California secondary schools and, in 2009 and 2011, was named Orange County's top middle school. For his leadership, Mike was named the Orange County Middle School Administrator of the Year by the Association of California School Administrators.

Mike has coauthored many best-selling books focused on multitiered systems of supports (MTSS) and PLCs, including *Learning by Doing: A Handbook for Professional Learning Communities at Work*; *Concise Answers to Frequently Asked Questions About Professional Learning Communities at Work*; *Simplifying Response to Intervention: Four Essential Guiding Principles*; *Pyramid Response to Intervention: RTI, Professional Learning Communities, and How to Respond When Kids Don't Learn*; *Uniting Academic and Behavior Interventions: Solving the Skill or Will Dilemma*; *It's About Time: Planning Interventions and Extensions in Secondary School*; *It's About Time: Planning Interventions and Extensions in Elementary School*; *Best Practices at Tier 1: Daily Differentiation for Effective Instruction, Secondary*; *Best Practices at Tier 1: Daily Differentiation for Effective Instruction, Elementary*; and *The Collaborative Administrator: Working Together as a Professional Learning Community*.

To learn more about Mike's work, visit AllThingsPLC (https://allthingsplc.info) and www .mikemattos.info, or follow him @mikemattos65 on X, formerly known as Twitter.

Austin Buffum, EdD, has fifty years of experience in public schools. His many roles include serving as former senior deputy superintendent of California's Capistrano Unified School District. Austin has presented in over nine hundred school districts throughout the United States and around the world. He delivers trainings and presentations on the RTI at Work model. This tiered approach to response to intervention centers on PLC at Work concepts and strategies to ensure every student receives the time and support necessary to succeed. Austin also delivers workshops and presentations that provide the tools educators need to build and sustain PLCs.

Austin was named Curriculum and Instruction Administrator of the Year by the Association of California School Administrators in 2006. He attended the Principals' Center at the Harvard Graduate School of Education and was greatly inspired by its founder, Roland Barth, an early advocate of the collaborative culture that defines PLCs today. He later led Capistrano's K–12 instructional program on an increasingly collaborative path toward operating as a PLC. During this process, thirty-seven of the district's schools were designated California Distinguished Schools, and eleven received National Blue Ribbon recognition.

Austin is coauthor with Suzette Lovely of *Generations at School: Building an Age-Friendly Learning Community.* He has also coauthored *Uniting Academic and Behavior Interventions: Solving the Skill or Will Dilemma*; *It's About Time: Planning Interventions and Extensions in Elementary School*; *It's About Time: Planning Interventions and Extensions in Secondary School*; *Simplifying Response to Intervention: Four Essential Guiding Principles*; and *Pyramid Response to Intervention: RTI, Professional Learning Communities, and How to Respond When Kids Don't Learn.*

A graduate of the University of Southern California, Austin earned a bachelor of music degree and received a master of education degree with honors. He holds a doctor of education degree from Nova Southeastern University.

To learn more about Austin's work, follow him @agbuffum on X, formerly known as Twitter.

Janet Malone has thirty-five years of experience in public schools, including two years in rural Australia. She spent most of her public school career in the Poway Unified School District in Southern California, where she retired as the director of professional development. As a teacher, teacher coach, principal, and central office administrator, Janet was able to meet the interests and needs of teachers, administrators, and support staff alike on topics ranging from assessment and effective grading to PLCs, team building, and more.

In retirement, Janet has presented at conferences, conducted professional workshops, and consulted with school districts throughout North America. Most recently, she has worked closely with Austin Buffum and Mike Mattos to co-create both the content of RTI at Work and the design of RTI at Work professional development offerings. Based on her range of experiences, she has made contributions to assessment, collaborative teamwork, leadership development, and facilitation of adult learning.

From her first teaching job to the leadership she demonstrates currently, Janet has always kept her focus on student learning. She passionately believes that in order for students to learn at their highest levels, the adults who serve them must be learning too.

Luis F. Cruz, PhD, is a sought-after consultant, coach, thought leader, and accomplished author in the field of education. His over thirty years of practical experience as a teacher and an administrator at the elementary, middle, and high school levels, coupled with his ability to effectively communicate research-based approaches focused on the need to ensure high levels of learning for all students, have earned him acknowledgment and praise from an array of education communities around the United States. Luis specializes in school culture and leadership, support for students learning English as an additional language, PLCs, and RTI.

Born to immigrant parents from South America, Luis blends his experience as a student learning English as an additional language in a low-income community of Los Angeles with his professional experience and insight to advocate that public school educators acknowledge the disconnect between the antiquated public school system they inherited and the diverse student population they aim to serve. He therefore advocates that public school educators learn and commit to redesigning a school system that is out of touch with the needs of today's students.

As a recipient of the Hispanic Border Leadership Institute's fellowship for doctoral studies, a fellowship focused on increasing the number of Latino leaders with doctorates, Luis earned a doctorate in institutional leadership and policy studies from the University of California, Riverside.

Luis is coauthor of the best-selling *Time for Change: Four Essential Skills for Transformational School and District Leaders*, which he wrote with Anthony Muhammad, and a contributing author to *It's About Time: Planning Interventions and Extensions in Secondary School*.

To learn more about Luis's work, follow him @lcruzconsulting on X, formerly known as Twitter.

Nicole Dimich has a passion for education and lifelong learning, which has led her to extensively explore, facilitate, and implement innovative practices in school transformation. She works with elementary and secondary educators in presentations, trainings, and consultations that address today's most critical issues, all in the spirit of facilitating increased student learning and confidence.

Nicole was a school transformation specialist, coaching individual teachers and teams of teachers on assessment, literacy, and high expectations for all students. She also was a program evaluator and trainer at the Princeton Center for Leadership Training in New Jersey. A former middle and high school English teacher, Nicole is committed to making schools places where all students feel invested and successful.

As one of the architects of Solution Tree's Assessment Collaborative, and a featured presenter at conferences internationally, Nicole empowers educators to build their capacity for and implement engaging assessment design, formative assessment practices, common assessment design and analysis, RTI systems, data-driven decisions, student work protocols, and motivational strategies. She was the executive director of Thrive Ed, a nonprofit working to fundamentally transform education by empowering students, teachers, and guiding coalitions to innovate and thrive.

Nicole is the author of *Design in Five: Essential Phases to Create Engaging Assessment Practice* and coauthor of multiple books, including *Jackpot! Nurturing Student Investment Through Assessment; Concise Answers to Frequently Asked Questions About Assessment and Grading; Motivating Students: 25 Strategies to Light the Fire of Engagement; Growing Tomorrow's Citizens in Today's Classrooms:*

Assessing Seven Critical Competencies; *Instructional Agility: Responding to Assessment With Real-Time Decisions*; and *Essential Assessment: Six Tenets for Bringing Hope, Efficacy, and Achievement to the Classroom*. She also contributed to the best-selling books *The Teacher as Assessment Leader* and *The Principal as Assessment Leader*.

Nicole earned a bachelor of arts degree in English and psychology from Concordia College and a master of arts degree in human development from Saint Mary's University.

To learn more about Nicole's work, follow her @NicoleDimich on X, formerly known as Twitter, or visit http://allthingsassessment.info.

Sarah Schuhl is an educational coach and international consultant specializing in mathematics, PLCs, assessment, school improvement, and RTI. She has worked in schools as a secondary mathematics teacher, high school instructional coach, and K–12 mathematics specialist.

Sarah was instrumental in the creation of a PLC in the Centennial School District in Portland, Oregon, helping teachers make large gains in student achievement. She earned the Centennial School District Triple C Award in 2012.

Sarah grows learning through large-group professional development and small-group coaching in districts and schools. Her work focuses on strengthening the teaching and learning of mathematics, having teachers learn from one another when working effectively as collaborative teams in a PLC at Work, and striving to ensure the learning of each and every student through instruction, assessment practices, and intervention. Her practical approach includes working with teachers and administrators to implement assessments *for* learning, analyze data, collectively respond to student learning, and map standards.

Since 2015, Sarah has coauthored many books related to both school improvement and the teaching and learning of mathematics. For priority schools and school improvement, her primary work includes coauthoring *Acceleration for All: A How-To Guide for Overcoming Learning Gaps* and *School Improvement for All: A How-To Guide for Doing the Right Work*. For Mathematics at Work™, she coauthored *Engage in the Mathematical Practices: Strategies to Build Numeracy and Literacy With K–5 Learners* and (with Timothy D. Kanold) the *Every Student Can Learn Mathematics* series and the *Mathematics at Work Plan Book*. She is also one of the editors of the *Mathematics Unit Planning in a PLC at Work* series.

Previously, Sarah served as a member and chair of the National Council of Teachers of Mathematics (NCTM) editorial panel for the journal *Mathematics Teacher* and secretary of the National Council of Supervisors of Mathematics (NCSM). Her work with the Oregon Department of Education includes designing mathematics assessment items, test specifications and blueprints, and rubrics for achievement-level descriptors. She has also contributed as a writer to a middle school mathematics series and an elementary mathematics intervention program.

Sarah earned a bachelor of science degree in mathematics from Eastern Oregon University and a master of science degree in mathematics education from Portland State University.

To learn more about Sarah's work, follow her @SSchuhl on X, formerly known as Twitter.

To book Mike Mattos, Austin Buffum, Janet Malone, Luis F. Cruz, Nicole Dimich, or Sarah Schuhl for professional development, contact pd@SolutionTree.com.

INTRODUCTION

The Urgency of
the Moment

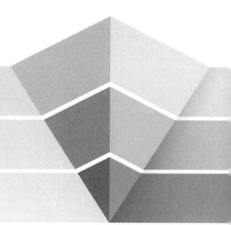

A child without education is like a bird without wings.

—Tibetan proverb

Since we wrote the first edition of this book (Buffum, Mattos, & Malone, 2018), the world has changed in radical, life-altering ways that have affected nearly every aspect of our personal and professional lives. At the eye of this storm is COVID-19. Within weeks of the virus being deemed a pandemic in 2020, nearly every state in the United States ordered school closures for the rest of the year (Education Week, 2020), and 1.6 billion students were impacted worldwide (UNESCO, 2022). What we hoped would be a temporary sacrifice became a protracted struggle with lasting consequences that continue to affect our society, our profession, and our students.

Beyond the most devastating consequences of the pandemic—the tragic loss of life and the extreme economic hardship it caused many families—it's clear it dramatically impacted students around the world. Each year from 2020 to 2022, U.S. students made about 80 percent of the academic progress they would typically make during a school year pre-pandemic (Goldhaber et al., 2022). This learning loss can be seen in the 2022 National Assessment of Educational Progress results. Post-pandemic, a record number of students scored in the lowest test performance category, *below basic*, in both mathematics and reading. Only 37 percent of fourth graders and 27 percent of eighth graders were proficient in mathematics, and fewer than one in three students read proficiently (Sparks, 2022a, 2022b). Collectively, this was the poorest aggregate performance on this assessment in the exam's history (Jimenez, 2022). And these academic declines were sweeping, spanning students of every income level, every gender, and every racial or ethnic group (Sparks, 2022a, 2022b).

The pandemic had an equally negative impact on students' social-emotional development. Post-pandemic, 50 percent of middle school students and 56 percent of high school students have reported consistent feelings of stress, anxiety, or depression (YouthTruth, 2022). Most schools are seeing an unprecedented wave of chronic absenteeism since the pandemic (Chang, 2023). Aside from physical illness and bad weather, high school students report that anxiety is the top reason why they miss school (Stanford, 2023).

Having *some* students enter a new school year with gaps in their learning or without some key behaviors is certainly not new to our profession. What is different is the scale of need the pandemic created. In virtually every classroom, most students lack prerequisite skills, knowledge, and behaviors needed for future success in school and beyond. If we, as educators, do not successfully close those gaps, these students will face continual hardship throughout their adult lives. Students who fail in the K–12 system are much more likely to be unemployed (U.S. Bureau of Labor Statistics, 2019), live in poverty (Statista, 2023), be incarcerated (Camera, 2021), and die prematurely (Lee-St. John et al., 2018).

This severe increase in student needs is a primary reason why many educators are dissatisfied with their job and are leaving the profession. A 2022 Merrimack College survey found only 12 percent of U.S. teachers report satisfaction with their job—a record low. Many teachers report they are experiencing frequent job-related stress and burnout, with more than a quarter saying they are experiencing symptoms of depression (Will, 2022). According to *The Wall Street Journal* (Dill, 2022), at least three hundred thousand public school teachers and other staff left the field between February 2020 and May 2022 (Smith, 2022), and 86 percent of public schools are struggling to fill teacher vacancies (Schermele, 2023). Effective teaching and timely intervention are our best hopes to close the learning gaps for students, but those are difficult to achieve without well-qualified educators who feel up to the tasks.

Our purpose for sharing these sobering facts is not to use a scared-straight tactic, nor to paint a picture that we are hopeless victims of historic circumstances. As Jim Collins (2017) states, "If we don't confront the brutal facts, they will confront us." As a profession, we face a moment of unprecedented urgency. If we do not effectively address students' educational gaps, we will have a lost generation—the "pandemic kids" who had vital years of their childhood disrupted, socially distanced, and sheltered in place. At the same time, successful intervention on behalf of students cannot come at the cost of educators, asking teachers to sacrifice even more of their personal time, resources, and well-being for the benefit of their students.

We must commit to practices that not only are proven to accelerate student learning but also are achievable within each site's current school day and with its resources. That was the exact purpose of the first edition of this book—to describe exactly how to create a highly effective process to ensure high levels of learning for every student. Creating such a system of supports is possible, and now absolutely essential to meet the daunting needs of our students.

A Deep Commitment to the Right Work

If we are going to successfully respond to this challenge, we must acknowledge that it will take a collective effort. There is no way individual teachers—working primarily in isolated classrooms—possess all the expertise required to meet the academic and behavioral needs of their assigned students. This "one-room schoolhouse" approach did not produce high levels of learning for all students *before* the pandemic and will most assuredly continue to fail students and educators in the future. Instead, site and district educators must work collaboratively and take collective responsibility for each student's success. Regular and special education teachers, administrators, and support staff must leverage their diverse knowledge and skills to meet the needs of all students. When done well, this level of collaboration creates a collective sum that is far greater than each individual educator's contribution.

Fortunately, our profession has near-unanimous agreement on how best to structure a school or district to collaboratively ensure student and adult learning—educators would deeply commit to being a professional learning community (PLC). When implemented well, the PLC process is the best way to build the learning-focused culture, collaborative structures, instructional focus, and assessment information necessary to successfully respond when students don't learn.

Equally important, we must acknowledge that interventions alone will be insufficient to close all the learning gaps the pandemic created. The depth and breadth of student need cannot be addressed by hiring additional interventionist staff, buying supplemental intervention programs, or creating an intervention period in the master schedule. Instead, we must rethink how we can strategically leverage every precious minute of the school day, restructure schools to ensure all students have access to grade-level essential rigor, and reconsider traditional intervention practices that have not consistently produced higher levels of learning for all students.

We are fortunate that our profession has decades of compelling research that the best way to systematically intervene is to leverage response to intervention (RTI) practices (Hattie, 2012, 2023). Austin Buffum, Mike Mattos, and Chris Weber (2012) state the following about RTI (also commonly referred to as a *multitiered system of supports*, or *MTSS*):

> RTI's underlying premise is that schools should not delay providing help for struggling students until they fall far enough behind to qualify for special education, but instead should provide timely, targeted, systematic interventions to all students who demonstrate the need. (p. xiii)

In a multitiered system of supports, all students have access to rigorous curriculum and effective initial teaching as part of their core instruction, *and* students are provided additional time and support to fill academic and behavior gaps based on each student's needs.

This is a critical point: we will not successfully close learning gaps by removing students from new essential grade-level curriculum. Students must learn this year's essential grade-level standards while we close their learning gaps. Such a process requires educators to collectively rethink and restructure their entire school day.

The PLC at Work Foundation

We call our approach to systematic interventions RTI *at Work* because we firmly believe that the best way to ensure high levels of learning for both students and educators is for schools or districts to function as a professional learning community. We specifically advocate the PLC at Work® process, which was first developed by Richard DuFour and Robert Eaker (1998). The PLC at Work process requires educators to work collaboratively to:

- ▸ Learn about the practices, policies, procedures, and beliefs that best ensure student learning
- ▸ Apply what they are learning
- ▸ Use evidence of student learning to evaluate, revise, and celebrate their collective efforts to improve student achievement

These outcomes are captured in the three big ideas of the PLC at Work process: (1) a focus on learning, (2) a collaborative culture, and (3) a results orientation (DuFour, DuFour, Eaker, Many, Mattos, & Muhammad, 2024).

A Focus on Learning

A PLC school's core mission is not simply to ensure that all students are *taught* but to ensure that they actually *learn*. The first (and the biggest) of the big ideas is based on the premise that the fundamental purpose of the school is to ensure all students learn at high levels (grade level or higher). This focus on and commitment to the learning of each student is the very essence of a learning community (DuFour et al., 2024). This seismic shift from a focus on teaching to a focus on learning requires far more than rewriting a school's mission statement or creating a catchy "learning for all" motto to put on the school's letterhead. This commitment to ensure student learning unites and focuses the collaborative efforts of the staff and serves as the organization's North Star when making decisions. The school's policies, practices, and procedures are guided by the question, Will this help more students learn at higher levels?

As stated in *Learning by Doing* (DuFour et al., 2024):

> The members of a PLC create and are guided by a clear and compelling vision of what the organization must become in order to help all students learn. They make collective commitments, clarifying what each member will do to create such an organization, and they use results-oriented goals to mark their progress. Members work together to clarify exactly what each student must learn, monitor each student's learning on a timely basis, provide systematic interventions that ensure students receive additional time and support for learning when they struggle, and extend [their] learning when students have already mastered the intended outcomes. (p. 18)

Creating consensus and commitment to becoming a learning-focused school or district is an essential prerequisite to successful RTI implementation. Likewise, any school already committed to the PLC process would heartily embrace RTI as an essential tool in achieving its commitment to guarantee every student's success.

A Collaborative Culture

The second big idea is a commitment to creating a collaborative culture. Because no teacher can possibly possess all the knowledge, skills, time, and resources needed to ensure high levels of learning for all their students, educators functioning as a PLC work collaboratively and take collective responsibility for student success. Instead of allowing individual teachers to work in isolation, the entire staff works collaboratively and takes collective responsibility for ensuring all students learn at high levels. Collaboration does not happen by invitation or chance; instead, frequent team time is embedded into the contractual day. Specifically, in our RTI at Work™ approach, we advocate three essential site teams: (1) a guiding coalition, (2) teacher teams, and (3) an intervention team.

Educators working collaboratively will not improve student learning unless their efforts focus on the *right work*. To this end, collaboration in the PLC at Work process is guided by four critical questions:

1. What knowledge, skills, and dispositions should every student acquire as a result of this unit, this course, or this grade level?

2. How will we know when each student has acquired the essential knowledge and skills?

3. How will we respond when some students do not learn?

4. How will we extend the learning for students who are already proficient? (DuFour et al., 2024, p. 44)

Question one requires teachers of the same course or grade level to collectively determine what they expect all their students to know and be able to do for future success. After all, a school cannot possibly create a systematic, collective response when students do not learn if individual teachers focus on different learning standards. By identifying essential standards, teacher teams prioritize, analyze, and teach what is most essential for students to know. Because the school is committed to all students' learning these essential standards, teams must be prepared to identify students who require additional time and support. This process is captured in the third big idea.

A Results Orientation

The third big idea focuses on evidence of student learning. To assess their effectiveness in ensuring all students learn, educators must use evidence of learning to inform and improve their professional practice and respond to individual students who need intervention and enrichment (DuFour et al., 2024).

After identifying the knowledge and skills that all students must learn, collaborative teams focus on the second critical question: "How will we know when each student has acquired the essential knowledge and skills?" (DuFour et al., 2024, p. 44). Educators functioning as a PLC must assess their efforts to achieve high levels of learning for all students based on concrete results rather than good intentions. Student assessment information constitutes the lifeblood of an effective system of interventions; teachers use it to identify students in need of additional time and support and to confirm which core instructional strategies are most effective in meeting students' needs.

By answering the first two critical questions, the school is now prepared to successfully intervene for students who need extra help mastering essential curriculum and to extend the learning for students who have shown mastery. These two outcomes are captured in critical questions three and four:

3. How will we respond when some students do not learn?

4. How will we extend the learning for students who are already proficient?
   (DuFour et al., 2024, p. 44)

Schools that function as a PLC should view MTSS not as a new initiative, but instead as a proven process to improve their responses when students don't learn. For schools that have not embraced PLC practices, RTI might seem like a nearly impossible undertaking. Trying to implement RTI without creating a school culture and structure that align with PLC practices is like trying to build a house starting with the roof—without a proper foundation, no building can stand.

Doing the Right Work *Right*

If you want to cook a delicious meal, you need more than a proven recipe and the right ingredients. These conditions are necessary but insufficient. You must prepare the recipe with a high level of cooking skill. Similarly, the PLC process and MTSS practices are the proven recipes needed to ensure all students learn at high levels, but to reap powerful results, schools must implement these practices at a very high level. That is the purpose of this book—to walk you through exactly how to create a highly effective multitiered system of supports within the framework of the PLC at Work process.

After providing a broad overview of the RTI at Work process in chapter 1, we divide this book into three parts.

> ▸ **Part one:** Part one includes chapters 2–4 and focuses on the essential actions necessary to build a highly effective Tier 1 core instructional program. Chapter 2 addresses how to create a schoolwide culture of collective responsibility, how to form the collaborative teams necessary to guide the RTI process, and how to deal with resistance. Chapter 3

digs deeply into the essential work of collaborative teacher teams at Tier 1, while chapter 4 describes leadership responsibilities of the guiding coalition.

▶ **Part two:** Part two targets Tier 2 interventions. Chapter 5 reviews how teacher teams should lead interventions for students who need additional time and support to learn team-identified essential standards. Chapter 6 describes the schoolwide actions of the guiding coalition at Tier 2, including scheduling time for supplemental help during the school day and utilizing site support staff to lead supplemental behavior interventions.

▶ **Part three:** Part three, chapters 7 and 8, addresses the schoolwide essential actions needed to plan and target Tier 3 interventions for students who need intensive reinforcement in foundational prerequisite skills. Chapter 7 examines the essential responsibilities of the site guiding coalition, while chapter 8 focuses on the essential actions of the school's intervention team.

Within each chapter, we describe the specific essential actions schools must take to create a highly effective multitiered system of supports. Consider for a moment the meaning of the word *essential*. When something is essential, it is so important to the whole that the whole cannot survive without it. The questions we like to ask to capture this definition are as follows: Is your arm essential to your whole body? Can you cut it off and live? Yes, so your arm is not essential. It's very useful but not essential. Now, is your heart essential? Yes. Every other part of your body can be perfectly healthy, but if your heart stops working, everything else soon follows. We are not suggesting that the steps we present at each tier are the only beneficial actions a school can take to improve student learning. Other elements (like arms) are good too! This book focuses on the *absolutely essential* elements— the hearts—that, if we skip any of them, will ultimately kill the effectiveness of the overall system. Many of these essential elements are the practices to which a school must also hold tight in the PLC at Work process.

For each essential action, we clearly and concisely address the following elements.

▶ **Here's Why:** We provide the research, evidence, and rationale behind the recommended action.

▶ **Here's How:** We provide a step-by-step process to successfully implement the essential element.

▶ **Helpful Tools:** We provide tools needed to support the implementation process and, in some cases, suggest other resources that dig deeper into specific aspects of the work.

▶ **Coaching Tips:** We provide reminders, ideas, and strategies for engaging and supporting educators in learning by doing. Based on the belief that staff members should solve their own most complex problems, it is essential to create a culture in which the adults effectively collaborate and learn together. These tips are meant to assist guiding coalition members as catalysts of change—promoting inquiry into current practices and, in turn, working to create an environment conducive to growth for teachers and students alike.

While we designed the content of this book to sequentially address each tier of the MTSS process, you do not have to read the book sequentially. We want this to be an ongoing resource, so we have written each chapter so it can stand alone. This design required us to repeat some key ideas more than once in the book, when specific content was relevant to multiple steps in the PLC and RTI processes. So, as you read the book, if you have a déjà vu moment and think, "I've read that idea already," you're right. We hope this repetition also helps solidify and reinforce key concepts.

Finally, in this book, we use the terms *RTI* (*response to intervention*) and *MTSS* (*multitiered system of supports*) interchangeably. As mentioned earlier, research on the topic of tiered supports spans decades, with dozens of researchers adding to our profession's collective knowledge of academic and behavior interventions. We find that some regions and systems refer to this research base as *RTI*, while others primarily use *MTSS*. This is why we use both terms. As practitioners, we have not based our approach exclusively on one researcher's terminology, nor have we written this book for a specific country, state, or education system. Instead, our recommendations are based on a collective analysis of the research and on what we have seen work in schools around the world. So, we suggest not focusing on the name—*RTI* or *MTSS*—and instead focusing on the process.

What's New in This Edition

Being a true PLC is a continual process in which educators work in recurring cycles of collective inquiry and action experimentation to increase the learning of the educators and students they serve (DuFour et al., 2024). As authors, we continue to practice what we preach. The goal of this second edition is not only to update the research behind our original recommendations, but to revise and expand on what we—as a profession—have learned. This edition includes the following major additions.

- ▸ Most schools and districts that struggle in becoming a PLC or implementing MTSS do not struggle because they lack understanding of what to do. Instead, they struggle due to ineffective leadership and staff resistance to the discomfort created by change. To this end, we are fortunate to add Luis F. Cruz to our team. Luis is an expert in transformational leadership and how to deal with resistance, and he has added specific steps and new tools to address these obstacles.

- ▸ Many schools and districts are drowning in data yet starving for timely information to guide their instruction and intervention. This problem is compounded when state or provincial assessment scores, district benchmark tests, and universal screening data are misused or used for unintended purposes. To address this need, we are honored to add assessment experts Nicole Dimich and Sarah Schuhl to our team. They have improved our recommendations and tools related to common formative assessments and their use to enhance instruction, guide interventions, and encourage student engagement and hope.

- ▸ While writing the first edition of *Taking Action* (Buffum et al., 2018), we debated whether we should address schoolwide grading practices as an essential action. Due to the strong disagreements we often see when educators discuss this topic—and the fear that these disagreements might jeopardize a faculty's commitment to the larger RTI at Work process—we decided not to include it. But we have seen too many schools create systems of interventions yet still cling to outdated grading practices that stop students from fixing their errors, that rank students into predetermined bands of achievement, and that fail to motivate the students who most need to improve. So, we added a new essential action that provides concrete steps for creating schoolwide grading practices that are proven to increase student engagement and learning.

- ▸ This is not a theory book—it is a *doing handbook*. It is designed to take research from ideas to action. This is why every essential action is supported with targeted tools. We have added numerous new protocols and activities to assist your efforts.

And as previously mentioned, we all have been immeasurably impacted by the COVID-19 pandemic. Every school, educator, and student is dealing with the social, emotional, and academic repercussions of this once-in-a-century event. It would be naive at best, and downright irresponsible at worst, not to address this reality and provide context to our previous recommendations.

Additional Resources

While the purpose of this book is to provide a step-by-step guide to create a highly effective system of interventions, no book is the be-all and end-all on PLCs or MTSS. We highly recommend the following complementary resources to go deeper into specific topics.

- ▶ **_Learning by Doing, Fourth Edition_ (DuFour, DuFour, Eaker, Many, Mattos, & Muhammad, 2024):** _Taking Action_ is modeled after this handbook for the PLC at Work process. We purposefully align critical concepts, essential actions, and vocabulary with this invaluable resource. Additionally, where appropriate, we reference chapters and tools in _Learning by Doing_ that will support and extend our RTI recommendations. We highly recommend this exceptional book to dig deeper into creating a true PLC.

- ▶ **AllThingsPLC (https://allthingsplc.info):** This free website—provided by Solution Tree—features hundreds of Model PLC schools and districts from across the world. Collectively, these schools represent the following.

  - ▪ PreK schools, elementary schools, middle and junior high schools, and high schools

  - ▪ Large schools with thousands of students and small schools with fewer than one teacher per grade or course

  - ▪ Large districts with dozens of schools and small districts comprised of a single school

  - ▪ Secondary schools that have block, five-period, six-period, seven-period, eight-period, nine-period, and ten-period schedules

  - ▪ Traditional, dual language, alternative, public, private, charter, and virtual schools

  - ▪ Schools that serve students who come from homes of poverty and schools that serve communities of significant wealth

  - ▪ Schools that represent tremendous variance in local, state or provincial, and national regulations, mandates, and assessment systems

  - ▪ Schools with active teachers' unions and schools with no unions

  - ▪ Schools with strong parental support and schools in which most parents lack the time and resources to be active partners in their children's education

  - ▪ Schools with significant supplemental funding and interventionist staff and schools with almost no additional resources

  - ▪ Schools with average class sizes in the single digits and schools with student-to-teacher ratios of more than thirty to one

Despite these tremendous differences, all these Model PLCs have developed effective systematic processes to intervene and extend student learning. In every case, these schools and districts created their systems of support and extension using their existing resources. And most important, there is contact information for each Model PLC, and they will gladly share what they are doing with you.

- ***Behavior Solutions* (Hannigan, Hannigan, Mattos, & Buffum, 2021):** For a much deeper dive into how to ensure all students learn essential academic and social behaviors, we highly recommend the book *Behavior Solutions*. This book is also built on the PLC at Work process and uses our RTI at Work pyramid to guide behavior processes at all three tiers. Equally important, it provides specific, proven behavior interventions.

- ***The Big Book of Tools for RTI at Work* (Ferriter, Mattos, & Meyer, 2025):** While this second edition of *Taking Action* provides targeted tools to implement every essential action, additional ideas and protocols will help with your journey. To this end, our colleague and award-winning educator Bill Ferriter led a team in creating a complementary resource, *The Big Book of Tools for RTI at Work*. It contains exactly what the title describes—lots of targeted tools that are purposefully designed to support specific essential actions featured in this book.

Getting Started

One challenge in writing an implementation book is that some readers might interpret the essential actions as a checklist of tasks. There are both important guiding principles that drive the work and essential actions that turn research into practice. But within these parameters, each school and district must be flexible regarding how it implements these practices to best meet the unique needs of the students it serves with its available resources. Additionally, schools must work within the laws and regulations of their district, state or province, and country. Understanding the right thinking empowers educators to be true to the process but flexible in implementation. In the PLC at Work process, this is referred to as being simultaneously "tight and loose" (DuFour et al., 2024). We must be tight about implementing the practices proven to increase student learning but loose on how each school implements each step in the process.

Finally, while we designed this book to specifically address and help you avoid the most common MTSS implementation mistakes, we know this to be true—you are going to make mistakes. To teach specific points in the book, we tell stories about our own mistakes on the journey. These mistakes were unintentional but ultimately critical to our subsequent improvement. However, one mistake is a sure death knell to the process—failing to put what you learn into action. This book is about *taking action*. The most powerful research—and the best of intentions—will not help a single student at your school unless you transform it from ideas to effort. And if there has ever been a time when our students needed us to act on their behalf, it is this moment. Our students don't have years to wait for the adults to get started.

To begin our journey, it is important to lay out a vision of the road ahead. Visually, we capture this with our RTI at Work pyramid, the focus of chapter 1.

CHAPTER 1

The RTI at Work Pyramid

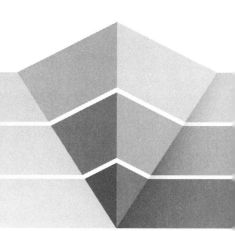

Where there is no vision, there is no hope.

—George Washington Carver

The use of graphic organizers is nothing new in education. Using a symbolic image such as a Venn diagram to compare and contrast multiple items or ideas can be a powerful tool to visually capture and guide thinking. A three-tier pyramid shape representing a school's systematic interventions is designed to be just that—a graphic organizer. But just as a Venn diagram would be useless to students who don't understand the thinking represented by interlocking circles, providing schools with a blank pyramid to build a site intervention process would be useless without ensuring that those using the tool understand the correct thinking behind it.

To this end, we find the traditional RTI pyramid can be both a blessing and a curse. When interpreted properly, it is a powerful visual that can help organize a school's time and resources to meet the learning needs of all students. Sadly, we find that many schools, districts, and states have misinterpreted the traditional pyramid, which has led to misguided thinking and ineffective practices that can be counterproductive to a school's goal of ensuring every student's success.

To address these misinterpretations, we have carefully rethought and revised the traditional RTI pyramid. We refer to our visual framework, shown in figure 1.1 (page 12), as the RTI at Work pyramid. We call it the RTI *at Work* pyramid because, as mentioned in the introduction, our recommendations leverage two research-based processes to ensure student learning: (1) the PLC at Work process and (2) RTI.

Because the RTI at Work pyramid serves as this book's culminating activity, let's answer some common questions about the pyramid and process by digging deeper into the guiding principles behind the design.

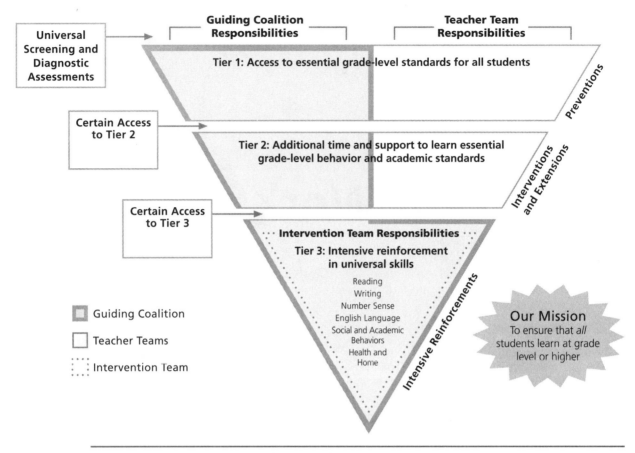

FIGURE 1.1: The RTI at Work pyramid.

Why Is the RTI at Work Pyramid Upside Down?

While we are not the first educators to invert the traditional RTI pyramid (Brown-Chidsey & Steege, 2010; Deno, 1970), our reason for this design is to respond to a common misinterpretation of the traditional RTI pyramid—that RTI is primarily a way to qualify students for special education. States, provinces, and school districts visually reinforce this conclusion when they place special education at the top of the pyramid, as illustrated in figure 1.2.

This incorrect application is understandable, as the traditional pyramid visually focuses a school's intervention system toward one point: special education. Consequently, schools then view each tier as a required step that they must document prior to assessing students for traditional special education services. Tragically, this approach tends to be a self-fulfilling prophecy because the organization starts interventions with protocols designed to screen and document students for this potential outcome.

To challenge this detrimental view of the traditional pyramid, we intentionally inverted the RTI at Work pyramid, visually focusing a school's interventions on the needs of individual students. See figure 1.3. With this approach, the school begins the intervention process assuming that every student is capable of learning at high levels, regardless of things like their home environment, ethnicity, native language, or previous success in school. Because every student does not learn the same way or at the same speed or enter school with the same prior access to learning, the school

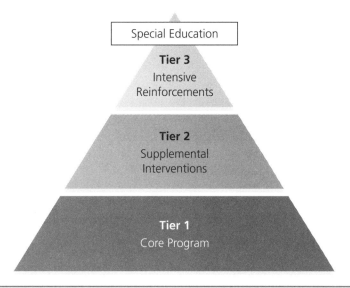

FIGURE 1.2: RTI pyramid with special education at the top.

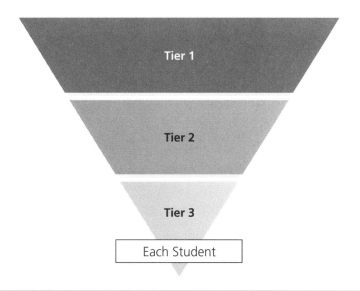

FIGURE 1.3: Inverted RTI at Work pyramid.

builds tiers of additional support to ensure every student's success. The school views these tiers not as a pathway to traditional special education but instead as additional layers of targeted supports to meet each student's individual learning needs.

What Are the Three Tiers of the RTI at Work Pyramid?

Our RTI at Work pyramid is a multitiered system of supports (MTSS) designed to meet four essential outcomes needed to ensure high levels of learning for all students.

1. If the ultimate goal of a learning-focused school is to ensure every student ends each year having acquired the essential skills, knowledge, and behaviors required for success

at the next grade level, then all students must have access to essential grade-level standards as part of their Tier 1 core instruction. While some students will undoubtedly need interventions, this additional time and support cannot deny or replace a student's access to the new essential curriculum.

2. Some students will not master every new essential grade-level or course-specific standard by the end of a unit of study, but all students must master this essential curriculum by the end of the school year to be ready for the next grade or course.

3. Some students enter each school year lacking foundational prerequisite skills they should have mastered in prior years—specifically, basic skills such as reading, writing, number sense, English language, and behavior. As these skills are foundational to learning in all grades and subjects, some students will require intensive reinforcement in these skills to succeed.

4. Some students require all three of these outcomes to learn at high levels.

    a. Access to essential grade-level standards for all students (Tier 1)

    b. Additional time and support to learn essential grade-level behavior and academic standards (Tier 2)

    c. Intensive reinforcement in universal skills (Tier 3)

These three outcomes collectively create a multitiered system of supports to meet the learning needs of all students.

The RTI at Work pyramid has three tiers to visually represent essential outcomes. The widest part of the pyramid represents the school's core instructional program. The purpose of this tier—Tier 1— is to provide *all* students access to essential grade-level curriculum and effective initial teaching. See figure 1.4.

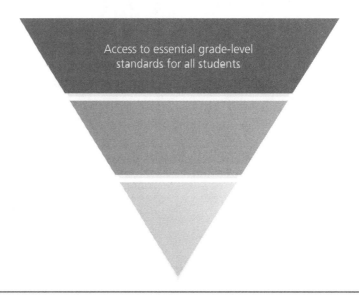

Access to essential grade-level
standards for all students

FIGURE 1.4: Core instructional program.

Many traditional RTI approaches advocate that the key to Tier 1 is effective first instruction. We don't disagree, but this teaching must include instruction on the skills, knowledge, and behaviors that a student must acquire during the current school year to be prepared for the following year. Unfortunately, many schools deem their most at-risk students as incapable of learning grade-level curriculum, so they place them in Tier 3 interventions that replace grade-level instruction with remedial coursework. So, even if the initial teaching is done well, a student will learn well below grade level if their core instruction is focused on below-grade-level standards.

If our mission is to ensure all students learn at high levels—grade level or better each year—then we must teach all students at grade level. Not every student might leave each school year having mastered every grade-level standard, but they must master the learning outcomes deemed indispensable for future success.

There is a point in every unit of study when most students will have demonstrated mastery of the unit's essential learning outcomes, and teachers must proceed to the next topic or unit. But because some students will not have mastered the essential curriculum by the end of the unit, the school must dedicate time to collectively provide these students with additional support to learn this essential curriculum *without missing critical new core instruction*. This supplemental help to learn essential grade-level curriculum is the primary purpose of the second tier—Tier 2—in the RTI at Work pyramid. See figure 1.5.

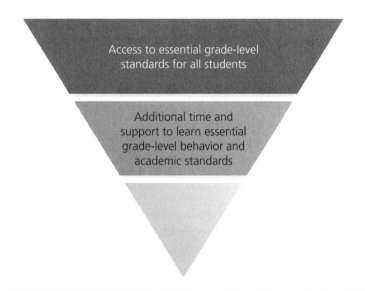

FIGURE 1.5: Supports to target essential grade-level standards.

The defining characteristics of Tier 2 are as follows.

▸ The highest priority of this time is to ensure all students learn the absolutely essential skills, knowledge, and behaviors needed for success in the next grade or course.

▸ Tier 2 help is provided in addition to Tier 1—access to new essential grade-level curriculum—not in place of it.

▸ Tier 2 is not regular education or special education—it must be available for any student who demonstrates the need.

▸ This additional support is systematic, meaning that *all* students can receive this targeted help as needed.

▸ Tier 2 is provided collaboratively, leveraging the experts on campus who are best trained to meet the outcomes of each intervention. It is unrealistic and ineffective to expect individual teachers to provide Tier 2 help solely through classroom differentiation.

Classroom teacher teams should be actively involved at Tier 2, as these outcomes directly relate to their areas of expertise. Because Tier 2 interventions are focused on very specific learning targets, placement into Tier 2 interventions must be timely, targeted, flexible, and most often guided by team-created common assessments aligned to essential grade-level or course-specific standards.

If a school provides students access to essential grade-level curriculum and effective initial teaching during Tier 1 core instruction, and targeted supplemental academic and behavioral help in meeting these standards at Tier 2, then most students should be succeeding. This is because when MTSS is done well, it should be a proactive process designed to catch student needs early, before students can fall too far behind.

However, there inevitably will be students who enter each school year lacking the foundational prerequisite skills needed to learn at high levels. These universal skills of learning include the abilities to:

1. Decode and comprehend grade-level text

2. Write effectively

3. Apply number sense

4. Comprehend the English language (or the school's primary language)

5. Consistently demonstrate social and academic behaviors

6. Overcome complications due to health or home

Like the foundation of a house, these skills are the foundational prerequisite skills needed to become a self-sufficient, lifelong learner.

As you may have noticed, these six skills are listed inside Tier 3 on our RTI at Work pyramid. They represent much more than a need for help with a specific learning standard; instead, they represent a series of skills that enable a student to comprehend instruction, access information, demonstrate understanding, and behave appropriately in a school setting. If a student is significantly behind in just one of these universal skills, they will struggle in virtually every grade level, course, and subject. And usually, students who are most at risk are behind in more than one area. Therefore, for students who need intensive reinforcement in foundational prerequisite skills, the school must have a plan to provide this level of assistance *without denying these students access to essential grade-level curriculum*. This is the purpose of Tier 3. See figure 1.6.

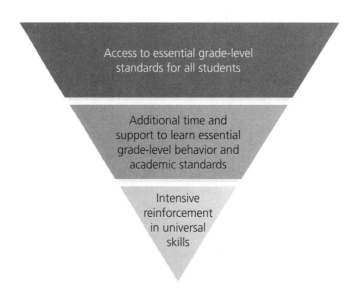

FIGURE 1.6: Intensive reinforcement in universal skills.

The essential characteristics of Tier 3 are as follows.

- ▸ Tier 3 is not regular education or special education—it must be available for any student who demonstrates the need.

- ▸ Like Tier 2, Tier 3 is provided collaboratively, leveraging the experts on campus who are best trained to meet the outcomes of each intervention.

- ▸ Tier 3 supports should be embedded into a student's schedule nearly every day.

- ▸ This intensive help must be in addition to Tier 1—access to new essential grade-level curriculum. It must also be in addition to Tier 2—extra support to learn essential grade-level standards.

- ▸ Reinforcement interventions must be targeted to individual student needs—not merely by broad universal screening scores.

Tier 3 should not be a life sentence. When it's done well, students needing Tier 3 intensive reinforcements should show multiple years of growth each school year, closing their learning gaps and transitioning them out of needing this level of help. Note we use the term *students in need of Tier 3 support* and not *Tier 3 students*. Naming students after tiers is a subtle, corrosive way to reinforce ability grouping. Students labeled *low*, *Tier 3*, or *special education* might be viewed as less capable. Any student receiving Tier 3 intensive reinforcements should also be in Tier 1 and probably Tier 2, so there is no such thing as a Tier 3 student.

Last and most important, some students need all three tiers to learn at high levels; this is why it is called a multitiered system of supports. Students do not move from tier to tier—the tiers are cumulative, value added. This is because of three factors.

1. All students need effective initial teaching on essential grade-level standards at Tier 1.

2. In addition to Tier 1, some students need supplemental time and support in meeting essential grade-level standards at Tier 2.

3. In addition to Tier 1 and Tier 2, some students need intensive help in learning essential outcomes from previous years. Students in need of Tier 3 intensive reinforcements in foundational prerequisite skills will probably also struggle with new essential grade-level curriculum the first time it is taught. This means these students need Tier 2 and Tier 3, all without missing new essential instruction at Tier 1.

There is no way individual teachers can effectively provide this level of support in their classrooms; in fact, a high-performing grade-level or department team cannot effectively provide all three tiers. Instead, it requires a schoolwide, collective, collaborative, coordinated all-hands-on-deck mentality. This is why structuring a school to function as a PLC—and specifically implementing the PLC at Work process—is necessary to provide highly effective interventions at all three tiers. In a PLC, we do not refer to each team as a "PLC." The entire school is the PLC because ensuring learning for all takes the expertise and collective efforts of the entire staff.

Why Is the RTI at Work Pyramid Split?

Another misinterpretation of RTI occurs when schools view Tier 1 as the classroom teachers' responsibility and interventions as primarily the responsibility of interventionist staff, such as instructional aides, categorically funded teachers, and the special education department. This approach means some classroom teachers assume that when students require help after initial teaching, their job is to refer them to someone else. According to Buffum and colleagues (2012), this practice can overwhelm site intervention teams and resources, especially at schools with a large number of students at risk:

> In response to this problem, many districts have responded by dictating that classroom teachers cannot refer a student for schoolwide interventions until they can document a set of predetermined interventions that must first be tried in their classroom. This [mandate] places the initial [responsibility] of Tier 2 interventions with the classroom teacher.
>
> The problem with this approach is that every student does not struggle for the same reason. The reasons [why students struggle] can vary from just needing a little extra practice on a new concept, to lacking necessary prerequisite skills, to requiring assistance with English language, to [having] severe attendance and behavioral issues. It is unlikely that each teacher has all the skills and time needed to effectively meet every need. . . . This approach fails students and educators.
>
> The answer . . . lies not in determining who is responsible for intervening when students don't learn [after core instruction]—classroom teachers or the school's intervention resources—but in determining the [lead responsibilities of each specific staff member]. . . . To visually capture this thinking, we have divided the RTI [at Work] pyramid into two distinct areas of responsibility: interventions led by collaborative teacher teams and interventions led by the schoolwide teams. (p. 12)

The upper-right portion of the pyramid in Tier 1 and Tier 2 represents responsibilities that collaborative teacher teams should lead. See figure 1.7.

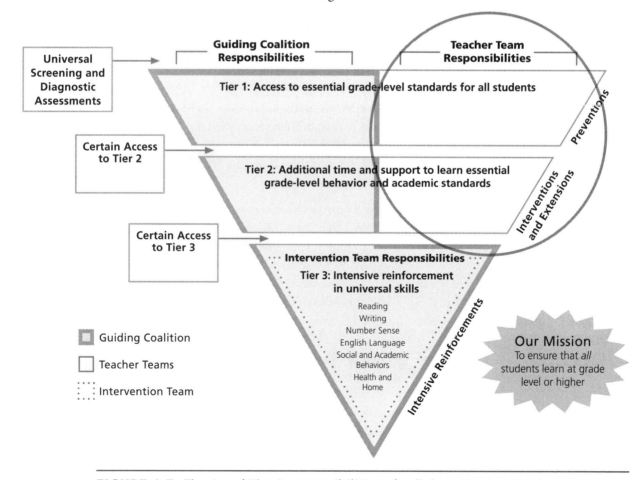

FIGURE 1.7: Tier 1 and Tier 2 responsibilities of collaborative teacher teams.

By *collaborative teacher teams*, we mean teams of educators who share essential learning outcomes for their students—the structure advocated in the PLC at Work process. At the elementary level, they are most likely grade-level teams, while at the secondary level, they are content and course specific. Teacher teams can also potentially be vertical, interdisciplinary, and virtual, as long as team members share essential curriculum. Chapters 3 (page 81) and 5 (page 201) of this book clearly identify the essential actions for which teacher teams should take lead responsibility at Tiers 1 and 2. These outcomes directly relate to the expertise, training, and job-embedded responsibilities of classroom teachers.

The left side of the RTI at Work pyramid at Tiers 1, 2, and 3 represents processes that the guiding coalition must coordinate. See figure 1.8.

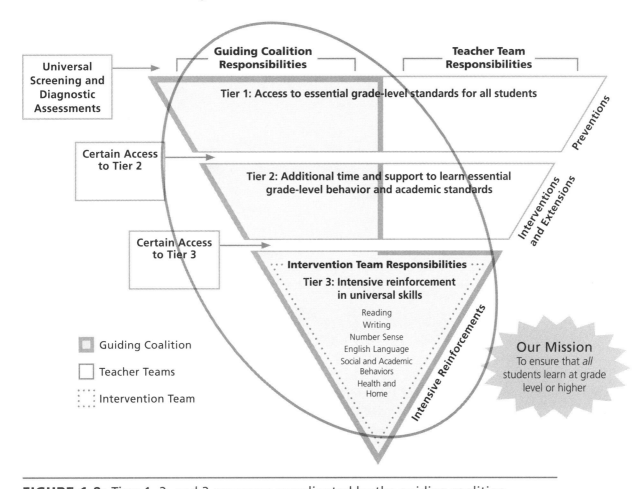

FIGURE 1.8: Tiers 1, 2, and 3 processes coordinated by the guiding coalition.

For this portion of the pyramid, a site guiding coalition takes lead responsibility for carrying out essential actions. This book clearly defines the exact responsibilities of the guiding coalition in chapters 2 (page 27), 4 (page 153), 6 (page 231), and 7 (page 263). An example is creating a master schedule that makes it possible for targeted students to receive all three tiers of support.

A second schoolwide team is needed to dive deeply into the specific needs of each student needing Tier 3 intensive reinforcements—the site intervention team. This team, which collectively should represent expertise in the universal skills listed in Tier 3, takes lead responsibility for determining, monitoring, and revising Tier 3 supports for individual students. Chapter 8 (page 293) digs deeply into intervention team responsibilities.

Figure 1.9 (page 20) shows how this book's chapters correspond with the RTI at Work pyramid.

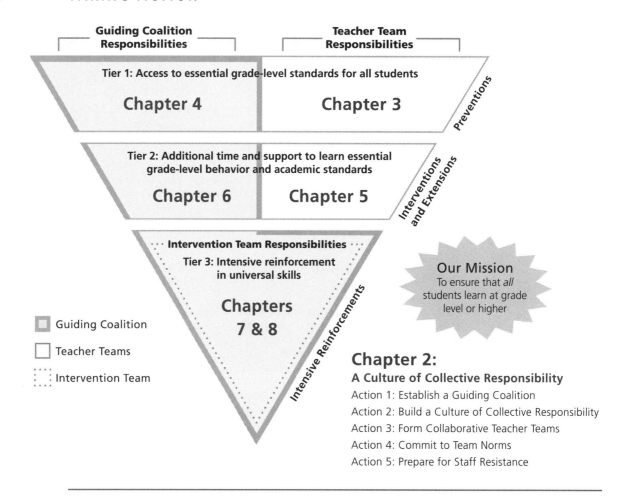

FIGURE 1.9: *Taking Action* chapter alignment with the RTI at Work pyramid.

In this book, we often use the phrases *lead responsibility* and *take the lead*. Do not suppose *lead responsibility* to mean *sole responsibility*. For example, we might recommend that a third grade teacher team take lead responsibility for planning Tier 2 interventions that reteach essential third-grade standards. We are not suggesting that third-grade teachers—and these teachers alone—are responsible for this outcome. If they're available, could a school utilize instructional aides, special education staff, peer tutors, or parent volunteers to help provide interventions for students who need additional time and support in mastering essential third-grade curriculum? Of course. But to ensure something happens, the buck must stop with specific people. It makes sense that the third-grade team is the best group on campus to know the specific learning needs of each third-grade student and thus would be the logical choice for taking lead responsibility to plan these interventions.

What Do the Boxes Represent?

Every school has interventions, but very few have systematic interventions. A school has a systematic intervention process when it can promise every parent that it does not matter which teacher their child is assigned to, as every student receives the additional time and support needed to learn at high levels (Buffum et al., 2012).

Failure to create a timely, systematic process to identify students in need of additional help makes the school's interventions an education lottery that leaves the question of intervention up to each teacher to resolve. The first step of any intervention is identifying students who need help. How can schools help students if they are ignorant of students' struggles?

The boxes down the left side of the pyramid represent the process a school uses to identify students for Tier 2 and Tier 3 assistance. See figure 1.10.

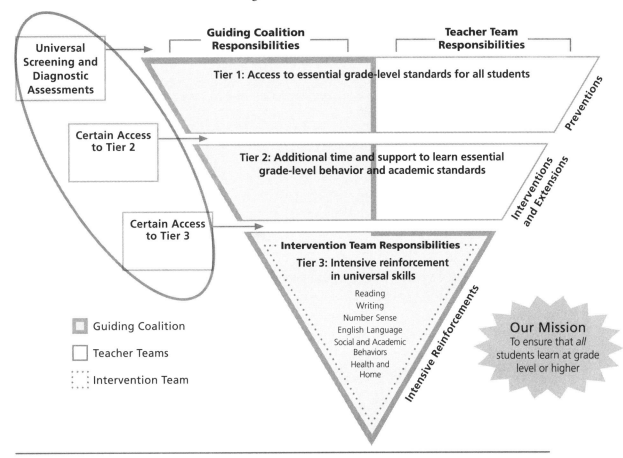

FIGURE 1.10: Process a school uses to identify students for Tier 2 and Tier 3 assistance.

A systematic identification process not only identifies which students need interventions and extensions but also utilizes the right kinds of information to best target each student's needs at each tier. Throughout this book, we clearly define the roles and uses of universal screeners, formative assessments, diagnostic tools, and staff recommendations in the MTSS process.

What Is the Role of Special Education?

If there were no labels in education—regular education, special education, Title I, English learner (EL), gifted, accelerated—how would a school target students for interventions? Wouldn't the school base its interventions on students who have the same need? Consider these examples.

- ▶ Students struggling with consonant-vowel-consonant (CVC) blends
- ▶ Students having difficulty multiplying exponents
- ▶ Students lacking organizational skills to keep track of assignments

Wouldn't it make sense to group students by need and not by label?

And how would a school determine which staff members should lead each of these interventions? Wouldn't the school base its determination on who has training and expertise in teaching each of the targeted outcomes of CVC blends, multiplication of exponents, and organizational skills? Although this approach is clearly logical, it is often not the norm, as many schools instead group students by labels first, then by needs.

We cannot stress these two points strongly enough.

1. If the purpose of an MTSS is to ensure all students learn at grade level or better, then *all* students must have access to all three tiers of support. Each tier is neither for regular education nor special education students—it is to serve the needs of every student, based on their individual needs.

2. Ensuring high levels of learning for all students requires the collective efforts of the entire staff. This means that regular education and special education staff must work collaboratively and take collective responsibility for the success of all students. Such an approach is encouraged in the federal reauthorization of special education (Individuals With Disabilities Education Improvement Act [IDEA], 2004) through early intervention services, which allow districts to use a percentage of special education resources to support students not currently in special education.

Until a school or district tears down the outdated barriers between regular education and special education and leverages the content knowledge of classroom teachers and the specialized training of special education staff for the benefit of all students, an effective system of interventions will remain painfully out of reach.

What Are Prevention, Intervention, and Reinforcement?

In a multitiered system of supports, the term *supports* represents all the different types of additional help that a school provides for students. We have found it helpful to add a bit more specificity to how we refer to the supports provided at each tier. In this book, we use the terms *prevention*, *intervention*, and *reinforcement*. See figure 1.11.

▶ **Tier 1:** When extra help occurs during Tier 1 core instruction, we call it *prevention*. Additional support works best when it is proactive, catching students' struggles early before the students have the chance to fail.

▶ **Tier 2:** The additional time and support provided to ensure all students master essential grade-level or course-specific standards is called *intervention*. Stretching student learning beyond minimum grade-level proficiency is called *extension*.

▶ **Tier 3:** When the causes of students' struggles are rooted in a lack of foundational prerequisite skills, we refer to efforts to fill in the gaps as *reinforcements*. These universal skills of learning include the ability to read and write, basic number sense, English language (or the native language spoken at the school), and significant behavioral needs.

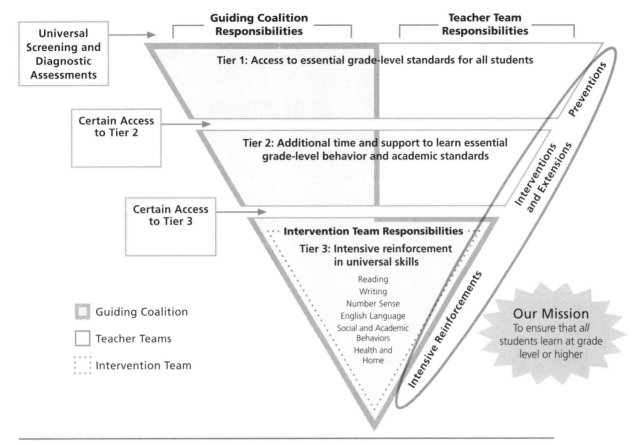

FIGURE 1.11: Supports addressed by teams at each tier.

What Is Extension?

Extension is when students are stretched beyond essential grade-level curriculum or levels of proficiency. An effective system of supports should not focus exclusively on supporting students who are struggling, nor should RTI come at the cost of students already learning at or above grade level. If a school is going to build flexible time, support, and collaboration into the school week, it can apply these efforts to support students in stretching their learning beyond grade-level proficiency and advanced coursework. The fourth critical question of the PLC at Work process captures this outcome: "How will we extend the learning for students who are already proficient?" (DuFour et al., 2024, p. 44).

What Is Enrichment?

There is an important difference between enrichment and extension. We define *enrichment* as students having access to the subjects that specials or electives teachers traditionally teach, such as music, art, drama, applied technology, and physical education. We strongly believe that this curriculum is essential for all students. When we pull students from enrichment to receive extra help in core curriculum, intervention turns into a punishment. Consequently, students' motivation and attitude can suffer. Finally, there is the equity issue. Often, students who need intervention come from economically disadvantaged homes. For many of these students, the only way they will learn a musical instrument or use advanced technology is through school. For these reasons, students should not be denied access to enrichment because they need additional time and support in core subjects.

What Is the Difference Between Immediate and Foundational Prerequisite Skills?

There is a significant difference between immediate prerequisite skills and foundational prerequisite skills. *Immediate prerequisite skills* represent discrete academic vocabulary, content, or skills from the previous year that students need in order to learn a current essential grade-level or course-specific standard. In comparison, *foundational prerequisite skills* represent universal skills used across the curriculum that students should have learned over previous years of school to access new content. Consider this example.

▶ **Essential grade 8 English language arts (ELA) standard:** "Determine the meaning of words and phrases as they are used in a text, including figurative, connotative, and technical meanings; analyze the impact of specific word choices on meaning and tone, including analogies or allusions to other texts" (RI.8.4; National Governors Association Center for Best Practices & Council of Chief State School Officers [NGA & CCSSO], 2010a).

  ▪ *Immediate prerequisite*—Understand how to use a process to figure out the meaning of a word and the difference among figurative, connotative, and technical meanings. (Grade 7)

  ▪ *Foundational prerequisite*—Know and apply grade-level phonics and word analysis skills in decoding words. Use context to confirm or self-correct word recognition and understanding, rereading as necessary. (Grades 3–5)

Immediate prerequisite skills are best addressed by teacher teams during Tier 1 prevention and Tier 2 intervention. Foundational prerequisite skills are targeted by the intervention team at Tier 3.

Conclusion

As captured in the title, this book is about *taking action*. Using the RTI at Work pyramid as our road map, we can now dig deeper into each tier and the essential actions schools must take to ensure every student succeeds. By the end of this book, if you complete each task, you will have created the structures needed for a highly effective multitiered system of supports to ensure high levels of learning for all students. In the next three chapters, we begin by focusing on Tier 1.

PART ONE

TIER 1 ESSENTIAL ACTIONS

CHAPTER 2

A Culture of Collective Responsibility

A small body of determined spirits fired by an unquenchable faith in their mission can alter the course of history.

—Mahatma Gandhi

RTI is not an end in itself but a means to an end. It is a tool. Consider that for a moment: *a tool*. You can use a hammer to help build a home for a family—what a positive, productive purpose. However, you can use the same hammer to tear a house down. A tool is only as effective as the hands that are guiding it and the purpose for which it is used.

We have seen many schools and districts approach RTI as an end in itself, viewing it as a mandate they must implement. When this happens, they see the critical elements of the process as steps on an implementation checklist—as actions to complete to achieve compliance. Top-down, mandate-driven reform efforts rarely create the deep levels of commitment and ownership necessary to truly transform an organization (Pink, 2009).

Why should a school commit to an MTSS process? What is the purpose of this tool? The first big idea of the PLC at Work process captures the answer to these questions—a focus on learning. See the highlighted piece of the RTI at Work pyramid in figure 2.1 (page 28). Richard DuFour, Rebecca DuFour, Robert Eaker, Thomas W. Many, Mike Mattos, and Anthony Muhammad (2024) state it this way:

> Whereas many schools operate as if their primary purpose is to ensure students are *taught* or are merely provided with *an opportunity* to learn, PLCs are dedicated to the idea that their organizations exist to ensure all students actually acquire the essential knowledge, skills, and dispositions of each unit, course, and grade level. Every potential organizational practice, policy, and procedure is assessed on the basis of this question: "Will this ensure higher levels of learning for our students?" (p. 18)

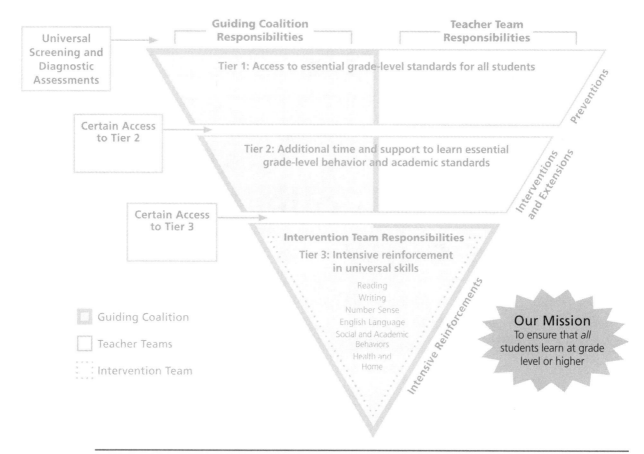

FIGURE 2.1: Focus on creating a culture of collective responsibility.

A school or district mission to ensure student learning is much more than a hopeful wish or a catchy motto on the organization's letterhead. An organization's mission does the following.

▸ States its fundamental purpose

▸ Guides decisions and actions

▸ Provides a path, framework, and context that the organization uses to formulate strategies

In other words, a school or district's mission serves as both a sacred promise to those it serves and the organization's highest priority when making decisions. It represents what is non-negotiable—what the school or district will not compromise.

Because the purpose of MTSS is to ensure high levels of learning for every student, one would expect educators to enthusiastically embrace the process. Would any educator be against proven practices that help all students succeed? Have some schools and districts adopted a mission statement in conflict with this goal? We have had the honor of working with schools around the globe, and we have never found mission statements that sound like the following.

▸ Our mission is to ensure that *most* students succeed.

▸ Our mission is to maintain a bell-shaped curve of student achievement.

▸ Our mission is to use students' perceived genetic abilities and home demographics to rank, sort, and track them.

Instead, what we see in school mission statements are the words *each*, *every*, and *all*.

- We will focus on *each* student's needs.

- We will maximize *every* student's potential.

- We are committed to the success of *all* students.

When the mission ensures student success, RTI is the perfect tool to achieve this goal.

Sadly, our experience is that many schools and districts struggle with implementing RTI because what they claim in their public mission statement conflicts with what they advocate in the privacy of the staff lounge and parking lot, faculty meetings, or district cabinet meetings. Propose to the school staff that they actually commit to practices aligned with their mission of ensuring that all students learn at high levels, and we find that many educators hedge on two words: *ensure* and *all*. Some claim it is unfair to hold educators responsible for student learning when so many factors outside of school impact each student's academic success. Others state it is a teacher's job to teach and a student's job to learn. Still others assume that some students are incapable of learning rigorous academic outcomes, or they lack sufficient resources to meet students' diverse needs. The underlying point in these concerns is this: some educators neither believe in nor support a mission that claims all students will succeed.

If the purpose of RTI is to ensure that all students learn at high levels, but a critical number of staff do not believe it is fair and reasonable to commit to this purpose, then it is unrealistic to expect educators to embrace the practices required to achieve this outcome. Likewise, if the reason why PLC members collaborate is to ensure every student's success, but a majority of the staff are unwilling to commit to this outcome, then team meetings are likely to digress and lose focus.

A successful journey begins not by taking a first step but by facing the right direction (Buffum et al., 2012). Likewise, transforming a school or district starts not with implementing a sequence of tasks but with clarifying the organization's direction—its fundamental purpose. This chapter focuses on how an organization builds agreement on a mission of collective responsibility and what foundational conditions must be in place to successfully build a multitiered system of supports to achieve this outcome. The five essential actions we discuss are as follows.

1. Establish a guiding coalition.

2. Build a culture of collective responsibility.

3. Form collaborative teacher teams.

4. Commit to team norms.

5. Prepare for staff resistance.

In this chapter, we explore each of these essential actions required to build the right school culture and the collaborative structures that serve as the foundation for a school's Tier 1 core instructional practices.

Action 1

Establish a Guiding Coalition

Creating a culture built around the concept of *every* student succeeding represents a major shift in thinking for many schools. In his book *Leading Change*, John Kotter (1996) asserts that such shifts in thinking (cultural change) often fail due to the lack of what he calls a "guiding coalition" (p. 52).

To achieve this goal, many schools need to redesign or repurpose their existing leadership team, as we find that most site leadership teams rarely function as a guiding coalition dedicated to ensuring high levels of learning for all students. Instead, traditional leadership teams—at the site or district level—often focus exclusively on managing the school's day-to-day operations. MTSS represents an almost overwhelming level of change compared to how schools have functioned for more than two hundred years. We know that even slight levels of change can be hard for people. Unless the right team—a team that focuses its efforts on the right work—leads the process, the anxiety and inevitable obstacles inherent in this level of change will overwhelm the best organization's intentions.

Here's Why

Regarding organizational transformation, John Kotter and Lorne A. Whitehead (2010) state:

> No one person, no matter how competent, is capable of single-handedly developing the right vision, communicating it to vast numbers of people, eliminating all of the key obstacles, generating short-term wins, leading and managing dozens of change projects, and anchoring new approaches deep in an organization's culture. . . . Putting together the right coalition of people to lead a change initiative is critical to its success. (p. 52)

In his book *Good to Great: Why Some Companies Make the Leap . . . and Others Don't*, Jim Collins (2001) similarly asserts that the first step to implementing successful change is to "get the right people on the bus" (p. 41). Collins (2001) says, "If we get the right people on the bus, the right people in the right seats, and the wrong people off the bus, then we'll figure out how to take it someplace great" (p. 41). The right people don't need to be closely managed or constantly fired up. Rather, they are capable, self-motivated, and eager to take responsibility for creating something great.

We find it both fascinating and tragic that many schools give more careful consideration to forming their varsity football coaching staff or school social committee than to forming the best possible school guiding coalition. Random practices, such as the following, often determine positions on the guiding coalition.

- ▸ **Seniority:** "I should be department chair because I have been here the longest."
- ▸ **Novice:** "Make the rookie do it. Pay your dues, kid!"
- ▸ **Rotation:** "It's Sally's turn to be grade-level leader."
- ▸ **Default:** "Bill is the only person who applied."

Forming an effective guiding coalition is unlikely to happen serendipitously. It takes carefully considering both the essential tasks that the leadership must accomplish and the research behind effective leadership.

Here's How

In selecting the right people for an effective guiding coalition, it is important to consider the essential tasks that this team will take responsibility for in the RTI at Work process. They include the following (Buffum et al., 2012).

- ▸ Build consensus on the school's mission of collective responsibility.

- ▸ Create a master schedule that provides sufficient time for team collaboration, core instruction, Tier 2 interventions, and Tier 3 intensive reinforcements.

- ▸ Coordinate human resources to support all three tiers, including the best use of school-wide staff, such as counselors, psychologists, speech-language pathologists, special education teachers, librarians, health services, subject specialists, instructional aides, and other classified staff.

- ▸ Allocate the school's fiscal resources, including school categorical funding, to best support all three tiers.

- ▸ Assist with articulating essential learning outcomes across grade levels and subjects.

- ▸ Lead the school's universal screening efforts to identify students in need of Tier 3 intensive reinforcements.

- ▸ Lead the school's efforts at Tier 1 for research-based teaching practices and schoolwide behavior expectations, including attendance policies and awards and recognitions.

- ▸ Ensure all students have access to essential grade-level (or higher) standards as part of their Tier 1 core instruction.

- ▸ Ensure sufficient, effective resources are available to provide Tier 2 interventions for students in need of additional time and support to master essential grade-level academic and behavior standards.

- ▸ Ensure sufficient, effective resources are available to provide Tier 3 reinforcements in the universal skills of reading, writing, number sense, English language, behavior, and health and home.

- ▸ Continually monitor schoolwide evidence of student learning.

- ▸ Proactively prepare to deal with both rational and irrational resistance from staff.

In addition to administrative representation, the guiding coalition should have teacher representatives from each collaborative teacher team because many of the listed outcomes relate to supporting and monitoring these teams' work. At the elementary level, the representatives most likely will be grade-level leaders; at the secondary level, they most likely will be department or course-level leaders. Additionally, representation from classified and support staff will help the guiding coalition best allocate schoolwide resources to support the school's system of supports.

Beyond positional representation, Kotter (1996) states a successful guiding coalition should consider four essential types of power.

1. **Positional power:** Individuals with positional power have a certain level of defined authority because of their title or office. For example, schools afford the principal the ability to make certain decisions because of the defined responsibilities of this position. Kotter (1996) says that if a guiding coalition does not have enough positional power, it

will not have the authority to carry out essential actions. In other words, are enough key players on board so those who disagree cannot easily block progress?

2. **Expertise:** Based on the previous list of essential tasks, what types of expertise must the guiding coalition possess to successfully achieve these outcomes? For example, because RTI requires coordinating data about specific students, we have found that having at least one member with a deep level of expertise in the school's education technology can be very helpful.

3. **Credibility:** Anyone with expertise in an organization knows that some individuals influence and sway decision making more than others. Some of these individuals use this credibility to advocate keeping the status quo, while others can use their influence to build support for a new change initiative. It is critical that a guiding coalition has sufficient levels of credibility with those it is trying to influence. An important question to ask is, Does your guiding coalition have enough people with credibility that its recommendations and decisions will be taken seriously, especially by the staff members you need to influence most? Moreover, would your guiding coalition be willing to invest in continuously learning more about the details and intricacies of the RTI at Work process to lead your staff more effectively?

4. **Leadership ability:** Leaders have the ability to convincingly articulate a position, unite others toward a common goal, build trust with others, and respectfully confront actions that do not align with the school's mission. If a guiding coalition lacks members with leadership ability, it is unlikely that the best-laid plans will be implemented successfully. Even if the school's principal possesses leadership ability, it would be unwise to always make the principal the spokesperson for the guiding coalition. When administrators always introduce new ideas, staff members often view them as top-down directives. Identifying other members—especially teacher leaders—with leadership ability is a powerful asset for an effective guiding coalition. The right question to ask is, Does the group include enough proven leaders to be able to drive the change process?

So, an effective guiding coalition should consist of people who collectively possess strong positional power, broad expertise, and high credibility with their peers. Moreover, the guiding coalition must consist of people who have strong leadership skills and not just the ability to organize and manage programs. In other words, the guiding coalition, along with the school administration, acts as a change agent relative to the mission and vision of the school, and therefore invests in developing skill sets aligned with consolidating staff commitment and tactfully addressing staff resistance to change.

While the previous examples focus on creating a guiding coalition, you should apply these same principles to forming a team to guide *districtwide* RTI implementation. Building a broad base of expertise, including representation from each school, special and regular education, classified support staff, the teachers' union, district and site administration, parents, and community resources, is important to the coalition's success.

As important as getting the "right people on the bus" is to establish an effective guiding coalition, it is equally important to establish a culture of collective responsibility within the team itself. In other words, all individuals on the guiding coalition must see themselves as leaders whose role it is to participate in such a culture, model it, and inspire a similar culture for the whole school. The team's work, therefore, must consistently have a dual focus—*internal* attention to how members are working together and *external* attention to coaching and inspiring others within the context of an ever-evolving healthy school culture.

To begin, the coalition must discuss and agree on its purpose—to unite and coordinate the school's collective efforts to help every student succeed and allocate the school's resources to best achieve this goal. It must also identify any nonpurposes—topics that will be off-limits during team meetings, such as complaints about students, parents, or staff members. Once the coalition clearly understands and agrees to its purpose, it then needs to reach consensus on team tasks, desired outcomes for each meeting, team norms, and team members' individual roles and responsibilities. The following tools and tips can help in this process.

Helpful Tools

The following tools will help you accomplish the work for this essential action.

- ▶ **"Building a School Guiding Coalition" (page 35):** This activity is designed to help a principal or administrative team create an effective school guiding coalition.

- ▶ **"Application for the Position of School Guiding Coalition Member" (page 36):** Use this form to communicate to staff members the purpose of your school's guiding coalition and to recruit potential members.

- ▶ **"Team Charter" (page 37):** Use this form to organize and set norms for any team that wishes to improve its effectiveness. It is an essential tool for establishing a guiding coalition.

- ▶ **"Meeting Agenda Template" (page 39):** Use this template to record the meeting agenda for your guiding coalition.

Coaching Tips

As stated previously, once the right people are on the schoolwide guiding coalition, the team has to embrace the importance of *doing* the work, not just leading the work. In other words, team members must establish and *live* a culture of collective responsibility among themselves in order to model, inform, and establish a similar culture in the school as a whole. It will be important, then, for the guiding coalition to understand and communicate the difference between climate and culture. While *climate* focuses on how staff feel, *culture* focuses on how adults in the school behave (Muhammad, 2018). While a healthy climate (staff feel content to come to work) is desirable, a healthy school culture (adults behave in a manner aligned with RTI) will be necessary if the objective is to create a multitiered system of supports for all students to learn at high levels.

An effective way to get started is to have the guiding coalition, once assembled, create a one-sentence purpose statement that defines its reason for existing. This purpose statement should capture three important characteristics.

1. We exist to support our staff in our collective quest to continuously generate high levels of learning for students.

2. We exist to learn and then share with our staff research-based practices that will continuously elevate high levels of learning for all students.

3. We exist to continuously ensure a healthy school culture focused on high levels of learning for all students.

Once a guiding coalition develops its purpose and shares it with the staff, we recommend that the coalition proceed to create a team charter, a document that outlines the foundation on which to base all team interactions and work. All team members must participate in the dialogue and discussion that result in consensus on the document itself. Once they reach agreement, all members sign and date the charter. As work progresses, the team might need to revisit, revise, or supplement the charter to meet its needs.

The success of the guiding coalition goes hand in hand with the success of its meetings. Every time the guiding coalition meets, there must be a clear path to action (goals and tasks), attention to culture building (collaborative work, norms, and all members' equal participation), exchange of information (structured conversations to ensure shared understanding), and tangible action steps.

A carefully planned and skillfully facilitated meeting agenda is the key to success. High-performing teams consistently use an agenda template, such as the "Meeting Agenda Template" (page 39). Using an agenda template ensures that each meeting begins with an overview of purpose, desired outcomes, and tasks to be accomplished, along with team member roles and the approximate time needed for each task. Remember, *less is more*. The most productive meetings often have fewer topics, which, in turn, allows all members to have greater participation.

We recommend that the guiding coalition commence each meeting by articulating its purpose statement. It must also conclude each meeting with consistency—reviewing tasks the team completed and decisions it made, clarifying team members' responsibilities to accomplish before the next meeting, evaluating the meeting's effectiveness, and brainstorming a list of topics to include on the next meeting agenda. Team members should compile and share notes after each meeting. This responsibility can be assigned to a specific team member or shared among team members. Assigning additional team member roles, such as facilitator, timer, norm enforcer, and public recorder, may also help team meetings run more smoothly.

Once the guiding coalition takes the foundational steps outlined previously in this section—creating a team purpose and charter, establishing routine protocols for meeting effectiveness, and sharing team member roles—work broadens to include paying ongoing attention to its own team culture and productivity as well as developing a similar culture in the school as a whole. Team members must model the purpose, beliefs, and behaviors of the guiding coalition both formally and informally. Daily conversations and interactions with colleagues, in addition to team and faculty meetings, are the most influential building blocks for changing culture. Mahatma Gandhi said it best: "You must be the change you wish to see in the world" (BrainyQuote, n.d.). Teachers, staff, and leaders can also be the change they want to see in their schools.

Building a School Guiding Coalition

This activity is designed to help a principal or administrative team create an effective school guiding coalition.

First, list the names of the current group members who you might consider to be your guiding coalition. If no such group currently exists, list the potential members who come to mind.

_____	_____
_____	_____
_____	_____
_____	_____
_____	_____

Then consider the following personal characteristics that will impact your team's success. Write the name of each team member under any characteristic that applies (a person may be listed under more than one). Eliminate any person from your list who possesses none of these characteristics. We recommend that a member of each teacher team be on the guiding coalition. Does your team have the necessary balance?

Positional Power	**Expertise**
_____	_____
_____	_____
_____	_____
_____	_____
_____	_____
Ask: Are enough key players on board so those who don't agree cannot easily block progress?	Ask: Are the various points of view—in terms of discipline, work experience, and so on—that are relevant to the task at hand adequately represented so informed, intelligent decisions will be made?
Credibility	**Leadership Ability**
_____	_____
_____	_____
_____	_____
_____	_____
_____	_____
Ask: Does the group have enough people with good reputations that its recommendations and decisions will be taken seriously?	Ask: Does the group include enough proven leaders to be able to drive the change process?

Source: Buffum, A., Mattos, M., & Weber, C. (2012). Simplifying response to intervention: Four essential guiding principles. *Bloomington, IN: Solution Tree Press.*

Application for the Position of School Guiding Coalition Member

Background

The fundamental purpose of our school is to continuously increase learning for all students. To achieve this goal, teachers and administrators must work together to accomplish the following.

- Guide and support the faculty and staff to embrace the need for all students to learn at high levels (grade level or higher).

- Learn and then share with the faculty and staff research-based best practices aligned with continuously increasing learning for all students.

- Continuously foster a school culture in which, through data analysis, the faculty and staff passionately strive to increase learning for all students.

Eligibility

Our school's guiding coalition will be composed of both administrators and teachers who intrinsically seek to work with other adults on campus to continuously increase learning for all students. While all teachers and administrators are welcome to apply, the guiding coalition will be composed to include representatives from academic departments or grade levels. Please note that the principal and a representative from the teachers' association will automatically be on our school's guiding coalition.

Characteristics

Interested applicants must possess the following characteristics.

- Optimism (positive thinking) in our quest to increase learning for all students (In short, a "Yes, we can" attitude is highly desired.)

- Honesty and the ability to focus on situations we, as a faculty and staff, can control when seeking to increase learning for all students, versus those challenges we cannot control (such as poverty, a lack of resources at home, and the lack of an academic foundation for students)

- A desire to work and assist other adults on campus to reach their fullest potential as professionals

Skills

Interested applicants must be willing to develop the following skills.

- The ability to positively influence other adults on campus to think differently and, therefore, do differently

- The ability to work with others to increase the productivity (learning) of our school

- The ability to support faculty and staff members to embrace and commit to change in policies, practices, and procedures aimed at increasing learning for all students

Interested applicants must apply by _____. Please submit a letter of interest detailing why you seek this position and what qualifications you feel you possess that will contribute to the overall purpose of the guiding coalition as described on this form. Please also include one letter of recommendation from any individual who can attest to the leadership skills sought for our school's guiding coalition.

Team Charter

Use this form to organize and establish norms for your guiding coalition.

Guiding coalition: _____ Date: _____

Team members: _____

_____

_____

_____

Team members' strengths: _____

_____

_____

_____

Team purpose: _____

_____

_____

_____

Team nonpurposes: _____

_____

_____

_____

Team norms or guidelines: _____

_____

_____

_____

page 1 of 2

Team tasks: _____

_____

_____

_____

Team questions or concerns: _____

_____

_____

_____

Signatures: _____   Date: _____

_____   _____

_____   _____

_____   _____

_____   _____

_____   _____

_____   _____

Meeting Agenda Template

Agenda: _____

Purpose:

_____

_____

Desired outcomes:

_____

_____

We will have the following by the end of this meeting:

_____

_____

Meeting Agenda			
What (content)	**How (process)**	**Who (facilitator)**	**Time (estimated minutes)**

Action 2

Build a Culture of Collective Responsibility

The guiding coalition's first and most important task is to establish what we refer to as a *culture of collective responsibility*. *School culture* is defined as the norms, values, rituals, beliefs, symbols, and ceremonies that produce a school persona (Deal & Peterson, 1999). If the fundamental purpose of collaboration in a PLC—and the very reason for creating a multitiered system of supports—is *to ensure all students learn at high levels*, then a school's culture must align with this mission.

Specifically, the staff must embrace two underlying cultural beliefs that are necessary to create a highly effective system of supports. The first belief is this.

1. **As educators, we collectively accept primary responsibility to ensure high levels of learning for every student:** While parental, societal, and economic forces influence student academic achievement, our collective expertise and efforts have the greatest impact on student learning. So, when students struggle, we will focus on what we can directly do to *ensure* every student succeeds.

While most schools and districts publicly state in their mission statements a commitment to high levels of learning for all students, we find that educators often privately protect a culture that is misaligned or contradictory to this outcome. This conflict is often expressed when faculty members hedge on the word *ensure* in their mission statement and instead suggest that the job of educators is to provide their students with the *opportunity* to learn.

Buffum and colleagues (2012) write that an opportunity-to-learn school believes:

> Its responsibility for student learning ends once the child has been given the opportunity to learn the first time. But a learning-focused school understands that the school was not built so that teachers have a place to teach; it was built so that the children of the community have a place to learn. Learning-focused schools embrace RTI, as it is a proven process to help them achieve their mission. (p. 18)

Research proves that RTI is twice as powerful as any single environmental factor that can impact student success (Bailey & Dynarski, 2011; Hattie, 2012, 2023; Reardon, 2011). Until educators stop blaming factors outside of school for why failing students have not learned essential academic curriculum or critical behaviors, and instead look internally at what they can control to ensure these outcomes, they will unlikely have success creating a highly effective system of supports.

The second belief is as follows.

2. **We, as educators, assume all students can learn at high levels:** Regardless of a student's demographic profile or home environment, we assume that with effective instruction and targeted supports, every student can learn at grade level or higher.

This belief requires educators to assume that all students are capable of learning at high levels. Yet, when we ask many educators to commit to a mission of ensuring that *all* students learn at high levels, a reasonable concern is, What about students with disabilities? Isn't it unfair to commit to a mission of learning for all when some students lack the cognitive ability to achieve this outcome?

Undeniably, there is a very small percentage of students with profound cognitive disabilities that make it impossible for them to learn the higher-level thinking skills required for postsecondary education. In the United States, we recognize these limitations and would not expect these individuals to become self-sufficient, independent adults. We are not suggesting that these students cannot learn or that schools are not responsible for their education. While almost all students must transition to postsecondary education to succeed in the global economy, these students are not expected to compete in this environment, so their curriculum in school might not meet our criteria of grade level or higher. Instead, our learning goals for students with profound disabilities should be to the best of their individual abilities so they can have adult lives that are as independent and option filled as possible.

So, when we ask educators to assume all students can learn at high levels, we should define *all* as any student who can or might be an independent adult someday. This reasonable definition means that most students currently in special education must learn at high levels. These students are not going to receive modified rent, accommodated bills, or an individualized education program (IEP) at work someday. They can and must leave the K–12 system with the skills needed to succeed in postsecondary education and in life.

Regardless of this reality, many educators refuse to assume all students—beyond students with profound disabilities—can learn at high levels because they believe that some students lack the innate ability to learn rigorous curriculum. These educators often point to students with IQ scores that are above the threshold of profound disabilities but much lower than the average. Yet we know IQ testing is an imperfect science that was not designed to definitively predict a child's future academic limitations. Also, IQ testing has been legally determined to be culturally biased (Powers, Hagans-Murillo, & Restori, 2004).

While working with schools, we hear some educators claim that the law of averages—the distribution of the bell-shaped curve—proves we must always expect some students to be below average. We should not be surprised that many educators feel this way, since this assumption is the foundation of the traditional K–12 school system in the United States. Because this system was preparing students for a farm- and factory-driven economy, people assumed that only a small percentage of students would learn beyond grammar school. Therefore, schools did not expect all students to learn at high levels. Instead, they ranked and sorted students on a bell-shaped curve, which identified those few expected to reach higher education. In this kind of system, it is reasonable to expect that "a few people will excel, most will be satisfactory or average, and a few will fail" (Fendler & Muzaffar, 2008, p. 63). Yet Benjamin Bloom (1971) states:

> The normal curve is not sacred. It describes the outcome of a random process. Since education is a purposeful activity in which we seek to have the students learn what we teach, the achievement distribution should be very different from the normal curve if our instruction is effective. In fact, our educational efforts may be said to be unsuccessful to the extent that student achievement is normally distributed. (p. 49)

The focused collaboration of a PLC is the purposeful activity that can flatten the bell-shaped curve and ensure all students succeed.

And most tragically, some educators tell us that a trained teacher can spot students who just don't have it—the capacity to learn at high levels. Overwhelming evidence would prove otherwise. We know that a student's ethnicity, native language, and economic status do not reduce their capacity for learning. Yet, across the United States, students of color, non-native language learners, and economically disadvantaged students are disproportionately represented in special education (Brantlinger, 2006; Ferri & Connor, 2006; Fish, 2019; Gopalan & Lewis, 2022; Skiba, Poloni-Staudinger, Gallini, Simmons, & Feggins-Azziz, 2006; Skiba et al., 2008) and underrepresented in gifted and honors programs (Donovan & Cross, 2002; Gopalan & Lewis, 2022; National Working Group on Advanced Education, 2023).

Why are these students being overidentified as learning disabled? Some educators assume these students are less capable, and these inaccurate judgments often become self-fulfilling prophecies for their students (Buffum et al., 2012). Educators typically view students who enter school with a head start from their home environment as being capable of learning at high levels, and these students are consequently placed in more rigorous coursework, taught at advanced levels, expected to achieve, and thus much more likely to learn at those levels. Conversely, students perceived as being incapable of learning at high levels are placed in below-grade-level curriculum, taught at remedial levels, expected to achieve at lower levels, and, to no one's surprise, most likely learn at low levels. These outcomes falsely confirm the school's initial assumptions and reinforce the misgiving some educators have to committing to a mission of learning for all.

Effective interventions begin by assuming all students are capable of learning at high levels. According to researcher John Hattie, one of the most powerful influences on increasing student learning is when educators believe a student is capable of learning at high levels and, in turn, set rigorous learning goals to achieve this outcome (Corwin Visible Learning Plus, 2023).

We could make a convincing argument that, regardless of how effective a school's system of interventions, some students might face cognitive challenges or environmental factors that prove beyond a school's ability to overcome. But here is the critical point: to start the journey, we must accept primary responsibility for what we can control—student mastery of academic skills, knowledge, and dispositions—and assume each student is capable of achieving these outcomes, regardless of their demographic background. Consider the alternative. If a school is unwilling to commit to the word *all*, then educators are, by default, accepting a mission that *most* students will succeed, but undoubtedly, some students are always going to fail. In other words, the school believes there will always be educational collateral damage, regardless of the school's policies and practices. If staff are unwilling to commit to a mission that embraces the words *ensure* and *all*, they are unlikely to fully commit to being a PLC and deeply implementing the RTI at Work process. As Larry Lezotte (2005), one of the original researchers of the Effective Schools Movement, states:

> Our experience verifies that the possibilities are unlimited once a dedicated school staff goes in search of research and best practices to advance their shared vision of learning for all. However, until they embrace the possibility that all children can learn, the obstacles and barriers they will find are virtually endless and will seem insurmountable. (p. 189)

Here's Why

In his book *Transforming School Culture*, Anthony Muhammad (2018) describes two types of school reform efforts: (1) *technical changes* and (2) *cultural changes*. Technical changes are made of tools such as a school's master schedule, instructional materials, and policies. Obviously, creating a multitiered system of supports requires a significant amount of technical change. However, Muhammad (2018) argues that technical changes "are definitely necessary to effect improvement in student performance, but they produce very few positive results when people who do not believe in the intended outcome of the change use them" (pp. 22–23). For the technical steps of RTI to work, you must execute them within a culture of high expectations for both educators and students.

To measure its organization's current culture, the guiding coalition should consider what will happen at the school if an educator asks, "Our school mission says we are committed to *all* students learning at high levels. Currently, we know that some students are failing. What are we going to do to fix this problem?"

Will the faculty meet the question with resistance? Will the question create a faculty debate? Will this person be ostracized, or will the question be a rallying cry for self-reflection and improvement? If this question creates significant staff division, it indicates that the school's culture misaligns with a mission of ensuring high levels of learning for all students. Change the setting for this question. What if someone raises this concern in a district cabinet meeting? How will central office leadership respond?

Here's How

Unfortunately, a learning-focused school culture is not a reality in most schools. Through our work at sites struggling to become a PLC and implement MTSS, schools often acknowledge that they lack a shared commitment. But then they ask the wrong question: How do we get buy-in from our staff? We don't care for the term *buy-in* because it conveys the wrong message. To say staff won't *buy into it* suggests that educators are resisting because they want to know what is in it for *them*. Having worked with thousands of educators around the world, we have hardly met an educator who does not work with the best interests of students in mind. What they have to give, not what they expect to receive, is what attracts educators to this field.

We suggest the correct term is *ownership*: How does a school create a sense of staff ownership of becoming a PLC and creating systematic supports, especially considering the cultural hurdles this chapter describes? We cannot achieve cultural change through force or coercion (Muhammad, 2018). Rational adults resist change for many reasons, and experienced educators often raise legitimate concerns regarding the professional conditions and personal commitments needed to ensure learning for all. Complex problems require multiple solutions.

Establishing this kind of culture requires much thought and planning by the guiding coalition, beginning with discussing the critical questions outlined in the reproducible "Creating Consensus for a Culture of Collective Responsibility" (page 47). The guiding coalition's initial work is also summarized in the following four steps. In considering the challenges of leading change, it is important to recognize that long-lasting and substantial change does not happen overnight. Rather, it is more of a one-thousand-step journey, with each step carefully and intentionally planned. As educational change expert Michael Fullan (1994) points out, "Leading change is a planned journey into uncharted waters with a leaky boat and a mutinous crew."

1. **Assess the current reality:** It is difficult to map a successful journey if team members are unsure of the school's current location. In this case, it is critical to determine the staff's current culture to ensure all students learn. Muhammad (2018) recommends using data to catalyze change in an inspirational way. We have found that many successful schools don't solely look at data such as the percentage of students below proficient on state assessments or the number of students reading below grade level. Instead, these schools connect data to individual students—rather than telling teachers that 12 percent of the school's students are below proficient in reading, they connect those numbers with a list of specific students who make up the 12 percent. These connections resonate with why we joined the profession—to help children.

2. **Provide a compelling case for change:** Too often when introducing change initiatives, schools describe what needs to be done without first providing a compelling reason why the alteration is necessary. In his study of educational *fundamentalists*, or members who

actively fight change, Muhammad (2018) finds that many resist because no one provides them with a clear rationale for change. If school leadership cannot provide a compelling *why*, the staff won't care about the *what*. Agreeing on the need for change results from assessing and confronting the current reality, celebrating what is right, identifying areas for growth, and learning together about new possibilities through research and dialogue.

3. **Create a doable plan:** The most compelling reason for change is irrelevant if the staff view the goal as impossible. It is critical that staff receive a doable plan that defines specific responsibilities and includes the resources needed to meet these expectations. If teachers view RTI as a demand requiring them to work beyond their current contractual hours, they have a legitimate right to resist.

4. **Build staff consensus:** Most people become committed to a process once they see that it works, not before. This creates an interesting dilemma—schools can't start until they build consensus, but they won't get true commitment until they start. Consequently, taking months and months to plan for change and get everyone to feel ownership over the process follows the law of diminishing returns. If schools wait for everyone to get on board before starting, the train will never leave the station. What it takes to start is consensus—everyone has had a say, the will of the group has emerged, and that will is evident, even to those who disagree (DuFour et al., 2024).

In short, building a culture of collective responsibility happens not by chance but by intentional and direct action taken by a guiding coalition. Anthony Muhammad and Luis F. Cruz (2019) identify transformational leadership as an approach required to simultaneously build a culture of collective responsibility and effectively confront resistance to change. The tenets of transformational leadership are introduced later in this chapter under Action 5: Prepare for Staff Resistance (page 69).

People tend to come to the same conclusions when they base their decisions on the same facts. Regrettably, many schools average opinions to make decisions. Because every staff member enters a discussion with different prior experiences, priorities, and perspectives, it is often difficult to reach consensus. More often than not, the loudest and most aggressive voices win, and those resistant to change are usually the most vocal in this debate process. Muhammad's (2018) research finds that fundamentalists are usually the most aggressive in stating their beliefs.

By contrast, team members in a PLC build shared knowledge instead of averaging opinions to arrive at consensus on vital questions. They engage in collective inquiry into best practices (DuFour et al., 2024). The guiding coalition members should serve as the lead learners. They must dig deeply into the areas of focus, identify powerful research and relevant information, and determine the best format for sharing this information with the staff.

Reaching true consensus begins with a shared understanding of what consensus actually represents. To get there requires time, trust building, structured conversations, and consistent monitoring along the way.

Helpful Tools

The following tools will help you accomplish the work for this essential action.

▶ **Chapter 2 of *Learning by Doing, Fourth Edition* (DuFour et al., 2024), "Defining a Clear and Compelling Purpose":** This chapter focuses on how to create the four pillars of the PLC process—common mission, vision, values, and goals.

- ▶ **"Creating Consensus for a Culture of Collective Responsibility" (page 47):** The guiding coalition can use this tool to help build consensus regarding a school mission to ensure high levels of learning for all students.

- ▶ **"Creating Consensus Survey" (for the guiding coalition; page 48):** The guiding coalition can use this tool to self-assess its readiness to build consensus and lead change.

- ▶ **"Forces at Work" (page 49):** Once the guiding coalition has self-assessed its current readiness, it can use this tool to identify its strengths, areas of weakness, and specific action steps for moving forward.

- ▶ **"Simplifying RTI Culture Survey" (for the entire staff; page 50):** All staff can use this tool to provide the guiding coalition with a more accurate picture of current cultural beliefs and norms.

- ▶ **"Building Consensus for Change and Bell Schedule Chart" (page 51):** This tool provides an example of how one school successfully surveyed and achieved consensus.

Coaching Tips

At its most fundamental level, the task of creating consensus for cultural change is all about building shared knowledge and understanding. As the guiding coalition works through and discusses the questions included on the reproducible "Creating Consensus for a Culture of Collective Responsibility," it must structure and facilitate the same discussions with the entire staff. Cultural change happens when all staff members reveal their beliefs and assumptions, read research, confront the current reality, explore the possibilities of a new vision for their work, and hear each other's thoughts and opinions. It is not enough for the guiding coalition to have these powerful discussions only among its members.

Building shared knowledge takes time, consistency of message, and multiple opportunities for dialogue. Team members must pay attention to both written and verbal communication, including emails, bulletins, meeting notes, one-on-one conversations, team and department meetings, and whole-staff meetings. It is also important to ensure that all stakeholders are included—administrators, counselors, instructional staff, support staff, parents, and, when appropriate, students.

As the guiding coalition engages in this work, it may choose to use the reproducible "Creating Consensus Survey" to formatively assess its progress. The reproducible "Forces at Work" is useful for ensuring discussions include evidence and data as their basis, not just opinions. It also helps the team develop a prioritized to-do list of next steps.

The most challenging steps in creating cultural change are those at the beginning and the end, in which team members explore assumptions and beliefs in a nonthreatening way and reach consensus about the proposed change.

Many tools are available for structuring and facilitating a discussion about assumptions and beliefs. The bottom line is that teams cannot ignore this step. The likelihood of reaching consensus on shared assumptions and beliefs is almost nil without first uncovering and discussing current beliefs.

As conversations take place, the guiding coalition needs to check progress toward consensus. A tool such as the reproducible "Simplifying RTI Culture Survey" is one means to do a temperature check along the way. You can use it more than once, as long as enough time and conversation take place between uses to show change.

Finally, two common obstacles to cultural change are (1) a lack of common understanding of consensus and (2) a lack of a clear tool or strategy to demonstrate consensus. Sharing the example highlighted in the reproducible "Building Consensus for Change and Bell Schedule Chart" (page 51) is one way to ensure everyone has a common definition of *consensus* and a common vision of how and when they'll know the school has achieved it.

Take note! The work described in this section—Action 2: Build a Culture of Collective Responsibility—never ends! In other words, creating and sustaining a healthy school culture is a topic of conversation that the guiding coalition must attend to in its own meetings, as well as each and every day. Culture is a dynamic and amoeba-like social organism that requires constant nurturing and care.

Creating Consensus for a Culture of Collective Responsibility

A culture of collective responsibility is based on two fundamental beliefs:

1. The first assumption is that we, as educators, must accept responsibility to ensure high levels of learning for every student. While parental, societal, and economic forces impact student learning, the actions of the educators will ultimately determine each student's success in school.

2. The second assumption is that all students can learn at high levels. We define high levels of learning as *high school plus*, meaning every student will graduate from high school with the skills and knowledge required to continue to learn. To compete in the global marketplace of the 21st century, students must continue to learn beyond high school, and there are many paths for that learning, including trade schools, internships, community colleges, and universities.

Discussing the following critical questions will assist the school leadership team in creating consensus for a culture of collective responsibility aligned with these beliefs.

1. **How will we provide a compelling case for change?** For someone to change, they first must see a compelling reason to change. In other words, one must show why there is a need to change. Raising test scores or meeting district, state, or federal mandates hardly meets this goal. Instead, look to paint a picture of what adulthood will likely look like for students who don't succeed in school.

2. **What must we do differently?** Besides a compelling reason to change, one must also provide a doable plan. The noblest cause is useless if the changes required are seen as unrealistic. Staff members want a clear picture of exactly what changes are necessary to achieve learning for all students.

3. **How do we know these changes will work?** Having experienced the pendulum of school change for the past decades, many educators are skeptical of change processes. What evidence is available to demonstrate the validity of the recommended changes? (Besides the research quoted in *Simplifying Response to Intervention* [Buffum, Mattos, & Weber, 2012], the website www.allthingsplc.info has dozens of schools and hundreds of pages of research validating the elements of PLCs and RTI.)

4. **What concerns do we expect, especially from staff members traditionally against change?** The leadership team should brainstorm the concerns staff members will have regarding the recommended changes. What will be the leadership's response to these concerns?

5. **What is the best setting or structure for the conversations needed to create consensus?** One of the leadership team's greatest leverage points is its ability to determine the location, structure, and timing of the conversations to create staff consensus. All stakeholders must have a voice in the process, but not necessarily in the same meeting. Sometimes the feelings of the silent majority can be drowned out by the aggressive opinions of a loud minority resistant to change. Consider a series of meetings with teams, grade levels, or departments. Also, set clear norms for the meeting, as professional, respectful dialogue is essential.

6. **How will we know if we have reached consensus?** Remember, it does not take 100 percent approval to get started; it takes consensus. Consensus is reached when all stakeholders have had a say and the will of the group has emerged and is evident, even to those who disagree. Consider how many key people will be needed to create the tipping point necessary for consensus.

In the end, true commitment comes when people see that the changes work. So the key is to build consensus, then get started doing the work. You will never get commitment until you start doing the work, but you cannot start until you get consensus.

Source: Adapted from Buffum, A., Mattos, M., & Weber, C. (2012). Simplifying response to intervention: Four essential guiding principles. *Bloomington, IN: Solution Tree Press.*

Creating Consensus Survey

A culture of collective responsibility is based on two fundamental beliefs.

1. The first assumption is that we, as educators, must accept responsibility to ensure high levels of learning for every student. While parental, societal, and economic forces impact student learning, the actions of educators ultimately determine each student's success in school.

2. The second assumption is that all students can learn at high levels. We define high levels of learning as *high school plus*, meaning every student graduates from high school with the skills and knowledge required to continue to learn. To compete in the 21st century global marketplace, students must continue to learn beyond high school. There are many paths for learning, including trade schools, internships, community colleges, and universities.

Collective Responsibility Survey

Respond to the following statements using the number scale.

1 = Never   2 = Seldom   3 = Sometimes   4 = Often   5 = Always, or almost always

Statement	1	2	3	4	5
1. We show teachers why there is a need for change. This need is not primarily tied to raising test scores or meeting district, state, and federal mandates. The need for change is tied to what the future looks like for students who do not succeed in school.					
2. In addition to providing compelling reasons to change, we make change doable. Our plans for change are realistic and scaffolded.					
3. We provide teachers with evidence that demonstrates the validity of recommended changes. We acknowledge that teachers are rightfully skeptical of change processes due to constant swings of the pendulum.					
4. We anticipate concerns staff members have regarding proposed change and prepare our responses in advance.					
5. We create a series of meetings and opportunities for staff to express their opinions. We are careful to structure meetings in a way that encourages professional dialogue rather than allowing a few voices to dominate.					
6. We define consensus so that it does not require 100 percent approval to get change started. The tipping point is reached when the will of the group is evident, even to those who still oppose it.					

Source: Adapted from Buffum, A., Mattos, M., & Weber, C. (2012). Simplifying response to intervention: Four essential guiding principles. *Bloomington, IN: Solution Tree Press.*

Forces at Work

Based on these critical questions, consider the forces in your team's favor and those working against you. Then, create a to-do list of next steps.

Critical Questions to Consider	Forces in Our Favor	Forces Working Against Us	Next Steps to Effectively Address These Questions
How will we provide a compelling case for change? ❏ Quantitative evidence ❏ Qualitative evidence			
What must we do differently? How doable is our plan? ❏ Clarity of changes needed ❏ Skills and resources needed to support change			
How do we know these changes will work? ❏ Research ❏ Experience			
What concerns do we expect, especially from staff members who are traditionally against change? ❏ Staff concerns ❏ Leadership response			
What is the best setting or structure for the conversations needed to create consensus? ❏ Meetings ❏ Clear norms			
How will we know if we have reached consensus? ❏ Evidence of consensus ❏ Implementation			

Simplifying RTI Culture Survey

Respond to the following statements using the number scale.

1 = Never   2 = Seldom   3 = Sometimes   4 = Often   5 = Always, or almost always

Question	1	2	3	4	5
1. Our school supports and appreciates staff sharing new ideas.					
2. When something at our school is not working, our staff predict and prevent rather than react and repair.					
3. Our school schedule includes frequent collaboration opportunities for teachers as well as staff.					
4. Staff use team time to work as collaborative teams rather than as separate individuals.					
5. Our teams write norms or commitments that govern their work with each other, and they review and revise norms as needed.					
6. Our school enjoys a rich and robust tradition of rituals and celebrations that honor the work of teams as well as individuals.					
7. It is evident that learning for all is our core purpose as a school.					
8. Our staff believe that all students are capable of learning at high levels.					
9. Our staff believe that what we do can overcome the effects of poverty, language barriers, and poor parenting.					
10. Our staff believe that it is our responsibility to help all students become successful, even if the cause of challenges originates outside of school.					

Building Consensus for Change and Bell Schedule Chart

Voices: I understand the current attached proposal, and my voice and opinion have been clearly heard and represented through this process. (Please circle the statement that reflects your position.)

I Veto	**I Strongly Disagree**	**I Agree**	**I Strongly Agree**
I have never seen the proposal.	I have many unanswered questions. I had no opportunity to express my views.	I was heard. I understand. I had the opportunity to express my views.	All my views and opinions were heard. All questions were answered.

- -

Proposal: It is proposed that _____ School adopt the following mission statement reflecting its commitment to ensure high levels of learning for all students.

_____

_____

Please circle the statement that reflects your position on this mission statement.

I Veto	**I Disagree**	**I Have Reservations**	**I Support It**	**I'm In**	**"You Had Me at Hello" (Absolutely)**
It's not good for students. Do not pursue.	It's not the best way. Let's keep trying.	But I'll support the will of the people.	Let's get moving.	I'll promote this proposal. I'll help.	I'll champion this proposal. I'll lead.

- -

Consensus: It's clear to me that the will of this school has emerged regarding this proposal. The staff have given a mandate to adopt this mission statement effective _____ (deadline).

Please circle the following statement that best reflects your position.

- I see clear disagreement, which communicates to me *not* to move ahead with this proposal.

- I see reservations, but the overall will of the group to move forward is evident.

- It is clearly the will of this staff to move forward with this proposal.

Action 3

Form Collaborative Teacher Teams

Achieving a learning-focused mission requires more than the belief that all students can learn at high levels—it also requires collaborative structures and tools to achieve this goal. In addition to the school guiding coalition, collaborative teacher teams form the engine that drives a school's PLC and RTI efforts. Collaborative teacher teams consist of educators who share essential curriculum and, thus, take collective responsibility for students learning their common essential learning outcomes.

Because the uniting characteristics of teacher teams are shared learning outcomes, the most common and preferred structures would be grade-level teams at the elementary level and course-based teams at the secondary level. It is likely that every school has some singleton educators, who are the only people teaching a specific grade, course, or subject. When this is the case, the following structures can be effective ways to form teams.

▶ **Vertical teams:** Vertical teams share common learning outcomes developed across consecutive years of school. Examples include a K–2 primary team at the elementary level and a high school language arts team at the secondary level. While grade-level standards are not identical from kindergarten to second grade, they have several essential skills in common, such as phonemic awareness and number sense, with increasing rigor over time. Students develop these skills across all three grades. Likewise, the members of a high school language arts team do not share identical content standards but do share essential skills, such as persuasive writing and analytical reading. Vertical teams can also ensure that prerequisite skills are taught in sequence. This team structure often works best at smaller schools, where there may be only one teacher who teaches a particular grade level, subject, or course.

▶ **Interdisciplinary teams:** Interdisciplinary teams consist of teachers who teach different subjects. While interdisciplinary teams do not share content standards, they can focus their team efforts on shared essential skills. For example, an interdisciplinary team can focus on the college-ready skills David T. Conley (2007) recommends, including—

  ▪ Performing analytical reading and discussion

  ▪ Demonstrating persuasive writing

  ▪ Drawing inferences and conclusions from texts

  ▪ Analyzing conflicting source documents

  ▪ Supporting arguments with evidence

  ▪ Solving complex problems with no obvious answer

These essential learning standards are not subject specific; therefore, each teacher on the interdisciplinary team can use their unique subject content as the vehicle to teaching these higher-level thinking skills. The team can clearly define these common learning outcomes, discuss effective Tier 1 core instruction, develop common rubrics to assess these skills, and respond collectively when students need additional help. This approach can work especially well at smaller secondary schools.

▶ **Regional and virtual teams:** It is possible that the previous teaming options might not work for a specific faculty member. When this is the case, the educator is unlikely the only person in the district, county, region, state or province, or country who teaches their curriculum content. Forming a collaborative team beyond the site is an option. This collaboration most likely will require virtual team meetings.

While there are numerous ways to structure collaborative teacher teams, all these structures have one characteristic in common—if the purpose of school collaboration is to improve student learning, then team members must share essential student learning outcomes. Ronald Gallimore, Bradley A. Ermeling, William M. Saunders, and Claude Goldenberg (2009) find that "successful teams need to set and share goals to work on that are immediately applicable to student learning. Without such goals, teams will drift toward superficial discussions and truncated efforts" (p. 549). These common learning goals are what unite and focus each teacher team's work. This focus on learning ensures that teacher teams are able to fulfill the vision of collective responsibility.

Here's Why

It is a universal truth that no one teacher has all the skills, knowledge, and time necessary to meet the needs of all students assigned to their classes. There is no evidence that having teachers work in isolation is an effective way to enhance student or teacher success.

The authors of the book *Concise Answers to Frequently Asked Questions About Professional Learning Communities at Work* provide four significant reasons why educators need time to collaborate (Mattos, DuFour, DuFour, Eaker, & Many, 2016).

1. Leaders in most professions consider time collaborating with colleagues as essential to success. As professionals, educators benefit from the expertise and collective efforts of a team. Collaboration is not a frill; it is an essential element of best practice.

2. The research supporting collaboration is extensive. The collaborative team is the fundamental building block of a learning organization, and the link between a collaborative culture and school improvement is well established.

3. U.S. educators have been criticized because their students do not score as well as Asian students on international tests. The fact is Japanese teachers spend much less time in front of students in the classroom than U.S. teachers do (Mehta, 2013; Organisation for Economic Co-operation and Development, 2014). In Japan, a teacher working with colleagues to perfect a lesson or review student work is engaged in highly productive activities that improve student achievement (Mehta, 2013; Organisation for Economic Co-operation and Development, 2018).

4. Finally, organizations show their priorities by how they use their resources. In a school, time is one of the most important resources. Knowing the strong correlation between meaningful collaboration and improved student achievement, any board of education should be willing to provide this precious resource.

The degree to which teachers depend on one another and interdependently help all students learn at high levels largely determines their school's success.

Here's How

The expectation for teachers to meet with colleagues, in either grade-level or department meetings, is nothing new in education. Yet, at most schools, these meetings rarely lead to increased student learning. This is because the act of meeting does not mean teachers are collaborating. They aren't doing the right work. As we emphasized previously, this book is about *doing the right work right*. Buffum and colleagues (2012) state the responsibilities of each teacher team in the RTI process are to:

- Clearly define essential student learning outcomes

- Provide effective Tier 1 core instruction

- Assess student learning and the effectiveness of instruction

- Identify students in need of additional time and support

- Take primary responsibility for Tier 2 interventions for students who have [not yet] mastered the team's identified essential [academic] standards (p. 33)

The key to team success lies in the development of *systematic processes*—foundational structures that promote consistency, honest communication, respect, and mutual accountability within each team. Tools and strategies, such as those listed and explained later in this chapter, are critical to establishing such processes. It's the guiding coalition's responsibility not only to facilitate dialogue and promote the development of a shared understanding of collaboration but also to *live* this work, thus modeling what it looks and sounds like to be a high-performing collaborative team.

In addition, the guiding coalition must support the staff by ensuring that a structure provides ample time for weekly teacher team collaboration. Buffum and colleagues (2012) state the guiding coalition, working within the district's and state or province's contractual agreements and regulations, must lead the process of creating sufficient collaboration time for each team. At a minimum, this collaboration time should meet the following criteria.

- ▶ **Frequency:** We recommend that teacher teams meet at least once per week. Likewise, we recommend that the site intervention team meet weekly, while the guiding coalition should meet at least twice per month.

- ▶ **Duration:** Each meeting should be at least forty-five minutes in length. If the meetings are twice monthly, then it's best to dedicate at least ninety minutes.

- ▶ **Attendance:** Participation must be mandatory. Collaboration by invitation does not work.

Occasionally, we encounter schools or districts that claim to be stumped in their efforts to find the time necessary for collaboration. We find this perplexing, as the average teacher is paid to be on campus six to seven hours a day, totaling thirty to thirty-five hours a week. Is it really impossible to carve out forty-five minutes of meeting time in a thirty-five-hour workweek? More often than not, the problem is that the school is trying to find extra time while keeping the current schedule unaltered. Very few schools have extra time in their schedule—that is, time currently unallocated to any particular purpose. For this reason, the task is not to find time for collaboration but rather to make collaboration time a priority.

Helpful Tools

The following tools will help you accomplish the work for this essential action.

- ▶ **Chapter 3 of *Learning by Doing, Fourth Edition* (DuFour et al., 2024), "Building a Collaborative Culture":** This chapter discusses different structures to create collaborative teams that share essential learning outcomes, including options for educators who are the only people on campus who teach their particular grade, course, or curriculum. In addition, it provides multiple options regarding how schools and districts create collaborative teams without needing added funding or lengthening the teachers' contractual workweek.

- ▶ **"Are We a Group or a Team?" (page 57):** This activity facilitates powerful dialogue about both the *what* and the *why* of collaboration. You can use the chart of team descriptors generated in this activity as the foundation for self-assessment and goal setting in moving from *group work* to *teamwork*. In addition, many books and articles are available for shared reading and dialogue, including *The Handbook for SMART School Teams* (Conzemius & O'Neill, 2014), *Learning by Doing* (DuFour et al., 2024), and *Collaborative Teams That Transform Schools* (Marzano, Heflebower, Hoegh, Warrick, & Grift, 2016).

- ▶ **"Stages of Team Development" (page 58):** This form highlights the stages that all groups go through as they transition from a group of individuals to a cooperative group and, finally, a high-performing collaborative team.

- ▶ **"Team Action-Planning Template" (page 60):** Teacher teams can use this template to ensure that their collaborative goals and tasks are based on data rather than opinions.

- ▶ **"The Trust on Our Team Survey" (page 61):** This survey helps the guiding coalition assess the current level of trust among team members.

- ▶ **"Team Collaboration Time: Planning Guide and Schedule" (page 62):** The guiding coalition can use this tool to plan team collaboration time.

Coaching Tips

The key tip to keep in mind here is to involve teachers in each and every step of creating time for collaboration. This includes building a shared understanding of *why* collaboration time is essential, *where* to find the time within the school day, and *how* to use that time. That said, the following are several strategies to consider for involving teachers in the process of creating time for collaboration.

- ▶ Incorporate into faculty meetings readings and discussions about professional articles that focus on the importance of collaboration.

- ▶ Create a teacher-led task force to explore options for creating time during the school day. This might entail research, visitations to other schools, or attendance at professional conferences focused on teacher collaboration.

- ▶ Ensure teachers understand the differences between *collaboration* (a systematic process in which people work together on a single shared goal) and *coblaboration* (people meeting with no structure or process for sharing knowledge, solving problems, or creating new ideas), *cooperation* (people meeting to accomplish individual yet common goals), and other forms of *collaboration lite* (any process with superficial levels of collaborative implementation). Professional reading and role play may be helpful.

- ▶ Model collaboration in faculty meetings by agreeing on the purpose and nonpurpose of meetings, brainstorming and setting meeting norms, reviewing the norms regularly, and holding each other accountable to the norms.

- ▶ Identify clear expectations for the products you will create as a team during collaboration time.

- ▶ Use a consensus decision-making process for establishing the schedule for collaboration time.

The more that teachers are involved in understanding, developing, and supporting the creation of collaboration time, the more likely they are to use that time well.

Once time for teacher team collaboration is accomplished, we find that, when asked, almost all teachers report they are working together collaboratively. The fact is, however, very few of these groups are actually engaged in true collaboration, and therefore, they have little chance of producing powerful results.

Investing time in activities that ensure a shared understanding of the differences between cooperation (groups) and collaboration (teams) can help you avoid this scenario. Once you reach consensus on the definition of collaboration, you might consider writing a charter of collaboration that all staff members sign as a symbol of support and commitment to active participation.

All the tools in this section are useful for helping team members understand themselves and how to work together as a team. Understanding where each group is in the process allows the guiding coalition to make better decisions about tools and strategies that will help each group progress to the next stage of development.

Most important, it is the guiding coalition's responsibility not only to facilitate dialogue and promote the development of a shared understanding of collaboration but also to *live* this work, thus modeling what it looks and sounds like to be a high-performing collaborative team.

Are We a Group or a Team?

Complete the following ten steps to understand the differences between cooperation and collaboration.

1. Give the following directions to teams: "I will show you a triangle graphic comprised of twenty-five randomly placed capital letters (twenty-five out of twenty-six—none repeated). You have ten seconds to study the triangle, and you may *not* write during those ten seconds. When I remove the triangle, record as much as you can remember. Score your work based on the number of correct letters in the correct location on the triangle."

2. Show the first triangle for ten seconds, and then remove it from view (see the sample triangles).

Y
Q Z D
P C F H I
R X V A M O G
T J E W U B L N K

3. When everyone is finished recording their response, show the triangle again. Have individuals score their recordings and find the average for their table team. Report out and chart the averages.

4. Using the same data, direct teams to determine their team score by compiling their individual results into a team total—there is still a total of twenty-five possible, so each letter only counts once, even if all team members got it correct. But every letter counts, even if only one member got it correct. Report out and record team scores. Point out the positive impact of cooperating—more heads are better than one.

5. Give the following directions to teams: "I will now show you a new triangle—same format, different letter placement. You have ten seconds to view it. The difference this time is that you only need to create one triangle as a team, and you will have one minute to figure out how you want to do it."

6. Monitor planning time (one minute). Give a cue, show the second triangle for ten seconds, and then remove it from view. Tell teams to compile their recordings for their team triangle.

F
K P D
V A G T O
E Q I L C W J
M U B R Y H N X S

7. Once everyone is finished, show the second triangle again. Have teams determine their team scores—report out and chart.

8. Ask participants to look at data and point out the significant gains between team totals and team results. Ask them to briefly talk about how and why their teams improved. Ask for individuals to share and chart their responses. Be sure to probe for ideas such as clear, common goal; clear individual expectations; individual strengths factoring into work division; data used for reflection and improvement; trust; accountability to teammates; communication; and strategies for sharing.

9. Once you chart all responses, ask participants to reflect on a team that they currently work with and answer *yes* or *no* to each question you are about to pose. Using the charted responses, ask a question based on each response. For example, "Does your team have a clear, common goal?"

10. Finally, suggest that the responses on the chart reflect the differences between cooperative teams and collaborative teams to conclude the activity. Highlight the potential of increasing student achievement (getting results no one is able to get when working alone or in cooperative groups) when educators understand and commit to true collaboration.

Stages of Team Development

While the process of developing a professional learning team may feel uniquely personal, certain stages of development are common across teams. By understanding that these stages exist—and by describing both the challenges and the opportunities inherent in each stage—school leaders can improve the chances of success for every learning team. Use the following quick reference guide to evaluate the stages of team development in your building and to identify practical strategies for offering support.

Characteristics of the Stage	Strategies for Offering Support
Stage: Filling the Time	
• Teams ask, "What exactly are we supposed to do together?" • Meetings can ramble. • Frustration levels can be high. • Activities are simple and scattered rather than part of a coherent plan for improvement.	❑ Set clear work expectations. ❑ Define specific tasks for teams to complete (for example, identifying essential objectives or developing common assessments). ❑ Provide sample agendas and sets of norms to help define the work.
Stage: Sharing Personal Practices	
• Teamwork focuses on sharing instructional practices or resources. • A self-imposed standardization of instruction appears. • Less-experienced teammates benefit from the planning acumen of their colleagues. • Teams delegate planning responsibilities.	❑ Require teams to come to consensus around issues related to curriculum, assessment, and instruction. ❑ Require teams to develop shared minilessons delivered by all teachers. ❑ Structure efforts to use student learning data in the planning process. ❑ Ask questions that require data analysis to answer.
Stage: Developing Common Assessments	
• Teachers begin to wrestle with the question, "What does mastery look like?" • Emotional conversations about the characteristics of quality instruction and the importance of individual objectives emerge. • Pedagogical controversy is common.	❑ Provide teams with additional training in interpersonal skills and conflict management. ❑ Moderate or mediate initial conversations about common assessments to model strategies for joint decision making. ❑ Ensure that teams have had training in how to best develop effective common assessments. ❑ Create a library of sample assessments from which teams can draw.

Stage: Analyzing Student Learning

• Teams begin to ask, "Are students learning what they are supposed to be learning?" • Teams shift attention from a focus on teaching to a focus on learning. • Teams need technical and emotional support. • Teachers publicly face student learning results. • Teachers can be defensive in the face of unyielding evidence. • Teachers can grow competitive.	❏ Provide tools and structures for effective data analysis. ❏ Repurpose positions to hire teachers trained in data analysis so they can support teams new to working with assessment results. ❏ Emphasize a separation of person from practice. ❏ Model a data-oriented approach by sharing results that reflect on the work of practitioners beyond the classroom (for example, principals, counselors, and instructional resource teachers).

Stage: Differentiating Follow-Up

• Teachers begin responding instructionally to student data. • Teams take collective action rather than responding to results as individuals. • Principals no longer direct team development. Instead, they serve as collaborative partners in conversations about learning.	❏ Ask provocative questions about instructional practices and levels of student mastery. ❏ Demonstrate flexibility as teams pursue novel approaches to enrichment and reinforcement. ❏ Provide concrete ways to support differentiation. ❏ Identify relevant professional development opportunities; allocate funds to after-school tutoring programs. ❏ Redesign positions to focus additional human resources on struggling students.

Stage: Reflecting on Instruction

• Teams begin to ask, "What instructional practices are most effective with our students?" • Learning is connected back to teaching. • Practitioners engage in deep reflection about instruction. • Action research and lesson study are used to document the most effective instructional strategies for a school's student population.	❏ Facilitate a team's efforts to study the teaching-learning connection. ❏ Create opportunities for teachers to observe each other teaching. ❏ Provide release time for teams to complete independent projects. ❏ Facilitate opportunities for cross-team conversations to spread practices and perspectives across the entire school. ❏ Celebrate and publicize the findings of team studies.

Source: Adapted from Graham, P., & Ferriter, W. M. (2010). Building a Professional Learning Community at Work: A guide to the first year. *Bloomington, IN: Solution Tree Press.*

Team Action-Planning Template

For novice learning teams, the decision to collectively analyze student learning data does not come naturally. To ensure that your team incorporates the analysis of student learning data into its work, include explicit references to data in any team action planning documents. By doing so, you will constantly reinforce the message that data are important. Use the sample action-planning template below as a guide.

Your Team: _____

1. What is your area of focus? Please identify both general content area and specific curricular objectives, and any appropriate student subgroups.

2. Why did you pick this area of focus? What data did you use in making your decision?

3. What is your SMART goal for this area of focus?

4. How will you regularly assess progress toward this goal? How will you respond to the results of these assessments? In your answer, please include the following elements.
    *   Use of common assessments
    *   Plans for analyzing data from common assessments
    *   Plans for making team-based instructional adjustments based on assessment data
    *   Clear timelines

5. What additional skills might your team need to accomplish the goal? What professional learning opportunities or resources would help your team acquire these skills?

Source: Adapted from Graham, P., & Ferriter, W. M. (2010). Building a Professional Learning Community at Work: A guide to the first year. *Bloomington, IN: Solution Tree Press.*

The Trust on Our Team Survey

This survey is designed to collect information about the levels of trust on our learning team. For each of the descriptors below, please indicate the extent to which you agree or disagree with each statement by circling one of the three letters (D, N, A), and the level of importance that you place on each indicator by circling one of the three numbers (1, 2, 3).

D = Disagree   N = Neutral   A = Agree

1 = Very important   2 = Somewhat important   3 = Not important

My colleagues willingly share their materials, resources, and ideas with me.	D	N	A	1	2	3
I feel welcome in my colleagues' classrooms before and after school.	D	N	A	1	2	3
I feel welcome in my colleagues' classrooms during their instructional periods.	D	N	A	1	2	3
I feel comfortable with my colleagues in my room during my instructional periods.	D	N	A	1	2	3
I believe that my colleagues have good intentions in their interactions with me.	D	N	A	1	2	3
I believe that my colleagues have good intentions in their interactions with students.	D	N	A	1	2	3
I know that I can count on my colleagues.	D	N	A	1	2	3
I believe that my colleagues are honest.	D	N	A	1	2	3
I am not afraid to share student learning results with my colleagues.	D	N	A	1	2	3
I believe that my colleagues are competent and capable teachers.	D	N	A	1	2	3
I believe that I can learn from my colleagues.	D	N	A	1	2	3
I believe that everyone on my team makes meaningful contributions to our work.	D	N	A	1	2	3
I believe that everyone on my team is pulling in the same direction.	D	N	A	1	2	3
Our team celebrates the personal and professional successes of individual members.	D	N	A	1	2	3
Our team celebrates our collective accomplishments.	D	N	A	1	2	3
I look forward to the time that I spend with my colleagues.	D	N	A	1	2	3

Final Thoughts: On the back of this page, please describe the kind of support you think your team would need in order to improve the overall levels of trust between teachers.

Source: Adapted from Graham, P., & Ferriter, W. M. (2010). Building a Professional Learning Community at Work: A guide to the first year. *Bloomington, IN: Solution Tree Press.*

Team Collaboration Time: Planning Guide and Schedule

Collaboration time is essential to the PLC and RTI processes. Without it, the work is virtually impossible. It is the guiding coalition's responsibility to ensure frequent collaboration for schoolwide and teacher teams. This time should be:

- **Frequent**—Each team should meet weekly, or once every other week at a minimum.
- **Scheduled**—Meetings should last at least forty-five to sixty minutes per week.
- **Embedded**—Time must be embedded in the contractual workweek.

Site Collaboration Schedule

Schoolwide Teams	Time and Day	Location
Guiding Coalition		
Intervention Team		

Teacher Teams	Time and Day	Location

Action 4

Commit to Team Norms

We cannot overemphasize the importance of setting team norms to guide professional behavior while collaborating. True collaboration often requires staff members to have difficult conversations and to trust colleagues with their students. People can feel vulnerable discussing the best ways to meet students' needs or the current reality of what is not working. For this reason, team members must set collective commitments regarding how they are going to act and interact with each other. Unfortunately, some schools struggle with building a collaborative culture because personal conflicts prevent teams from functioning efficiently.

Team norms should address three types of outcomes.

1. **Procedural meeting expectations** to address such things as meeting attendance, punctuality, preparedness, division of labor, and the follow-through of team decisions

2. **Behavior expectations** to explain how the team makes decisions and addresses disagreements between team members

3. **Protocols** to successfully address when team norms are violated

Here's Why

Collaborative teacher teams form the engine that drives a PLC and leads critical elements at Tier 1 and Tier 2. Team meetings, in turn, provide the vehicle within which the engine can thrive, and team norms ensure that both the engine and the vehicle function at maximum productivity.

Robert J. Garmston and Bruce M. Wellman (2009) remind us, "Meeting success is influenced more by the collaborative norms of the group than by the knowledge and skill of the group's facilitator" (p. 56). In other words, when team members develop norms to which they hold themselves accountable, they make better use of meeting time, maintain their focus on student learning challenges, confront conflicts more effectively, and produce greater results.

Garmston and Wellman (2009, 2016) also point out that professional communication is at the heart of getting work done in schools. With that in mind, additional experts also highlight the importance of establishing team norms.

- ▸ Business writer Patrick Lencioni (2002) says, "Having clear norms gives teams a huge advantage when it comes to ensuring the exchange of good ideas" (p. 43).

- ▸ Susan K. Sparks (2008) shares, "[Norms] help us take risks, work through issues, and communicate well" (p. 45).

- ▸ Kathryn Parker Boudett and Meghan Lockwood (2019) point out, "Setting and sticking to shared agreements can transform team dynamics."

- ▸ Michael Roberts (2020b) states, "Without clearly laid out and agreed upon norms, there is no commitment from team members for how they will conduct their work, how they will treat one another, and what each professional will be held accountable for."

Here's How

There are many ways for teams to create and enforce their norms. Fundamental to any process a team might choose are the following six key considerations.

1. Team members must understand the purpose of their meetings. Ensuring that all team members have a clear, shared understanding of why they are meeting helps the rationale for establishing team norms gain leverage. Asking the question, "How do we need to work together to accomplish our goals?" is much more substantive than asking, "How do we need to behave?"

2. All team members need to participate in brainstorming, clarifying, and reaching agreement on team norms. Without full participation in the process, members will unlikely be willing to hold themselves or others accountable to the norms.

3. Team norms need to include a commitment to confronting behaviors that violate the norms. Teams often identify and agree on a specific signal as a norm check that causes everyone to stop and self-assess their own behavior. For example, a middle school guiding coalition printed its norms on bright pink bookmarks and agreed to raise one whenever anyone noticed a norm being violated. Instead of pointing it at an individual, someone would simply raise the bookmark in the air as a signal to everyone.

4. Make the norms visible at all meetings once your team agrees to the norms. To accomplish this, you can post the norms on a chart or table tent or include them on each meeting agenda.

5. Review the team norms at each meeting. A single norm might be highlighted at the beginning of each meeting, or individual members can take turns highlighting a norm that they believe to be in place and a norm that they suggest for reflection and improvement.

6. Assess the team norms for celebration or revision at least twice a year. Team members can respond to an individual survey to assess how well the team is living its norms or participate in a group assessment during a team meeting. For example, give each team member a set of red and green dots. Have them post the dots on a charted list of the norms (green for *in place* and red for *needs improvement*). Once they post all the dots, team members can discuss which norms are working well and should stay as they are, and which ones need to be reinforced or revised.

Helpful Tools

The following tools will help you accomplish the work for this essential action.

▶ **Chapter 2 of *Learning by Doing, Fourth Edition* (DuFour et al., 2024), "Defining a Clear and Compelling Purpose":** This chapter provides research regarding the importance of team norms and specifics on how to create and enforce these collective commitments.

▶ **"Steps for Establishing Team Norms" (page 67):** Teams can use this reproducible to follow a step-by-step process for establishing team norms and behaviors.

▶ **"Sample Team Norms" (page 68):** This sheet provides sample norms to help teams understand the types of behaviors to address when establishing team norms of their own.

Coaching Tips

Most important, schools and teams need to embrace the concept of *go slow to go fast*. One of the biggest mistakes teams can make is to ignore how essential it is to develop norms. Yes, establishing norms takes time. It might only take a single meeting, or it might require more extensive discussion and multiple meetings to reach agreement. The payoff, however, occurs when teams become more efficient and productive because they have clearly articulated their collective commitment to working together.

Based on our many experiences with multiple teams, two additional tips stand out.

1. Clarify why the team is meeting and what it seeks to accomplish through collaboration. As noted previously, this allows the conversation to center on *how we need to work together to accomplish our goals* rather than *how we need to behave*. Working together to accomplish goals feels more professional than simply setting rules for behavior.

2. To begin the brainstorming process, have members reflect on the behaviors they are willing to commit to as individuals. Consider the following.

   • Pose an open-ended question such as, "How can I best support my team and the accomplishment of our goals?" Ask each person to silently record a brief list of the behaviors they need to bring to each team meeting.

   • Following that, pose an additional question: "What do I need from my teammates to help us accomplish our goals?" Each person draws a line under their first brainstormed list and then adds behaviors they need from others.

   • After everyone completes the written brainstorming (without talking), a facilitator collects and charts ideas from members' initial list of personal behaviors. Challenge members to share only those behaviors from their own lists that are not already noted on the chart.

   • Review and clarify the list, and then ask members to offer any additional behaviors they identified as needs from others. Often, there are very few additions, thus reinforcing the idea that team norms start with individual commitments.

A team's first efforts at developing norms are often quite simplistic. This is normal. As team members strengthen their collaborative skills and begin to experience success, team members' norms typically strengthen and go beyond surface behaviors. For example, a high school English team was into its third year as a team before members became ready to identify "Check your ego at the door!" as a norm that they could all agree on and commit to.

Of course, challenges are always part of this process. Educators often ask us this question regarding RTI and collaborative teams: "How do you deal with a staff member who refuses to commit to this work?" Once reluctant staff members learn the compelling reasons to change and receive a doable plan and every opportunity to succeed, they have no professional, logical, or ethical justification to resist the proposed changes that most of the staff deem necessary for the welfare of their students. By this point, they have neither the right to stop the plan from proceeding nor the option of refusing to participate. Leaders must be willing to confront these resisters and demand that they meet their responsibilities to the school's collective efforts. In the next action, we provide more detail on how to successfully address resistance. Failure to do so empowers resisters to continue their destructive ways and damage trust with the majority of staff members who support the changes.

While the school administration must take the lead in confronting hard-core resistant members, our experience is that the greatest coercive pressure comes from peers who are willing to take a stand. Simply stated, teachers have more influence than administrators when seeking commitment from other teachers.

At most schools, a silent majority is willing to change, and an aggressive minority does whatever it takes to stop change. Many of these extreme resisters mistakenly believe that they speak for most of the staff because when they share their combatant opinions in the staff lounge every day, their peers sit quietly and don't say a word. That silence seemingly condones the comments and emboldens the resisters. The individual actions of each staff member shape the collective culture of an entire school. Unless the silent majority begins to have some courageous conversations with the aggressive minority holding their school hostage, truly transforming the school's culture will be difficult.

Steps for Establishing Team Norms

As a team, use the following five steps to establish behaviors for your team to operate under. These are the standards to which you must commit to accomplish your goals.

1. Discuss and agree on your team's purpose, goals, and desired products.

2. Post the question, "How do we need to work together in order to accomplish our goals?"

   a. Individually, brainstorm or record responses to "What do I need to do to ensure my team's success?"

   b. Underline the responses, and then individually brainstorm and record responses to "What do I need from my teammates in order to best contribute to my team's success?"

3. Collect and publicly record responses from all team members, beginning with individual needs and adding needs from others to complete the list.

4. Clarify, prioritize, and narrow the list to five to eight norms.

5. Reach consensus on the norms. Confirm commitment to norms from all members, and agree to give feedback.

6. Post norms, review them, and assess their use frequently. Modify as needed and agreed to.

Sample Team Norms

NORMS

Standards of behavior we commit to in order to accomplish our goals

---

The following are sample team norms.

1. Be honest and share what you think and feel.

2. Participate in the conversation. It is your responsibility to get your voice in the room.

3. Focus on the task.

4. Think creatively and comprehensively.

5. Treat one another as equals.

6. Listen and hear one another's viewpoints—one's perspective is one's truth.

7. Ensure equal airtime for all participants.

8. Come to meetings ready to work and learn.

9. Honor time limits and commitments.

Source: Adapted from Malone, J. (2006, August 17). Are we a group or a team? 2006 Getting Results Conference—The impact of one, the power of many *[Handout]. Accessed at http://results.ocde.us/downloads/JMalone-Group_Team_Handout.pdf on April 17, 2017.*

Action 5

Prepare for Staff Resistance

A guiding coalition should expect staff to resist change. It would be surprising if they didn't. Because resistance is inevitable, the guiding coalition members must not ask themselves, "Why are we experiencing resistance?" but instead ask, "Is the resistance to change rational or irrational?" As alluded to earlier in this chapter, when a school commits to implementing the RTI at Work process, educators are committing to redesigning a traditional school system that historically was not structured to ensure high levels of learning for all students. Therefore, staff who commit to implementing RTI at Work must be willing to change certain behaviors and professional responsibilities and align with the following.

▸ Commit to working collaboratively instead of independently.

▸ Collectively identify essential standards and unpack them to pinpoint essential knowledge and skills students must learn.

▸ Create and follow a scope and sequence whereby learning targets that staff unpack from essential standards guide their team's pacing and collective commitment to student learning.

▸ Formulate common formative assessments that all collaborative team members will use, analyze, and assess.

▸ Develop a bell schedule that allows additional time and support during the day for students who are not mastering essential standards.

▸ Share students, resources, and instructional practices to ensure all students succeed.

This list is not how most schools—and most educators—function. And in all organizations—especially schools—even the smallest change can be difficult for some to bear. As former teachers and administrators, we recall passionate discussions among educators regarding what font to use on staff T-shirts for the upcoming school year, and emotional debates about whether hot dogs or tacos should be served at the back-to-school barbeque. So, it is realistic to expect some degree of resistance to implementing RTI, a process that will alter your school's master schedule and people's professional responsibilities. And as the best intervention is prevention, it behooves a guiding coalition to take a proactive stance and prepare accordingly.

Here's Why

Guiding coalition members shouldn't immediately interpret staff's initial resistance to implementing a PLC or RTI as a lack of commitment to diligently working to help all students learn at higher levels. Fullan (2003) recognizes that those who choose to educate students largely do so because of a moral imperative. Why, then, would educators resist the implementation of research-based practices, such as RTI? Sociological and psychological perspectives can help leaders understand the conflicting scenario wherein hardworking and well-intentioned educators adamantly resist changes intended to serve students more effectively.

Sociologically, it is important to realize that schools do not exist in a vacuum. Cultural and political ideologies of the time have always influenced education reform. Thus, schools must prepare students to function within the context of a rapidly changing society (Spring, 2001). Likewise, rapid technological advancements have created a more interconnected global economy that requires students to leave postsecondary school career ready.

Schools are not immune to these changes, and well-intentioned educators are caught in the middle of this quandary. They begin each year with noble intentions to help students flourish academically, only to discover that traditional policies, practices, and procedures are misaligned with meeting many academic challenges. Muhammad (2024) states that understanding the gap that exists between what society expects of its citizens and what schools can deliver requires an honest assessment of the purpose of public education, who should have access to high levels of learning, and the quality of learning in U.S. schools.

In his theory of apprenticeship of observation, Dan C. Lortie (2002) further provides a psychological perspective as to the possible origins of educators' resistance to change. Lortie (2002) concludes that since most educators succeeded in the traditional public school system, they have been conditioned to believe that student success has less to do with a need to change a misaligned school system and more to do with external factors that influence achievement (student apathy to learning, parent involvement, and district and state support, to name a few).

As a result, rather than commit to changing an archaic public school system not designed to generate high levels of learning for diverse student populations, educators might subconsciously try to fit a square peg in a round hole; that is, they focus on, and put most of their energy into, factors beyond their control. Over time, they experience professional exhaustion and form a fixed, rather than growth, mindset (Dweck, 2006, 2017) about the effort required to change their school system.

Due to these sociological and psychological factors, educators may experience anxiety and frustration when leaders introduce a change in practice with limited context. Frustration eventually morphs into feelings of unhappiness and misery, and misery loves company, as the adage goes. For this reason, the guiding coalition must equip itself with the knowledge and skills to effectively navigate the discomfort created by change and proactively address staff resistance. Educators will not intrinsically commit to implementing the RTI at Work process—this commitment requires effective leadership (Muhammad & Cruz, 2019).

Here's How

Transformational leadership is the most effective approach a guiding coalition can use to generate collective commitment to the PLC and RTI at Work processes. According to Langston University (n.d.):

> Transformational leadership is defined as a leadership approach that causes change in individuals and social systems. In its ideal form, it creates valuable and positive change in the followers with the end goal of developing followers into leaders. Enacted in its authentic form, transformational leadership enhances the motivation, morale and performance of followers through a variety of mechanisms. (p. 1)

Muhammad and Cruz (2019) expand on the tenets of transformational leadership by identifying four specific skills transformational leaders must develop and consistently practice with a staff struggling with change.

1. The ability to communicate effectively

2. The ability to generate trust

3. The ability to build capacity

4. The ability to generate results through tactful confrontation

The following sections elaborate on these four skills.

Communicate Effectively

Transformational school leaders are effective communicators who make sure that staff members are keenly aware of why changes they advocate are necessary. They know that if they do not provide continuous, fact-based communication, staff will get lost and confused and, as a result, jump to conclusions based on assumptions or past negative experiences. For transformational leaders, effective communication encompasses the ability not only to share information, but also to interpret and respond to body language, listen to those expected to carry out change, and effectively provide honest and tactful feedback (Muhammad & Cruz, 2019). In addition, transformational leaders react to perceived breakdowns in communication and are proactive in their approach. In short, transformational leaders ensure that those expected to change understand the why that aligns with the change initiative.

There are four types of whys that transformational leaders can use to explain why change is needed based on their assessment of staff's climate and culture: (1) institutional, (2) professional, (3) societal, and (4) personal. When guiding coalitions use data and research to communicate change initiatives, they help staff intrinsically commit. As leading management thinker and economist W. Edwards Deming states, "Without data, you're just another person with an opinion" (Wikiquote, n.d.). Therefore, a guiding coalition must never use data as condemnation but rather as information (Muhammad & Cruz, 2019), and then align accumulated data with the appropriate why to persuade the staff. The following briefly describes the four whys.

Institutional

Transformational leaders utilizing an *institutional* why leverage their organization's fundamental purpose to guide necessary adult behaviors. Schools and districts typically publicize this fundamental purpose in the form of a mission statement. For example, if a school declares in its mission statement a commitment to ensure all students learn, and data indicate that specific cohorts of students are not learning at desired levels, professional educators have an obligation to explore ways to accomplish the articulated fundamental purpose.

Further, a guiding coalition has a responsibility to avoid organizational hypocrisy by ensuring staff uphold that mission statement. The guiding coalition can guide faculty and staff in realizing that helping only *some* students learn is out of the question, and therefore, the research-based practices that constitute PLC and MTSS can support them in accomplishing the desired outcomes stated in their mission statement. The guiding coalition should prepare for staff resistance by keeping up to date with student achievement data and using them as a means of both celebrating student achievement and reminding the faculty of its commitment as a school via its publicly declared mission.

Professional

When a guiding coalition incorporates a *professional* why, it tactfully reminds staff that they are not amateurs but rather professional educators. As professional educators, they are expected to develop expertise in techniques and methods that allow students to grasp new information. In short, professional educators utilize research and evidence of student learning to identify the practices proven to increase student achievement (Marzano, 2017; Simms, 2024). They have a responsibility, not an option, to implement techniques that help students continuously learn at higher levels, and RTI is grounded in research-based practices (Bailey & Dynarski, 2011; Hattie, 2012, 2023; Reardon, 2011). The guiding coalition must continuously couple its recommendations with compelling research that proves the recommendations' potential impact on student learning.

Societal

Creating a sense of urgency is a powerful way to inspire change (Kotter, 2007; Muhammad & Cruz, 2019). As teachers, administrators, and global educational consultants, we have extensive experience that confirms most school professionals exhibit great dedication and concern for students. Therefore, transformational leaders on a guiding coalition might use a *societal* why to articulate to faculty the unfortunate outcomes that students will experience should they leave school lacking the essential academic knowledge, skills, and behaviors needed for future success.

For example, the guiding coalition might first ask the faculty, "Shouldn't we want for every student the kind of future we want for the children in our own lives—our children, nieces and nephews, and grandchildren?" If so, then here is what we know about the likely futures of students who fail in the K–12 system: they are much more likely to be unemployed (U.S. Bureau of Labor Statistics, 2019), live in poverty (Statista, 2023), be incarcerated (Camera, 2021), and die prematurely (Lee-St. John et al., 2018). Is this the type of future we want for our own children? If not, then it is not good enough for any of your students.

In this example, the guiding coalition is leveraging a societal why. Our need to ensure high levels of learning for all students is far greater than what is measured by high-stakes tests—it is about the long-term well-being of our students and our collective prosperity as a society.

Personal

Educators don't enter the teaching profession to be wealthy or to have an extended summer vacation; instead, they choose the teaching profession out of a *personal* desire to help students achieve. Hence, educators are prone to experience a personal and natural high when their students succeed! Teachers' moral imperative to pursue a challenging and often underappreciated profession diminishes over time when they are repeatedly unsuccessful in achieving the desired outcomes for the students they serve (Education Week, 2024; Fullan, 2003).

Likewise, working within traditional structures, practices, and processes not proven to generate high levels of learning for all students further contributes to a sense of professional disappointment and disillusionment. Transformational leaders can prepare for resistance by reminding staff of their personal why—a reintroduction of sorts to why they chose the teaching profession in the first place. For example, during staff meetings, teachers can articulate the reasons why they chose the profession. Staff can share photographs and stories of times in their careers when their work with students was successful. And during this collective epiphany, the guiding coalition can seek to re-energize the staff's commitment to learn about new structures, processes, and procedures that can lead to stronger learning outcomes for all the students they serve.

The guiding coalition's ongoing assessment of the current climate and culture of the school will help it determine which of the four whys it should communicate to help staff stay committed to the right work.

Generate Trust

Transformational school leaders are aware that, in addition to cognitive needs, staff have emotional needs that can create resistance. Simply stated, school staff will not commit to RTI if they do not trust those who are advocating necessary changes (Muhammad & Cruz, 2019). Therefore, the guiding coalition should prepare for resistance by combining empathy and credibility to generate authentic trust among the staff.

The guiding coalition must know the difference between empathy and sympathy to effectively generate trustworthiness. Colleen Seward Ryan (n.d.) makes the following distinction:

> To discover what empathy is, let's first talk about what it is not. Empathy is not sympathy. It does not mean you have to agree with how someone is feeling, or even relate to their feelings. Instead, empathy is all about the awareness of other people's feelings—even when you can't sympathize with them!

As it pertains to RTI implementation, the guiding coalition must dedicate time to listening to the staff—especially resistant colleagues—as they grapple with embracing new ideas, practices, behaviors, and expectations.

Becoming a true PLC and creating an effective system of supports impacts every aspect of your school. As mentioned previously, this level of change inevitably creates discomfort, so taking the time to listen to individual concerns and offer support along the way is a worthwhile investment toward trust. In addition, the guiding coalition should continuously invest in its own learning by engaging in professional reading, attending conferences, and visiting schools further along in the process. When a guiding coalition invests in learning, it creates credibility and trustworthiness with those it leads and supports.

Build Capacity

Transformational leaders are keenly aware that there is a difference between understanding the need to embrace change and providing those expected to implement change with the knowledge, skills, and resources to do so effectively. If school staff lack the knowledge and skills required to turn PLC and RTI into day-to-day practice (the *how*), leaders should expect rational resistance to implementation (Muhammad & Cruz, 2019). The guiding coalition can prepare for resistance by:

▶ Clearly identifying the essential knowledge, skills, and behaviors that each faculty member needs in order to successfully contribute to team collaboration and systematic interventions

▶ Assessing current levels of competence

▶ Providing targeted training and support

Staff will not embrace what they do not understand, which is why a guiding coalition ensures the staff continuously have time to learn the knowledge and skills aligned with RTI at Work, even if that requires tactfully staggering implementation of the process.

In addition to providing staff with spaces and opportunities conducive to learning, the guiding coalition should prepare for resistance by inviting staff members to discuss and solve aspects of the process that are not working. People are less likely to tear down a bridge they helped build; thus, including staff voices in problem solving can empower the staff to take ownership of the changes required and, as a result, lessen the degree of resistance to implementation (Muhammad & Cruz, 2019).

The golden rule of transformational leadership is that support must always precede accountability (Muhammad & Cruz, 2019). Transformational leaders invest in various forms of support when they address cognitive needs by using data to persuade (the why), emotional needs by using empathy coupled with credibility to generate trustworthiness (the who), and functional needs by creating learning opportunities and also inviting followers to share their thoughts and opinions on change implementation (the how). In short, a guiding coalition takes solid steps to prepare for rational resistance, which is part of the change process.

But when some staff members persistently resist change—despite the continuous investment of support to meet staff's cognitive, emotional, and functional needs—the guiding coalition must demand a return on investment. We cannot stress this point too strongly: the guiding coalition must hold irrational resisters on staff accountable to the practices proven to ensure high levels of learning for all students. Anything less is malpractice.

Generate Results Through Tactful Confrontation

Members of a guiding coalition must be prepared to initiate two types of accountability.

1. **A culture of accountability:** This is achieved when the guiding coalition inundates staff with continuous support in the form of why, who, and how and, as a result, creates an environment that empowers staff members without positional authority to speak up and support RTI implementation. Lencioni (2005) describes a culture of accountability as a culture where team members are willing to "remind one another when they are not living up to the performance standards of the group" (p. 61). All members of the guiding coalition—administrators and teacher leaders—can use positive peer pressure with the minority of staff who continue to resist.

2. **Direct accountability:** Direct accountability should be implemented for any staff members who continue to resist despite the existence of a strong culture of accountability. In this context, direct accountability is the process of communicating to an individual or group that their resistance to research-based strategies that can help all students learn at high levels is unacceptable and will no longer be tolerated. Direct accountability requires positional authority, so it is usually ceded to administration.

Unfortunately, school leadership training programs often do not include the skills needed to initiate direct accountability in a tactful, professional manner. As former administrators, we recall how our administrative credential programs prepared us to manage our schools by learning the state laws for governing schools (also known as the "educational code"), creating functional bell schedules, and maintaining balanced school budgets. Programs provided little, if any, training on what to do when staff members refuse to embrace practices that generate high levels of learning. Hence, the ability to manage a school and lead a staff requires a different set of skills.

Muhammad and Cruz (2019) attempt to fill this void by showing school leaders how they can use the RESIST protocol to effectively initiate direct accountability for change. The RESIST protocol, as it pertains to RTI implementation, is as follows.

▸ **Recognize** that ignoring behavior that is not in line with RTI implementation subtly endorses this behavior and may communicate a lack of importance or emphasis to those grappling with the discomfort of RTI implementation.

▸ **Evaluate** whether you have provided enough support in the form of why, who, and how aligned with RTI implementation. If you are not providing enough support, begin providing additional support.

▸ **Select** the language you will use and the location (classroom, parking lot, and so on) where direct accountability emphasizing the need to implement the RTI process will occur.

▸ **Initiate** direct accountability with the individual or individuals, and **inquire** why behaviors aligned with RTI implementation are not apparent.

- ▸ **Select** your response to their response. If they reveal a perceived lack of support for RTI implementation, then begin by offering the support they have communicated is lacking. If they refuse to contribute to RTI implementation regardless of support provided, then only a leader with positional authority, such as an administrator, proceeds to the last step.

- ▸ **Tell** the individual or individuals refusing to comply with RTI implementation that their behavior is unacceptable and refusal to engage in behaviors aligned with the RTI process may lead to disciplinary consequences, including behavior monitoring until compliance is observed.

Initiating the RESIST protocol requires courage on the part of leaders. Muhammad (2018) reminds us that "illogical resistance . . . will eventually call leaders into a battle of will. This is a fight that the school leader must win, because to allow [resisters] to operate in a school culture in the midst of effective transformation is akin to sanctioning the behavior" (p. 113).

Guiding coalition members must also keep in mind that efforts to initiate a culture of accountability or direct accountability are attempts to change staff behaviors. While irrational resisters' pessimistic attitudes may persist, efforts to change adult behaviors (not attitudes or feelings) aligned with RTI implementation must remain the focus of the guiding coalition because behavior is congruent to culture.

Helpful Tools

The following tools will help you accomplish the work for this essential action.

- ▸ **Chapter 6 of *Time for Change: Four Essential Skills for Transformational School and District Leaders* (Muhammad & Cruz, 2019), "Tying It All Together":** This chapter provides a summary of the skill sets required by transformational leaders in schools.

- ▸ **"Understanding the Whys" (page 77):** Teams can use this reproducible to determine how best to meet cognitive needs and prepare for initiating each of the four whys—institutional, professional, societal, and personal.

- ▸ **"Tilling the Soil" (page 78):** Teams can use this reproducible to reflect on how best to initiate staff support and accountability for RTI implementation.

Coaching Tips

A fundamental initial step to preparing for resistance is to ensure that guiding coalition members understand their role as coaches. As David B. Peterson and Mary Dee Hicks (1996) point out, "Coaching is the process of equipping people with the tools, knowledge, and opportunities they need to develop themselves and become more effective" (p. 14). In other words, preparing for and effectively addressing resistance requires an ability to facilitate growth rather than demand or direct change.

Beginning with a self-assessment may help the guiding coalition members become aware of their personal assumptions, biases, strengths, and challenges in preparing for resistance. The four essential skills of transformational leaders described in this section provide a framework for such a self-assessment. Have the members ask themselves how well they currently do the following.

- ▸ Do we communicate consistently and clearly about why it is important to implement RTI processes and practices?

▸ Do we build our trustworthiness as leaders by demonstrating knowledge, listening to others, and providing support for change?

▸ Do we invest in building capacity and creating opportunities for shared decision making?

▸ Do we tactfully and effectively confront negativity?

Each member of the guiding coalition must answer these questions and be ready to share their responses with the rest of the team. After reviewing and discussing the data from all members, the guiding coalition can develop action steps for increasing its readiness for resistance.

Another key to becoming skilled at responding to resistance is practice! Muhammad and Cruz (2019) include a broad range of scenarios in their book, *Time for Change*. Each scenario begins with a description of a realistic interaction that might occur on campus and is accompanied by questions for reflection. As the guiding coalition role-plays and discusses each scenario, the members may collaboratively identify strategies for moving forward.

In summary, preparing for and effectively responding to resistance requires that all the guiding coalition members see themselves as growth agents. This means that, both individually and collectively, they understand when to consult (share information, advice, or tools), collaborate (co-develop ideas or solutions to problems), and coach (support others' ideas, decisions, and reflections). Coaching is challenging work, but the effort it requires is worth the results it generates.

Understanding the Whys

Institutional Why An *institutional why* reminds us that no one is an independent contractor, and we must work collaboratively to achieve our school's mission. 1. What student achievement data indicate that not all students are learning at high levels? 2. How committed are we, both individually and collectively, to ensuring *all* students learn at high levels? 3. Based on our data and current level of commitment, what changes might we need to make in order to achieve our mission?	**Professional Why** A *professional why* reminds us that we, as professional educators, have a responsibility to implement research-based best practices. 1. What research will we use to inform ourselves and best increase student learning? 2. How will we hold ourselves accountable to using research-based best practices? 3. How might we link current research to our responsibility as educators to implement RTI practices?
Societal Why A *societal why* reminds us that failure to ensure all students learn at high levels has dire life consequences. 1. What student achievement data indicate that some of our students may be facing life-threatening consequences? 2. What skills and tools do we have to ensure that none of our students become victims of negative statistics? 3. How might our collective sense of urgency contribute to our implementation of RTI practices?	**Personal Why** A *personal why* reminds us of our moral imperative and the reasons we became educators. 1. What strategies or tools might we use to share stories, pictures, and artifacts of our journeys to becoming educators? 2. How might we create a safe environment for each of us to be heard? 3. How might we build on our collective moral imperative to strengthen our resolve for implementing RTI practices?

Tilling the Soil

The challenge of leading RTI implementation requires that a guiding coalition consider four key questions: *Why? Who? How?* and *Do?* Reflect on these four questions and respond to them in the space provided. Be ready to share your responses with the rest of the team.

Cognitive Investment *Why?* How will we continuously incorporate the four whys throughout the school year?	Emotional Investment *Who?* How will we continuously and consistently create trustworthy relationships with one another and our staff?	Functional Investment *How?* How will we ensure that all staff members are consistently engaged in professional learning and shared decision making?	Return on Investment *Do?* What will we do to create a culture of accountability and ensure we are prepared to tactfully confront resistance?

Conclusion

Muhammad (2018) uses a gardening analogy to describe the complementary relationship between school structure and school culture. Proven practices are like good seeds, while a healthy school culture is like good soil. Planting good seeds in toxic, barren ground stunts and kills off the heartiest plants. Likewise, the powerful practices of PLCs and RTI wither and die in a school culture of isolation, negativity, and low expectations. Many schools and districts spend hours planning the schedules, assessments, and timelines that support successful RTI implementation but fail to properly prepare the soil before planting the seeds of RTI.

The five essential actions in this chapter are not recommendations or suggestions; they are necessities. Beyond the research provided throughout this chapter, common sense dictates that a highly effective system of interventions requires transformational leadership, a learning-focused school culture, high-performing teams, and a commitment to adult behaviors that foster trust and mutual accountability. In the next chapter, we focus on the essential actions of collaborative teams at Tier 1.

CHAPTER 3

Tier 1 Teacher Team Essential Actions

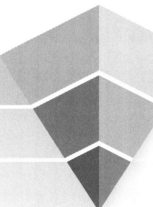

> Why [does] knowledge of what needs to be done frequently fail to result in action or behavior consistent with that knowledge?
>
> **—Jeffrey Pfeffer and Robert I. Sutton**

In this chapter, we focus on the top-right portion of the RTI at Work pyramid (see figure 3.1, page 82). Again, we want to stress that this pyramid is merely a graphic organizer designed to guide thinking and clarify roles and responsibilities. Let us reconsider what this portion of the pyramid visually represents.

▶ This portion is part of Tier 1, which represents what all students receive. Any action or outcome a team places in this box is going to be part of the core instructional program for every student.

▶ Because it's on the right side of the pyramid, this portion represents outcomes led by the school's collaborative teacher teams. The essential actions in this chapter directly relate to the core instruction for each grade level or course a school offers, so the teachers who teach these classes have the best training and are positioned to take lead responsibility.

This top-right portion of the pyramid—and the essential actions that collaborative teams must successfully engage in at Tier 1—is most important to a school's ability to create a highly effective system of interventions. Teacher teams are the engine that drives the entire RTI process. If teacher teams sputter, so will the school's efforts to achieve the mission of high levels of learning for all students.

Besides forming the right teams, allocating frequent meeting times, and committing to norms of behavior, teacher teams must focus their efforts on the right work. In this chapter, we discuss the essential actions and responsibilities of collaborative teacher teams that provide the foundation of RTI academic content and skills.

The five essential actions are as follows.

1. Identify essential standards.

2. Design a unit assessment plan.

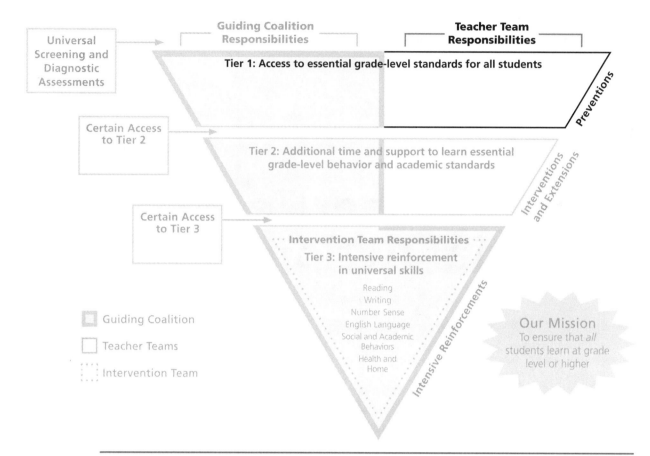

FIGURE 3.1: Focus on Tier 1 teacher team essential actions.

3. Create common assessments and begin instruction.

4. Foster student investment.

5. Analyze and respond to common assessment data.

To align this book with the common language of the PLC at Work process, we use the term *common end-of-unit assessment* rather than *common summative assessment*. Here's why: for some educators, the term *summative* mistakenly signals the end of the learning process—a time to record grades and move forward with instruction. We use the term *end-of-unit* to remove any doubt that, although the assessment comes at the end of a period of instruction, learning continues afterward. Teachers use the information from the common end-of-unit assessment *formatively* when they help students who are still struggling to master essentials and *summatively* when they extend learning for those students who demonstrate mastery of the essential standards.

DuFour and colleagues (2024) emphasize that team-developed common formative and end-of-unit assessments are the most powerful elements of a balanced assessment system for monitoring and ensuring student learning. Such a system also includes assessments individual teachers create and use in their own classrooms on a regular basis; end-of-course or end-of-year summative assessments teacher or district teams create; and occasional district, state, or provincial benchmark assessments. All these assessments play roles in monitoring and improving student learning. (See chapter 4, action 3, page 174, for more about creating a balanced assessment approach.)

Tier 1 represents what all students receive in their core instruction, so we must consider the outcomes identified here on a school's pyramid as promises to every student. A school cannot simply invite teacher participation in these essential actions or hope that teachers actually carry out the activities in core instruction. Instead, teacher teams must engage in these activities as a process of ensuring learning, which needs to be supported with school resources, monitored frequently, and celebrated often.

Schools must also empower and support teacher teams to make critical decisions about these promises, including identifying the essential standards and working together to ensure students learn them. Without teacher teams' commitment to them, these promises become merely possibilities, and student achievement becomes dependent on which teacher a student has been assigned to. As Stephen R. Covey (1989) states, "Without involvement, there is no commitment. Mark it down, asterisk it, circle it, underline it. No involvement, no commitment" (p. 143).

Teacher teams collaboratively create common assessments, design quality lessons, and collectively respond to evidence of student learning focused on essential standards. Figure 3.2 shows how the five essential collaborative team actions in this chapter (and the essential actions in chapter 5, page 201) work together as a process for ensuring student learning, called the *teaching-assessing-learning cycle*. Each essential action is part of the teaching-assessing-learning cycle or is a planning action needed to implement part of the cycle. Note that the actions in boxes represent team actions that require planning, making sense of student learning, and responding as a team. The actions outside the boxes represent when the planning is enacted (give a common formative assessment, let all students continue to learn, repeat as needed, and so on).

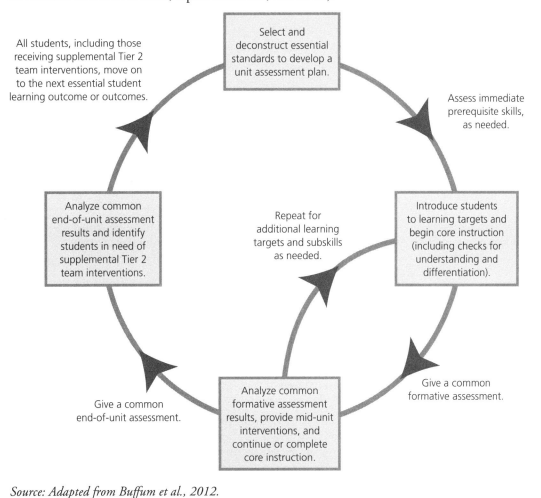

Source: Adapted from Buffum et al., 2012.

FIGURE 3.2: Team teaching-assessing-learning cycle.

It is not enough to teach and assess; these actions must *produce* student learning. Therefore, we added *learning* to the name of the teaching-assessing-learning cycle to emphasize that teachers implement quality instruction and assessments to monitor and respond to student learning. This cycle serves as a graphic and conceptual framework for moving from theory to action. The connections between this chapter's five essential actions for collaborative teacher teams and the team teaching-assessing-learning cycle are shown in table 3.1.

TABLE 3.1: Connections Between Tier 1 Teacher Team Essential Actions and the Team Teaching-Assessing-Learning Cycle

Tier 1 Teacher Team Essential Action	Connections to the Teaching-Assessing-Learning Cycle
1. Identify essential standards.	• Select and deconstruct essential standards to develop a unit assessment plan. *The focus is on making sense of immediate prerequisite and grade-level skills.* • Assess immediate prerequisite skills, as needed.
2. Design a unit assessment plan.	• Select and deconstruct essential standards to develop a unit assessment plan. *The focus is on assessment design.* • Determine when to give common formative assessments during the unit and the common end-of-unit assessment.
3. Create common assessments and begin instruction.	• Select and deconstruct essential standards to develop a unit assessment plan. *The focus is on creating common formative and end-of-unit assessments.* • Introduce students to learning targets and begin core instruction (including checks for understanding and differentiation). • If applicable, move all students, including those receiving supplemental Tier 2 interventions, to the next essential student learning outcome or outcomes.
4. Foster student investment.	• Introduce students to learning targets and begin core instruction (including checks for understanding and differentiation). *The focus is on having students make sense of learning targets.* • Analyze common formative assessment results, provide mid-unit interventions, and continue or complete core instruction. *The focus is on engaging students to reflect on their strengths and next learning steps, and using learning targets to frame Tier 1 mid-unit interventions.* • Analyze common end-of-unit assessment results and identify students in need of supplemental Tier 2 team interventions. *The focus is on engaging students to reflect on their strengths and next learning steps, and using learning targets to frame Tier 2 interventions.*
5. Analyze and respond to common assessment data.	• Analyze common formative assessment results, provide mid-unit interventions, and continue or complete core instruction. • Analyze common end-of-unit assessment results and identify students in need of supplemental Tier 2 team interventions.

We added some details within the Connections to the Teaching-Assessing-Learning Cycle column as clarification. In Tier 1, teacher teams focus on instruction and a team response to student learning that happens during core instruction. Chapter 5 will address the teacher team actions needed for an effective Tier 2 response, when teams use additional time and support during the school day to ensure student learning. Tier 2 re-engagement is most often designed using the student learning results from each common end-of-unit assessment, while Tier 1 responses most often occur throughout each lesson and after common formative assessments.

This chapter may represent a sort of "handwashing" example for you and your school. Consider how a hospital lowered its infection rate from 11 percent to 0 percent by simply and continuously reminding all staff to wash their hands. As a result of this effort, in two years, the hospital prevented eight deaths and saved approximately $2 million (Sickbert-Bennett et al., 2016). Just as hospital staff already knew to wash their hands, you have already heard or read about the ideas we discuss here, such as the need to create a guaranteed and viable curriculum, and the use of common formative assessments. Indeed, you may already consider these things done. However, *knowing* and *doing* are different concepts!

Action 1

Identify Essential Standards

The mission of a learning-focused school is to ensure that all students learn at high levels. We define *high levels of learning* as grade level or better, so essential standards represent the absolutely essential knowledge, skills, and behaviors every student must acquire to succeed in the next unit, semester, year, and course—and ultimately, in life.

We know it is a folly to expect all students to master every standard that district, state, or provincial curriculum guides require us to teach. That would be impossible. Some standards that we teach each year are *nice to know*; that is, if students do not master them this year, it will not hurt their chances of future success. But we know some standards are absolutely *have-to-know* learning outcomes. They represent content and skills that keep students from progressing in that subject if students don't master them.

For example, if you asked kindergarten teachers, "Is letter recognition important for your students to learn?" they would chuckle at this ridiculous question. In our work with schools throughout the United States, we have never heard a single kindergarten teacher respond to that question with this answer: "Letters, shmetters. Who cares if kids know their letters?" Kindergarten teachers know that letter recognition is absolutely essential to a student's future success in reading, in first grade, in all future subjects, and in life.

However, are *all* the kindergarten ELA standards essential? Of course not. In California, a required kindergarten ELA Common Core standard is "With prompting and support, name the author and illustrator of a story and define the role of each in telling the story" (RL.K.6; NGA & CCSSO, 2010a).

Will a kindergartner make it in first grade if they can't yet name the illustrator of the book the class is reading? Probably. So, identifying the absolutely essential learning outcomes—year by year, subject by subject, and unit by unit—is a critical first step in focusing a school's core instruction and intervention process. Yet while the need to create a guaranteed and viable curriculum is obvious, achieving this outcome has proven elusive at best, like handwashing in a hospital.

Rather than focusing on how they might cover content (for example, a copy of the state or provincial standards, a district pacing guide, or a curriculum map), each collaborative teacher team must receive the time to examine such materials and then decide what skills and concepts are essential and, thus, what every student must master. In other words, identifying essential standards means clarifying what each student must *learn*, not simply what teachers will *teach* and when they will teach it. So, the first step in the teaching-assessing-learning cycle is for teams to identify what is most essential for students to learn and to deconstruct the standards to make sense of that learning (see figure 3.3). Before instruction begins, teams may assess prior skills to inform how best to support students in accessing essential grade-level standards.

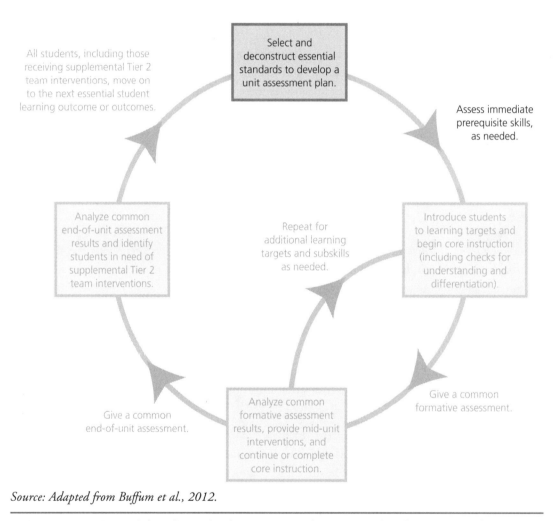

Source: Adapted from Buffum et al., 2012.

FIGURE 3.3: Essential action 1 in the team teaching-assessing-learning cycle.

While we believe that the district and state or province have roles to play in this discussion, teacher teams must ultimately commit to the standards they will prioritize, teach, reteach, and use for intervention. Without the teacher teams' involvement and the resulting ownership that comes from committing to intervene, the implemented curriculum and the intended curriculum are seldom the same.

Here's Why

The research supporting the need to identify essential standards and engage every teacher in the identification process is compelling and conclusive. In *Concise Answers to Frequently Asked Questions About Professional Learning Communities at Work*, Mattos and colleagues (2016) argue:

Merely providing teachers with a copy of the state standards for their grade level does not ensure all students will have access to a guaranteed curriculum that can be taught in the amount of time available for teaching. Teachers may ignore the standards, assign different priorities to the standards, vary dramatically in how much time they devote to the standards, see huge discrepancies in what the standards look like in terms of student work, and possess significant differences in their ability to teach the standards. (p. 77)

Having analyzed more than 2,100 meta-analyses involving millions of students, Hattie (2023) says:

Both learning intentions *and* success criteria are needed to maximize the impact on achievement. The bases of many claims about the value of student self-assessment, self-evaluation, self-monitoring, and self-learning are that students have a reasonable understanding of where they are at, where they are going, what it would look like when they get there, and where they will go to next: that is, they have learning intentions and success criteria. (p. 313)

Carol Ann Tomlinson and Jay McTighe (2006) state that the first step in curriculum development is to "identify desired results. What should students know, understand, and be able to do? What content is worthy of understanding? What 'enduring' understandings are desired? What essential questions will be explored? . . . [This step] calls for clarity about priorities" (pp. 27–28).

More emphatically, Robert J. Marzano, Philip B. Warrick, and Mario I. Acosta (2024) claim that a High Reliability School provides students with a guaranteed and viable curriculum focused on enhancing student learning. The curriculum is focused enough that teachers can adequately address it in the time available to them, and students are taught by teachers committed to ensuring they learn the critical content. Individual teachers do not have the option to disregard or replace content that has been designated as essential (Marzano et al., 2024).

While a preponderance of education research, conventional wisdom, and common sense would tell us that creating a guaranteed and viable curriculum increases student learning, few schools and districts have fully committed to it. Instead, most have settled for shortcuts in the process or have actually promoted practices that are counterproductive to this goal. Consider these examples.

▶ The district office hand-selects a few teachers to produce lists of essential or power standards. The school distributes these standards to all teachers with the explanation that these are teacher-created documents. Since not all teachers were involved in the selection and prioritization process, the teachers have little ownership of or commitment to the lists. Heidi Hayes Jacobs (2001) states that most district curriculum guides are "well-intended but fundamentally fictional accounts of what students actually learn" (p. 20). Additionally, Mike Schmoker (2011) confirms schools' continuing need for a coherent and rich curriculum focused on what is most essential and their continuing struggle to prioritize their efforts to ensure effective implementation.

▶ The district office asks teachers to prioritize standards, but they do nothing more than place a check mark next to standards they believe are important for students to learn. This approach does little to clarify what the standards actually mean. Because standards are often written in a way that leaves much room for interpretation, teachers need to give more than a headshake when making critical decisions about student learning. Schmoker (2011) puts it this way: "Though the national standards for language arts are better than the state standards they would replace, there are still too many of them, and many are poorly and confusingly written" (p. 41).

Shortcuts lead schools and districts to generate lists of standards that collect dust on a shelf or get lost in the abyss of online documents. Clarity comes when teacher teams engage in the process of prioritizing and identifying essential standards. It is the *process*, not the list, that creates clarity and sets the stage for schools to create a schoolwide system of supports that ensures learning for all students at high levels.

If we are to build a solid foundation of essential skills and knowledge for students at Tier 1, we must be crystal clear about what those skills and knowledge are and what mastery looks like. If we plan to build a schoolwide system of supports for students when they struggle to learn, we must recognize that the system will never be systematic until teacher teams are clear on what each student must master. If not, schools will reteach different things or focus on work completion and send students for Tier 2 interventions for inconsistent reasons, while experiencing large numbers of students falling so far behind that they require Tier 3 support. Schools suffer this frustrating fate simply because they never gain clarity on what they want each student to learn.

Here's How

Teacher teams prioritize and select what all students must learn for a grade level or course. Then, they identify the essential standards to be mastered in particular units of study or during a particular time period (such as a trimester or quarter). The first step in this process is for teams to determine the criteria they will use to make decisions about what is essential and should be prioritized. Based on the work of Douglas Reeves (2002) and Larry Ainsworth (2013), Ted Horrell and his colleagues in Shelby County, Tennessee, created the REAL acronym as a practical application for teams to use when identifying essential standards (Many, Maffoni, Sparks, Thomas, & Greeney, 2022).

▶ **R—Readiness:** Will this standard provide students with knowledge and skills essential for success in the next grade or level of instruction?

▶ **E—Endurance:** Are the knowledge and skills in this standard so valuable that students will need them to last beyond a single test date?

▶ **A—Assessed:** Will this standard support students to achieve what is prioritized on the state, provincial, or national external assessments?

▶ **L—Leverage:** Does this standard include knowledge and skills that are valuable in multiple disciplines?

The REAL criteria help teacher teams make important decisions regarding what is essential, the standards teacher teams promise to ensure students learn. *Essential standards* are those for which teams first design interventions when students are not yet learning grade-level standards. The remaining standards are *supporting standards*, which teams categorize as those that are still part of core instruction (*important-to-know standards*). Finally, those that may or may not be covered are called *nice-to-know standards*.

Teams can use the reproducible tool "Process for Selecting Essential Standards" (page 91) to guide their process discussions for prioritizing standards. Rather than simply placing check marks next to standards deemed essential or creating a list, teacher teams develop a shared understanding of each essential standard using the "Essential Standards Chart" reproducible (page 93). The dialogue and process generated by the essential standards chart help teams clarify what proficiency looks like as they discuss and determine the following five elements for each essential standard.

1. Clarify the wording of the standard without reducing the cognitive level required.

2. Agree on the level of rigor required at grade or course level (and give an example of that rigor).

3. Identify the prerequisite skills and vocabulary needed for students to be successful in mastering the standard.

4. Agree on when students are expected to have learned the standard and how to most accurately assess their learning at the end of the unit.

5. Determine how to meaningfully extend learning for students who demonstrate early in the unit that they have already mastered the standard.

We believe this kind of discussion leads teams to a deeper understanding of what they are expecting all students to learn, and a deeper commitment to making sure every student learns it. Once they choose essential standards, teacher teams should revisit and re-evaluate their essential standards yearly to make sure they have the most appropriate ones. The list of essential standards may change slightly over time as student learning improves from year to year.

Helpful Tools

The following tools will help you accomplish the work for this essential action.

▸ **Chapter 6 of *Learning by Doing, Fourth Edition* (DuFour et al., 2024), "Establishing a Focus on Learning":** This chapter provides foundational content knowledge as well as tools that can help schools accomplish the action steps outlined in this section.

▸ **"Process for Selecting Essential Standards" (page 91):** Teams can use this tool to guide their discussions regarding the determination of essential standards.

▸ **"Essential Standards Chart" (page 93):** Teams can use this chart to bring greater clarity to the essential standards they expect students to learn.

Coaching Tips

As teams begin this work, it is worthwhile to remind them of Lencioni's (2002) quote, "If everything is important, then nothing is" (p. 106). So true, and so challenging to accomplish! To agree on what is truly essential for students to learn requires time, structure, patience, and courage. Teachers need to be prepared to speak up for their own views, and to keep an open mind and truly listen to their colleagues. The guiding coalition's role, then, is to provide a balance of support and accountability.

In order to identify essential standards successfully and efficiently, team members should follow these steps to clarify and establish their team and task, time to do the work, and tools to support their collaboration.

1. **Clarify the context of collaborative teams:** Who will be collaborating with whom? What tasks will they be collaboratively working on? What shared goals will they be seeking to accomplish in support of increased student learning?

2. **Designate time for teams to engage in doing the work:** Two options for providing this time have generally proven successful.

   a. Provide teacher teams with large chunks of student-free time before the school year begins. During this time, they can create a draft of their agreed-on essentials for an entire semester or more. As they teach each instructional unit, teachers should discuss and re-evaluate this draft with the goal of having a completed essential standards chart for the entire year at the time school ends.

b. Have teacher teams discuss and identify essentials one unit at a time. In this case, teams set aside at least one meeting several weeks before each instructional unit to agree on the essential standards for that particular unit. By the end of the school year, the teams are ready to reflect on the year as a whole and evaluate their work to ensure the essentials they identified sequence appropriately and best support student success. Tackling this work unit by unit can help focus the work and reduce feelings of overwhelm. It also allows teams to reflect on what is working in the process and what might need to be revised.

3. **Help teams use digital and artificial intelligence (AI) tools:** Teams can use generative AI to guide them to identify essential standards, unwrap standards into learning targets, find good questions and tasks to assess learning, and even locate instructional strategies for misconceptions that emerge. Choose these tools thoughtfully so as to promote efficient and accurate recordkeeping and to support the work itself. Teacher teams must also be critical consumers of what they find, ensuring that the information is accurate, contextual, and reasonable. As with any efficiency tool, teachers should not copy and paste anything that pops up, or take anything at face value, but use their generative AI tool as a launching point for discussion. They must ensure that they have clarity and intention in both what is to be learned and how it will be assessed.

Teams must consistently review and re-evaluate their decisions to ensure that their essential standards chart represents what is most important for students to learn.

As teams do this work, we hear two questions: (1) "How many essential standards should we select?" and (2) "If a standard is not essential, does that mean we don't teach it at all?" Our response to the first question is both a gift (no one right answer) and a challenge (no one right answer!). In other words, teams must find their own right answer—enough standards to ensure students master what is most important, but few enough standards to allow teachers and students to truly focus their work. Regarding the second question, if a team identifies standards as not essential, it does not mean that teachers ignore them. Rather, the team looks at the remaining standards to determine whether they are "important to know" or "nice to know." Individual teachers should continue to teach and assess supporting standards that are important to know. All standards are mapped across units. Standards not included on the essential standards chart, however, are not the focus of collaborative teamwork, common assessments, and team-provided interventions.

As teams seek consensus, they must use a structured tool and process; we cannot stress enough the importance of this. The essential standards chart is the tool, but teachers must determine how to best complete it together. That said, not all the work takes place during team meetings. Teams are most productive when they divvy up the work and come to each meeting with individual recommendations for review, rather than starting each meeting with a blank slate.

Finally, don't forget the value of vertical articulation and celebration. It is time well spent to designate faculty meeting time, two or three times per year, for teams to share their work with each other, check for continuity between grade levels and subject areas, and cheer each other on. According to an ancient Chinese proverb, "The journey of a thousand miles begins with a single step." Celebrate every step!

Process for Selecting Essential Standards

Essential standards play an integral role in helping all students achieve at high levels. Teachers work in collaboration to identify essential standards, map them across units or cycles of instruction, and share them with students to focus learning. Then teachers analyze assessments that measure the essential standards so they can plan Tier 1 and Tier 2 re-engagement to ensure students learn them. Essential standards are what teachers promise students will learn, and thus, collaborative teams consistently analyze and respond to them to ensure students learn them, no matter how long it takes. This process leads to higher achievement and more student investment in learning.

The following steps guide the process of identifying essential standards. As a grade level or course, review the REAL criteria (see Here's How, page 88). Discuss any clarifications or other contextual considerations to add to the list.

1. Using the REAL criteria, individually identify essential standards that meet at least two or three of the established criteria. If your team struggles to come to consensus after you start identifying essential standards individually, go standard by standard together and discuss them, skipping this step.

2. Choose among the several options for guiding the logistics of this process.

   - To set up this process, some teams copy and paste all their standards into the first column of a spreadsheet or table and then have additional columns for each of the REAL criteria. See the Essential Standards Spreadsheet Model (page 92) as an example.

   - Some teams print out copies of the standards, have team members individually highlight the essential standards on their own copy, and then create one document that captures their consensus.

   - Some teams copy and paste all standards into a Word document and bold the standards that are essential.

3. As a grade level or course, share your lists, and have one person record the selections on one master copy of the standards—in print or on a spreadsheet.

4. As a grade level or course, examine the commonalities. Come to consensus on the most essential standards or big ideas. Are there discrepancies? Discuss your reasoning. Remind one another that these are the standards on which you will focus your collaboration, common assessments, data analysis, and team interventions. You will also teach other important standards. However, you must commit and respond to the essential standards to ensure all students learn them.

5. Meet in vertical teams to share your lists. How do they align? Are you missing any essential standards? Did you identify essential standards that may not need to be essential?

Essential Standards Spreadsheet Model

Course or grade level: _____

For each standard, dialogue with colleagues to identify which criteria it meets, and place a checkmark in the corresponding box. Those that meet the most criteria become your essentials.

- **R—Readiness:** Will this standard provide students with knowledge and skills essential for success in the next grade or level of instruction?

- **E—Endurance:** Are the knowledge and skills in this standard so valuable that students will need them to last beyond a single test date?

- **A—Assessed:** Will this standard support students to achieve what is prioritized on the state, provincial, or national external assessments?

- **L—Leverage:** Does this standard include knowledge and skills that are valuable in multiple disciplines?

Standard	Readiness	Endurance	Assessed	Leverage	Critical as a Team Intervention Focus

Source: Adapted from Buffum, A., & Mattos, M. (2014, May). Criteria for selecting essential standards *[Presentation]. Simplifying Response to Intervention Workshop, Prince George, British Columbia, Canada; Kramer, S. V., & Schuhl, S. (2023).* Acceleration for all: A how-to guide for overcoming learning gaps. *Bloomington, IN: Solution Tree Press; Reeves, D. B. (2002).* The leader's guide to standards: A blueprint for educational equity and excellence. *San Francisco: Jossey-Bass.*

Essential Standards Chart

Working in collaborative teams, examine all relevant documents—which may include state or provincial standards and district-, state-, or province-identified essential standards—and then apply the REAL criteria (*readiness, endurance, assessed,* and *leverage*) to determine which standards are essential for all students to master. Remember, *less is more.* For each standard selected, fill out the remaining columns. Complete this chart in advance of teaching the standard.

Grade:	Subject:	Semester:	Team Members:		
		What Do We Expect Students to Learn?			
Description of Standard	**Example of Grade- or Course-Level Rigor**	**Immediate Prerequisite Skills**	**When Proficiency Is Expected**	**Common Formative and End-of-Unit Assessments**	**Extension**
What is the essential standard to be learned? Describe it in student-friendly language, but avoid reducing the cognitive level of the standard.	What does proficient student work look like? Provide an example or description of the items and tasks that demonstrate proficiency.	What prior knowledge, skills, and vocabulary from earlier this year or last year are needed for a student to master this standard?	When will this standard be taught, and when will proficiency be expected with part, or all, of the standard?	What common assessments will be used to measure student mastery?	What will we do when students have already learned this standard?

Source: Adapted from Buffum, A., Mattos, M., & Weber, C. (2012). Simplifying response to intervention: Four essential guiding principles. Bloomington, IN: Solution Tree Press.

Action 2

Design a Unit Assessment Plan

Once a team prioritizes and identifies essential standards, it needs to create a road map describing how it will get all students to the destination of mastery—not of everything, but of those standards it deemed essential. We call this road map the *unit assessment plan.*

In preparation for an upcoming unit of study, the team discusses and agrees on the essential standards students will learn and whether to include any supporting standards or prior knowledge standards. Some teams will have access to district or school documents when planning the standards students learn in each unit, which can be helpful to reference. If not, teams can start with the "Essential Standards Chart" tool (page 93) in their planning for each unit.

Deconstructing the essential standards into learning targets to use for instruction and assessment is another critical part of the team teaching-assessing-learning cycle (see figure 3.4) as well as the unit assessment plan. Additionally, as part of a unit assessment plan, teams determine the learning targets to use with students and the design of their common assessments, and create a team calendar specifying when to give and respond to common formative and end-of-unit assessments.

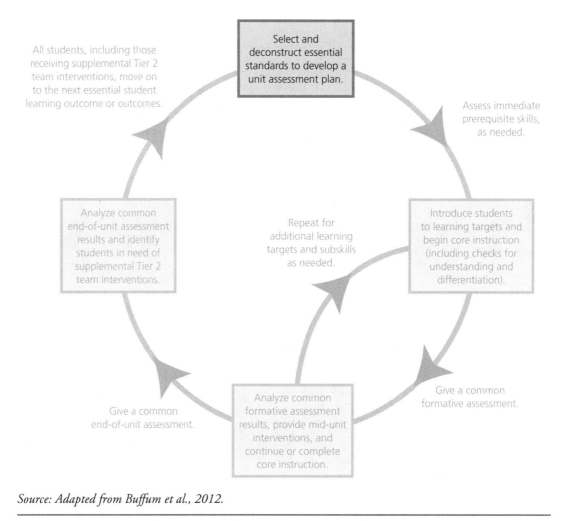

Source: Adapted from Buffum et al., 2012.

FIGURE 3.4: Essential action 2 in the team teaching-assessing-learning cycle.

At this point, teams are ready to map out a plan for ensuring all students master each essential standard. The four-step plan should include the following.

1. Identify and deconstruct each essential standard to select the learning targets for the unit (see the "Deconstructing Standards" reproducible, page 113).

2. Organize the learning targets into a sequenced learning progression for instruction, assessment, and student investment. The learning progression consists of the learning targets, placed in order of learning complexity, that clearly create the pathway to achieving the standard. To create a manageable number of student-friendly learning targets (*I can* statements) for student investment throughout the unit, your team may need to group together some learning targets that are tightly connected.

3. Collaboratively create or select common assessments to administer at the end of and throughout the unit.

4. Create a team calendar and agree on when to administer each common assessment.

As a result of the dialogue and decisions needed to create a unit assessment plan, team members are ready to create their common assessments, share the learning targets with students, begin implementing instruction with collective clarity on the intended outcomes, and identify when and how they expect students to demonstrate progress.

Here's Why

As schools shift from a focus on teaching everything to a focus on learning and mastery, each step teams take to create a unit assessment plan helps establish a foundation for success. This is because of the following.

▸ Understanding the connections between essential standards and any supporting standards in the unit helps teams create a meaningful unit that emphasizes essential standards and a focused plan for when to respond to students who need additional time to learn and when to let it go. To begin, focus as a team on the essential standards to make the work manageable. As your team deepens the work, discuss how some supporting standards connect and support essential standards.

▸ Identifying the learning targets in each essential standard gives the team information it needs to create the learning progression for the unit and develop common assessments that will provide targeted and specific feedback to the teacher team and students.

▸ Converting standards to student-friendly language and sharing them with the class invites students to actively partner with teachers on the learning journey. As a result, students are better able to self-assess, set goals, and respond appropriately to feedback and evaluation. As curriculum and assessment specialists Jan Chappuis and Rick Stiggins (2020) state, "Students can hit any target they can see and that holds still for them" (p. 49).

▸ Collaboratively creating and selecting common assessments ensure that teams collect the detailed information needed to effectively monitor and support each student's learning. Common assessments provide the information critical to implementing an effective system of interventions.

▸ Determining when to give each common formative assessment as a team and when to respond to its data allows teams to ensure students have team-created re-engagement learning experiences during Tier 1, prior to any common end-of-unit assessment.

Teams can then analyze common end-of-unit assessment data and design any team Tier 2 interventions and extensions. When teams successfully create re-engagement learning experiences at Tier 1, fewer students will need additional time and support in Tier 2 interventions.

In summary, it is important to remember that Tier 1 of the RTI process requires teacher teams to clearly define what students must learn, implement quality instruction, use common formative assessments to identify effective instructional practices, and plan for specific students to re-engage in learning the targets in essential standards as needed. The process of creating unit assessment plans positions teachers to intentionally teach, assess, and proactively respond to student learning struggles prior to the conclusion of any unit. This helps teachers actualize this powerful premise: *the best intervention is prevention.*

Here's How

Creating a unit assessment plan is truly the most important task for educators seeking to transform themselves into high-performing teams that take collective responsibility for high levels of student learning. Each step of this four-step process requires designated time, a shared understanding of the task, and a commitment to collaborative work.

Step 1: Identify and Deconstruct Each Essential Standard to Select the Learning Targets for the Unit

To begin the process, teams need to clarify which essential standards students will learn in the unit and record them in the unit assessment plan. Essential standards will be the focus for common formative assessments, informing any Tier 1 re-engagement for prevention and Tier 2 intervention for students needing additional time.

Once the essential standards in the unit are identified, teams deconstruct each one to select the specific learning targets underpinning it and record their thinking in the unit assessment plan for future reference. Teams review standards documents as well as bring their own knowledge of the content to this discussion. They pay careful attention to the verbs in each standard (stating what students must do) and the connections of those verbs to the nouns or noun phrases (stating what students need to know) to create the specific learning targets inherent to the standard. This language informs what assessment methods, or items and tasks, will accurately assess student learning on the standard. For example, consider the grade 9 Common Core ELA standard, "*Write* arguments to *support* claims in an analysis of substantive topics or texts, *using* valid reasoning and relevant and sufficient evidence" (W.9-10.1, emphasis added; NGA & CCSSO, 2010a). The text in the standard points out several learning targets.

▸ Analyze a topic by *developing a claim* to focus an argument.

▸ Support claims using *valid reasoning*.

▸ Support claims using *relevant and sufficient evidence*.

Writing an argument is the overall standard, followed by more specific sub-standards. The team may also choose parts or all of the sub-standards as essential. For example, a team might choose sub-standards A and B:

- W.9-10.1a—Introduce precise claim(s), distinguish the claim(s) from alternate or opposing claims, and create an organization that establishes clear relationships among claim(s), counterclaims, reasons, and evidence.

- W.9-10.1b—Develop claim(s) and counterclaims fairly, supplying evidence for each while pointing out strengths and limitations of both in a manner that anticipates the audience's knowledge level and concerns. (NGA & CCSSO, 2010a)

To learn this essential standard, students need to explore a topic by reading or viewing multiple sources on that topic and identifying different perspectives and sources. Based on exploring different perspectives and sources, students develop a claim. This means students need to explore what it means to make a claim and what contributes to a strong claim when making an argument. Then, students must learn what quality evidence is, including how to make sure their evidence is relevant and they have enough to strongly support their claim. After that, students need to focus on explaining how the evidence supports their claim, including ensuring that their explanation shows valid reasoning. Finally, students organize their claim, the supporting evidence, and the counterclaims to fully build their argument. Learning targets for this essential standard include the following.

▸ I can introduce precise claims.

▸ I can develop claims and counterclaims fairly and thoroughly.

  ▪ I can use valid reasoning and relevant, sufficient evidence.

  ▪ I can explain strengths and limitations of the evidence.

▸ I can organize and establish clear relationships among claims, counterclaims, reasons, and evidence.

Once the team members understand the standard, they agree on the method of assessment students can use to demonstrate their ability to write this argument. The method helps further determine what proficiency looks like. In this example, the team may design an essay, a short written response, a presentation, or an infographic.

Similarly, a third-grade mathematics unit focused on fractions might include two essential standards.

- 3.NF.A.3b—Recognize and generate simple equivalent fractions, e.g., $\frac{1}{2} = \frac{2}{4}, \frac{4}{6} = \frac{2}{3}$. Explain why the fractions are equivalent, e.g., by using a visual fraction model.

- 3.NF.A.3d—Compare two fractions with the same numerator or the same denominator by reasoning about their size. Recognize that comparisons are valid only when the two fractions refer to the same whole. Record the results of comparisons with the symbols >, =, or <, and justify the conclusions, e.g., by using a visual fraction model. (NGA & CCSSO, 2010b)

To learn the first essential standard, students need to (1) recognize simple equivalent fractions, (2) generate simple equivalent fractions, and (3) explain why fractions are equivalent. When deconstructing the standard, the team discusses how students might explain equivalent fractions and agrees on methods such as number lines, fraction tiles, and pictures. Additionally, to learn the second essential standard, students will (1) compare two fractions with the same numerator; (2) compare two fractions with the same denominator; (3) recognize fractions can only be compared if they refer to the same whole; (4) record the results of comparisons using >, =, or <; and (5) explain the comparison of the fractions. Team members may agree, when deconstructing the standard, that the justification in the second standard matches the explanation in the first and includes number lines, fraction tiles, and pictures.

In the unit assessment plan, this first step of identifying standards and deconstructing them into learning targets is recorded at the top of the plan. The top part of the unit assessment plan is shown in figure 3.5 (page 98).

Unit:	Start and End Dates:
Essential Standards	**Deconstruct to Identify Skills and Concepts**

FIGURE 3.5: Step 1 of the unit assessment plan—Identify and deconstruct each essential standard to select the learning targets for the unit.

As teams deepen their work, they may also include some of the supporting standards (important-to-know standards) connected to the essential standards in a unit as part of their unit assessment plan and corresponding learning targets. However, it all starts with the essential standards.

Step 2: Organize the Learning Targets Into a Sequenced Learning Progression for Instruction, Assessment, and Student Investment

Once a team determines learning targets for its essential standards, it puts the learning targets in sequential order for teaching and learning. Which targets will students learn first? Which targets will follow? The learning targets grow in complexity throughout the progression. See figure 3.6.

Unit:	Start and End Dates:
Essential Standards	**Deconstruct to Identify Skills and Concepts**
Learning Target Progression With Student-Friendly Targets *List skills and concepts from least complex to most complex. Clarify targets for student reflection and assessment.*	

FIGURE 3.6: Step 2 of the unit assessment plan—Organize the learning targets into a sequenced learning progression for instruction, assessment, and student investment.

After organizing learning targets into a learning progression, the team converts the learning targets to student-friendly language so they can help students invest in learning. Team members must agree on the most important targets and identify any potentially unclear or confusing language. After they clarify the targets' language and meaning, the team members must reach consensus on learning target statements to share with students. These statements often begin with *I can*.

As an example, let's return to the third-grade fraction standard stating students need to recognize and generate equivalent fractions. Keeping in mind that this is a third-grade standard, teachers might agree on the following definitions.

- ▸ **Recognize:** Identify equivalent fractions.
- ▸ **Generate:** Create or find equivalent fractions.

The learning progression of targets tells teachers specifically what they must teach and work to have students learn. However, if there are too many learning targets, converting every target to student-friendly language can sometimes confuse students, especially a third grader in the example who is learning fractions for the first time. The team may want to cluster or group learning targets and create a single student-friendly *I can* statement for student reflection and as a focus for common assessments. The specific learning targets can be used as success criteria when teaching each student-friendly *I can* statement. For example, in the third-grade fraction unit, the team may create three student-friendly *I can* statements and then group the learning targets under each one in a learning progression, as follows.

1. I can identify and create equivalent fractions. *This means I can:*
   - Identify equivalent fractions and show why they are equivalent
   - Create equivalent fractions and show why they are equivalent

2. I can compare two fractions and explain why my answer is correct. *This means I can:*
   - Recognize fractions can only be compared if they refer to the same whole
   - Compare two fractions with the same numerator and explain why my answer is correct
   - Compare two fractions with the same denominator and explain why my answer is correct

3. I can record my answer when comparing fractions using >, =, or <.

Teams record student-friendly learning targets, along with the corresponding learning targets from the deconstructed standards, in the shaded section of the unit assessment plan (see figure 3.6, page 98).

As they are teaching, educators can use anchor charts to share the success criteria and examples and descriptions of what it looks like when students achieve each student-friendly learning target. Teams should identify, discuss, and evaluate student-friendly targets on a regular basis. This helps students see the targets and recognize that the targets are "holding still" for them; in other words, the targets are a consistent part of instruction, rather than constantly changing or moving.

Step 3: Collaboratively Create or Select Common Assessments to Administer at the End of and Throughout the Unit

The next important step when creating a unit assessment plan is to collaboratively create or select assessments to administer at the end of the unit and throughout the unit and to agree on when to give each assessment. The good news is that teams already did half the work when developing the essential standards chart (see page 93). They have already identified the common end-of-unit assessment to use at the unit's conclusion.

The unit assessment plan focuses on common assessments teams will administer to measure the extent to which students are learning the student-friendly learning targets during the unit and at its conclusion. In addition, teachers may independently assess less critical targets, often including those from any important-to-know supporting standards, to assess student learning throughout the unit. The common end-of-unit assessment generally includes essential standards and may include supporting important-to-know standards to check on as a team. Regardless, assessment information on the essential standards informs who needs Tier 2 interventions, and on what skill or learning target they need the interventions. When starting this work, focus on assessing the essential standards.

It is important to identify which learning targets might need extra instructional attention. There is no one right number of assessments needed in a unit plan. That said, all students can benefit from a minimum of one risk-free opportunity to demonstrate and revise their learning. We therefore recommend that teams include at least one common formative assessment during each unit of instruction. A common formative assessment is only formative if teams use it to inform instruction, so teams should administer only as many common formative assessments as they can collectively respond to. For each one, they align the assessment with the end-of-unit assessment and determine the date to give the assessment. This information appears at the bottom of the unit assessment plan, as shown in figure 3.7.

Unit:	Start and End Dates:
Essential Standards	**Deconstruct to Identify Skills and Concepts**
Learning Target Progression With Student-Friendly Targets	
List skills and concepts from least complex to most complex. *Clarify targets for student reflection and assessment.*	

Common Assessments		
Learning Targets *Which targets are being assessed?*	**End-of-Unit Assessment** *What assessment methods will you use? How many questions will there be for each target being assessed on the end-of-unit assessment?*	**Targets Assessed on a Common Formative Assessment** *Choose those you will intervene on, and determine where students need more feedback.*

FIGURE 3.7: Step 3 of the unit assessment plan—Collaboratively create or select common assessments to administer at the end of and throughout the unit.

Team members now have collective clarity on learning targets, student-friendly versions of the targets to share with students, and agreement on when and how to assess. As a result, students in each teacher's classroom benefit from equal access to the essential standards.

Step 4: Create a Team Calendar and Agree on When to Administer Each Common Assessment

Teams finalize their planning by creating a calendar to show the dates or date ranges for each common assessment as well as the dates for re-engaging students in learning during core instruction after a common formative assessment (see figure 3.8, page 102). This ensures that common formative assessment (CFA) data are used and seen as part of lesson planning and student learning. Teams also identify when, during their team meetings, they will create each common assessment and analyze the assessment data.

Helpful Tools

The following tools will help you accomplish the work for this essential action.

- ▶ **"Unit Assessment Plan" (page 104):** This reproducible template for putting together a unit assessment plan includes all the elements illustrated in the preceding sections.
- ▶ **"Sample Grade 3 Mathematics Unit Assessment Plan" (page 107):** This reproducible provides a sample unit assessment plan for mathematics.

Calendar

- On the calendar, note meeting days so you are clear on when you will analyze the assessment information (common formative assessments and common end-of-unit assessment).
- Note when you will respond to your analysis and instruction or intervention planning.
- Note the focused learning target to address at team meetings and on each common assessment.

Monday	Tuesday	Wednesday	Thursday	Friday

FIGURE 3.8: Step 4 of the unit assessment plan—Create a team calendar and agree on when to administer each common assessment.

> ▸ **"Sample Grade 9 ELA Unit Assessment Plan" (page 110):** This reproducible provides a sample unit assessment plan for English language arts.

> ▸ **"Deconstructing Standards" (page 113):** Teams can use this template to deconstruct, or unwrap, each essential standard to identify the learning targets that underpin it.

Coaching Tips

The best advice for supporting this challenging work is to remember how to eat an elephant—one bite at a time! The guiding coalition needs to teach, discuss, and practice each step of the plan in a whole-staff setting before assigning individual teams to complete the task. This allows teachers time to ask questions and learn with and from each other. It may also be less overwhelming for teams to use the templates for individual steps of the process before they are required to complete the entire unit plan.

Once the guiding coalition teaches, discusses, and practices each step in a whole-staff setting, each team should set a date for completing a unit assessment plan with standards of its own for an upcoming unit of study. To lend support and assist with facilitating the process, guiding coalition members should drop in on teams as they collaborate to complete each task. It may also be helpful to have teams bring finished products to staff meetings for sharing and problem solving with other teams.

To provide the most impactful support, the guiding coalition should pay attention to each team's level of experience and expertise. Those teams new to planning may only have identified their essential standards, while others may already have identified connected supporting standards to teach targets. Following the four outlined steps and using the templates provided in Helpful Tools (page 101) will help teams stay focused and productive. Additionally, it is best to advise teams to select a unit of study that needs improvement rather than a unit that is already working well. More advanced teams may be ready to describe their plan for each common assessment in more detail and fill in their team calendar with a focused target for each day.

As work progresses, be sure to gather teams' feedback on how the unit assessment plan is helping guide and focus their work, as well as what, if any, challenges are emerging. Sharing and discussing reflections help ensure that each unit assessment plan becomes a living document and learning process, rather than a compliance-driven task that resides in cyberspace or on a shelf collecting dust. Once each unit is completed, you must assess the process. What worked well, and what might need to be revised or tweaked? With guidance, collective reflection and assessment can help teams become more invested and can ensure that unit assessment planning becomes a meaningful part of helping all students learn at high levels.

In a perfect world, teams would have a full student-free day (or more) to learn together and try out this process. However, if teams must use their weekly collaboration time to work through the process, ensure that teachers continue to give formative and end-of-unit assessments, even if they have not yet implemented other steps of the process. Teachers must not hold up or sacrifice student learning as they gain mastery of new tools and strategies.

In conclusion, participating in a step-by-step process that has been carefully taught, guided, and monitored means teachers are more likely to fully understand both the logistics of the work and each step's importance and relationship to instruction and student learning. They also begin working much more independently and efficiently. As a wise person once said, "Go slow to go fast!"

Unit Assessment Plan

Use the following four-step process to complete the unit assessment plan.

1. Identify and deconstruct each essential standard to identify the learning targets for the unit.

2. Organize the learning targets into a sequenced learning progression for instruction, assessment, and student investment.

3. Collaboratively create or select common assessments to administer at the end of and throughout the unit.

4. Create a team calendar and agree on when to administer and respond to each common assessment.

Unit:	Start and End Dates:
Essential Standards	**Deconstruct to Identify Skills and Concepts**
Learning Target Progression With Student-Friendly Targets *List skills and concepts from least complex to most complex. Clarify targets for student reflection and assessment.*	

Common Assessments		
Learning Targets *Which targets are being assessed?*	**End-of-Unit Assessment** *What assessment methods will you use? How many questions will there be for each target being assessed on the end-of-unit assessment?*	**Targets Assessed on a Common Formative Assessment** *Choose those you will intervene on, and determine where students need more feedback.*

Taking Action © 2018, 2025 Solution Tree Press • SolutionTree.com
Visit **go.SolutionTree.com/RTIatWork** to download this free reproducible.

Calendar

- On the calendar, note meeting days so you are clear on when you will analyze the assessment information (common formative assessments and common end-of-unit assessment).

- Note when you will respond to your analysis and instruction or intervention planning.

- Note the focused learning target to address at team meetings and on each common assessment.

Monday	Tuesday	Wednesday	Thursday	Friday

Sample Grade 3 Mathematics Unit Assessment Plan

This is a sample unit assessment plan for grade 3 mathematics. The verbs are bolded for emphasis.

Unit: Comparing Fractions	Start and End Dates: February 22–March 26
Essential Standards	**Deconstruct to Identify Skills and Concepts**
3.NF.A.3b: **Recognize** and **generate** simple equivalent fractions, e.g., $\frac{1}{2} = \frac{2}{4}$, $\frac{4}{6} = \frac{2}{3}$. **Explain** why the fractions are equivalent, such as by **using** a visual fraction model.	• **Recognize** (**identify**) equivalent fractions. • **Generate** equivalent fractions. • **Explain** why fractions are equivalent **using**: ◦ Number lines ◦ Pictures ◦ Fraction tiles
3.NF.A.3d: **Compare** two fractions with the same numerator or the same denominator by **reasoning** about their size. **Recognize** that comparisons are valid only when the two fractions refer to the same whole. **Record** the results of comparisons with the symbols >, =, or <, and **justify** the conclusions, such as by **using** a visual fraction model.	• **Compare** two fractions with the same numerator. • **Compare** two fractions with the same denominator. • **Recognize** fractions can only be compared if they refer to the same whole. • **Record** comparisons using >, =, or <. • **Explain** the comparison of fractions **using**: ◦ Number lines ◦ Pictures ◦ Fraction tiles

Learning Target Progression With Student-Friendly Targets
List skills and concepts from least complex to most complex.
Clarify targets for student reflection and assessment.

I can identify and create equivalent fractions.

This means I can:

• Identify equivalent fractions and show why they are equivalent.
• Create equivalent fractions and show why they are equivalent.

I can compare two fractions and explain why my answer is correct.

This means I can:

• Recognize fractions can only be compared if they refer to the same whole.
• Compare two fractions with the same numerator and explain why my answer is correct.
• Compare two fractions with the same denominator and explain why my answer is correct.
• Record my answer when comparing fractions using >, =, or <.

Common Assessments		
Learning Targets *Which targets are being assessed?*	**End-of-Unit Assessment** *What assessment methods will you use? How many questions will there be for each target being assessed on the end-of-unit assessment?*	**Targets Assessed on a Common Formative Assessment** *Choose those you will intervene on, and determine where students need more feedback.*
I can identify and create equivalent fractions. *This means I can:* • Identify equivalent fractions and show why they are equivalent. • Create equivalent fractions and show why they are equivalent.	Two multiple-choice items: Identify equivalent fractions. Three constructed-response items: Given a fraction, create equivalent fractions.	Common Formative Assessment 1: One multiple-choice item with more than one correct answer: Show six pairs of fractions and ask which are equivalent. Four constructed-response items: • One question: Explain why two fractions are equivalent. • Three questions: Generate a fraction equivalent to one given and justify.
I can compare two fractions and explain why my answer is correct. *This means I can:* • Recognize fractions can only be compared if they refer to the same whole. • Compare two fractions with the same numerator and explain why my answer is correct. • Compare two fractions with the same denominator and explain why my answer is correct. • Record my answer when comparing fractions using >, =, or <.	One constructed-response item: Show a large and small pizza and explain why fractional parts of the pizzas cannot be compared using only fractions. Three items: Give two fractions with the same denominator; students compare them using >, =, or < and explain their reasoning. Three items: Give two fractions with the same numerator; students compare them using >, =, or < and explain their reasoning.	Common Formative Assessment 2: • Compare two fractions with the same denominator and write the answer using >, =, or <. • Compare two fractions with the same numerator and write the answer using >, =, or <. Four constructed-response items: • Two comparisons of fractions with common denominators. Record the answer using >, =, or <. Provide a number line or picture, and students show why their answer is correct. • Two comparisons of fractions with common numerators. Record the answer using >, =, or <. Provide a number line or picture, and students show why their answer is correct.

Taking Action © 2018, 2025 Solution Tree Press • SolutionTree.com
Visit **go.SolutionTree.com/RTIatWork** to download this free reproducible.

Calendar

Words in bold are agreed-on team actions.

- On the calendar, note meeting days so you are clear on when you will analyze the assessment information (common formative assessments and common end-of-unit assessment).

- Note when you will respond to your analysis and instruction or intervention planning.

- Note the focused learning target to address at team meetings and on each common assessment.

Monday	Tuesday	Wednesday	Thursday	Friday
2/22	2/23	2/24	2/25 Team meeting: **Plan** CFA 1: I can identify and create equivalent fractions.	2/26
3/1	3/2	3/3	3/4 Team meeting: **Plan** CFA 2: I can compare two fractions and explain why my answer is correct.	3/5
3/8	3/9 **Administer** CFA 1: I can identify and create equivalent fractions.	3/10	3/11 Team meeting: **Analyze and plan** a team response to CFA 1.	3/12 FLEX DAY **Respond** to CFA 1.
3/15	3/16	3/17 **Administer** CFA 2: I can compare two fractions and explain why my answer is correct.	3/18 Team meeting: **Analyze and plan** a team response to CFA 2.	3/19
3/22 FLEX DAY **Respond** to CFA 2.	3/23	3/24 **End-of-Unit Assessment**	3/25 Team meeting: **Plan** Tier 2 interventions.	3/26

Source for standards: National Governors Association Center for Best Practices & Council of Chief State School Officers. (2010b). Common Core State Standards for mathematics. Washington, DC: Authors. Accessed at https://learning.ccsso.org/wp-content /uploads/2022/11/ADA-Compliant-Math-Standards.pdf on January 11, 2024.

Sample Grade 9 ELA Unit Assessment Plan

This is a sample unit assessment plan for grade 9 English language arts. The verbs are bolded for emphasis.

Unit: Writing an Argument	Start and End Dates: March 1–26
Essential Standards	**Deconstruct to Identify Skills and Concepts**
W.9-10.1: **Write** arguments to support claims in an **analysis** of substantive topics or texts, **using** valid reasoning and relevant and sufficient evidence. W.9-10.1a: **Introduce** precise claim(s), **distinguish** the claim(s) from alternate or opposing claims, and **create** an organization that establishes clear relationships among claim(s), counterclaims, reasons, and evidence. W.9-10.1b: **Develop** claim(s) and counterclaims fairly, supplying evidence for each while **pointing out (explain)** strengths and limitations of both in a manner that anticipates the audience's knowledge level and concerns.	**Write** an argument. **Analyze** a topic by developing (introducing) a claim to focus an argument. **Use** valid reasoning to support claims. **Use** relevant and sufficient evidence to support claims. **Explain** (develop/supply) the evidence, including the strengths and limitations of the evidence as applicable. **Distinguish** and explain the counterclaim, including an opposing or opposite stance. **Organize** (create) the argument effectively and logically.

Learning Target Progression With Student-Friendly Targets
List skills and concepts from least complex to most complex.
Clarify concepts for student reflection and assessment.

I can write an argument.

I can introduce precise claims.

I can develop claims and counterclaims fairly and thoroughly.
This means I can:

- Use valid reasoning and relevant, sufficient evidence.

- Explain strengths and limitations of the evidence.

I can organize and establish clear relationships among claims, counterclaims, reasons, and evidence.
This means I can:

- Use evidence and reasons that make sense and are logically ordered to support the claim.

- Clearly explain the supporting evidence and reasons.

- Clearly explain the counterclaims or opposing viewpoints.

Common Assessments		
Learning Targets *Which targets are being assessed?*	**End-of-Unit Assessment** *What assessment methods will you use? How many questions will there be for each target being assessed on the end-of-unit assessment?*	**Targets Assessed on a Common Formative Assessment** *Choose those you will intervene on, and determine where students need more feedback.*
I can introduce precise claims. I can develop claims and counterclaims fairly and thoroughly. • Use valid reasoning. • Use relevant and sufficient evidence. • Explain strengths and limitations of the evidence. I can organize and establish clear relationships among claims, counterclaims, reasons, and evidence. • Evidence and reasons to support the claim make sense and are logically ordered. • Evidence and reasons are clearly explained. • Counterclaims or opposing viewpoints are clearly explained.	Essay (assessed with rubric): Students choose from a list of topics or create their own. They read multiple sources on their topic from different perspectives and then develop a claim, supporting it with evidence and explaining the counterclaim.	Common Formative Assessment 1: 1. Students choose from two possible claims regarding the influence of artificial intelligence. 2. Students read two sources or articles on artificial intelligence. 3. Students use a graphic organizer to name evidence that supports the claim, their reasoning, and each piece of evidence's strengths and limitations. Common Formative Assessment 2: Students create a draft of their essay.

page 2 of 3

Calendar

Words in bold are agreed-on team actions.

- On the calendar, note meeting days so you are clear on when you will analyze the assessment information (common formative assessments and common end-of-unit assessment).
- Note when you will respond to your analysis and instruction or intervention planning.
- Note the focused learning target to address at team meetings and on each common assessment.

Monday	Tuesday	Wednesday	Thursday	Friday
3/1	3/2	3/3	3/4 Team meeting: **Plan** CFA 1: I can develop claims and counterclaims fairly and thoroughly.	3/5
3/8	3/9 **Administer** CFA 1.	3/10	3/11 Team meeting: **Analyze and plan** a response to CFA 1.	3/12 FLEX DAY **Respond** to CFA 1.
3/15	3/16	3/17	3/18 Team meeting: **Check in** to discuss how the response to CFA 1 went and plan an additional response if needed. **Plan** CFA 2: I can organize and establish clear relationships among claims, counterclaims, reasons, and evidence.	3/19 FLEX DAY **Respond** to CFA 2.
3/22	3/23	3/24	3/25 Team meeting: **Analyze** essay drafts to identify one criterion that each student needs to review before they revise. **Review for End-of-Unit Assessment** Review drafts of essays and identify one criterion for students to use to revise. They go to the station where others are working on the same criterion. Students review and revise their essays based on those criteria, and the teacher works with students still needing support with developing their claims.	3/26 **End-of-Unit Assessment** **Revised essays are due.**

Source for standards: National Governors Association Center for Best Practices & Council of Chief State School Officers. (2010a). Common Core State Standards for English language arts and literacy in history/social studies, science, and technical subjects. Washington, DC: Authors. Accessed at https://learning.ccsso.org/wp-content/uploads/2022/11/ELA_Standards1.pdf on April 30, 2024.

Deconstructing Standards

As a team, use the following chart to deconstruct, or make sense of, each essential standard to identify the learning targets that underpin the standard and the student-friendly targets to use in class.

1. Highlight or circle the verbs that describe what students must do in the standard. Underline the noun phrases to determine the concepts students need to learn.

2. List the noun phrases in the Concepts column. Clarify them if needed. (For example, if the phrase is *Causes of World War I*, list the causes to have clarity as a team.)

3. List the verbs from the standard in the Skills column.

4. Group the skills (learning targets) into student-friendly learning targets. The skills become the success criteria and inform daily teaching objectives. The student-friendly learning targets are used for student investment throughout the unit and after each assessment.

Essential standards:		
Concepts *What do students have to know?*	**Skills** *What do students have to be able to do?*	**Student-Friendly Learning Targets** *I can . . .*

Action 3

Create Common Assessments and Begin Instruction

Assessment evidence—the quizzes, the presentations, the products, and the observations—helps teachers understand the extent to which students have mastered the essential standards. Once teams complete actions 1 (identify essential standards) and 2 (design a unit assessment plan) to create an intentional plan, they are ready to breathe life into their plan. These actions help teachers begin to reculture their classrooms from a focus on grading and evaluating to a focus on learning that will facilitate greater engagement, more targeted instruction, and, therefore, higher levels of student learning. The structure teams choose for assessment design contributes to the ease with which teams can identify what students need to focus on to reach the essential standards. Data analysis is simpler when the assessments are targeted and organized by learning target and standard.

Creating and giving common assessments is another critical part of the team teaching-assessing-learning cycle, as shown in figure 3.9. Once the unit assessment plan and common assessments are created, instruction can begin more effectively because each teacher on the team is clear about the standards being assessed and the level to which students need to learn them to demonstrate mastery. In the teaching-assessing-learning cycle, the assessments are administered in the flow of instruction, and teams build in time to analyze the results and use those insights to respond instructionally to students' identified learning needs. In essence, common formative assessments are used to plan lessons.

Since teachers make such important decisions based on assessment data, it is critical that the assessments themselves adhere to professional standards of quality all team members agree to. These include:

- Clarity of purpose
- Clarity of learning targets (derived from standards)
- Effective assessment design
- Calibration of the level of rigor the team expects students to demonstrate

When teams attend to these quality indicators in the design and use of their assessments, they get more accurate and reliable information about where students are toward achieving the desired learning.

Here's Why

Assessment evidence is critical to understand (1) the effectiveness of instruction and (2) which students need more time and different instruction to learn the essential standards. Assessment is the only way we can know whether students learn what we teach. In a very real sense, therefore, assessment is the bridge between teaching and learning (Andrade & Cizek, 2009). As such, assessments need to be accurate and meet standards of high-quality design and use. These include clarity of purpose, clarity of learning targets, effective assessment design, and calibration of the level of rigor the team expects students to demonstrate, as detailed in the following sections.

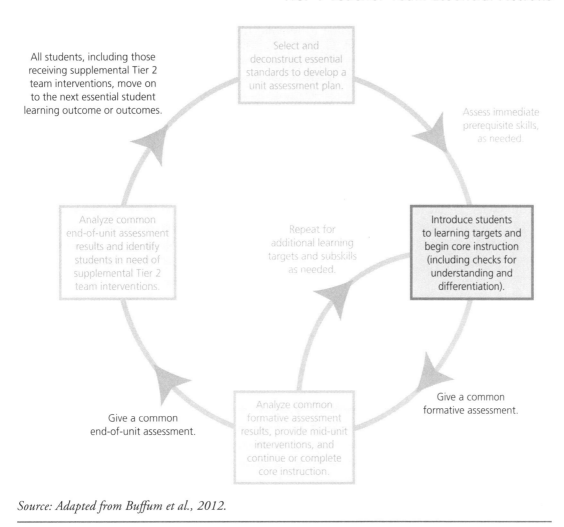

All students, including those receiving supplemental Tier 2 team interventions, move on to the next essential student learning outcome or outcomes.

Select and deconstruct essential standards to develop a unit assessment plan.

Assess immediate prerequisite skills, as needed.

Analyze common end-of-unit assessment results and identify students in need of supplemental Tier 2 team interventions.

Repeat for additional learning targets and subskills as needed.

Introduce students to learning targets and begin core instruction (including checks for understanding and differentiation).

Give a common end-of-unit assessment.

Analyze common formative assessment results, provide mid-unit interventions, and continue or complete core instruction.

Give a common formative assessment.

Source: Adapted from Buffum et al., 2012.

FIGURE 3.9: Essential action 3 in the team teaching-assessing-learning cycle.

Clarity of Purpose

Understanding the purposes, or uses, of common end-of-unit assessments, common formative assessments, and checks for understanding helps both teachers and students understand what is expected before, during, and after instruction to maximize success. Any assessment can be used formatively or summatively; it is what teams and students do with the information that makes the assessment so. Teams analyze data and student work from an end-of-unit assessment to understand what students need to work on during Tier 2 intervention if the students have not yet learned the essential standards. Interventions are more focused when team members have a common understanding that the end-of-unit assessment is only summative for students who have shown mastery. For those students who need more time to master the essentials, the end-of-unit assessment is used formatively to understand what learning or misconceptions need to be addressed in Tier 2 intervention.

Throughout the unit, team members formatively assess targets from the essential standard, as agreed on and planned in advance in the unit assessment plan. When teams analyze common formative assessment student work and data, they develop new lessons and instruction—which is different from reteaching the same way (just louder and slower) to help guide core instruction, or Tier 1 prevention.

Teachers use checks for understanding to respond to students in real time. Gathering information from ongoing checks for understanding (exit slips, responders, whiteboards, questioning strategies, and so on) enables teachers to give frequent, meaningful, and differentiated feedback to students without having to wait for results from a team-developed common formative assessment. Figure 3.10 illustrates the timing of and relationships among the end-of-unit assessment, common formative assessments, and checks for understanding.

Clarity of Learning Targets

When students receive frequent feedback on how they are doing relative to learning targets, they are empowered to take responsibility for their own learning. When learning targets appear on the assessment and students begin to link what they are learning with how they are being assessed, they can identify their specific strengths and next steps. This clarity creates a sense of hope and possibility, as instruction and intervention are connected to learning and not just getting assignments done and accumulating points. This clarity is foundational to assessment design; it ensures teacher teams are crystal clear about the essential learning and what it looks like when students reach proficiency.

Effective Assessment Design

As learning targets become clearer and more defined, teacher teams generate valid and reliable evidence of learning through the creation of a common end-of-unit assessment and common formative assessments. For the assessments to be valid (meaning they measure what you intended students to learn), the assessment design, or method, must closely align with the learning targets, or the verbs, being assessed. It is important that whatever method is chosen requires students to do the actions of the verbs.

This assessment design informs the subsequent teacher instruction before, during, and after each assessment. For example, if an assessment asks students to explain their thinking using a problem-solving strategy, the instruction must have students practice and learn how to do this type of explaining. For the assessment to be reliable, it must have enough items or enough diversity of evidence to ensure the results are consistent, giving teachers confidence that students can show mastery consistently and not just on one assessment or item that is an anomaly.

Calibration of the Level of Rigor the Team Expects Students to Demonstrate

Creating assessments also includes defining the expected level of rigor. Teacher teams decide that level of rigor before beginning the unit and provide instruction that maximizes student success on the end-of-unit assessment, or student learning of the most essential standards. It is one thing to identify an essential standard, but it is another to choose the assessment items and tasks for determining mastery; this is what signals the teams' expectations.

While choosing or designing items, teams ensure the items meet the desired cognitive level. After administering the assessment, team members analyze student work to ensure the items meet the level of rigor and revise the items as needed. It is the process of aligning items and reviewing the results that ensures consistent calibration of what high levels of learning look like. This calibration is essential in ensuring equitable access and achievement.

	Unit Starts ⟶				Unit Ends ⟶
Used to inform Tier 2 intervention *Team designs and responds.*					End-of-Unit Assessment
Used to inform Tier 1 prevention and sometimes Tier 2 intervention *Team designs and responds.*	Common Formative Assessment			Common Formative Assessment	
Used to inform Tier 1 prevention throughout lessons *Individual teachers design and respond.*	Check for Understanding	Check for Understanding	Check for Understanding	Check for Understanding	Check for Understanding

FIGURE 3.10: Timing of and relationships among the end-of-unit assessment, common formative assessments, and checks for understanding in a unit.

Here's How

When teams determined essential standards (action 1), completed the essential standards chart (action 1), and developed a unit assessment plan (action 2), they laid the groundwork for accurate assessment design. As they consider accuracy, teacher teams learn and explore the characteristics of the design of a high-quality assessment. Teams achieve accuracy by doing the following.

▶ Align items and tasks to learning targets identified in the unit assessment plan.

▶ Align items and tasks to grade-level rigor agreed on as a team.

▶ Choose methods that match the student actions in the verbs.

▶ Maintain awareness of bias and assumptions of knowledge needed on the assessment.

▶ Ensure the assessment is organized so it is clear which items and tasks provide information on which learning targets.

The "Assessment Design Checklist" reproducible (page 122) can help guide the critique and design of end-of-unit and common formative assessments.

To address accuracy, teams look at the verb in a learning target and standard and then choose a method, or type of item or task, that ensures students do the action of the verb. For example, any method chosen for the learning target, "I can use evidence to support my claim," must require students to produce the evidence and explain how it supports the claim. A constructed response, a graphic organizer, or an interview would be effective, but a multiple-choice item would not, as the item would be limited to identifying the evidence.

Assessment items must also be clearly written and easy for both teachers and students to understand. The goal is to accurately assess what students have learned, not to create a guessing game of expectations. The more reasons that students can get something wrong, other than they don't understand or don't have mastery, the lower the validity of that item. Teacher teams plan for this level of alignment in the unit assessment plan (action 2) when identifying the types of methods and items that align with the learning targets.

Teams select a cognitive framework to determine complexity. Some teams use Webb's Depth of Knowledge (DOK; Hess, 2018; Webb, 2002), but there are many other frameworks to help guide and define rigor. Using their chosen framework, teams ensure their items match the intended level. Team members design or choose and agree on these items and tasks together. Teams also decide on the conditions in which they will administer the assessment, so students are assessed in similar contexts or with the same level of support. Having clearly defined conditions ensures that when teams share data and look at student work from the assessments, teachers can be confident they are comparing apples to apples rather than apples to oranges.

Assessment design also must attend to sampling, which is part of reliability. The assessment plan and the assessment itself must include enough items for each target to ensure accuracy and confidence that students' work effectively indicates their level of mastery. Teams can use the "Assessment Design Checklist" reproducible to guide their creation and review of end-of-unit and common formative assessments.

The process of reviewing the assessment data (see Action 5: Analyze and Respond to Common Assessment Data, page 138) ensures that teachers are scoring the items and tasks similarly. Equally important, it ensures students experience the assessment as fair and equitable because performance expectations are the same in all classrooms. This process of looking at student work to calibrate rigor and clarity of expectations increases the assessment's validity and strengthens instruction. This means that teams can be confident that their scores are accurately measuring student learning on grade-level essentials.

When the data are analyzed and adjustments are made to reduce bias or error (students get something wrong for reasons other than they don't know it, or they get it right for reasons other than they know it), the accuracy of the assessment increases. To catch those items that may inadvertently assess something other than the learning targets, teacher teams analyze the data and toss out any items that may have caused confusion, often seen when most students get an item wrong. Teams can revise the item for the next time they give the assessment.

Teams also intentionally plan the use of the assessment. Essential action 2 asks teams to articulate not only when they will administer a common formative assessment, but also when they will analyze the student work and respond. Timing and response are key to ensuring high levels of learning. So, understanding the relationship between common formative assessment use and end-of-unit assessment use is central to ensuring timely and targeted responses to assessment design.

Decisions made about when to give common formative assessments are primarily based on student need. On which targets will you plan to intervene? Which targets are most challenging to students? When might students benefit most from teachers working together to adjust instruction? Agreeing to give a common formative assessment means that team members have also agreed to the targets assessed, the assessment tool or task used, and the format for sharing the results.

Teams use learning targets to inform instruction in the team teaching-assessing-learning cycle. Each teacher can use the knowledge gained about standards and mastery to design quality lessons, introduce students to the learning targets, and better differentiate and check for understanding— all part of the team teaching-assessing-learning cycle *during the unit* as well as during instruction that starts in the next unit while Tier 2 interventions take place.

Helpful Tools

The following tools will help you accomplish the work for this essential action.

- ▸ **Chapter 7 of *Learning by Doing, Fourth Edition* (DuFour et al., 2024), "Creating Team-Developed Common Formative Assessments":** This chapter provides foundational content knowledge as well as tools that can help schools accomplish the action steps outlined in this section.

- ▸ **Chapter 4 of *Acceleration for All* (Kramer & Schuhl, 2023), "An Assessment System That Accelerates Learning":** This chapter shares strategies for creating and different methods for giving common assessments designed to grow student learning.

- ▸ **Chapters 4 and 5 of *Design in Five* (Dimich, 2024), "Crafting an Assessment Plan" and "Creating the Assessment and Gathering the Materials":** These two chapters describe how to develop an assessment plan and choose or create both formative and end-of-unit assessments to ensure the assessment methods align to the intended learning. This includes characteristics of different types of assessment items, such as selected-response items, constructed-response items, performance tasks, and rubrics.

- ▸ **"Assessment Design Checklist" (page 122):** This reproducible checklist helps teams create their common end-of-unit and common formative assessments and critique them for quality.

> ▶ **"CFA 1: Grade 9 ELA Unit—Developing Claims and Counterclaims" (page 125):** This reproducible common formative assessment is an example of how to create an aligned and easy-to-administer common formative assessment to ensure students are practicing and getting feedback on the most essential parts of the standards before the unit ends. (We describe this assessment in the reproducible "Sample Grade 9 ELA Unit Assessment Plan," page 110.) Note that the rubric for this common formative assessment is the same as for the end-of-unit assessment, ensuring alignment of criteria and expectations.

> ▶ **"CFA 2: Grade 2 Mathematics Unit—Two-Step Addition and Subtraction Word Problems" (page 128):** This reproducible grade 2 mathematics common formative assessment is an example of an assessment based on the most essential learning target from an essential standard.

> ▶ **"Sample Grade 9 ELA End-of-Unit Assessment":** This reproducible end-of-unit assessment is an example of how to create this kind of assessment to ensure students master the most essential standards. It also includes student self-reflection and a note about how students get additional support if they don't meet mastery on the essential standard. (Visit **go.SolutionTree.com/RTIatWork** to download this free reproducible. We describe this assessment in the reproducible "Sample Grade 9 ELA Unit Assessment Plan," page 110.)

Coaching Tips

As is almost always the case, moving from theory (framework) to action (implementation) is very challenging. It is one thing to understand the needed changes in practice and something else entirely to implement them. At this point, the knowing-doing gap rears its head. In other words, knowing what to do does not always translate into acting on that knowledge.

To maximize success, guiding coalition members must put on their coaching hats and work alongside their teams. As Peterson and Hicks (1996) write in *Leader as Coach*:

> Approach your coaching like a gardener who does not try to motivate the plants to grow, but who seeks the right combination of sunlight, nourishment, and water to release the plant's natural growth. A gardener provides an environment conducive to growth, much as a coach creates the conditions in which personal motivation will flourish. (p. 55)

Equally important to successful implementation is a shared understanding of the coach's role between teachers and guiding coalition members (Peterson & Hicks, 1996). All parties must challenge themselves to interact in a nonevaluative, learning-focused manner, with all conversations centering on student learning, never teacher evaluation.

Coaching teacher teams in the design and creation of assessments can be an engaging and complex process. Fundamentally, all students must have access to grade-level essentials, and therefore, all common formative and end-of-unit assessments must accurately reflect them. In turn, analyzing assessment results helps teams determine what instruction is needed to ensure all students achieve at grade level or above. Guiding coalition members contribute to assessment accuracy by assisting teams with the following.

> ▶ Guide teams to critique their end-of-unit assessment items to ensure all items are aligned to grade-level learning targets and standards. If teams use items and tasks from their

curriculum materials, they must also verify alignment to grade-level standards. When engaging in this alignment process, teams may benefit from creating and using a table. In the first column, they list the learning targets to be assessed. In the second column, they identify which assessment items match which learning targets. This process can quickly lead to a reflective conversation about the validity of the assessment.

▶ Guide teams to determine the cognitive level of each essential standard they want students to achieve. Review assessment items to ensure they match the intended level, and revise any items that do not match.

▶ Help facilitate conversations about what to grade as teams are developing common assessments. Providing a minimum of one ungraded common formative assessment in a unit of instruction ensures students have at least one risk-free opportunity to test their understanding of the learning targets. Not grading the formative assessment can help focus the team's collaborative analysis of how best to support high levels of learning for all students, versus just having students do work for a score. (See chapter 4, action 4, page 184, for more on how to co-create schoolwide grading practices.)

Ultimately, coaching is all about promoting reflective thinking. To do so, coaches utilize strategies and language that support teams' or teachers' planning and decision-making skills, their ability to reflect on practice, and their development as self-directed learners. Table 3.2 highlights several key strategies and language that good coaches use.

TABLE 3.2: Key Strategies and Language Good Coaches Use

Coaching Strategies	Coaching Language
Maintaining a nonjudgmental stance	• Let me see if I understand . . . • In other words . . .
Listening	• Tell me what you mean when you say . . . • Let's review the key points so far . . .
Inquiring and probing for specificity rather than telling	• To what extent . . . ? • What might be another way . . . ? • What do you see as your next steps . . . ?

Finally, as busy as guiding coalition members will be supporting teachers to implement the team teaching-assessing-learning cycle, it is critical that the guiding coalition continues to meet regularly. These meetings provide a forum for sharing challenges, finding solutions, and celebrating successes. Coaching is hard work!

Tom Landry says it best: "A coach is someone who tells you what you don't want to hear, who has you see what you don't want to see, so you can be who you have always known you could be" (Goodreads, n.d). This type of sharing and transparency is crucial to building an environment in which both teachers and leaders can truly thrive and grow.

Assessment Design Checklist

Review the statements in the following checklist for creating, critiquing, and revising assessments. The statements in this checklist fall into two categories.

1. The design statements reflect qualities or criteria that lead to accurate information from the assessment evidence.

2. The use statements capture the assessment qualities that lead both students and teachers to take action based on what they learn from assessment evidence.

Next to each statement, record your comments on the quality of the design or use of your assessments.

Accurate Design	
Statement	**Response and Comments**
1. The team clarifies the standards, targets, and skills being assessed and determines grade- or course-level expectations for each.	
2. The team matches the assessment method to the learning targets. This means the items or tasks ask students to "do" the verb to show mastery. For example, if the verb in the target is *explain*, the item ensures students produce an explanation and don't just select one.	
3. The team ensures there are enough items to determine with confidence the level of proficiency.	
4. The team determines the cognitive level and grade- or course-level expectations for each item. (If critiquing or revising an already designed assessment, identify the cognitive level and learning target for each item to be sure it reflects the cognitive demand in the standards.)	
5. The team ensures the structure, layout, and setup of the questions create the best possible conditions for students to show their understanding, and revises what might contribute to student confusion.	

Taking Action © 2018, 2025 Solution Tree Press • SolutionTree.com
Visit **go.SolutionTree.com/RTIatWork** to download this free reproducible.

6. The team ensures directions are present, clear, and concise and the visual layout of the assessment is easy to understand and read.	
7. If utilizing a technology tool, the team ensures that students have the training needed to use the tool in a meaningful way and that they have access to and an understanding of what they need to utilize the tool.	
8. The team ensures the tasks, items, and questions or exercises are written well. • The assessment is clear, succinct, and generally not confusing. • The team identifies the vocabulary and background knowledge needed to engage successfully in the assessment.	
9. The team collaborates with colleagues who have expertise in special education, language learning, and any other specialized expertise to ensure appropriate accommodations or modifications are made for students who need them so they have equitable access and can demonstrate grade- or course-level learning.	
10. The team ensures scores communicated directly on the assessment are provided by learning targets or standards. Or, the scoring rubric indicates the qualities of the work.	
11. The team agrees on how to administer the assessment to students (for example, which resources students can use, what posters can be on the walls, and the length of time given to complete the assessment).	
12. The team creates a tool or plan for students to reflect and, as needed, learn from their assessment results and feedback.	

Taking Action © 2018, 2025 Solution Tree Press • SolutionTree.com
Visit **go.SolutionTree.com/RTIatWork** to download this free reproducible.

Intentional Use	
Statement	**Response and Comments**
13. The team analyzes data from the common assessment (formative or end-of-unit) by standard, target, or skill and by student to determine effective instructional practices and identify next steps for students. The team also identifies who needs intervention and extension to achieve the targeted essential standard and learning target.	
14. The team analyzes student work from the common assessment to identify the strengths, errors, and next steps for students related to the essential standard, target, or skill.	
15. The team develops an agreed-on instructional plan for intervention and extension from data analysis and student work. This plan may be executed as a Tier 1 prevention or Tier 2 intervention and extension based on the common assessment the team is analyzing.	
16. The team determines how it will know whether students learned through Tier 1 or Tier 2 responses. In other words, when and how will the team reassess the essential learning that is the focus of the response?	
17. The team agrees on how to evaluate student learning on the assessment (how to score student work for consistent feedback and grading).	

As a team, discuss the following.

- What are the strengths of your team's common assessment based on your alignment to the design-quality checklist?

- What, if any, revisions to the assessment are needed based on your alignment to the design-quality checklist? Decide how those revisions will be made.

CFA 1: Grade 9 ELA Unit—Developing Claims and Counterclaims

Name: _____ Date: _____

Directions:

1. Read two sources to explore the topic: How does artificial intelligence enhance or diminish learning in school?

2. The following two statements represent a claim and a counterclaim. Circle the one you want to use as your claim.

   a. Artificial intelligence enhances learning in school.

   b. Artificial intelligence diminishes learning in school.

3. Use the following table to record one piece of evidence from each source to support the claim you chose. Explain how it supports the claim. Explain its strengths and limitations.

Name the source (author's name and year).	Name the evidence that supports the claim you chose.	Explain how the evidence supports the claim.	Explain the strengths and limitations of the evidence.
Source 1			
Source 2			

Taking Action © 2018, 2025 Solution Tree Press • SolutionTree.com
Visit **go.SolutionTree.com/RTIatWork** to download this free reproducible.

4. Describe the claim that is counter to yours, and use one piece of evidence to explain its reasoning. Include why you refute that stance.

_____

_____

_____

_____

_____

_____

_____

_____

_____

_____

5. How confident are you about each of the following criteria? Use the rubric to help determine your confidence level. Check the box that best matches how you feel about the learning you can demonstrate on this assessment.

	I've got this.	I have questions about how to do this.	I am unsure about what this means.
I can develop claims fairly and thoroughly. _This means I can:_ • Use valid reasoning. • Use relevant and sufficient evidence. • Explain the strengths and limitations of the evidence.			
I can develop counterclaims thoroughly. _This means I can:_ • Identify the counterclaim. • Clearly explain the counterclaim.			

Taking Action © 2018, 2025 Solution Tree Press • SolutionTree.com
Visit **go.SolutionTree.com/RTIatWork** to download this free reproducible.

Criteria	10 9	8	7 6	5 (Not Yet)
I can develop claims fairly and thoroughly. *This means I can:* • Use valid reasoning. • Use relevant and sufficient evidence. • Explain the strengths and limitations of the evidence.	Uses valid reasoning; clearly explains how the evidence supports the claim Uses relevant and sufficient evidence that strongly supports the claim Clearly and thoroughly explains the strengths and limitations of the evidence	Clearly explains how the evidence supports the claim Uses enough evidence that makes sense and accurately supports the claim Explains the strengths of the evidence	Explains the evidence but not necessarily how it ties to the claim Uses some evidence that generally supports the claim Explains with some reference to the claim	Explanation is general or not present. Use of evidence that accurately supports the claim is limited. Explanation is lacking or doesn't tie evidence to the claim.
I can develop counterclaims thoroughly. *This means I can:* • Identify the counterclaim. • Explain the counterclaim.	Clearly identifies and explains the counterclaim with supported evidence	Identifies and explains the counterclaim	References the counterclaim	The counterclaim is missing or contradictory to the position.

CFA 2: Grade 2 Mathematics Unit—Two-Step Addition and Subtraction Word Problems

Name: _____ Date: _____

Learning Target: I can solve word problems and show how I know my answers are correct.

Directions: Solve each word problem. Show your thinking using pictures or equations.

1. Javier walks to the park and sees many animals. He sees 27 birds, 8 squirrels, and 12 dogs. How many more birds does Javier see than squirrels and dogs put together? (4 points)

2. Ariel has 15 stickers. Her friend Amy has 32 stickers. How many more stickers do Ariel and Amy need to collect to have 60 stickers altogether? (4 points)

3. Caroline has a basket of 50 blueberries. She uses 22 blueberries to make pancakes and 15 blueberries to make muffins. How many blueberries does Caroline have left in her basket? (4 points)

Scoring Criteria

For each word problem, the student earns:

- 1 point for a picture or equation to show the first step of the word problem
- 1 point for an accurate answer to the first step of the word problem
- 1 point for a picture or equation to show the second step of the word problem
- 1 point for the answer to the second step, which answers the question

Or, if using a rubric:

1 Minimal Understanding	2 Partial Understanding	3 Proficient Understanding	4 Advanced Understanding
Student draws a picture or writes an equation for some of the word problem. Student guesses at an operation to solve one step of the two-step word problem.	Student shows a picture or equation and: 1. Solves the first step but forgets the second OR 2. Uses incorrect computation when solving one step of the two-step word problem	Student shows a picture or equation and solves each step. Student's work may include a minor error.	Student shows a picture or equation and solves each step accurately. Student checks their answer.

Action 4

Foster Student Investment

Too often, students feel like intervention, or additional time, is a punishment for not learning fast enough or not understanding or doing the work the first or second time—no matter what the cause. This perception can cause students to disengage and develop mindsets of "I don't care," "I'm not doing this. It isn't going to matter anyway," or "The teacher doesn't like me, so what I do won't make a difference."

Students should understand and experience intervention as teachers' belief that they can and will learn with a little more time and a little twist in instruction. Providing additional time and requiring multiple opportunities to learn essential standards are two direct actions that signal to students their teachers believe in them and won't give up on them; these actions occur when schools authentically embrace the mindset that all students will learn, without exception. Sometimes, we need to believe in our students before they can believe in themselves. When students start to see success, their confidence grows, and achievement will follow (McMillan, 2020).

Fostering student investment, and not just involvement, is about "a reciprocal relationship between student and teacher, one that leads to students taking the reins and beginning to own and value their own learning" (Dimich, 2024, p. 25). However, students often describe school as something that is done *to* them versus *with* them. When students feel that school is done *to* them, success depends on students' figuring out how to get enough points, be compliant, do what the teacher wants, get all the work done, and do the work in a structured amount of time. When school is done *with* students, they work with teachers to develop the ability to articulate *what* they are learning and *where* they are in achieving that learning. And they believe that the actions they take will help them learn more. Action 4 focuses on having teacher teams partner with students to foster their investment as the teams ensure high levels of learning for all.

Students can reflect on their learning and next steps within daily lessons and data from common mid-unit and end-of-unit assessments—all parts of the team teaching-assessing-learning cycle, as shown in figure 3.11 (page 130). When students are using their own assessment data to understand what they have learned and not yet learned, and teachers are explicitly tying Tier 1 and Tier 2 instruction to this learning, students begin to make the connection that this additional time or instruction is helping them learn a particular skill. This focus helps students see that learning is doable because they know *why* they are working to learn a specific target.

Teacher teams can't achieve high levels of learning alone. They must partner with students to help them recognize the learning they need to achieve, reflect on their assessment evidence to understand their strengths and next steps, and take action to grow toward the essential standards and develop confidence in their abilities.

Here's Why

Educator and researcher D. Royce Sadler (1989) studied the idea of students being front and center in their learning. He found that students invested in their learning when they were able to answer the following questions through their assessment and instructional experience in school: "What am I learning?" "Where am I now (in relation to the grade-level goal)?" and "How can I

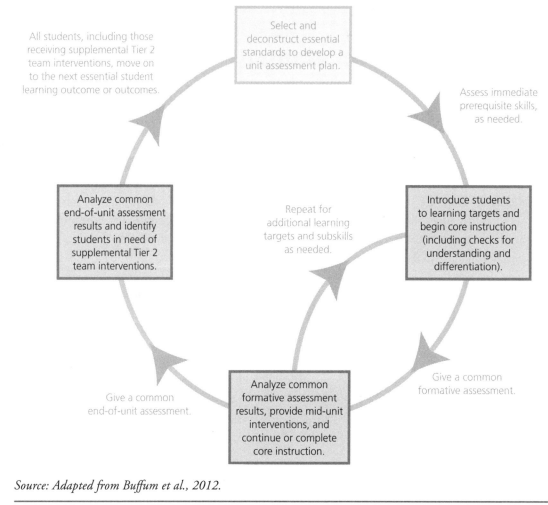

All students, including those receiving supplemental Tier 2 team interventions, move on to the next essential student learning outcome or outcomes.

Select and deconstruct essential standards to develop a unit assessment plan.

Assess immediate prerequisite skills, as needed.

Analyze common end-of-unit assessment results and identify students in need of supplemental Tier 2 team interventions.

Repeat for additional learning targets and subskills as needed.

Introduce students to learning targets and begin core instruction (including checks for understanding and differentiation).

Give a common end-of-unit assessment.

Analyze common formative assessment results, provide mid-unit interventions, and continue or complete core instruction.

Give a common formative assessment.

Source: Adapted from Buffum et al., 2012.

FIGURE 3.11: Essential action 4 in the team teaching-assessing-learning cycle.

close the gap (or what action do I take or am I guided to take to improve along the path toward learning)?" Rick Stiggins (2007) further articulates the role of students in investment:

> The students' role is to strive to understand what success looks like, to use feedback from each assessment to discover where they are now in relation to where they want to be, and to determine how to do better the next time. As students become increasingly proficient, they learn to generate their own descriptive feedback and set goals for what comes next on their journey.

It is the teacher team that sets the stage for students to be able to answer these questions and develop this level of investment as the team designs and analyzes common formative and end-of-unit assessment evidence.

Assessment is about not only gathering evidence of how students are progressing toward achieving the essential standards, or knowledge and skills, but also understanding students' emotions, confidence, and perceptions of their likelihood of achievement (McMillan, 2020). If a student lacks belief that anything they do will help them learn, they require a different intervention than a student who believes they can learn something with a little more time. Teacher teams must understand students' belief about their capacity to learn and their emotional state as much as what students know and can do in relation to the essential standards. Jacqueline Leighton (2020) writes:

Although classroom assessment results may lead to inferences about whether a student has acquired specific knowledge or skills, these inferences do not provide diagnostic information about *why* students might have underperformed or provide much context for how a feedback intervention might be designed to address an existing knowledge gap. This is because classroom assessment results only narrowly inform teachers about acquisition of cognitive skills but do not shed light on the foundation for learning—students' states of emotion and relatedness. Therefore, measures of socio-emotional learning should be incorporated to contextualize students' classroom assessment results. (p. 38)

When the assessment clearly articulates what is being learned and allows students to share how confident they are about that learning, it is easier for students to self-assess where they are currently and where they are going.

Teachers need to deeply understand and respond to assessment information and data. But just as important, students should also be essential users of assessment information (Chappuis & Stiggins, 2020): "Students' thoughts and actions regarding assessment results are at least as important as those of adults. The students' emotional reaction to results will determine what they do in response" (Stiggins, 2007). A student's emotional reaction could be as simple as seeing an F or a 60 percent and having a sinking feeling that trying to figure out what happened would just take too much effort. Teacher teams need to understand how students experience assessment results so they can keep the focus on learning, not quantities or grades. Assessment responses should be framed so students understand that additional support is to help them learn essential standards or specific skills, not because they had an overall poor score on an assessment.

When collaborative teams analyze data from their common formative and end-of-unit assessments, they reflect on what worked in their instruction and what didn't. They identify the misconceptions and next steps individual students need, and they plan their Tier 1 preventions and Tier 2 interventions and extensions, so all students achieve the essential standard and beyond. Stiggins (2007) and Leighton (2020) highlight the importance of analyzing students' confidence and the extent to which their emotional state influences their learning. This analysis helps teams get clear on where students are and what they, the educators, need to do to ensure students achieve essential standards.

While analyzing data or looking at student work is one of the highest-leverage practices in which collaborative teams engage (McMillan, 2020; Reeves, 2008; Willis, Adie, Addison, & Kimber, 2023), how teachers guide students to reflect on that learning and act on what they don't know is where learning occurs—that's where student investment takes root. Optimism and success breed more optimism and success.

Student investment is about helping students make connections to and gain information about their learning through the work they do in class, their reflections on their errors, and the actions they take to learn more (engage in teachers' instructions and intervention). When teachers use the most recent and frequent scores to determine students' grades and scores, students see that when they learn more, their grade reflects it. Students start to believe that what they put into their learning and work leads to growth and success. When we can make these connections and help students see the positive impact of their actions, student investment is not only possible but intentionally cultivated.

Ultimately, students must meaningfully engage in our instructional plans and interventions. Our response to the assessment data attends to both what students understand and how confident they are about their learning. With this more comprehensive picture of learning, intervention and instruction can target the root cause of where students are and intentionally move them forward in learning the essential standard and investing in their learning (and not just getting the work done or achieving a number of points). When students begin to understand their strengths and not just their evaluative grade, they start to build confidence and take more risks to grow more.

Here's How

Before we highlight key actions for fostering student investment, it is worthwhile to point out that teams have already completed most of the work necessary to put the team teaching-assessing-learning cycle in motion. They have identified essential standards, deconstructed them into learning targets, converted the targets to student-friendly language, collaboratively created or selected assessments, and determined how they will use those assessments. The only missing piece is the development of instructional plans and intentional ways they will engage students with team-designed student investment tools to guide students' reflection on their learning and the action they must take to ensure learning.

With the clarity that comes from completing the previous steps, teachers will find that instructional planning and student investment actions, whether done individually or collaboratively, fall into place very quickly. The following actions foster student investment as teams plan units, review assessment results, and implement instructional responses. The specific actions are framed as three sets of questions students must answer as educators build investment in their learning.

1. Where am I going? What am I learning?

2. Where am I now? What have I learned? What do I still need to learn?

3. How do I close the gap? What will I do next to learn?

Where Am I Going? What Am I Learning?

Teacher teams began preparing for students to answer these questions when they wrote student-friendly learning targets as part of action 1 in the essential standards chart and action 2 in the unit assessment plan.

1. Introduce students to learning targets on the first day of unit instruction, and continue to discuss and build clarity on what mastery of these learning targets looks like. Consider the following actions to build students' understanding of where they are going.

   - Post learning targets in the classroom so students can connect instructional activities to what they are learning.

   - Put those same learning targets on assessments so students connect their assessment evidence to learning and can more easily identify their strengths and next steps. Figure 3.12 is an example of an assessment tool with learning targets in it.

   - Ask students to reflect on their learning targets as instruction continues throughout the unit. Exit tickets or small-group discussions can help teachers understand students' confidence in achieving the learning target that day, what questions are coming up, and what might be working or not working.

   - Consider posting the learning progression so students see how all the individual targets fit into the bigger picture. You can give this progression to students so they can track their progress.

Learning Target	Items	Points
I can formulate a testable hypothesis. This means I can identify a question to test and predict the results.	1–2	5 out of 5 points
I can organize data from an experiment. This means I can take the data and visually display them in an accurate, clear, and concise form.	3–4	8 out of 10 points
I can draw conclusions to either defend or refute my hypothesis. This means I can justify my conclusions by citing evidence gathered during an experiment.	5–6	3 out of 10 points
Overall		**16 out of 25 points, or 64%**

FIGURE 3.12: Student assessment tool showing scores for learning targets.

2. Build and share the success criteria, or qualities, needed to achieve learning targets and essential standards.

   • Share examples of strong and weak work.

   • Have students sort anonymous examples of student work from strongest to weakest and discuss why they sorted them the way they did.

Where Am I Now? What Have I Learned? What Do I Still Need to Learn?

Teams began this work when they outlined the assessments in the unit assessment plan. Then, through their common assessment design (action 3), teams ensured the learning targets were tightly aligned to the assessment items and tasks on each common formative and end-of-unit assessment. Such alignment means teachers can provide more targeted feedback to help students grow. Consider the following four actions to help students understand where they are now.

1. Engage students in reflecting on their strengths and next learning steps from their assessments using learning targets (self-assessment). Develop ways for students to self-assess their assessment evidence to determine their strengths and next steps. Because the assessment items and tasks are tightly aligned to the learning targets (which are usually embedded in the assessment or attached as a cover page), students can easily review their assessment results for strengths and next steps.

   For example, a student who gets a 64 percent on their assessment may feel overwhelmed or resigned to failure if they don't have confidence or specific actions to take to move forward. However, a student who gets the assessment scores shown in figure 3.12 can see their strengths and targets not yet learned. This helps both the teacher and the student know what's next.

2. Provide specific, descriptive feedback to students. Use the qualities, or criteria, your team generated when clarifying what students are learning. Target one strength and one

or two actions for students to take. Build in time for students to act on this feedback and revise their work.

Feedback from teachers can help students understand where they are: "Feedback is arguably the most important source of assessment information that supports learning (Hattie, 2023; Ruiz-Primo & Brookhart, 2018) or formative assessment information" (Brookhart, 2020, p. 64).

When teachers provide targeted feedback that is descriptive and actionable, student learning increases. However, feedback is only effective to the extent students act on it.

3. As a team, generate feedback as you examine student work and systematically identify students who need similar feedback (see action 5, page 138). Students who need similar feedback can work together to ensure they act on that feedback.

4. Implement frequent, ongoing checks for understanding, and give students differentiated feedback so they can deeply understand their strengths and next steps in relation to the criteria to achieve the learning targets (and grade-level standards) in real time.

How Do I Close the Gap? What Will I Do Next to Learn?

As noted previously, once students use learning evidence to determine their strengths, they can determine their next learning steps. Investing students in their next steps places a focus on learning and lets students know they have simply not learned something *yet*. Consider the following four actions to help students understand how to close any learning gaps.

1. Ask students to name actions they will take to address the area (or areas) they need to work on, whether it's a target not yet learned or a target partially learned. Teachers may generate options to help guide students' actions.

2. Frame re-engagement instruction (Tier 1 and Tier 2) around learning targets and essential standards so students know what learning targets they are working on when they get additional time and support.

3. Build in time to ensure students know how to act on the feedback and follow through. Focus this required action on the essential standards. Teams can identify students who need to act on the same feedback, and they can develop instruction and intervention to guide students in acting on that feedback.

4. Build in reassessment, or another assessment opportunity on the learning targets students worked on during their Tier 1 or Tier 2 instruction. Ensure students receive full credit for the revised work.

What role do teachers and teacher teams have in fostering student investment? It requires deep understanding of students—not just of what they know, but of who they are, how they learn, and where they make connections. Katie White (2017) articulates this need:

Knowing our students enables us to understand when and how to encourage risk taking and provides insights into their beliefs about themselves and their abilities. When we know our students, we understand the roadblocks preventing their success and can identify the best supports to help them create new stories about their potential. (p. 19)

As teacher teams plan student investment actions, they notice and reflect on the impact these actions have on student learning and confidence. They adjust their strategies and actions to continuously develop an understanding and practice where students own their learning.

Helpful Tools

The following tools will help you accomplish the work for this essential action.

▸ **"Student Reflection Planning Tool" (page 137):** This planning guide is designed for teams to ensure students can reflect on their learning from any assessment. This type of reflection requires that results or scores be broken down by learning goal or have learning descriptions so students can reflect on their strengths and next steps.

▸ *You Can Learn! Building Student Ownership, Motivation, and Efficacy With the PLC at Work Process* **(Brown & Ferriter, 2021):** In this resource, Tim Brown and William M. Ferriter provide strategies for building confidence and investment, including practical examples to build ownership.

▸ *Jackpot! Nurturing Student Investment Through Assessment* **(Dimich, Erkens, & Schimmer, 2023):** This resource provides practical tools for building investment, including examples of how to systematically use instruction and assessment to build confidence, efficacy, and hope in learning.

▸ **"Sample Grade 9 ELA Reflection for a Common Formative Assessment":** Teams can use this sample reflection to guide students' reflection on common formative assessments. This common formative assessment was outlined in the "Sample Grade 9 ELA Unit Assessment Plan" reproducible (page 110). (Visit **go.SolutionTree.com/RTIatWork** to download this free reproducible.)

▸ **"Sample Grade 7 Mathematics End-of-Unit Reflection for Proportions":** Teams can use this sample reflection to guide students' reflection on common formative assessments. (Visit **go.SolutionTree.com/RTIatWork** to download this free reproducible.)

Coaching Tips

As teams deepen their work in responding when students do and don't learn, utilizing strategies that increase student investment is essential. Creating transparency in what students are learning and providing them with information about their strengths and next steps empowers them to take ownership of their learning.

▸ First and foremost, teams need to understand various ways to foster student investment. This may be challenging since most adults, as learners, have had little personal experience with formative assessment and student investment strategies. To engage teams in understanding the three sets of key questions (see Here's How, page 132), include investment activities in staff meetings and professional development settings. As adults reflect on their own learning experiences, their understanding of student investment strategies and their commitment to utilizing these strategies in their instruction will grow.

▸ Creating and facilitating opportunities to hear from students can be very powerful. At staff meetings, teams can share informal or short surveys that ask students what helps them learn and what gets in the way; older students may also be willing to share their insights by participating on panels. In turn, teams can use surveys, panels, or exit tickets to gather similar feedback in their classrooms. Students are very intuitive and can provide direction for teachers, both individually and collectively.

▶ Providing consistent and targeted feedback is a powerful strategy for increasing student learning. Help teams view feedback as a systematic process in which they review student work and group students who need the same intervention. This helps teams avoid spending hours outside of class marking comments on assignments and assessments that students may or may not implement to improve their learning.

▶ Finally, celebrate! Highlight the power of student investment by having teams regularly share their strategies and results with one another.

Student Reflection Planning Tool

Teacher teams can develop a reflection tool using the following two steps.

1. Communicate what students have learned. You might design a cover page or table to show items by learning goal or develop a proficiency scale to ensure students are clear about what their score means in terms of learning.

Learning Goal	Score Needed for Proficiency	Student Score

2. Develop reflection tools and questions to guide students' understanding of assessment information in terms of their learning strengths, misconceptions, next steps, and learning strategies that will help them persist and learn more.

   Consider including questions like the following on assessments to facilitate student reflection and action.

   - **Strengths:** What are my learning strengths? On which learning goals did I reach proficiency?

   - **Challenges:** What was most challenging about this assessment?

   - **Next steps:** Which learning goal or goals do I need to work on?

   - **Action plan:** What actions will I take?

Action 5

Analyze and Respond to Common Assessment Data

In completing the first four essential actions of a collaborative team, team members have identified essential standards; created a unit assessment plan that includes a progression of learning targets, assessments, and dates for common assessments; developed common assessments; and determined how to invest students in their learning. The remaining essential teacher team action at Tier 1 is to collectively analyze student learning from common formative assessments and the common end-of-unit assessment to design targeted and specific Tier 1 and Tier 2 re-engagement learning experiences for students.

Analyzing common assessment data to determine the most effective ways to re-engage students in learning, as needed, is integral to the team teaching-assessing-learning cycle (see figure 3.13). It is the team's analysis that fuels the process of ensuring learning.

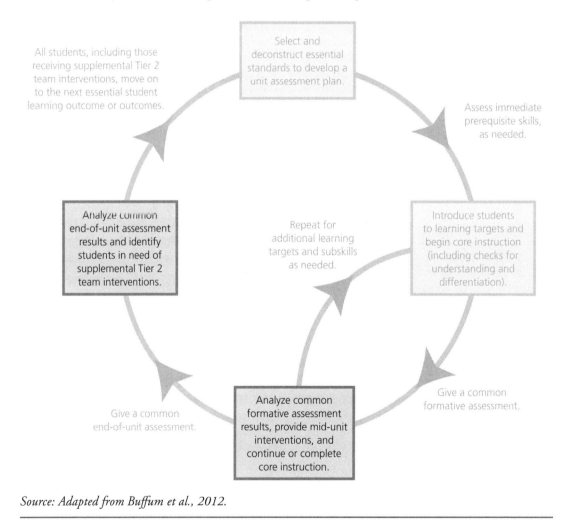

Source: Adapted from Buffum et al., 2012.

FIGURE 3.13: Essential action 5 in the team teaching-assessing-learning cycle.

The team teaching-assessing-learning cycle shows the connection between instruction and common formative assessments (analysis and response during Tier 1) as well as common end-of-unit assessments (analysis and response for additional time and support, or Tier 2). At the start of the unit, teachers share the student-friendly learning targets with students. During the unit, teachers design lessons and respond instructionally to student learning using checks for understanding and differentiated feedback through exit slips, questioning strategies, whiteboards, and so on. Also during the unit, teachers give common formative assessments to collectively check on and analyze student learning of essential standards to plan a team response for instruction in Tier 1, if needed. Team actions may repeat throughout a unit of study, meaning the team may be able to administer, analyze, and respond to several common formative assessments, but the key is to ensure all three parts happen—administer, analyze, and respond.

At the end of the unit, the team administers a common end-of-unit assessment, and the teachers analyze the results to determine, by student and by target, how to utilize Tier 2 additional time and support for ongoing student learning of essential standards, as needed. Students continue to learn essentials not yet learned in Tier 2, while Tier 1 instruction often moves on to the next unit.

Analyzing common assessment evidence has four purposes.

1. Understand students' learning strengths and next steps, specifically related to achieving the essential standards.

2. Plan instruction and intervention as a team to ensure students take the next steps and learn the essential standards.

3. Reflect on teachers' instructional practices, specifically the effectiveness of their instruction to date.

4. Create more valid and reliable assessment through revisions to the assessment itself.

Analyzing common assessment data and student work is the highest-leverage part of the process because it is where teachers gain clarity on what proficiency looks like and develop targeted, specific instruction and intervention that will lead students to high achievement (Brookhart, 2020; Willis et al., 2023).

Teams must analyze student data and work so they get the information they need to design specific team interventions by target and by student. The re-engagement learning experiences in Tier 1 and Tier 2 that follow common assessments are designed to accelerate student learning to grade or course level and above.

Here's Why

The team teaching-assessing-learning cycle is the foundation of Tier 1 instruction. It is what makes RTI, or MTSS, such a powerful approach to ensure high levels of learning for all students. Rather than waiting to discover which students failed a summative assessment and then sending them off to someone else for Tier 1 prevention or Tier 2 interventions, the collaborative team accepts collective responsibility for each student's success by partnering with students to respond proactively throughout the unit and reduce the number of students who need additional time and support at the end. When students do need additional time and support, they receive it, and the team ensures that students engage in the Tier 2 support without consequence.

The biggest teacher pushback to formalizing the use of formative assessments is often, "I don't have time to reteach!" To address this challenge before the teachers start teaching the unit, the team schedules a day for responding to formative assessment results so time for reteaching or extending learning is already available. These days are strategically placed for use after the team has given a common formative assessment and analyzed student learning. In the Action 2: Design a Unit Assessment Plan section (page 94), the example ELA and mathematics unit assessment plans showed calendars with flex days—days the teams accounted for to re-engage students in learning after they gave them a common formative assessment and analyzed the data.

Common end-of-unit assessments are fundamental to both the PLC at Work process and a school's entire system of interventions. They provide information that identifies who needs to participate in Tier 2 interventions and what skills they must focus on within those interventions. Equally important, data from common end-of-unit assessments provide a window into the effectiveness of Tier 1 instruction, for both individual teachers and the team as a whole. Too often, schools fall into the trap of implementing interventions not explicitly linked to classroom instruction and the learning that needs to take place. Using data from team-based common end-of-unit assessments ensures interventions and classroom instruction align and, in turn, establishes a firm foundation of support for students who need it most. (See chapter 5, page 201, for more information about Tier 2.)

Once instruction for a unit of study is complete, the team gives the common end-of-unit assessment on its essential standards chart. The common end-of-unit assessment clearly defines the end in mind and provides the benchmark against which formative assessment data help teachers and students ensure they are moving in the right direction throughout the unit.

In learning-focused classrooms, teachers use all types of assessments to support learning. They provide students with ongoing and consistent formative opportunities to reflect on their learning and decide how best to move forward. Students also have multiple opportunities to demonstrate proficiency. In turn, teachers can continually gather data to determine their instruction's effectiveness and identify students who need additional time and support to master the essentials. Once students have demonstrated proficiency and teachers have evidence of this mastery, grading practices must ensure that students get credit for this new level of proficiency without penalty. (See chapter 4, Action 4: Co-Create Schoolwide Grading Practices, page 184.)

Essential standards represent the knowledge, skills, and dispositions all students must master to be successful in the current school year, subsequent school years, and life. Something is essential when the whole cannot exist without that part. While arms are very useful, your heart is truly essential! If we deem anything essential, it is the way teams analyze and respond to student work and data; this signals to students and the community that teams commit to help all students achieve at high levels. The process of analyzing data is what teachers need to collaboratively engage in to make this learning happen for students, many of whom have not been successful in a traditional system.

Because prioritized standards are essential and represent the heart of what students must know and be able to do, they are the focus of Tier 1 instruction, or re-engagement and Tier 2 interventions. Yet we must never allow students to flounder short of mastery while their class moves on to the next unit of instruction. Tier 2 interventions provide students with a little more time and targeted, scaffolded supports that help them attain proficiency in the essentials (see chapter 5, page 201, for more information about Tier 2 team interventions and extensions).

Here's How

Putting the team teaching-assessing-learning cycle into practice requires teachers to do what they do best: teach! With the clarity they each gain through collaboratively identifying essential standards and creating a unit assessment plan, teachers begin instruction by sharing the unit's destination with students (student-friendly learning targets). Teachers display and include targets in unit documents with such consistency that students cannot possibly miss seeing and understanding them. Informal conversations with students during instruction quickly shed light on whether they know where they are headed.

Depending on the complexity of the essential standards identified for the unit, the teaching-assessing-learning cycle may take several weeks or more to complete. As the unit progresses, teachers should regularly check for understanding and frequently give feedback to students as to how they are progressing toward the targets, allowing students to adjust as needed. Because students move through the learning sequence at different rates, it is unnecessary for every teacher on a team to be in the same place on the same day. It is essential, however, that each teacher instructionally prepares their students and administers the common formative assessment (or assessments) on the same day or within their team's agreed-on time frame.

Once teachers administer the common formative assessment and the team meeting begins, follow a standardized protocol to maximize productivity. As team members work through the protocol, their dialogue and inquiry should include reviewing the assessment, identifying which students need to work on which learning targets, distinguishing specific errors to inform instruction, reviewing which instructional strategies worked best, and intentionally planning how each student will get the instruction or extension needed to take their next step in achieving the essential standard.

Review How Assessment Items and Tasks Worked for Students

It's one thing to plan assessment items and tasks by learning target to ensure teachers assess what they want students to learn, but it's another to review the assessment results to see what, if anything, prevented students from showing what they know. Sometimes, students get an item or two wrong, and when teacher team members review the assessment, they realize the items were flawed. This realization influences how the team responds. In addition, sometimes teachers inadvertently administer the assessment with different expectations or conditions, so be sure each teacher is on the same page in their scoring, and if they aren't, they adjust accordingly.

Analyze Assessment Data by Student and by Target or Standard

As teams of teachers analyze the data, they look at the items by student and by target or standard, noting which students need to work on which targets. Also, as they identify the targets students need to work on, teams review student work to understand why they need to work on those targets. The following are items teams should analyze in each student's work.

Simple Mistakes

Simple mistakes in their work are things students can usually review and fix on their own (Fisher & Frey, 2014). It is imperative to require students to fix simple mistakes, as this ensures they will slow down and pay close attention to these things the next time around. However, teachers do not need to plan a new instructional lesson; they only have to carve out a little time for students to do that revision.

Larger Errors

Larger errors need additional instruction. These types of errors often include misconceptions, conceptual errors, and reasoning errors.

- **Misconceptions:** Teachers may identify misconceptions; these can be items students have wrong, inaccuracies in student thinking, or information students believe to be true but is not (for any number of reasons). Students sometimes bring misunderstandings into a lesson or unit from times past. They could have learned concepts that have changed or evolved, like the number of planets. Or they could firmly believe something to be true and the instruction doesn't help them connect new ideas or change their thinking. When teachers identify a misconception, the instruction must help students unlearn what they learned before and relearn a new way or a new concept. Marzano's high-impact strategy of examples and non-examples can help students see their current thinking (non-examples) and the accurate information (examples) and compare the old with the new to relearn (Goodwin & Rouleau, 2022). For instance, if students don't understand how to identify or describe a character in literature, a teacher might show examples of general language that identifies a character and examples of descriptive language that helps the reader understand more about a character. The teacher asks students to articulate the differences and then make revisions in their work. This is just one example of a misconception and an instructional strategy that aligns with the identified error.

- ▶ **Conceptual errors:** Conceptual errors are misunderstandings of concepts, and often misunderstandings of the relationships between and among ideas, that thus make it difficult for students to transfer the concepts to multiple situations. For example, students may mix up independent and dependent variables and struggle to explain their understanding. When students have conceptual errors, teachers can choose from many strategies to show these relationships; one example is they can use analogies to help students understand the relationships among ideas in a concept. Strategies that show relationships and explain concepts in unique ways help students with conceptual errors.

- ▶ **Reasoning errors:** Reasoning errors occur when students don't have enough evidence to support what they are thinking or why they are solving a problem in a certain way. Students' reasoning can also be too general or contradictory. Providing specific feedback and requiring revision, or showing students examples of strong and weak reasoning, can help students increase the quality and accuracy of their reasoning.

Again, there are many strategies teams can use in response to mistakes in student work. Thoughtful and intentional instructional planning can meet students where they are in their learning and take them to the next level.

Review Data to Determine the Strengths in Initial Instruction

Reviewing data helps teachers examine the instruction that worked as well as the instruction that may not have met the mark for some students. Reviewing data to understand the effectiveness of instructional strategies is helpful because strategies are dependent on context, relationships with students, and the ways students process information. As a result, the same strategy may work for one student but not another.

This is the creative part of our work. Sometimes, one teacher's results on a particular target are stronger than those of the rest of the team, and this review can aid team members to discover the most effective strategies and materials to try next in helping students master each target. These results are an evaluation not of teachers' effectiveness but of the instruction that worked and didn't work for students. It is important to clearly discern the difference between teacher evaluation and instructional evaluation. This process is designed for teams to evaluate the effectiveness of their instruction and how to collectively move forward. Teachers should freely share strategies and materials as they work toward team consensus on how best to respond to the data.

As noted, teams need to schedule instructional time for responding to common formative assessment results before they begin unit instruction. Instead of plowing ahead to address the next targets, teachers can use the day following their team meeting to deliver mid-unit interventions and extensions for the targets already assessed. Examples of mid-unit interventions designed to re-engage students in learning include the following.

▶ Have a flex day when students work in team-created stations in their own class or in another team member's classroom for a class period or block of time by specific targeted need. A team often accounts for this day as part of its unit calendar when it is planning the unit.

▶ As a team, design warm-ups for a given number of minutes each day, and implement them for one or two weeks.

▶ Identify a new strategy to use while continuing to address the essential standard in future lessons because the essential standard has not yet been fully learned.

These mid-unit interventions might also be called *preventions* because they help students close learning gaps prior to the end-of-unit summative assessment. Another way of thinking about mid-unit interventions comes from a mission statement seen in the waiting room of a primary care physician: "The mission of this practice is to prevent illness, not just to treat it." These preventive instructional actions are the very remedies that stop so-called academic illness and help all students succeed.

Depending on the number and complexity of targets, as well as the time available for team meetings, teams should repeat the common formative assessment cycle as many times as necessary. Once students receive instruction on all the essential learning targets and have opportunities to self-assess and adjust their understanding, teachers administer a common end-of-unit assessment.

It is also critical to collect data from a common end-of-unit assessment in a timely and efficient manner. Like data from a common formative assessment during a unit, common end-of-unit assessment data must be formatted so they reflect individual student results, specific standard and learning target results (item by item), and classroom results. Teachers can easily score, aggregate, and display selected-response items using technology tools. They also need to score open-ended questions using agreed-on scoring guidelines, or criteria, that student work examples support. Last, the team must schedule a meeting for analyzing results as soon as possible after teachers administer the assessment. This maximizes the time and opportunity teachers and students have to act on the results. In action 2 (page 94), the team members planned for this timing when they designed a calendar along with their unit assessment plan.

Consistently following a standardized protocol helps team members learn to adhere to team norms, maximize use of time, and ensure all necessary steps to evaluate the assessment, analyze data, and create effective interventions take place. To that end, any protocol must facilitate identifying individual students who need additional time and support, determining effective instructional practices, discussing strengths and needed revisions of the assessment, and preparing for appropriate interventions and extensions.

Teachers should identify students for Tier 2 support at least every three weeks. Students who are struggling to attain essential standards or skills should not have to wait longer than this for help to arrive. If we wait longer, students sink deeper and deeper into learning holes from which it becomes increasingly difficult to extract them. It is faulty thinking to wait for the benchmark assessment or end-of-quarter grades to find out which students need help. In ten weeks, they can fall so far behind that they never catch up!

We cannot overstate the importance of having teams look at student work when analyzing common assessment data for targeted and specific Tier 1 and Tier 2 responses. Calibrate scoring so one teacher is not grading for grammar and conventions on a science test while another is only looking at the science learning evidenced. Scoring differences create chaos when teams determine interventions. Teams may use a rubric, points, or some other scoring method, but regardless of scoring agreements, they must be clear on how to score to have meaningful results to analyze. Student work shows the instructional strategies that proved effective for learning and reveals student errors, misconceptions, or mistakes in reasoning or application to design a targeted and specific re-engagement learning experience.

Sort student work into piles showing students who excelled or are proficient, students who are nearly proficient, and students who are minimally proficient. Determine trends for each group of assessments, and use the trends to design targeted interventions for moving those students from minimally proficient to nearly proficient, nearly proficient to proficient, and proficient to advanced.

Together, team members determine which students need specific interventions or extensions using common formative assessment data and respond in Tier 1. This essential action (analyze and respond to common assessment data) focuses on teams creating an instructional plan for Tier 1 using common formative assessment results. Teams can also use the data analysis tools provided in this action to identify students in need of Tier 2 interventions after the common end-of-unit assessment, which we further explain in chapter 5, action 1 (page 203). (This action addresses how teams create Tier 2 learning experiences and monitor their effectiveness.)

Helpful Tools

The following tools will help you accomplish the work for this essential action.

▶ **Chapter 7 of *Learning by Doing, Fourth Edition* (DuFour et al., 2024), "Creating Team-Developed Common Formative Assessments":** This chapter provides foundational content knowledge as well as tools that can help schools accomplish the action steps outlined in this section.

▶ **"Sample Data From Grade 9 ELA Common Formative Assessment: Writing an Argument" (page 146):** This reproducible shows a sample common formative assessment and demonstrates that this kind of assessment is often short, easy to administer, and closely linked to instruction.

▶ **"Team Protocol for Analyzing Common Assessment Data" (page 147):** Teams can use this reproducible to establish a consistent protocol for collaboratively analyzing common formative and end-of-unit assessment results and determining collective responses to them.

▶ **"Team Response to Common Formative Assessment" (page 148):** This template helps teams agree on their collective response to common assessment results: Which students need additional support on which targets, and how will you provide that instruction? Which students need extension, and what will that look like?

▶ **"Team Protocol for Reviewing Student Work to Plan Tier 1 or Tier 2 Responses" (page 149):** Teacher teams can use this protocol to plan Tier 1 or Tier 2 responses by looking at student work from common formative or end-of-unit assessments. Team members bring in random samples (not ranked as high, medium, or low level, because a judgment is already made in that case). They then calibrate their scoring with a sample and determine common misconceptions. After completing this sample, team members review the rest of the student work with much more efficiency, as they are looking for the same thing in the same way.

▶ **"Essential Standards Student Tracking Chart" (page 151):** Teacher teams can use this reproducible chart to record steps toward the mastery of essential standards by tracking progress student by student, standard by standard, and target by target.

Coaching Tips

Supporting teachers to give and analyze common formative and end-of-unit assessments is all about working next to them as they take ownership of the process. The types of actions teachers often find most useful include proctoring classes during assessment administration, assisting with data collection and formatting, providing facilitation support during team meetings, helping identify strategies for targeted interventions, and advocating team decisions with the guiding coalition as a whole. The best way to find out what teams need is to ask them!

Learning to collaborate, share assessment results, and take collective responsibility for student learning challenges is a process. It takes time! Initial efforts don't always go smoothly, and they require lots of listening and patience on the part of guiding coalition members. Just as some students require additional time and support to be successful, some teams require additional time and support to become effective. It is the guiding coalition's role to ensure that teacher teams share a vision for their work's outcomes, guide and coach teams to that vision, and celebrate successes, both big and small, along the way. Providing protocols for sharing data and student work can help create focused dialogue and promote emotional safety. Remind teachers that this is a learning process, not a judgment process.

Coaches can also help teams take action by facilitating team meetings during analysis or just sitting alongside team members. When teams get stuck overanalyzing data, try to move the conversation to identifying instructional strategies for addressing any misconceptions exposed by the data. Monitoring team time to ensure there is space to talk about the best ways to collectively respond and develop new instructional strategies is critical to the analysis process.

Equally important, coaches must ensure teacher teams don't reduce the rigor of their assessments. Sometimes, if students aren't achieving at high levels on the assessments, these teams tend to change the assessments or make them easier rather than develop instruction to help students reach those levels. Coaches can help guide team conversations to ensure assessments remain at grade level and the teacher teams develop intentional steps to help students reach new levels.

As teacher teams move to identifying students in need of Tier 2 interventions, an important action the guiding coalition can take to support the teams is to ensure that the process is student and teacher friendly, not overreliant on filling out forms. A helpful strategy is for guiding coalition members to role-play a teacher team in the process of identifying students in need of Tier 2 interventions. They can do this during a schoolwide faculty meeting. To focus everyone's attention on key aspects of the process, the guiding coalition may also provide essential questions for follow-up discussion. Example questions include:

▶ What data and tools do you see the team using?

▶ How does the team maximize the use of its collaboration time?

▶ How do we inform students about and involve them in Tier 2 participation?

Once teachers have the opportunity to collectively observe and discuss this process, they are ready to identify students on their own. It is important to remember that mastering the process takes time, and leaders should regularly collect feedback from the teams. Continued coaching and facilitation support, as well as regular opportunities to have a voice in streamlining the process, assists teams as they progress toward productively identifying students who need Tier 2 help.

Sample Data From Grade 9 ELA Common Formative Assessment: Writing an Argument

The following chart is an example of how teams can collect common assessment data in a way that shows individual student results and collective classroom results based on specific learning targets. Students need to score an 8, 9, or 10 to demonstrate proficiency.

	Teacher 1	Teacher 2	Teacher 3	Teacher 4	Team Overall Data (Out of 100 students)
I can make a claim.	100% (25 students)	96% (24 students)	76% (19 students)	88% (22 students)	90 students
I can develop claims fairly and thoroughly.	96% (24 students)	68% (17 students)	84% (21 students)	68% (17 students)	79 students
I can organize data.	80% (20 students)	80% (20 students)	84% (21 students)	84% (21 students)	82 students

Each classroom will have its own sheet with students' scores by learning target. The following sheet features Teacher 1's data. The online spreadsheet will contain all the other classroom data as well.

Student	I can make a claim.	I can develop claims fairly and thoroughly.	I can organize data.	Student	I can make a claim.	I can develop claims fairly and thoroughly.	I can organize data.
1	10	10	10	14	9	10	Not yet
2	10	7	7	15	10	10	Not yet
3	10	7	7	16	10	10	10
4	10	9	7	17	10	7	7
5	9	10	10	18	10	7	Not yet
6	9	10	7	19	10	7	9
7	9	10	7	20	10	10	10
8	9	10	7	21	10	9	10
9	8	10	10	22	10	10	10
10	9	7	Not yet	23	10	10	7
11	10	7	10	24	8	10	7
12	10	7	10	25	9	7	10
13	8	Not yet	Not yet				
				Percentage Proficient	100%	96%	80%
				Number Proficient	25	24	20

Team Protocol for Analyzing Common Assessment Data

This protocol is designed to help a teacher team quickly and efficiently discuss student learning using a common assessment. If each teacher reviews their assessment data prior to the team meeting, then the team should be able to collectively complete this activity within a typical team meeting of forty-five to sixty minutes.

1. Which students did not demonstrate mastery on which specific standards? Which students mastered the standards and need extension? (Identify this by the student, by the standard, and by the target.)

2. Which learning targets require more of our attention as a team?

3. Which instructional practices proved to be most effective? How do we know?

4. What patterns can we identify from students' errors? What were the students' misconceptions?

5. What instruction and intervention are needed for students who need additional time and support? (Use the "Team Response to Common Formative Assessment" tool, page 148, to plan by specific need or misconception.)

6. How will we extend learning for students who have mastered the standards?

7. How can we improve this assessment?

Source: Buffum, A., Mattos, M., & Weber, C. (2012). Simplifying response to intervention: Four essential guiding principles. Bloomington, IN: Solution Tree Press.

Team Response to Common Formative Assessment

Follow these instructions for responding to common formative assessments.

1. After implementing and analyzing a common formative assessment as a team, identify students who need additional time and support (demonstrate minimal or partial mastery), students who are on target (demonstrate adequate understanding), and students who need extension (demonstrate mastery of grade-level standards).

2. Design and agree on an instructional plan for each group. Be sure to brainstorm and design the instructional responses together to ensure thoughtful new strategies (and not just more of the same) that match students' targeted needs. Teachers may individually refine the ideas brainstormed by the team.

3. Share lesson plan outlines and materials with all team members. Sometimes, individual teachers implement these instructional plans in their classrooms. Other times, one teacher takes one group of students (from multiple classes) based on their needs, another teacher takes another group of students, and so on. Deploying and shuffling students is effective when there is protected time for the response and the team has developed the process to respond in a meaningful way.

Essential standard:		
Needs Additional Time and Support *Demonstrates Minimal or Partial Understanding*	**On Target** *Demonstrates Adequate Understanding*	**Needs Extension** *Demonstrates Mastery of Grade-Level Targets*
Students:	Students:	Students:
Instructional Plan:	Instructional Plan:	Instructional Plan:

Team Protocol for Reviewing Student Work to Plan Tier 1 or Tier 2 Responses

As a teacher team prepares to analyze common assessment data (from a common formative or end-of-unit assessment), team members gather five to seven random samples of student work from the assessment. (These should be randomly selected and not already leveled at high, medium, and low so you have not yet judged the samples.) Work does not need to be scored prior to the meeting, and in some cases, it is best to do this protocol before teachers score all the work. This process ensures teachers calibrate their scoring, making the rest of their scoring more accurate and efficient.

When gathering student work, consider the following.

- Make electronic copies or take digital pictures of the student work and put them in your virtual team folder. Take names off of them, and number each piece of work.

- Place three or four videos of student work in the team folder. Number each video.

- Organize data from the assessment by student and by target. Additionally, organize the data by question on the assessment along with the results and responses.

Assign a facilitator (to guide you through the protocol and help you not get stuck in one step for too long) and a recorder (to capture the insights and ensure implementation of the plan).

Plan With Student Work From Common Assessments
1. Clarify the learning targets or standards being assessed, including the criteria or qualities to observe in student work and the criteria used to score student work.
2. Individually, review the student work samples, usually five to seven pieces. Identify a strength of each piece and a next step to improve it, or score each piece using an accompanying rubric. Write the score or descriptive feedback on a sticky note, and place it on the back of the student work. Pass the student work to a colleague to review; this colleague also completes a sticky note with a score or descriptive feedback, without looking at the other sticky note. Each team member reviews each sample in this manner.
3. Together, come to a consensus on the strengths and next steps or rubric scores for the pieces. Review the sticky notes on the back of each piece of work.
4. Categorize student work based on next steps or similar errors.
5. Develop an instructional response (Tier 1 prevention or Tier 2 intervention) for each of the next steps identified in student work. This plan helps students achieve their next steps.
6. Sort the student work by next steps.
7. Determine when and how to decide whether your instructional plan or intervention worked.

Next Step (What Students Need to Work On)	Misconceptions	Design for an Intervention to Help Students Revise Work or Take Next Steps	Students Needing to Revise Work or Take Next Steps

Source: Adapted from Dimich, N. (2024). Design in five: Essential phases to create engaging assessment practice *(2nd ed.). Bloomington, IN: Solution Tree Press, pp. 169–170.*

Essential Standards Student Tracking Chart
By Student, By Standard, By Target

Student Name	Essential Standards										
	Standard or Outcome	Target 1	Target 2	Target 3	Target 4	Standard or Outcome	Target 1	Target 2	Target 3	Target 4	

Conclusion

This chapter may be the most important part of this book and the RTI, or MTSS, process. We should think of RTI as response to instruction, or RTI² (response to instruction and intervention). Rather than waiting until students fail the end-of-unit test and then sending them to Tier 2 intervention, uncovering which students need additional time and support *before they fail* is much more effective. It is this practice and responsiveness that leads to high levels of learning for all students. Consider the classroom a rehearsal hall where students receive daily feedback and time to practice, which helps them succeed at the final performance, the end-of-unit assessment.

You may have noticed we haven't addressed assessing immediate prerequisite skills on the team teaching-assessing-learning cycle (see figure 3.2, page 83). (For a deeper discussion on immediate prerequisite skills, see chapter 5, Action 2: Identify and Target Immediate Prerequisite Skills, page 211.) While we believe this to be a powerful part of the process, we are concerned that all the details associated with it may overwhelm teams and potentially lead to instruction and assessment that target learning below grade level. Therefore, we plan for essential grade-level standards and instruction and then introduce this concept to further support students to learn at high levels, which may mean supporting them in immediate or foundational prerequisite skills.

These prerequisite skills are already identified on the "Essential Standards Chart" reproducible (page 93) in the Immediate Prerequisite Skills column. As teams become more familiar with the teaching-assessing-learning cycle, they may create small pretests to determine which students have the academic vocabulary and prerequisite skills needed for the new unit of instruction. Using the information from these pretests, teachers can introduce vocabulary and prerequisite skills as sponge activities at the beginning of class instruction to provide scaffolding for new learning several weeks before the unit begins. (Chapter 5, Action 2: Identify and Target Immediate Prerequisite Skills [page 211] explores in detail how teams can support students needing more work on prerequisite skills in Tier 2.) Again, the best intervention is prevention!

While reading this chapter, you may have thought, "I've heard this all before—this is nothing new." If so, we remind you of the handwashing analogy earlier in this chapter. While you may have heard similar ideas, is every grade-level or course-alike team in your school systematically doing the essential actions described in this chapter? We believe the team teaching-assessing-learning cycle is the absolute bedrock principle on which all RTI rests, not just something teams do when they want to create essential standards unit maps.

In the next chapter, we discuss the essential actions that must be coordinated across the entire school rather than by each collaborative team independent of the others.

CHAPTER 4

Tier 1 Guiding Coalition Essential Actions

Leadership and learning are indispensable to each other.

—John F. Kennedy

In this chapter, we focus on the top-left portion of the RTI at Work pyramid (see figure 4.1, page 154).

▸ This section of the pyramid is part of Tier 1, which represents what all students receive as part of their core instruction.

▸ Because this portion is on the pyramid's left side, it represents outcomes that educators must coordinate across the entire school. Neither grade-level nor department teams should make these decisions in isolation, nor should the administration dictate these outcomes. The guiding coalition—as described in chapter 2 (page 27)—takes lead responsibility for these essential outcomes. At a smaller school with limited staff, the faculty should work on these decisions collectively.

The guiding coalition takes primary responsibility for five essential actions at Tier 1.

1. Ensure access to essential grade-level curriculum.

2. Identify and teach essential academic and social behaviors.

3. Create a balanced assessment approach.

4. Co-create schoolwide grading practices.

5. Provide preventions to proactively support student success.

In this chapter, we examine each of these essential actions in depth and provide targeted tools to assist your efforts.

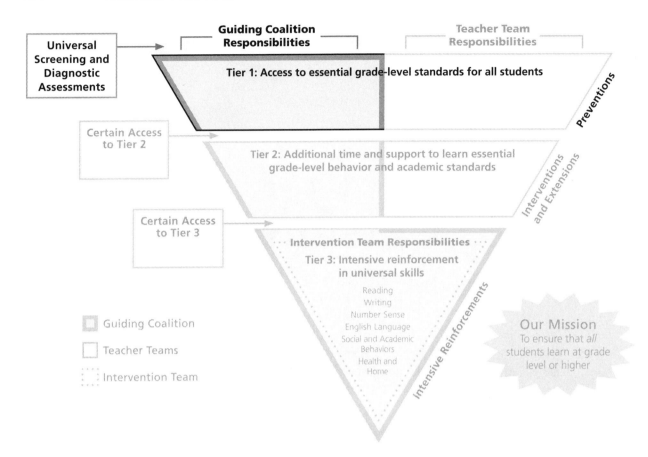

FIGURE 4.1: Focus on Tier 1 guiding coalition essential actions.

Action 1

Ensure Access to Essential Grade-Level Curriculum

If our mission is to ensure all students learn at high levels—grade level or higher—every year, then *all* students must be taught at high levels as part of their core instruction. While students will not master every standard introduced in the core curriculum, *all* students must learn the essential academic standards and behaviors deemed indispensable for success in the next grade or course. To this end, there is no realistic way a student can learn at grade level if they are:

▶ Pulled from class for additional support while essential grade-level or course-specific curriculum is being taught

▶ Deemed too "low" to learn grade-level curriculum, so instead are placed in below-grade-level remedial coursework for Tier 1 core instruction

This is a critical point we will continue to emphasize: Tier 2 and Tier 3 support cannot compensate for teaching students below grade level in core instruction. Ensuring all students have access to essential grade-level or higher curriculum at Tier 1 is the foundation of a highly effective MTSS process. This outcome is achieved—or denied—through the school's master schedule design.

The first step in ensuring this access is to identify the essential curriculum needed for success in the next grade or course. In chapter 3, action 1 (page 85), we outlined a process in which teacher teams work collaboratively at Tier 1 to identify the essential academic outcomes. But identifying the essential curriculum is not enough. A student can't learn these essential academic outcomes if their Tier 1 core instruction consists of below-grade-level remedial coursework or if they are pulled from instruction on these standards to receive additional support. Interventions at Tier 2 and Tier 3 must be provided *in addition to* Tier 1 essential grade-level instruction, not in place of it.

To achieve this outcome, a school must purposefully and strategically create a master schedule that ensures all students have access to essential grade-level curriculum. Because a school's master schedule impacts every grade level, department, and program in the school, creating such a schedule requires a schoolwide collaborative effort. Schools must consider coordination among classroom teachers and specialist staff, as well as special education services and classified support services (such as lunch and transportation schedules). This is why a school's guiding coalition, which comprises representation across the school, is in the best position to take lead responsibility for this action step.

Here's Why

When we work with educators, we often ask this question: "If you take a student out of grade-level curriculum and place them in a remedial class so the student is taught below grade level all day, where will this student end up at the close of the school year?"

The resounding answer we receive is, "Below grade level!" Research, evidence, and common sense confirm this reality. We then ask if all the students in their school currently have access to essential grade-level curriculum. More often than not, the answer is, "No."

This honest assessment is not a surprise, as most schools perpetuate a traditional 19th century master schedule—designed for only a select few to reach postsecondary education. Reflecting on secondary schools' purpose, Harvard University president Charles Eliot, chair of a national commission on the topic, reported to Congress in 1893:

> Their main function is to prepare for the duties of life that small proportion of all the children in the [United States]—a proportion small in number, but very important to the welfare of the nation—who show themselves able to profit by an education prolonged to the eighteenth year, and whose parents are able to support them while they remain so long at school. (as cited in Dorn, 1996, p. 36)

In such a system, educators sorted students into tracks based primarily on perceived ability and prior academic success. Students deemed to have greater academic potential were placed in more rigorous tracks to prepare them for college, while students viewed as less gifted or accomplished were relegated to lower tracks that prepare them for immediate entry into the workforce. This approach is captured in the traditional bell-shaped curve of student achievement shown in figure 4.2 (page 156).

If a student struggled in a higher track, the solution was not to provide additional time and support but instead to lower the student's academic expectations and demote them to a lower track. While this master schedule design denied most students access to postsecondary opportunities, the economic reality at that time was undeniably different. In the United States, most people either farmed or worked in factories throughout the 20th century—careers that did not require a high school diploma or a college degree—so ensuring high levels of learning for all students was not necessary or desirable.

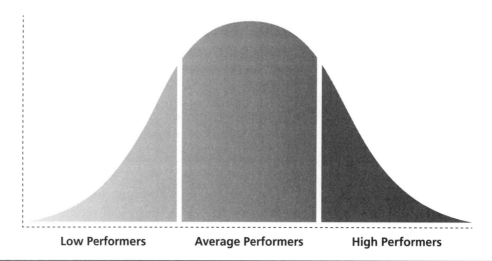

Low Performers   **Average Performers**   **High Performers**

FIGURE 4.2: Bell-shaped curve of student achievement.

While the economic demands in the United States have changed dramatically since the 1800s, the practice of tracking students in school has not. As Jeannie Oakes (2005) finds in her landmark study *Keeping Track: How Schools Structure Inequality, Second Edition*:

> The deep structure of tracking remains uncannily robust. Most middle and high schools still sort students into classes at different levels based on judgments of student "ability." This sorting continues to disadvantage those in lower track classes. Such students have less access to high-status knowledge, fewer opportunities to engage in stimulating learning activities, and classroom relationships less likely to foster engagement with teachers, peers, and learning. (p. 4)

Through our work with schools around the world, we have found that most of them continue to intervene when students struggle by merely lowering academic expectations. For example, are some students not succeeding in their grade level algebra 1 class? Place them in a two-year algebra class. Are some students still struggling? Remove them from algebra altogether and place them in a remedial mathematics class. Are a few students still struggling? Perhaps they have dropped far enough behind to qualify for special education. At the elementary level, educators demonstrate these same practices when they identify a student's ability as too low to succeed and beg the administration to get the student out of the classroom during certain times so they can work "at their level."

Many schools also apply this antiquated bell-shaped-curve thinking to their implementation of RTI. For example, a school starts each year by using universal screeners to document a baseline of each student's abilities in foundational skills. These results are then used to place students into their proper tier or track of expectations. See figure 4.3.

In such an approach, the three tiers represent traditional ability groups.

1. High-performing students have access to the most rigorous curriculum and enrichment opportunities at Tier 1.

2. Average performers, those who score at or near grade level, are placed in "regular classes" and might need some Tier 2 support.

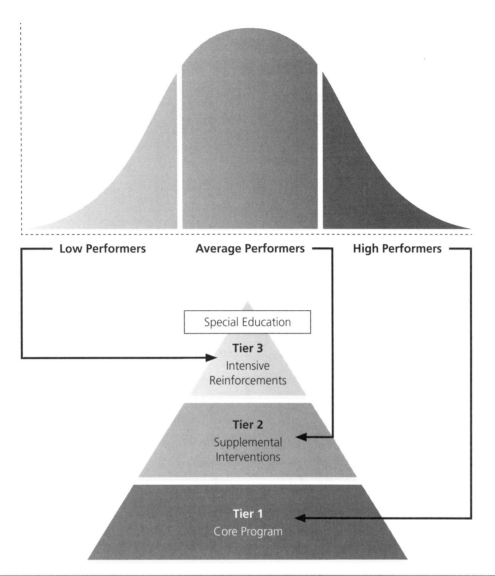

FIGURE 4.3: Ineffective MTSS implementation based on a bell curve.

3. The lowest-performing students are often deemed incapable of learning new essential grade-level standards and are subsequently placed in less rigorous curriculum, and enrichment is replaced with more Tier 3 remedial support.

This detrimental thinking is reinforced when a school or district moves students from tier to tier in their MTSS process instead of seeing the tiers as value added.

When we ask educators why they continue the practice of tracking students, they often claim they are differentiating for individual student needs. Yet research proves that ability grouping is an ineffective instructional practice. Hattie's meta-analysis on ability grouping finds that the practice of tracking has minimal effects on student learning—producing just a 0.09 standard deviation— and can have *profoundly* negative effects on equity, as the students who educators perceive to have the lowest ability are most often traditionally marginalized students, English learners, and students from poverty (Corwin Visible Learning Plus, 2023).

If professional educators want to challenge this research, they must reflect on these questions about their current reality: If the school or district currently tracks or ability-groups students, are the students in the lowest track catching up to their peers? Are they closing their achievement gaps? Are they transitioning to a more rigorous curriculum? Are they leaving K–12 education well prepared to succeed in postsecondary education and beyond?

Research and evidence supporting tracking is virtually nonexistent and represents the antithesis of an organization dedicated to high levels of learning for all.

Here's How

There is no universal, one-size-fits-all master schedule that ensures all students access to essential grade-level curriculum. The basic structures of elementary and secondary master schedules have significant differences. Additional factors that impact a school's scheduling needs include the school's size; demographics; available resources; and state, province, or district requirements. So, while we can't offer a specific model schedule to implement, we can provide the following five-step process for steering the guiding coalition's efforts to ensure access to essential grade-level standards.

1. Identify essential standards.

2. Dedicate specific times in the master schedule for teaching essential standards.

3. Eliminate below-grade-level learning tracks.

4. Guarantee all students receive essential grade-level curriculum as part of Tier 1 core instruction.

5. Identify and provide preventions for students needing Tier 1 support in essential grade-level curriculum.

Identify Essential Standards

If the goal is to ensure all students have access to essential curriculum as part of their core instruction, then a school must have absolute clarity on the skills, knowledge, and behaviors the students must master in each grade and course. And every teacher must commit to teaching these standards aligned to their teaching assignment. While teacher teams take the lead in determining the specific essential standards for their grade or course (as described in chapter 3, page 81), the guiding coalition has important responsibilities too. These include the following.

▶ Provide each teacher team with the time and resources necessary to:

- Study the intended curriculum and agree on what is essential for all students to learn for success in the next grade or course

- Clarify the specific knowledge and skills needed for students to learn each essential standard

- Determine student proficiency on each essential standard

- Establish common pacing for each essential standard

- Commit to one another that they will teach the curriculum

- Review and revise these decisions as needed

▶ Monitor and support each team's progress.

▶ Determine a process for vertical articulation to ensure that the essential learning outcomes from one grade or course provide students with the prerequisite skills, knowledge, and behaviors needed to succeed in the next grade or course.

▸ Coordinate with specialist staff, including special education and English development staff, to ensure that they clearly understand the essential standards of each grade or course for which they support students.

▸ Plan for revisions. As discussed in chapter 3, identifying essential standards is not a singular act but a continuous process.

Dedicate Specific Times in the Master Schedule for Teaching Essential Standards

Once a school creates a guaranteed and viable curriculum, it must dedicate enough time in the school's master schedule to teach that curriculum effectively. At the elementary school level, this requires the guiding coalition to designate specific times every day or week to teach essential curriculum at each grade level. Educators should consider these blocks of time sacred, during which they keep classroom interruptions to a minimum and don't pull students from class. Because essential standards do not represent all core curriculum to be taught, the times educators dedicate for teaching essential standards do not represent all the times allocated for Tier 1 instruction in the school's master schedule.

At the middle school level, there is usually state- or province-required grade-level coursework that students should complete to be prepared for the next course in each subject. For example, in 2008, when Mike Mattos was a middle school principal in California, the state's required eighth-grade curriculum was:

▸ English language arts 8

▸ Algebra 1

▸ U.S. history

▸ Physical science

▸ Physical education

Each of these courses had adopted the state curriculum. Schools could offer accelerated learning tracks above this rigor, and each school and district had the option of providing different electives and supplemental classes. But the preceding classes were deemed required for success in the state's ninth-grade curriculum. This meant at the middle school level, all students must have access to the essential curriculum for each of these classes as part of their Tier 1 scheduled coursework.

At the high school level, multiple pathways of learning usually lead to postsecondary education, such as Advanced Placement (AP) classes, the International Baccalaureate (IB) program, vocational programs, and career pathway academies. Secondary educators frequently ask whether ensuring high levels of learning means all students must be on the highest collegiate track that the school offers or if some students may meet this outcome by taking vocational coursework. We recommend that all students successfully complete at least the minimum sequence of coursework required for a realistic opportunity to apply to a four-year university.

For example, many states have minimum requirements to apply to a state college. In California, a student must successfully complete the equivalent of algebra 2 to apply to a state college—achieving less would disqualify them from even applying to a state-sponsored four-year university. In this case, we recommend that a high school offer no track or sequence of mathematics classes that restricts students' ability to successfully pass algebra 2 by the time they graduate. Anything less would not meet the goal of ensuring all students access to high levels of learning.

Obviously, high schools should continue to offer pathways that go beyond this minimal expectation, such as mathematics tracks that exceed algebra 2, and use their Tier 2 supports to assist students in these classes. Offering vocational pathways is equally acceptable. By ensuring all students have access to the minimum sequence of classes required to apply to a university, the schools give every student the option of deciding their own path—university, community college, trade school, or an internship process.

Once the guiding coalition determines, for each grade level, the required minimum coursework necessary for students to be at grade level on a college-prep learning track, it should then allocate the classes (course sections) necessary to ensure all students can take these or higher-level courses.

Eliminate Below-Grade-Level Learning Tracks

Most schools have what we refer to as a *phantom track*. It is a learning track that a school knows is below grade level but doesn't call it that, nor does the school usually tell students on this track (or their parents) that they are being taught below grade level and do not have a realistic chance of reaching grade level. For example, we have seen high schools place most of their ninth-grade students in a grade-level algebra 1 course but then place their lowest-performing mathematics students in an alternative class with a modified name, like *algebra basic*. This course has *algebra* in its name, giving the impression that these students are in an algebra class. But in reality, the curriculum for the course is below-grade-level remedial mathematics. From the first day students are in the class, the school knows they will not end the year prepared for the next grade-level mathematics class.

Sadly, the most prevalent and pervasive example of replacing grade-level expectations with remedial core instruction is the way many schools and districts implement traditional special education. While a vast majority of special education students will be independent adults someday, often their IEP goals and core instructional program focus on remedial outcomes. This is especially the case for students placed in self-contained special day classes. Educators sometimes claim that their school is legally bound to the student's IEP, which requires the student to receive these services, to justify these practices. But the school and the education experts in the building are who primarily write the IEP, so they have both the authority and the obligation to recommend revisions to the plan when a special education student is not achieving.

The school's guiding coalition must honestly examine all the classes and tracks provided as part of its core instructional program and revise or eliminate those that deny access to essential grade-level curriculum. We are not suggesting that no students will need intensive reinforcement or special education services built into their daily schedules, but educators must provide this support in addition to their essential grade-level curriculum.

Guarantee All Students Receive Essential Grade-Level Curriculum as Part of Tier 1 Core Instruction

Creating a school's master schedule is like being asked to plan a monthlong vacation in a weekend's worth of time—you want to do lots of things, but you don't have nearly enough time and resources to fit them all in. When creating a master schedule, the guiding coalition's first priority must be to ensure all students have access to essential grade-level curriculum. When we say they *have access*, we are not suggesting that students are merely *given the opportunity* to take college-prep classes or that the school *hopes* educators are teaching students essential grade-level curriculum. Instead, the guiding coalition creates processes to assign all students to Tier 1 classes and coursework that meets or exceeds essential grade-level standards, and it monitors that educators are following through. Achieving this goal takes vigilance and accountability. The school staff who schedule students for their core classes must be involved in this process and committed to ensuring this outcome for every student.

It's important to point out that while all students must have access to essential grade-level curriculum, this access does not necessarily have to be provided in a general education classroom. The goal should always be to serve students in the least restrictive environment, but some students may have unique learning needs that require a more specialized classroom setting. When this is the case, these students must still master the same essential curriculum. This is why it is critical that regular education teachers, special education staff, and other specialist staff collaborate when identifying, teaching, and assessing essential standards. Building shared knowledge on what students must learn and taking collective responsibility for student success are foundational requirements for an effective multitiered system of supports.

Finally, we define the phrase *all students* as those who can or might be independent adults someday. For the very small percentage of students who have profound cognitive disabilities (and will not be asked to function fully as independent adults), the school should work with highly trained professional experts and each student's family to determine how best to maximize the student's abilities and teach the skills necessary for the student to live as independent an adult life as possible. However, these individualized outcomes will most likely fall short of our definition of high levels of learning, so these students might not require access to all the essential grade-level curriculum as part of their core instructional program.

Identify and Provide Preventions for Students Needing Tier 1 Support in Essential Grade-Level Curriculum

Most schools remove students from grade-level coursework because they believe these students lack the prerequisite skills needed to succeed. This concern is understandable. When all students have access to essential grade-level curriculum, there will undoubtedly be those who are significantly below grade level in the foundational prerequisite skills of reading, writing, number sense, or proficiency in the school's native language. While tracking these students in remedial classes is not the answer, throwing them into grade-level curriculum to either sink or swim can set them up to fail.

A critical practice in the RTI process is universal screening. Its primary purpose is to proactively identify students who need Tier 3 intensive reinforcement so educators can begin these supports immediately. A student should not have to fail Tier 1 and Tier 2 to qualify for Tier 3 support when the school can realistically predict most students who need this level of support due to dramatic gaps in their foundational prerequisite skills at the end of the previous year. (We go deeper into the specifics of how to conduct universal screening in chapter 7, page 263.)

While universal screening has traditionally focused on identifying students for Tier 3 help, educators should also use this information to provide students support in Tier 1 core instruction. The guiding coalition should assume that students identified for Tier 3 reinforcements also need additional support at Tier 1 when learning essential grade-level curriculum. Examples of proactive, preventive core support include, but are not limited to, the following.

- ▸ **Strategic teacher assignments:** Douglas Reeves's (2009b) research concludes that one of a school's most effective learning strategies is to have highly trained teachers work with the students most at risk. Unfortunately, many schools do the exact opposite. Part of creating a master schedule is determining teacher assignments—what classes, subjects, and students educators teach. The guiding coalition should ensure that students the most at risk have access to the best-trained teachers in their area of need.

▶ **Scaffolded instruction and targeted accommodations:** Scaffolded instruction and accommodations are targeted supports that help students access grade-level curriculum and more accurately demonstrate what they know. For example, we can assume that a student reading multiple years below grade level might struggle with reading grade-level textbooks independently. Providing this student with alternative ways to access this information, such as an audio textbook and a pair-share reading buddy, can reasonably help them with essential grade-level content.

Planning for these types of preventions is best achieved when special education and regular education teachers collaboratively arrange teaching for new essential grade-level curriculum. Often, the faculty members with the most training and experience in scaffolded instructional practices and accommodations are special education teachers, as most students receiving special education services qualified due to foundational gaps in reading, writing, or mathematics. These same instructional practices are appropriate for students who don't have disabilities but have similar gaps in learning. An IEP or 504 plan is not required to receive accommodations and targeted instruction.

When providing these supports, educators must offer students accommodations, *not* modifications. Accommodations are supports that help students access and learn essential grade-level curriculum, while modifications alter the actual learning goal, usually lowering the bar to make it easier for students to succeed.

▶ **Sheltered classes:** Offering sheltered classes is an effective practice for supporting students with foundational gaps, especially in English language. For example, if a targeted student group has significant gaps in English language development—including a lack of academic vocabulary and basic reading and writing structures—it could be beneficial to group these students together for targeted Tier 1 core instruction.

A teacher who is highly trained in the students' area of need can proactively plan lessons that consider the English skills gaps and compensate for them through lesson design. Again, we must stress that if students are placed in an alternative Tier 1 core setting, the essential standards are the same as in the regular classroom. What is different is how educators teach and support students; the essential learning targets are the same.

▶ **Push-in supports:** A common practice to support students in Tier 1 core instruction is to "push in" specialized staff who support targeted students in their regular education classrooms. When done effectively, this service can provide embedded Tier 1 support for students who need intensive help in learning essential grade-level standards.

The guiding coalition is probably not the best group to determine the specific Tier 1 supports for each identified student; teacher teams and the school intervention team are best qualified to take the lead. (We discuss the school intervention team in depth in chapter 8, page 293.) The guiding coalition's responsibility is to take support recommendations from the intervention team and allocate the resources and scheduling necessary to achieve these outcomes. It then regularly evaluates if these resource allocations are working. (We dig deeper into providing preventions in action 5, page 192.)

Helpful Tools

The following tools will help you accomplish the work for this essential action.

- **"Ensuring Access to Essential Grade-Level Curriculum" (page 165):** This activity provides a template to help teams identify and discuss their responsibilities regarding access, assess their current reality, and gather and present recommendations.

- *It's About Time: Planning Interventions and Extensions in Elementary School* **(Buffum & Mattos, 2015):** This book features model elementary schools that offer explanations of how they make their schedules work. While there is no universal master schedule that can achieve the outcomes previously outlined, many schools successfully achieve these outcomes without lengthening their school day, receiving additional funding, or hiring additional staff.

- *It's About Time: Planning Interventions and Extensions in Secondary School* **(Mattos & Buffum, 2015):** This book offers chapters from model secondary schools that outline how these schools make their schedules work.

- **AllThingsPLC (https://allthingsplc.info):** This website offers hundreds of examples of model schools that have successfully created master schedules, giving all students access to essential grade-level standards and intervention. The resources include a description of each school and contact information. (Visit **go.SolutionTree.com/RTIatWork** to access live links to the websites mentioned in this book.)

Coaching Tips

Guiding coalition members should be the school's lead learners. A guiding principle we repeatedly emphasize in this book is that achieving these essential actions is an ongoing process, not a singular act. The steps are difficult to accomplish, as they represent dramatic shifts in how schools have operated for decades. A school does not get there overnight, nor are all its initial actions likely to work perfectly.

Cycles of collective inquiry and action research capture the essence of PLC at Work. Professionals first learn together about their current reality and better practices to improve student learning. Then they apply what they have learned. Finally, they collect evidence to determine whether these changes have achieved the goal—more students learning at higher levels. They validate actions that are working and discontinue practices and policies that are not improving learning. Then the cycle begins again.

As site practitioners, we can honestly admit that we never developed the perfect master schedule, but we did come closer and closer to this goal over time. Keeping in mind the guiding principle previously described, the guiding coalition reviews the process for ensuring access to essential grade-level curriculum for all students. This quickly makes it clear that every step in the process directly impacts the day-to-day lives of teachers and support staff. It is critical, therefore, to remember that gaining people's commitment to achieving schoolwide goals requires their involvement in decisions that affect their daily work experiences.

How, then, should the guiding coalition proceed? To begin, it needs to realize that increasing involvement in decisions also means sharing information, authority, and responsibility. The key to effectively facilitating involvement in decisions is to determine the maximum level of involvement appropriate to the situation. Types of involvement to consider include the following.

▸ **None:** In these situations, the guiding coalition makes the decision and announces it.

▸ **Recommendations from individuals:** In these situations, the guiding coalition randomly solicits input from a variety of individual stakeholders and then makes the decision.

▸ **Recommendations from teams:** In these situations, the guiding coalition seeks input from all stakeholders via their participation in team meetings. Each team forwards its recommendations, and then the guiding coalition makes the final decision.

▸ **Consensus:** In these situations, the guiding coalition facilitates opportunities for all stakeholders to personally participate in the decision-making process. Once they achieve a shared understanding of the situation, and all voices are heard, the guiding coalition facilitates a public process for stakeholders to show their level of support. When the whole group's view is apparent to all, they have reached consensus. At this point, all stakeholders must support the decision.

There is no single right way to make decisions. The guiding coalition needs to carefully consider the following questions to determine how best to make decisions.

▸ How much do stakeholders need to be involved to support the decision?

▸ How much time is available to make the decision?

▸ How important is the decision to stakeholders?

▸ Who has the information or expertise to maximize the quality of the decision?

▸ How capable (currently) are stakeholders in participating as decision makers?

▸ What is the potential for using this decision-making opportunity to strengthen the school culture of collaboration and shared leadership?

Clearly, there are benefits and risks to each level of involvement. Therefore, it is imperative that the guiding coalition carefully consider all aspects of each step in the process for ensuring access to essential grade-level curriculum. Once members determine the maximum appropriate level of involvement for each step, including a designated lead from the guiding coalition and expectations and desired outcomes, they can determine the timeline and deadline for completing the work. If committees are formed, committee members must be informed of their role (level of involvement) in the decision-making process.

The process and steps this section outlined provide an excellent vehicle for building all stakeholders' capacity to participate effectively in the decision-making process. Teachers and support staff members gain understanding of schoolwide challenges, broaden their perspectives beyond their individual classrooms' walls, and learn to accept collective responsibility for all students. In turn, shared leadership becomes the school norm and allows the guiding coalition to effectively tap stakeholders' expertise throughout RTI implementation.

Ensuring Access to Essential Grade-Level Curriculum

Review all guiding coalition responsibilities. For each responsibility, designate a member (or two) to form and lead a committee of stakeholders for discussing the responsibility, assessing the current reality, and gathering and presenting recommendations. Designate a time frame and deadline for each committee. Reach consensus on decisions and action steps, with the understanding that all decisions and actions must be revisited and re-evaluated for effectiveness over time.

Guiding Coalition Responsibility	Guiding Coalition Lead	Current Reality	Committee Input	Time Frame for Committee Work	Decisions and Action Steps
1. Identify essential standards.					
2. Dedicate specific times in the master schedule for teaching essential standards.					
3. Eliminate below-grade-level learning tracks.					
4. Guarantee all students receive essential grade-level curriculum as part of Tier 1 core instruction.					
5. Identify and provide preventions for students needing Tier 1 support in essential grade-level curriculum.					

Action 2

Identify and Teach Essential Academic and Social Behaviors

The fundamental mission of a PLC—and the reason why a school must create a highly effective multitiered system of supports—is to ensure all students learn at high levels. Undoubtedly, some students will struggle to learn new essential curriculum because they lack critical behaviors. If a school is going to ensure learning for all, it must guarantee all students acquire the essential behaviors they need for future success. Achieving this outcome begins with the guiding coalition creating a schoolwide process to identify and teach essential academic and social behaviors.

To achieve this outcome, a school can leverage its foundational PLC practices. As mentioned previously, four critical questions drive collaboration in the PLC at Work process:

1. What knowledge, skills, and dispositions should every student acquire as a result of this unit, this course, or this grade level?

2. How will we know when each student has acquired the essential knowledge and skills?

3. How will we respond when some students do not learn?

4. How will we extend the learning for students who are already proficient? (DuFour et al., 2024, p. 44)

These same questions can guide collaboration focused on essential behaviors. But whereas for academic standards, each teacher team takes lead responsibility to answer these questions for their shared grade or course, staff should collectively answer these questions regarding behavior outcomes. This is because essential core behaviors should be taught and reinforced across the entire school—in every grade, subject, and location on campus (Hannigan et al., 2021). Such behaviors can be categorized into two groups: (1) academic behaviors and (2) social behaviors. These behaviors include those listed in table 4.1.

TABLE 4.1: Examples of Essential Academic and Social Behaviors

Academic Behaviors	Social Behaviors
In addition to academic skills and knowledge, some academic behaviors are critical to school and career success.	Success in school and career requires the ability to consistently demonstrate socially appropriate behaviors.
Metacognition: Knowledge and beliefs about thinking **Self-concept:** A student's belief in their abilities **Self-monitoring:** The ability to plan and prepare for learning **Motivation:** The ability to initiate and maintain interest in tasks **Strategy:** Techniques for organizing and memorizing knowledge **Volition:** The efforts and techniques needed to stay motivated and engaged in learning (Many educators refer to this as demonstrating grit.)	**Responsible verbal and physical interactions with peers and adults:** Skills that demonstrate social responsibility, honesty, compassion, respect, self-regulation, and self-control **Appropriate language:** Skills that demonstrate self-awareness, communication, civility, and character **Respect for property and materials:** Skills that demonstrate empathy and respect **The ability to independently stay on a required task:** Skills that demonstrate on-task behavior **Regular attendance:** Skills that demonstrate punctuality, time management, and accountability

Source: Adapted from Buffum et al., 2018, p. 139.

Essential academic and social behaviors are not acquired genetically; they are taught, modeled, developed, and reinforced over time. Many students' parents first teach and reinforce these behaviors at home. To teach social behaviors, many families expect children to respect their elders and siblings, keep their hands and bodies to themselves, share with others, take turns, solve disagreements with their words instead of their fists, and not abuse their toys or family belongings. Families often expect children to complete assigned chores and memorize their home address and telephone number to develop academic behaviors like motivation and responsibility. And in many cases, they teach specific scholarly behaviors needed to succeed in school. They take their children to purchase school supplies before school starts, help them organize these materials, check daily for homework, set up the best home conditions to study, and require their children to demonstrate the effort needed to succeed.

Equally true, some students come from home environments where family members don't teach these behaviors and, in some cases, they model behaviors counterproductive to success in school. For a child who watches a family member physically respond to another over a disagreement, it makes sense that they would model the same behavior over a disagreement on the playground. Likewise, students who grow up in an unsafe neighborhood might have families that teach them walking away from a disagreement is a sign of weakness that only promotes future bullying. Regarding academic behaviors, many parents and guardians of students at risk did not excel in school, and it is difficult to teach scholarly behaviors that one has never mastered. Finally, some parents and guardians would love to check their children's homework every night, but working a second job to pay the rent is a higher-priority need for their families.

Despite these realities, many schools either consider teaching academic and social behaviors primarily the families' responsibility or fall into the trap of exclusively applying negative consequences to students who misbehave without teaching the desired behaviors in the first place. This approach is akin to having a zero-tolerance policy on illiteracy and devising an increasingly negative set of consequences for students who lack reading ability, all the while never actually teaching struggling readers how to read. If educators want students to demonstrate the social and academic behaviors needed to succeed in school, then they must first identify these behaviors, systematically teach them, and prepare to give some students additional time and support until they master them.

Here's Why

Effective educators know that a successful classroom begins with effective classroom management. Decades of research back this universal truth. The effective schools research from Larry Lezotte, Wilbur Brookover, George Weber, and Ronald Edmonds finds that a common characteristic and an essential correlate of highly effective schools is a safe and orderly environment conducive to teaching and learning (Effective Schools, n.d.). Likewise, level 1 of Robert Marzano's High Reliability Schools model is a safe, supportive, and collaborative culture. Students learn best when they feel safe and can focus on their work (Marzano, Warrick, Rains, & DuFour, 2018).

Research also confirms that mastering academic and social behaviors is not only required in school but also critical for success in the 21st century workplace. Due to an increasingly competitive global economy, successful businesses have moved from a hierarchical leadership structure with layers of management to a more flattened organizational structure in which employees work in teams that take projects from concept to completion. Due to this flattening out of the organizational structure, employees are now expected to take greater responsibility for their work (Jerald, 2009). This means employees must be able to organize and self-monitor their work, hold themselves accountable to complete tasks and meet deadlines, and collaborate with others. In his book

Future Skills: The 20 Skills and Competencies Everyone Needs to Succeed in a Digital World, Bernard Marr (2022) identifies the top-ten skills and competencies as follows.

1. Curiosity and continuous learning
2. Critical thinking
3. Creativity
4. Digital literacy
5. Data literacy
6. Emotional intelligence
7. Collaboration
8. Flexibility
9. Leadership skills
10. Time management

Half of this list is composed of behavior skills needed to thrive in a technology-driven global economy.

Finally, the need for schools to systematically and effectively teach behavior was exponentially compounded by the impact of the COVID-19 pandemic. As we have worked with educators around the world during these post-pandemic times, we have heard a chorus of concerns about students struggling with attendance, motivation, and mental health. This should hardly be surprising. As the world shut down for months, so did students' opportunities to develop socially and emotionally due to shelter-in-place and social distancing requirements. And, more tragically, some students felt the extreme grief of losing family members and loved ones to this deadly virus. It was hard on adults, but just imagine what it would have been like if the pandemic happened when you were five or fifteen years old.

Here's How

To systematically identify and teach essential academic and social behaviors at Tier 1, we recommend that the guiding coalition take the following seven steps.

1. Assign a team, committee, or task force to lead the school's focus on academic and social behaviors.
2. Learn together.
3. Identify a limited number of essential academic and social behaviors.
4. Determine how students will demonstrate mastery of each essential behavior.
5. Design a process to teach essential behaviors systematically and explicitly across the school.
6. Design targeted privileges and recognitions to promote positive behavior.
7. Monitor essential social and academic behaviors.

Assign a Team, Committee, or Task Force to Lead the School's Focus on Academic and Social Behaviors

If teaching essential behaviors should be a schoolwide effort, then a group made up of schoolwide representatives should lead the process. Because the school's guiding coalition is purposefully made up of representatives from every grade level or department, this team could take lead responsibility in organizing the school's focus on behavior.

The guiding coalition already has many other responsibilities in the MTSS process, so some schools find that forming a behavior committee is a more effective way to study, design, promote, and monitor the school's behavior efforts. Still other schools form a behavior task force to study the topic and report back to the faculty with recommendations on how to proceed. Finally, for smaller faculties, it might make the most sense to use faculty meeting time to identify schoolwide behaviors.

Regardless of the format, the ultimate responsibility to ensure a school identifies and teaches essential academic and social behaviors rests with the school's guiding coalition; it can directly lead the process or delegate the process to another group. But if the guiding coalition determines that a committee or task force is desirable, the coalition is still responsible for:

- Ensuring that this behavior subcommittee is clear on the desired outcomes

- Providing the time and resources needed to achieve these goals

- Monitoring that the goals are being achieved

- Revising the process as needed

Learn Together

The authors of the book *Behavior Solutions* (Hannigan et al., 2021) find that a school must create a list of essential behaviors that have the following three characteristics.

1. **Research based:** In the PLC at Work process, professionals make decisions by first committing to collective inquiry—learning together. They do not guess when determining which specific behaviors are most important to their students' future success, nor do they average opinions. Instead, they seek relevant research on which to base their decisions.

2. **Site relevant:** The ethnic, regional, religious, and historical uniqueness of the students and community must be considered to help students bridge the expectations of home and school. For example, we worked with Native American schools where everyone honored the local tribes' values when selecting essential behaviors. Also, we worked in schools where most of the students came from neighborhoods of deep ethnic diversity. Sometimes, these differences resulted in violent confrontations in the community. These schools determined that respecting cultural diversity was an essential social behavior.

3. **Doable:** When a school selects essential behavior standards, educators do not just list or teach them; the staff make a collective commitment to ensure every student masters every behavior. A school's collective list of essential behaviors—academic and social— must be succinct enough for students to memorize them all and for the school to be able to intervene on all of them.

Identify a Limited Number of Essential Academic and Social Behaviors

Based on what educators learned in the previous step, the school should identify the specific social and academic behaviors all students must learn and consistently demonstrate. The guiding coalition, behavior committee, or task force could create a draft proposal and then bring it to the entire faculty to gain input and build consensus. Alternatively, staff meeting time could be dedicated to creating a proposal together.

These essential behaviors should be stated in the positive, meaning the statements express the actions the school wants its students to demonstrate. Traditionally, schools often write their behavior rules in the negative, such as the following.

- ▶ Don't be late to class.
- ▶ Don't bully others.
- ▶ Don't steal.
- ▶ Don't interrupt class instruction.

It is better to teach the positive, such as the following.

- ▶ Be on time to class.
- ▶ Treat others with respect.
- ▶ Honor the property of others.
- ▶ Stay on task in class.

Determine How Students Will Demonstrate Mastery of Each Essential Behavior

When teacher teams identify an essential academic standard—such as persuasive writing—it is equally important that they determine how students demonstrate they have learned this outcome. To achieve this, teachers can develop a grading rubric and an assessment process to measure student learning in comparison to the rubric. Essential behaviors are no different. Once a school determines its essential academic and social behaviors, the staff must agree on how students demonstrate these behaviors, considering differences in student ages and learning environments.

For example, if a school determines that demonstrating respect is an essential social behavior, how should students demonstrate this behavior in the classroom during whole-group instruction? During cooperative learning time? On the playground? In the cafeteria? During a pep rally? Also, students' ability to self-monitor this behavior will vary between kindergartners and fifth graders, for example. Teachers must discuss these considerations before they can explicitly teach, monitor, and intervene in the essential behaviors. Teachers can capture demonstrated behaviors in a rubric that they then teach to students and clearly and strategically post around campus to remind them of schoolwide expectations.

Design a Process to Teach Essential Behaviors Systematically and Explicitly Across the School

It is unfair to hold students accountable for behaviors that the school did not effectively teach. Merely posting classroom rules or providing them in a student-parent handbook is insufficient. Consider for a moment the steps a teacher might take to effectively teach a new essential academic standard. In a direct instruction approach, teachers might follow a process such as the following.

1. Clearly identify the specific skill you want all students to learn.
2. Introduce the skill to the students and provide context regarding why it is important to learn.
3. Explicitly teach—step by step—how to do the skill.
4. Have students practice the skill.
5. Assess each student's proficiency in the skill.
6. Provide targeted feedback and support to students.

This same type of process applies to teaching essential behaviors too. The guiding coalition, working with the faculty, should develop a way to teach the essential social and academic behaviors systematically. This process should undoubtedly begin at the start of the school year. Moreover, in the same way effective teachers regularly remind and prompt students about classroom procedures, so too should the school plan to revisit its behavior expectations throughout the year. Because some students arrive after the start of school, there should also be a process to teach these behaviors to new students.

Here is an example of what this process might look like from a Model PLC middle school. The staff identified six essential academic behaviors they wanted all students to master.

1. Take notes.
2. Research, including determining the validity of sources and citing appropriate references.
3. Maintain a calendar of responsibilities, assignments, and due dates.
4. Keep work organized and come to class prepared.
5. Memorize information.
6. Set goals and reflect on progress.

To teach these academic behaviors systematically and explicitly across the school, the faculty decided that teacher teams in every subject would teach one of the essential academic skills in the school year's first month. For example, the ELA team taught Cornell note taking during the first month of school. This ensured that every student at every grade level learned the skill. The mathematics department taught students how to use a calendar to keep track of assignments and then reinforced the skill throughout the first month. The science department taught students internet research skills and how to cite information. This collective process took a limited amount of classroom instructional time but guaranteed that every student knew how to demonstrate these expectations.

Design Targeted Privileges and Recognitions to Promote Positive Behavior

There should be more positive reasons for students to demonstrate the right behaviors than threats and punishments to deter negative behaviors. To this end, we recommend that schools develop some standards-based privileges or recognitions that reward all students who demonstrate specific essential behaviors. We call them *standards based* because many schools have award processes that recognize a very limited number of winners: student of the month, athlete of the year, and valedictorian, to name a few. Many good students know it is unlikely they will ever win these awards, so they assume a *why try?* attitude.

Meanwhile, a standards-based behavior privilege sets an expectation and defines the award or recognition students earn for meeting this outcome. If ten students meet the expectation, then ten students earn the privilege. If two hundred students achieve the outcome, then two hundred students earn the recognition. Not all positive behavior awards need to be standards based, but the school's goal is to make many winners.

Monitor Essential Social and Academic Behaviors

The guiding coalition should determine processes to monitor whether students are learning and consistently demonstrating essential behaviors. Regularly reviewing information on who is earning positive behavior recognitions and where behavior infractions are most often occurring can help the school to evaluate its efforts to teach essential behaviors, and to target resources to intervene when some students don't consistently demonstrate these essentials.

Our behavior expectations for students should be nothing less than what the adults in the building would want for themselves. A teacher would expect those who evaluate them to know the school's staff expectations, to understand how the teacher may demonstrate the expected behaviors, to provide positive reinforcement when the teacher does demonstrate them, and to use frequent monitoring and support if they do not. Our students deserve nothing less.

Helpful Tools

The following tools will help you accomplish the work for this essential action.

- ▸ **"Our School's Preliminary Essential Academic and Social Behaviors" (page 173):** This simple template can help guide a school's conversation around identifying, teaching, and assessing its essential academic and social behaviors.

- ▸ *Behavior Solutions* **(Hannigan et al., 2021):** We highly recommend this book for digging much deeper into creating a highly effective system of behavior supports at Tiers 1, 2, and 3. It is aligned with the PLC at Work process and our RTI at Work recommendations. It also provides many more examples and tools to assist your efforts.

Coaching Tips

The steps outlined in chapter 2, action 2's Here's How section (page 43) on creating consensus for school culture are the same ones needed for the task of identifying schoolwide behavior expectations. Those three steps are as follows.

1. Provide a compelling case for identifying expectations.
2. Create a doable plan for sharing, monitoring, and rewarding expectations.
3. Build consensus to ensure shared commitment to and responsibility for implementation of the plan.

Do *not* overlook the importance of the first step. Lacking understanding of *why* this task is necessary, the potential for success with steps 2 and 3 dramatically decreases. A compelling case for identifying schoolwide expectations requires sharing experiences as both students and educators, learning from and visiting other schools, and exploring current research on this topic. It is important to assess staff's understanding and readiness to support a possible plan before creating one.

A doable plan includes multiple attributes, such as the following.

- ▸ Clearly defined behavior expectations
- ▸ Strategies and resources for recognizing and rewarding positive behaviors
- ▸ Strategies and resources for intervening to address misbehaviors
- ▸ Leadership communication and instruction on the plan to all stakeholders
- ▸ Systems for monitoring, evaluating, and adjusting the plan

The good news about creating multiple pieces of a doable plan is that there are opportunities to involve stakeholders. Inviting staff, students, and parents to actively participate in plan development means the plan will be stronger and potentially result in greater consensus. As you develop and share each part of the plan, you have the opportunity to check the level of understanding and support. You can use the formative feedback gathered along the way to address any misunderstandings and adjust the plan, thus facilitating greater commitment to and ultimately shared responsibility for its implementation.

Our School's Preliminary Essential Academic and Social Behaviors

List the essential academic and social behaviors you want students to demonstrate at your school. This tool is designed to help the guiding coalition assess what is currently in place at the school. Don't worry if your answers are unclear or incomplete; include what you can based on your background knowledge.

What essential academic and social behavior skills do you want students to demonstrate?	
Academic Behaviors	**Social Behaviors**
What evidence will show that students are learning these behavior skills?	
How will you ensure students are learning these essential academic and social behavior skills?	

Source: Hannigan, J., Hannigan, J. D., Mattos, M., & Buffum, A. (2021). Behavior solutions: Teaching academic and social skills through RTI at Work. *Bloomington, IN: Solution Tree Press.*

Action 3

Create a Balanced Assessment Approach

The guiding coalition's third essential action at Tier 1 is to ensure all educators in the system understand the purpose and use of each type of assessment. Educators do not lack data. In fact, many teachers—and students—lament the feeling of being over-tested. As a profession, educators have become quite proficient in collecting and analyzing data of all kinds, including different types of assessment evidence. The trickier part is determining what data to analyze and what action to take, including who will take the lead on the response that results in high achievement, all while maintaining a doable workflow.

Some data are best used at the classroom level to understand the efficiency of initial instruction for individual and targeted groups of students, including identifying specific students who need additional support. Other data are best used to understand how the larger system—the entire school or district—is serving groups of students and what needs to change to ensure access and equity. In a balanced approach, educators use specific types of assessments in a purposeful way to "monitor and enhance student learning in relation to the state standards and to the state's goals for student proficiency" (Schneider, Egan, & Julian, 2013, p. 61).

Here's Why

The guiding coalition takes the lead in making the purpose of assessments clear and ensuring all educators in the system understand their role and how to use the assessment data well. How educators talk about and use assessment data can lead to a firm belief that their actions make a difference in student learning and are more powerful than any outside influence. This belief is the idea of collective efficacy, one of the highest-leverage indicators of high achievement (Hattie, 2023; Reeves, 2008).

Mindset matters. Reeves (2008) asked over three thousand teachers and administrators what they believed to be the single biggest influence on student learning. Those who named something in their control had three times higher achievement in their schools than those who named something out of their control. Given this reality, it is critical for all teams—the guiding coalition, the intervention team, and teacher teams—to routinely review assessment data and reflect on the actions that are leading to the results they are getting.

When educators use data for purposes they weren't intended for, they can become frustrated at the amount of data analysis and feel they don't have time to respond in a meaningful and impactful way. Prioritizing who analyzes what type of assessment data and then what action to take can be paralyzing without a clear understanding of the best use of different assessment data types. In addition, if teacher teams, guiding coalitions, and district teams do not see results during data analysis, they can feel defeated. Utilizing assessments for unintended purposes can cause teachers and students to feel that the purpose of school is to do well on tests rather than to learn essential skills and knowledge. Guiding coalitions ensure all types of assessments are clearly defined in terms of what they are used for and by whom and, probably as important, what they are *not* used for. This is a balanced assessment approach.

When systems have a balanced assessment approach, educators know who uses the data and how, and they also have a deep understanding of what actions lead to results. They commit to focus on research-based practices and relentlessly pursue action and response as they monitor and adjust to how students are doing. This agility is what leads to a culture of learning, in which students are learning at high levels and developing confidence.

It is the guiding coalition's job to help cultivate a balanced assessment approach. The guiding coalition must identify the most prioritized work and ensure a reasonable and intentional workflow for teams. The guiding coalition can also guide the faculty to identify things to stop doing to make room for high-priority actions. How educators analyze assessment data and respond to results leads to a belief that what they are doing has an impact.

Here's How

A guiding coalition looks at the best use of different types of data, along with who is best positioned to learn from the information and take action. The coalition should look at a wide range of quantitative and qualitative data to understand not only what is working and what is not, but also why the results are the way they are. Following are the different types of data the guiding coalition should examine.

Large-Scale Assessments

Large-scale assessments are most often administered once a year and include end-of-year state and provincial tests and ACT, SAT, IB, and AP exams. The best use of these data is to help adults in the system understand for which students the current structures, curriculum, and instruction are working and for which students something different is needed. Large-scale data are not intended to reveal individual achievement indicators—they are not to be analyzed to understand what instruction specific students need and on what skills they need it. These data are too far away from the flow of classroom instruction.

One snapshot on one day, given the conditions under which tests are administered, does not provide sufficient information about why students didn't achieve in a particular strand or area. Large-scale assessments include items that are field-tested with large numbers of students, so making inferences about the effectiveness of systems is possible, but for individual students, it is challenging.

The site intervention team may look at end-of-year assessment data for students over multiple years; students who consistently score below grade level may need Tier 3 intensive reinforcements. However, these can't be the only data that determine the need for Tier 3 supports. The intervention team should pair large-scale assessment data over time with benchmark data, teacher team–level common assessment data, and teacher observation and classroom data to ensure the students have a true need for foundational skill support and not just a test anxiety issue or one bad testing day.

Large-scale assessment data are best used by guiding coalitions and district leadership teams to reflect on what is working in the system and what needs support. This includes guiding teacher teams to understand these data but not to overanalyze them. If these data are analyzed and used well, the system will, of course, see gains, and the educators and students will talk about the essential learning they are doing more than the scores.

Finally, when large-scale data are overused, educators may emphasize designing many assessments to look like end-of-year or state or provincial exams. They assume that if students get a lot of practice in the methods of the large-scale exams, they will do better. Unfortunately, this leads to testing fatigue, so students often burn out and may not take the assessments seriously, skipping items or just giving up when they get to something they don't know. The focus becomes testing over learning.

Benchmark Assessments

Benchmark assessments are often administered and analyzed two or three times per year. Like large-scale assessments, they are best used by adults in the system to understand the effectiveness of instruction and curriculum and predict how students are progressing toward end-of-year standards. Some benchmark assessments are outsourced progress-monitoring assessments that show growth on a set of skills, but they usually do not tightly align with specific essential standards.

Adults in the system can review these data to help them understand who is growing and who isn't, but students should not set goals based on these data, as they do not have tight ties to students' day-to-day learning or essential standards. Instead, students should set goals for essential standards and use common end-of-unit assessments and common formative assessments—places where they have time and support to work on specific essential learning—to reflect on their progress. Data from benchmark assessments can be among the data points used to identify students who need more support with immediate prerequisite skills in Tier 1 or Tier 2 or with foundational prerequisite skills at Tier 3.

When benchmark assessments are designed to measure each student's current level of proficiency in a universal skill—such as reading or number sense—their data could be used as part of a school's universal screening process. The primary purpose of universal screening is to identify students who need Tier 3 help in foundational prerequisite skills, which leads to Tier 3 support. Consequently, this information is not designed to guide Tier 2 interventions.

If benchmark assessments tightly align with the standards students are expected to master at the time the assessments are administered, teacher teams may use the data to determine who needs additional time and support at Tier 2. However, benchmark data should not be the first time that teacher teams intervene on essential standards.

Most often, benchmark assessments are aligned to the end-of-year assessment, so an analysis of a benchmark assessment may include essential standards or learning targets educators haven't taught yet, making any response difficult or inefficient at the least.

Common End-of-Unit Assessments

For each unit, teacher teams identify the essential standards to teach as a focus for instruction, common assessments, intervention, and extension. Teams may also agree to teach some connected supporting standards in a unit. Teacher teams analyze the results from common end-of-unit assessments and identify students who need additional time and support to learn essential standards. They analyze what misconceptions students have and what next steps students need, and they provide support and intervention during Tier 2 instructional time.

Common Formative Assessments

Educators create common formative assessments to gather evidence and information during the unit regarding what students understand and what they still need to work on to achieve the essential standards (see chapter 3, action 3, page 114). Teacher teams analyze the data by student, by standard, and by learning target to determine the instruction's effectiveness and the next steps for individual students and groups of students (see chapter 3, action 5, page 138). Teacher teams analyze student work to understand students' strengths in terms of the learning targets and students' errors or misconceptions that lead to targeted and specific interventions. Looking at student work helps teams match students with the best instruction to re-engage them in learning and achieve the standards before the unit ends.

Checks for Understanding or Ongoing Formative Assessment

Teachers notice when students understand content and when they need support. These moment-to-moment responses happen every day during class. Checks for understanding can be informal, using something like an exit ticket or observation at a station to get quick feedback on how students are doing on daily learning targets. Checks for understanding take place in the moment; this is when some of the most powerful and effective learning occurs (Brookhart, 2020; Ruiz-Primo & Brookhart, 2018; William & Leahy, 2015).

The most timely and targeted site-level information to guide interventions for specific students comes from common end-of-unit assessments and common formative assessments. This information should be the lifeblood of Tier 1 and Tier 2 (see figure 4.4).

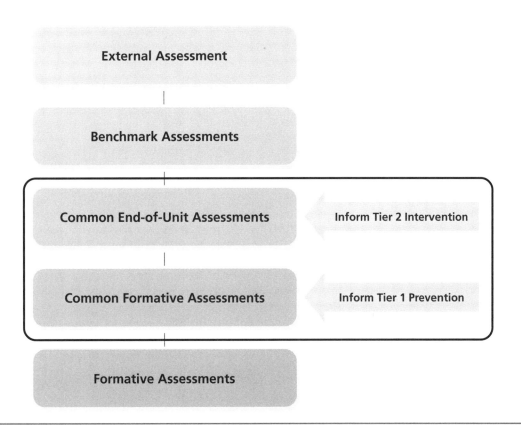

FIGURE 4.4: Teacher team assessments that best guide Tier 1 and Tier 2.

The guiding coalition identifies all the assessments administered at each level of the system. This includes identifying the purposes of the assessments, who is using them, and how they are using them. From this review, the guiding coalition considers the assessment balance on campus. It ensures large-scale assessments are used to understand system effectiveness without impacting the time teacher teams need to design and use common end-of-unit assessments and common formative assessments, and teacher checks for understanding inform instruction and intervention. Members of the guiding coalition learn from one another by sharing team common assessments.

The guiding coalitions at both the school and district levels determine which data to analyze, when to analyze the data, and how to analyze the data to identify what in the system is or is not working. Together, they create a school's assessment blueprint, noting which assessments must be used by which teams in the school. As they identify these assessments, guiding coalitions support and monitor assessments that are tight (or non-negotiable), ensuring the data are analyzed and acted on.

Figure 4.5, from Nicole Dimich's (2024) *Design in Five*, illustrates the move from unbalanced and over-tested to balanced and informed.

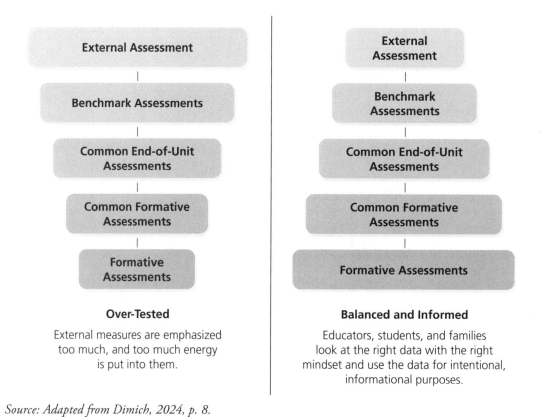

Source: Adapted from Dimich, 2024, p. 8.

FIGURE 4.5: From over-tested to balanced and informed.

Helpful Tools

The following tools will help you accomplish the work for this essential action.

▸ **"Balanced Assessment: Types and Purposes" (page 180):** This table facilitates conversation to help systems—districts, schools, and teams—identify the assessment data being collected and for what purpose.

▸ **"Types of Assessment Data to Inform System Effectiveness" (page 181):** This table identifies different types of data used for different tiers and different teams. It also provides guidance on questions to ask about these data.

▸ **"Team Response to Common Formative Assessment" (see chapter 3, action 5, page 148):** This template helps team members agree on their collective response to common assessment results.

▸ **"Team Protocol for Reviewing Student Work to Plan Tier 1 or Tier 2 Responses" (see chapter 3, action 5, page 149):** Teacher teams use this protocol to plan Tier 1 or Tier 2 responses by reviewing student work from common formative or end-of-unit assessments.

Coaching Tips

The greatest challenge to creating a balanced assessment approach is understanding that this essential action is as much about leading cultural change as it is about establishing systematic protocols for analyzing and responding to assessment data. A truly balanced assessment approach is based on the same two assumptions that were highlighted in chapter 2, Action 2: Build a Culture of Collective Responsibility (page 40).

1. Educators assume primary responsibility to ensure high levels of learning for every student.

2. Educators assume that all students can learn at high levels.

These assumptions are fundamental to shifting school culture from a focus on teaching and grading to a focus on learning and balanced assessment. As the guiding coalition begins working toward creating and implementing a balanced assessment approach, it may need to revisit these assumptions to ensure common understanding of how and why they are foundational.

As stated in chapter 2's second essential action, creating consensus for cultural change is about building shared knowledge and understanding. The advantage the guiding coalition may have in this case is that teacher teams understand the power of classroom assessments and are likely more than ready to reduce the emphasis too often placed on large-scale and benchmark assessments. The "Balanced Assessment: Types and Purposes" tool provides a strong framework for discussing types, purposes, and users of a range of assessments.

Fundamental to a balanced assessment approach is accurate and appropriate analysis and response to all types of assessments. Here are five additional guidelines to consider.

1. Assist teams in reviewing end-of-unit assessments to ensure all assessment items and tasks are at grade or course level and at the cognitive level required by the essential standards being assessed.

2. Guide teams to review all assessments being used to avoid duplication. If the teams already have data relevant to specific standards, an additional assessment is not needed.

3. Ensure data analysis conversations focus on identifying gaps, strengths, and next steps rather than hypothesizing causes and blaming previous grade-level teachers.

4. Encourage teams to spend one-third of their time analyzing the data and two-thirds of their time planning the action they will take in response.

5. Provide and support the use of protocols that feature intentional questions designed to help keep data discussions on track. Protocols need to include what action will be taken and by whom. Additionally, following up to understand the impact of actions is essential to creating a system that is responsive to students' needs—a system that ensures high levels of learning for all.

Balanced Assessment: Types and Purposes

Assessment Category	Best Use of the Information From This Type of Assessment	What Assessments Are Administered in Each Category (by Grade Level or Course)?	What Is the Best Use of These Data?	How Often Is the Assessment Given?	How Do Learners Get Feedback?	What Instructional Decisions Are Made Based on the Data?
• Large-scale external assessments (standardized tests) • Student perception data (surveys, focus groups)	Analysis: policy, district, whole school, department, or grade-level team					
• Benchmark assessments • Universal screeners	Analysis: district or system, whole school, department, grade-level team, or individual teacher					
End-of-course assessments	Analysis: whole school, department, grade-level team, or individual teacher					
End-of-unit assessments (common or individual)	Analysis: department, grade-level team, or individual teacher					
Common formative assessments	Analysis: department, grade-level team, individual teacher, or student					
Formative assessments or checks for understanding	Analysis and response by individual teachers on a daily basis					

Source: Adapted from Vagle, N. (2009). Finding the meaning in numbers. In T. Guskey (Ed.), The principal as assessment leader (Reissue ed.; pp. 149–173). Bloomington, IN: Solution Tree.

Types of Assessment Data to Inform System Effectiveness

Directions: The following table describes different types of assessment data with examples that may be useful to analyze at different levels of the system. It also includes the most appropriate people and teams who use the data and questions to ask about the different types of assessment data.

Large-Scale Assessment Data Often Used to Inform System Effectiveness
• State or provincial assessment results • Benchmark assessments • ACT and SAT results • AP and IB exam results • Universal screener results (formal or informal) • Students in rigorous courses and by subgroups such as AP and IB • Failure rates • Graduation rates • Dropout rates • MAP or other growth measures • Student and family surveys (on communication, classroom practices, assessment results, or instructional practices) • Student and family perception measures, such as focus groups or interviews
Questions to Consider • How do these data currently inform system effectiveness? • What subgroups are examined? How does the system respond when subgroups (for example, students of certain genders or ethnicities, students from homes of poverty, students with certain mobility needs, English learners, gifted and talented education students, and special education students) are not served well? • How are student voices and perceptions gathered and used to deeply understand what works and what does not?
Assessment Data Often Used to Inform Tier 1 Prevention
• Universal screening information • Formative assessment results • Results from collaborative teams and common formative assessments • Common end-of-unit assessment results if all or most students need additional time and support
Questions to Consider • How often do collaborative teams meet to analyze common formative assessment data to inform Tier 1 preventions? • What do teams currently use to inform Tier 1 preventions for students they identify as needing additional time and support on grade-level standards? What do they use to determine which instructional practices are effective and which are not? Is time scheduled for reteaching during a unit of study? • Do assessment results target preventions by student, by standard, and by learning target? • How do teams check the effectiveness of Tier 1 preventions? Do they reassess targeted learning?
Assessment Data Often Used to Inform Tier 2 Intervention
• Common end-of-unit assessments • Sometimes common formative assessment data during the unit of study

Questions to Consider

- What do teams currently use to inform Tier 2 interventions for students they identify as needing additional time and support on grade-level standards? What do they use to determine which instructional practices are effective and which are not?
- Do assessment results target interventions by student, by standard, and by learning target?
- How do teams check the effectiveness of Tier 2 interventions? Do they reassess targeted learning?
- Can identified students receive Tier 2 interventions without missing instruction in new essential curriculum at Tier 1?
- Can identified students receive Tier 2 intervention in addition to Tier 3 intensive reinforcement?

Assessment Data Often Used to Inform Tier 3 Intensive Reinforcements

- Universal screener results assessing foundational prerequisite skills
- Targeted diagnostic assessments to determine each student's needs for an identified universal skill
- Previous large-scale assessment results over time
- Teacher observations by identified foundational prerequisite skill

Questions to Consider

- What assessments currently inform Tier 3 reinforcement for students identified as needing additional time and support on foundational prerequisite skills?
- Has the school identified schoolwide essential social and academic behaviors? How are behaviors systematically taught across the school?
- What diagnostic assessments help determine a student's specific learning needs?
- How well trained are the faculty or staff who provide intensive reinforcement?
- Do all students who receive Tier 3 intensive reinforcement also have access to the Tier 1 essential grade-level curriculum? Can these students also receive Tier 2 support in the essential grade-level curriculum?
- Are the school's behavior interventions reteaching targeted essential behaviors or punishing students for not mastering them?
- Are the behavior interventions working? Do fewer students need additional behavior support after receiving targeted help?
- How do teachers check the effectiveness of Tier 3 reinforcement? How do they monitor progress? How do they assess foundational skills to determine whether students achieve grade-level standards?

Assessment Data Often Used to Inform Academic and Behavior Interventions

Quantitative Academic and Behavior Skills Data

- Number of discipline referrals
- Number of parent conferences for discipline
- Number of in- or out-of-school suspensions
- Expulsions
- Reasons for family meetings or phone calls
- Average daily attendance
- Number of students involved with athletics
- Number of students in clubs
- Number of students in community service
- Number of students in leadership roles
- Minutes or percentage of time on task

Qualitative Academic and Behavior Skills Data

- Student and family surveys (on communication, classroom practices, assessment results, or instructional practices)
- Student and family perception measures, such as focus groups or interviews
- Student, teacher, and family perceptions of discipline responses

Questions to Consider

- How do these data currently inform system effectiveness?
- What subgroups are examined? How does the system respond when student groups (for example, students of certain genders or ethnicities, students from homes of poverty, students with certain mobility needs, English learners, gifted and talented education students, and special education students) are not served well?
- How are student voices and perceptions gathered and used to deeply understand what works and what does not?
- What are the top three reasons students get referrals?
- When in the school day or year and where on campus are most referrals written?

Assessment Data Often Used to Monitor Systems and Structures

Artifacts for Analysis

- Clear learning targets (teachers, students, and instruction)
- Analysis of the cognitive demand and grade-level standards of instructional learning activities and assessments
- Observations of teacher responses to student learning (differentiation through formative assessment)
- Significant classroom time allocated for student discussions, explorations, and sense making

Structures

- Regular collaborative team time for teachers to analyze assessment evidence to plan instruction and ensure learning
- Scheduled time for Tier 2 and Tier 3 intervention that ensures students do not miss core instruction

Perceptions

- Student perceptions of learning and safety (homework, grading, assessment, questioning, and so on)
- Family perceptions of learning and safety
- Community perceptions of learning and safety
- Teacher perceptions of learning and safety
- Teacher voices in establishing learning goals, instruction, and assessment

Questions to Consider

- How do these data currently inform system effectiveness?
- What student groups are examined? How does the system respond when student groups (for example, students of certain genders or ethnicities, students from homes of poverty, students with certain mobility needs, English learners, gifted and talented education students, and special education students) are not served well?
- How are student voices and perceptions gathered and used to deeply understand what works and what does not?

Action 4

Co-Create Schoolwide Grading Practices

The fourth essential action for the guiding coalition at Tier 1 is to co-create schoolwide grading practices. Too often, grading practices are defined individually by teachers and vary from one teacher to the next. This variability causes students, parents, guardians, teachers, and administrators to be unclear about the relationship between a student's grades and their learning. Yet letter grades A–F persist. The school and larger community interpret them as good or bad and use them to determine who learned and who did not learn since they most likely were also graded this way.

In the teaching-assessing-learning cycle (see figure 3.2, page 83), there is no mention of grades. Student common formative and end-of-unit assessments are used to determine possible Tier 1 preventions or Tier 2 interventions and extensions. In chapter 3, action 5 (page 138), we shared the importance of using student work to reveal instructional practices that worked across a collaborative team and the student thinking that leads to targeted interventions. We did not mention grades. We did not say any student with a D or an F should be in an intervention. Instead, teachers use evidence of student learning on specific essential learning outcomes to target additional support, not grades.

That said, grades and report cards are a reality in schools. The guiding coalition must actively clarify the purpose and meaning of grades schoolwide to ensure they are meaningful and consistent and promote student learning. The coalition works with staff to understand that the purpose of grades is to communicate learning at a particular moment in time, ideally as tied to standards (Guskey, 2015b, 2022; Schimmer, 2016, 2023). As the guiding coalition explores these high-level and critical practices, it uses research, educational books, and articles to challenge historically ineffective grading policies and identify practices that motivate and improve student learning across the school. Without such leadership, some of the following may occur.

- A student may earn extra credit, which might raise their grade without them learning the essential standards.
- A student may be marked down for behaviors, such as not participating or missing a deadline, in a final grade even though they have learned the essential standards.
- A student who initially did not learn but eventually learned by the end of the unit may have their grade negatively impacted by formative activities and assessments used in class when learning was not yet fully expected.
- A student who learns essential standards after Tier 1 or Tier 2 additional time and support may not have this learning reflected in their grade.

Traditional grading practices that rank student achievement, punish students for initial failure, deny students opportunities to fix mistakes, value promptness over learning, and demotivate students who are struggling undermine a school's intervention efforts. Grades should represent *what a student learned*, not if they learned it first, fastest, or in the most behaved way. Any school committed to a mission of ensuring all students learn at high levels can no longer justify and perpetuate these practices. As defenders of the school's mission, guiding coalition members should build shared knowledge on grading practices that promote and support opportunities for students to learn from their mistakes, try again, and ultimately demonstrate what they learned.

Here's Why

When asked to justify their grading practices, teachers often say that they are grading the way they have always graded or grading the way they were taught to grade during student teaching. In other words, teachers across a collaborative team may have different policies to determine grades from personal experiences, not research-affirmed practices. Some teachers might allow student reassessment, while others do not; some might give greater consideration to students' recent work than to their previous work, while others do not; and some might give students extended time and grade solely on student work, while others do not.

Yet in a school committed to high levels of learning for all students, teachers across a team analyze student work and collectively determine which students are proficient and which are not yet proficient. Why would they not evaluate student work the same way, or not have grades mean the same thing, for any student in the grade or course (or any student on campus, in the guiding coalition's case)? Can any person explain the meaning of a letter grade in a traditional system? For example, what does a C tell someone about student learning? Did the student learn at a C level? Did they learn at a B level but not turn in work? Or did they learn at a D level but try hard? Left up to each teacher, these grading variances and more exist. A guiding coalition analyzes grading traditions and determines whether they still hold in a system working to have every student learn.

Here's How

A guiding coalition can gain great insight from gathering the grading policies of teachers on campus and seeing the variance in letter grades possible for a student. Often, such an activity causes some urgency to co-create grading practices.

As a school strengthens its RTI process and focuses on student learning, the guiding coalition often starts wrestling with two ideas: (1) "Should we count common formative assessments in a student's grade?" and (2) "Should we give retakes, and if so, how should we grade them?" Whether in a traditional letter-grade model or a standards-based grading model, these two questions apply and impact student learning results. In a letter-grade model, if a student earns 0 percent on an assessment and then 100 percent on an assessment, the average is 50 percent, an F. The 0 percent has much more influence on the final averaged grade than the 100 percent. And if a student earns a zero for work not turned in or completed by a given date, their grade may be negatively impacted and not accurately reflect their *current* learning. The guiding coalition must analyze and address these types of issues.

As your team addresses grading, discuss the following three areas as they relate to student learning.

1. Define the purpose for grading.

2. Use research-based evidence of effectiveness to determine shifts in grading practices.

3. Identify the learning evidence to include in a student's grade.

Define the Purpose for Grading

Traditionally, grades are one piece of data used to, among other things, complete college applications, rank seniors at graduation, and justify course placement at the secondary level. One challenge related to grades is that teachers often use a single letter grade to communicate student learning *and* student behavior. Another challenge for some teachers occurs when they have a student doing below-grade-level work and they want the student's grade to reflect what they learned *below grade level* rather than *at grade level*. Grading is also sometimes seen as compensation to students—

a payment for doing well and working hard, or a deduction for not doing well or not behaving as desired. In other words, it's a mess!

Thomas Guskey (2015b), professor of educational policy studies and evaluation at the University of Kentucky, states, "Most of the difficulties schools experience in their efforts to reform grading policies and practices can be traced to the lack of a well-defined and commonly understood purpose" (p. 15). Tom Schimmer (2016) shares:

> We must change how we think about grading—our mindset—before we can make any physical changes to our grade reporting structures and routines. We need a completely new paradigm to replace the traditional view of grades as a commodity or reward. The new grading paradigm shifts grades from something the teacher randomly doles out to a reflection of learning the student earns. (p. 3)

Susan M. Brookhart (2011) clarifies further: "Grading on standards for achievement means a shift from thinking that grades are what students earn to thinking that grades show what students learn" (p. 13). When the purpose of grading shifts to a reflection of student learning, the guiding coalition examines teachers' policies for assigning grades for late work and any reassessments, among other issues. Should a student turn in work late, the grade reflects the evidence of learning, not the timing. Should a student be reassessed after having done additional learning, why average the scores or limit the grade to a certain percentage? Often, the more recent evidence of student learning is a more accurate portrayal of that student's learning. Defining the purpose of grading as a guiding coalition guides teams and teachers to more accurately and consistently use grades as feedback. Grades reflect students' learning of standards and targets and therefore provide information to monitor through teacher teams' implementation of Tier 1 and Tier 2 learning experiences.

Use Research-Based Evidence of Effectiveness to Determine Shifts in Grading Practices

Several educational authors and researchers have addressed grading. As a guiding coalition, gather the sources and information to learn how grading decisions impact students' motivation and learning, as well as teachers' focus on learning. The content points toward a standards-based grading model to give students, parents, and guardians meaningful and accurate feedback about student learning.

In *Leading a High Reliability School*, Robert J. Marzano, Phil Warrick, Cameron L. Rains, and Richard DuFour (2018) include indicators for standards-referenced reporting. Indicator 4.1 discusses using proficiency scales for standards and determining how to evaluate student learning at levels of proficiency 1–4. The numbers can be translated into language such as the following: 1 is *minimally proficient*, 2 is *partially proficient*, 3 is *proficient*, and 4 is *highly proficient*. Students receive information about their learning of an essential standard and can measure growth in their learning as well. This means there is less variability with grades in a gradebook, as each grade reflects a student's learning of a standard.

Schimmer (2016) shares the following three components of a standards-based mindset that, when put together, reshape the grading paradigm.

1. Give students full credit for what they know.

2. Redefine accountability.

3. Repurpose the role of homework. (p. 4)

Whether teachers use a standards-based report card or not, a gradebook can show standards-based learning of standards and targets. Teams emphasize information related to essential standards to inform Tier 1 and Tier 2 learning experiences.

Identify the Learning Evidence to Include in a Student's Grade

The guiding coalition ensures collaborative teams have time to meet, uninterrupted time to teach in Tier 1, and time to address Tier 2 interventions. The goal, at a minimum, is to have students learn the essential standards. Ideally, students and teachers can monitor learning progress, and the guiding coalition can also check in on student learning. Some clarity may be needed as to the number of times, or consistency, that suffices for a teacher or student to know learning has occurred.

If a team uses percentages and a student earns 100 percent and 90 percent on the common formative assessments but 65 percent on the end-of-unit assessment, what is the grade? If another student earns 60 percent and 75 percent on the common formative assessments but 90 percent on the end-of-unit assessment, what is the grade? If all scores are simply averaged, the first student earns 85 percent and the second 75 percent. Is that accurate? If the team uses proficiency levels, the first student most likely earns 3, 3, and 2. The second earns 2, 2 or 3, and 3. Looking at the trend, we see the second student has evidence suggesting proficiency, while the first student may end up with a partial understanding. The most recent evidence shares the students' full and current level of understanding and gets more emphasis when student learning of a standard is evaluated (Marzano, 2017).

End-of-unit assessment data are used formatively for students who need additional time and support to master the essentials (Tier 2 intervention) and summatively for students who have mastered the essentials. If end-of-unit assessments are part of students' overall grade, students receive a grade on their assessment once they have reached mastery. If they get a grade prior to reaching mastery, then subsequent evidence of proficiency or mastery replaces the earlier grade (Schimmer, 2016). The earlier grade and the most recent grade (when assessing the same essential standard) are not averaged. In addition, students do not receive less credit for taking more time to learn the essentials. This grading practice ensures students understand that when they have evidence of learning, it will "equally count" toward their overall grade.

When students have reason to ask, "How much is this worth?" or "Is this graded?" it can lead them to feel unmotivated and focus on points instead of learning. When we can say, "It is graded when you show mastery, and it is worth full credit," our grading practices set up a culture of learning and engagement, so students don't opt out for reasons that are within our control. *Accurate and consistent grading practices are within our control.*

As a guiding coalition, clarify the purpose of a grade, use research to challenge grading practices, and clarify how teachers should interpret and share student learning using a grading system created by their team. Align grading practices and policies to ensure every student learns, even when some students need additional time and support to demonstrate that learning.

One final, critical piece of advice: having led this process on-site, we have learned that discussing and changing teachers' grading practices can be a volatile process. *How a teacher determines grades often represents what they value, and values are often deeply personal.* We have seen faculty meetings, collaborative teams, and RTI processes disintegrate because grading discussions turned into personal attacks, creating mistrust and deep staff divisions. Ignoring the topic of grading is not an option, as failure to address detrimental grading practices undermines student learning. But it might not be the place to start one's RTI journey. Instead, it is a mountain that might need to wait until the school builds the learning processes and trust needed to scale this peak.

Helpful Tools

The following tools will help you accomplish the work for this essential action.

> ▸ **"Report Card Discussion" (page 189):** This tool offers the guiding coalition an example report card and questions to consider and discuss.

> ▸ **"Grading Reflection" (page 190):** This tool offers a list of reflection questions about grading to discuss as a guiding coalition.

> ▸ **"Process for the Guiding Coalition to Draft Grading Practices and Policies" (page 191):** This tool provides the guiding coalition with steps to consider when clarifying a school grading policy.

> ▸ **"Proficiency Rubric":** This tool shows an example of a proficiency rubric for an essential standard, used for grading purposes. (Visit **go.SolutionTree.com/RTIatWork** to download this free reproducible.)

Coaching Tips

As mentioned previously, grading is very personal and often difficult to discuss. Too often, grading conversations turn into debates and teachers become defensive. When coaching about grading, consider how to initiate discussions by showing the disconnect between what grading practices could be and what they currently are. Determine the evidence and research you might share to begin or support conversations about grading. For example, gather the grading policies of various teachers on campus, and choose one or two students to show how different their grades might be based on which policy was used.

Collect articles related to grading, and use reading protocols to discuss the authors' purposes and any possible grading shifts needed. Also, initiate a grading-focused book study to have the guiding coalition engage in grading discussions. You might consider a book such as *Formative Assessment and Standards-Based Grading* (Marzano, 2010), *Grading From the Inside Out* (Schimmer, 2016), or *Grading Reform That Lasts* (Schimmer, Knight, & Townsley, 2024).

Ultimately, have the guiding coalition and collaborative teams work to align grading policies and practices with RTI and a focus on learning. Ask questions such as, "How might formative assessments factor into grading, if at all?" "How will a student's grade be affected by late work or a reassessment?" and "What is this grade telling the student, parent, or guardian about the student's learning?" Work with the guiding coalition to clarify what is tight and what is loose related to grading across campus.

Finally, think about the impact grades have on a student. Engage students in a survey or focus group to gather their feedback regarding what a grade means and how grades influence their thinking about learning and the actions they take. How do grades impact students' belief in their ability to learn? How do students see grades as reflections of their learning? Students provide insights the guiding coalition can use to shift thinking and practices related to grading.

Report Card Discussion

As a guiding coalition, complete the following activity. Members should first answer the questions individually and then engage in a discussion to begin questioning current grading practices and the shifts in practices and policies that may be needed.

Luke's First-Semester Report Card (Freshman)

REPORT CARD		
	First Semester	Second Semester
World Studies	B	
Biology	A	
Physical Education	C	
Algebra 1	D	
Freshman English	A	
Spanish 1–2	A	

1. In which subject areas is this student proficient or advanced? What evidence supports your answer? Which factors may contribute to an inaccurate determination of their proficiency?

2. What type of mathematics student is this? What evidence supports your answer? How could the evidence be flawed?

3. What assumptions might a future teacher or college make about this student?

4. Suppose Luke had three algebra 1 tests with scores of 90 percent, 95 percent, and 20 percent, which averaged to 68.3 percent. How accurately does the mark of D reflect his knowledge of the subject?

5. Suppose Luke retakes the third algebra 1 test (different test, same standards) and earns 88 percent. What should his grade in the course be?

6. In world studies, Luke earned test scores of 90 percent, 91 percent, 94 percent, and 90 percent, but had a homework score of 50 percent. The teacher averaged all the grades to 83 percent, a B. How accurately does this reflect Luke's knowledge of the standards covered in the first semester of world studies? What could be changed in this grading policy?

Grading Reflection

First, read and answer the questions individually. Then, as a guiding coalition, discuss your answers and develop a shared understanding of grading. These questions can inform how you mobilize the school to create a shared purpose and practice in grading.

1. What is the meaning of a grade at our school? For example, what does a C mean related to student learning?

2. How similar is your grading policy to the policies of others on your team?

3. Which grades are feedback showing student grade- or course-level learning?

4. How aligned are our grading practices with our focus on student learning?

5. What should be included in a student's grade?

6. When a student demonstrates a high level of learning but turns in work late, what should their grade reflect?

7. When a student is reassessed and shows proficiency, what should their grade reflect?

8. What in our grading needs to be tight (non-negotiable) and what can be loose (determined by team or teacher) in our grading system across campus?

Process for the Guiding Coalition to Draft Grading Practices and Policies

Use the following process to review and define grading practices and policies. The listed elements, often applied in the order suggested here, help with laying a foundation and then developing an implementation approach that leads to important student and family investment and clear communication.

1. **Start with team-calibrated grading of student work to reflect learning of essential standards.**

   - *Element 1:* Define essential standards and what proficiency looks like (in either deconstructed standards, rubrics, or items matched to learning goals).

   - *Element 2:* Make sure assessments clearly match the learning targets.

   - *Element 3:* Analyze student work to calibrate scoring.

2. **Engage in grading discussions for informing grading practices and report cards.**

   - *Element 4:* Engage teachers in learning more about and discussing different grading practices. Facilitate dialogue and pilot different practices. Reflect on these practices' impact on student learning and engagement. For example, try not to grade formative assessments for one unit; instead, only grade them when students show mastery. What follows are some additional questions to consider exploring.

     - Which rubrics should we use across teams and vertically through grades or courses to strengthen grading practices and student understanding of scores (for example, writing rubrics)?

     - How are we entering an assignment or assessment into the gradebook (for example, by learning success criteria, rubric criteria, or essential standards)? Will we do multiple entries for assignments or assessments? How do we label assignments so students know what their score means in terms of learning an essential standard or demonstrating proficiency with rubric criteria?

     - What categories will we establish in the learning management system to communicate externally how students are doing? What are the statements of how we do this as a school?

     - What assignments or assessments get multiple opportunities? How will we report the final score (for example, the most recent score)?

     - What do we do about behavior and work habits? How should we define what behavior and work habits we want to teach, provide feedback for, and hold students accountable to (schoolwide, class specific)? How do we report and record progress on behavior and work habits?

   - *Element 5:* Clearly define work habits and social and academic behaviors. Report work habits and achievement separately. Some assignments or assessments may include an achievement score and a work habit score. Work toward reporting them separately on the report card too.

   - *Element 6:* Decide on a process for determining a grade. Use guidelines such as most recent, most frequent, and most consistent, and avoid averaging assignments and assessments measuring the same learning.

   - *Element 7:* Communicate with parents, families, and students at the beginning and as policies and practices are piloted and adopted. Throughout the process, gather feedback about how families and students are experiencing these practices. Ensure parents, families, and students understand that effective communication about progress is not just the grade or report card, but a comprehensive system of feedback, newsletters, conferences, informal communication, student self-assessment, and the report card.

Action 5

Provide Preventions to Proactively Support Student Success

When it comes to identifying students for interventions in the timeliest way, consider the following three critical questions.

1. Can we identify students who may need additional time and support *before* they fail?

2. Can we identify students who might need help before the school year even begins?

3. Can we predict specific mistakes that students are going to make—academically and behaviorally—before their first day of a new school year?

We have asked these questions of thousands of educators at our trainings, and the overwhelming response to each is a resounding "Yes!" This means that if a school can accurately predict specific students who need extra help, and identify common mistakes students make every year, then a school can proactively provide support so students don't fail in the first place.

This proactive approach to interventions is captured in the mantra, The best intervention is prevention. In *Uniting Academic and Behavior Interventions*, our colleague Chris Weber says it this way: "If it's predictable, it's preventable" (Buffum, Mattos, Weber, & Hierck, 2015, p. 66). It is always better to proactively support student success than to wait for students to fail to give them additional support.

This is why in our RTI at Work pyramid (refer to figure 1.1, page 12) we call additional time and support provided at Tier 1 *preventions*—proactive help for targeted students before they fail.

Here's Why

The most prevalent example of the negative effects of requiring failure before providing additional help is special education. Special education has traditionally been a wait-to-fail model, meaning that most students must demonstrate a deep level of failure before the school gives them this systematic support. Because students are required to fail before help arrives, their large deficits in learning make it difficult for them to catch up. Nipping problems and closing gaps when they are small make catching up much more doable.

While special education usually requires long-term failure, even a short delay in providing additional time and support can potentially have severe consequences for students. For example, a study of high schools in the Chicago area found that 70 to 80 percent of students who fail at least one course their freshman year of high school do not graduate (Wyner, Bridgeland, & Diiulio, 2007).

So, a ninth grader who fails a required class the first semester of their freshman year is significantly more likely to later drop out of school than a student who is on track in credits entering their sophomore year. Yet how do many high schools identify freshmen who need additional help? They do it with failing grades on the students' first report card. The first weeks of high school can have a long-lasting impact on future years of success. As a team, ask the following.

▶ Can a high school staff proactively identify incoming freshmen who might need extra help, even before their first day of ninth grade?

▶ Can they predict the types of mistakes freshmen make every year?

Absolutely! This means preventions can be systematically planned and targeted to support freshmen beginning on the first day of school.

Here's How

While we can't proactively predict every student who might need additional help, we can use four reliable criteria to catch many students before they fail.

1. **Previous struggles:** If a student ended a school year with clearly identified concerns, shouldn't the educators who will serve the student the following year expect to provide additional help? How many students at risk return from summer break all caught up and ready to succeed? A guiding coalition can proactively identify these students at the end of each school year and plan for preventions starting day one of the next year. (We discuss this process in more detail in chapter 7, action 2, page 271.)

2. **Gaps in prerequisite skills:** Immediate prerequisite skills, knowledge, and behaviors are usually required in order to learn new essential grade-level curriculum. If a student lacks a specific prerequisite skill, they will likely struggle with mastering the next essential standard in that learning progression. Teacher teams can screen students on specific immediate prerequisite skills before they begin instruction on new essential standards, and then use this information to target preventions to specific students. (We go deeper into how to provide these preventions in chapter 5, action 2, page 211.)

3. **Developmental needs:** Children develop physically and cognitively in certain stages. With these stages come the acquisition of both certain abilities and certain challenges that can disrupt a student's success in school. For example, we know that the human brain develops the ability to think abstractly during adolescence or puberty. So, if an essential middle school academic standard requires abstract thinking, we should be able to predict that some students will struggle with learning this skill if we present information through abstract representations. It is not that these students can't learn an abstract thinking standard, but we must represent it in a concrete way, such as through the use of a physical model or visual representation.

4. **Transitional needs:** If there is one grade level that best understands the power of prevention, it is kindergarten. Kindergarten teachers know many of their students are transitioning to a school setting for the first time, and they expect many to start the year lacking several skills and behaviors needed to function in a classroom setting. Experienced primary teachers can predict the common mistakes that students make every year. The simplest tasks, like lining up or sitting on the floor for instruction, are foreign concepts to some students. So, while kindergarten teachers would prefer to begin teaching the required curriculum the first day of school, they know that taking the time to proactively teach these behaviors ultimately saves time. They have students repeatedly practice getting in and out of a line, walking in a line, and keeping their hands and bodies to themselves while in the line, and they praise students for forming the best line they have ever seen.

The following is a real-life example of prevention thinking and action.

The guiding coalition at Pioneer Middle School in Tustin, California, reviewed its end-of-year intervention data and noticed this trend: the incoming sixth-grade class made up about one-third of the school's enrollment, but during the first semester, over half the students identified for Tier 2 academic and behavior interventions were sixth graders. This was hardly surprising, as incoming sixth graders primarily came from feeder elementary schools structured around self-contained class-rooms, and now they were transitioning to a seven-period schedule and multiple teacher expectations. The guiding coalition decided that if sixth graders struggled with this transition every year, its school could proactively address these needs. Over a couple of years, the school developed the following Tier 1 preventions to address predictable concerns when new students enrolled.

▶ **Fifth-grade orientation:** Five district elementary schools sent students to Pioneer Middle School. Pioneer's administrative team worked with these schools to design an orientation process that began in March to prepare next year's sixth graders. The orientation process included three site visits to Pioneer, a fifth-grade parent night, and a sixth-grade registration day before the first day of school.

▶ **Sixth-grade mentors:** Through sixth-grade English classes, the school placed each sixth grader in a small group of about seven to ten fellow students. Then it assigned each group an upper-grade mentor. Upper-grade students applied to be mentors and were selected based on their ability to model and teach the school's essential academic and social behaviors. Mentors met with their groups every week throughout the year. The counseling staff designed the topics of discussion for each week, and they helped students learn the "Wildcat Way."

▶ **New student buddies:** The school assigned a student buddy to each student who was new to Pioneer as an upper-grade student. These buddies, arranged by the counseling staff, helped the new students transition to the school.

This is an example of planning for proactive support. If we can predict what might challenge students, and proactively remove these obstacles, then more students will have immediate success and fewer will need additional help at Tier 2. We offer these options not as specific preventions to copy, but instead as samples of a process that can be replicated at any school.

Helpful Tool

The following tool will help you accomplish the work for this essential action.

▶ **"Preventions to Proactively Support Student Success" (page 196):** This tool can help teams identify student needs that require preventive support and then identify strategies to determine the students who should receive that support.

Coaching Tips

Who better to proactively plan preventive strategies to support students' success than the teachers who will be working with those students daily? No one! That said, the guiding coalition should take the lead, designating time for staff to build a shared understanding of the need for preventions and brainstorm possible solutions. This discussion should take place annually—before the school year begins and once teachers have received their class lists. While they are still together as a staff, we recommend having teams spend thirty to forty minutes together to begin their work. This allows for cross-team sharing and vertical articulation before they head off to plan on their own.

As noted in previous sections, the basic processes for facilitating the development of a schoolwide culture of collective responsibility and for building a schoolwide system in support of all students learning at high levels are the same. Consider the following five steps.

1. Dialogue and learn together to build shared understanding.

2. Ensure opportunities for teachers to brainstorm ideas and provide input.

3. Facilitate sharing of information across teams.

4. Establish and communicate clear implementation expectations for all staff and teams, and articulate how you will hold teachers and teams accountable.

5. Revisit action plans to celebrate successes and modify plans as needed.

Keep in mind that none of these steps produces results unless all guiding coalition members hold themselves and others accountable for following through. Jonathon Saphier (2005), founder and president of Research for Better Teaching, writes:

> Day after day in schools across America, change initiatives, instructional improvement, and better results for children are blocked, sabotaged, or killed through silence and inaction. . . . This lack of follow-through results from the avoidance or inability to face conflict openly and make it a creative source of energy among educators. (p. 37)

To summarize, without commitment to and accountability for decisions made about schoolwide changes, the result may be inaction. A significant part of the guiding coalition's role is to collectively agree on strategies for addressing resistance or sabotage.

Preventions to Proactively Support Student Success

As a team, brainstorm typical skills and needs for preventive support and strategies or tools for identifying students requiring that support. Review information on incoming students, assess as necessary, and identify those who require proactive preventions. Create a team plan of action, and forward recommendations to the guiding coalition for additional schoolwide support. Revisit prevention planning quarterly to ensure no student slips through the cracks.

Team: _____

Reliable Criterion	Strategy or Tool for Identifying Students and Their Needs	Students Needing Support	Skills or Needs Requiring Support	Team Actions	Recommendations to the Guiding Coalition
Previous Struggles					
Gaps in Prerequisite Skills					
Predictable Developmental Needs					
Transitional Needs					

Conclusion

The essential actions in chapters 2, 3, and 4 are the critical building blocks needed to develop an effective Tier 1 core instructional program. Building this foundation takes time, and attacking every essential action in the first year might not be doable or prudent. If you are just starting the journey, a realistic goal for the first year would be to address the following.

- ▶ **Chapter 2:** Essential actions 1, 2, 3, 4, and 5
- ▶ **Chapter 3:** Essential actions 1, 4, and 5
- ▶ **Chapter 4:** Essential actions 1 and 2

When Tier 1 is implemented well, most students should be successfully learning essential grade-level curriculum and consistently demonstrating essential behaviors. But no matter how well a school implements these essential actions, some students will need additional time and support. In the next two chapters (part two), we discuss the essential actions needed at Tier 2 to ensure all students master the essential grade-level standards for future success.

PART TWO

TIER 2 ESSENTIAL ACTIONS

CHAPTER 5

Tier 2 Teacher Team Essential Actions

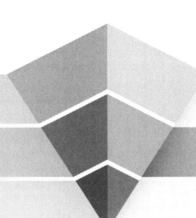

> After forty years of intensive research on school learning in the United States as well as abroad, my major conclusion is: What any person in the world can learn, almost all persons can learn if provided with appropriate prior and current conditions of learning.
>
> **—Benjamin Bloom**

In this chapter, we focus on the middle-right portion of the RTI at Work pyramid (see figure 5.1, page 202). Let us reconsider what this portion of the pyramid visually represents.

▶ This box is part of Tier 2, which represents how a school provides targeted students with the additional time and support needed to master the standards deemed absolutely essential to success in the next grade or course.

▶ This box is on the right side of the pyramid, which represents outcomes that the school's collaborative teacher teams lead. The essential actions in this chapter directly relate to the essential academic standards for each grade level or course offered in a school, so the teachers who identified these standards and teach these classes are best trained and positioned to take lead responsibility for these interventions as well as extensions for students who have already learned the essential standards.

Note that Tier 2 is divided into two sections—teacher team responsibilities and guiding coalition responsibilities. This is because there are two primary reasons why students struggle in school—academic needs and behavioral needs.

1. **Academic interventions:** These provide additional time and support for targeted students who have not yet mastered how to achieve specific academic essentials. For example, an essential academic standard in a student's mathematics class might be the ability to solve and graph a linear equation. At the end of the unit on this standard, if the student has not yet mastered the mathematical skills needed to demonstrate proficiency, additional learning happens through team-designed Tier 2 learning experiences.

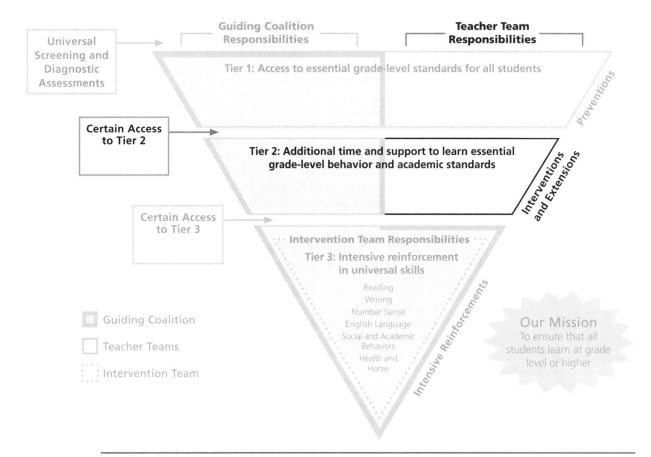

FIGURE 5.1: Focus on Tier 2 teacher team essential actions.

2. **Behavior interventions:** These provide additional time and support for targeted students who have not mastered specific essential behaviors.

We often ask educators, "How many of you have academic and behavioral needs in the same intervention?" Usually, most of the educators raise their hands. Combining academic and behavioral needs in the same intervention group is like putting together gasoline and a match. While a student can have both academic and behavioral needs, each requires a different intervention. An important guiding principle of effective interventions is this: target the cause of the problem, not the symptom. Students may fail the same test, but it does not mean they struggled for the same reason. Some students fail due to lacking academic skills, while others fail because of deficits in essential behaviors. Target the right cause, and the intervention is much more likely to be effective.

In this chapter, we discuss the actions collaborative teacher teams (not just individual teachers) can take when students have not mastered essential academic outcomes as part of Tier 1 instruction. Teachers must move on to the next unit of instruction or next set of skills even when some students have not yet demonstrated learning of what the teachers identified as essential. Rather than let these students struggle, the school must provide a system of Tier 2 interventions through which these students receive the additional time and support they need to master the essentials without missing initial instruction in the new set of essentials.

The essential actions that teacher teams must lead at Tier 2 are as follows.

1. Design and lead Tier 2 interventions for essential academic standards.

2. Identify and target immediate prerequisite skills.

3. Monitor the progress of students receiving Tier 2 academic interventions.

4. Extend student learning.

Let's consider the specifics of each essential action.

Action 1

Design and Lead Tier 2 Interventions for Essential Academic Standards

In chapter 3 (page 81), we demonstrated the importance of having teacher teams identify essential standards, unwrap them into learning targets, and develop a unit assessment plan, which includes a common end-of-unit assessment. For this first essential action (led by teacher teams), teachers have given the common end-of-unit assessment and analyzed the results, and some students are still not able to demonstrate mastery of specific essential standards—the learning outcomes that have been deemed indispensable for success in the next grade or course (see chapter 3, action 5, page 138). If a school is truly committed to ensuring all students learn at grade level or better every year, it must have a systematic process to guarantee the extra time and support needed to learn these vital learning outcomes by the end of the school year. This is the purpose of Tier 2—targeted interventions that supplement the instruction and proactive prevention that were part of the teams' Tier 1 instruction.

Teacher teams take the lead in designing Tier 2 interventions for identified essential standards because they are the same educators who:

▶ Are credentialed and trained in particular grade levels and disciplines

▶ Help prioritize the essential standards for their course or grade level

▶ Deconstruct the essential standards into learning targets

▶ Build, administer, and score the common formative assessments and common end-of-unit assessments at the target level

▶ Teach students each day

Who else would take the lead in this important work? Teachers who have the expertise to teach and to ensure essential grade- and course-level standards are best positioned to develop new and different interventions to support students in learning essential standards.

Additionally, we cannot stress these two points strongly enough.

1. **Team members take collective responsibility for each student's success:** Team members do not keep their own students. Students are grouped across classrooms by need, and teachers are assigned by expertise. This is a much more efficient and effective way to intervene in comparison to keeping one's own students and trying to differentiate to multiple needs in each class.

2. **Tier 2 support is provided in addition to Tier 1, not in place of it:** Students cannot miss instruction on new essential curriculum to receive Tier 2 interventions.

This means teacher teams must have a streamlined way of scheduling students into flexible time that does not involve laborious paperwork. Many schools are increasingly utilizing technology, such as shared Google Docs, Google Sheets, or purchased computer programs, to reduce the paperwork load in targeting Tier 2 interventions and also keep a record of their efforts for each student to guide future interventions. During flexible time, teachers can help students who demonstrate mastery extend their learning (action 4 in this chapter, page 223), thereby answering PLC critical question four: "How will we extend the learning for students who are already proficient?" (DuFour et al., 2024, p. 44). (We address how to dedicate Tier 2 time in your master schedule in chapter 6, action 1, page 232.) This action step supports teacher teams in how to best plan and implement Tier 2 academic interventions.

Here's Why

The purpose of planning and implementing Tier 2 interventions goes back to our fundamental assumptions: some students will need more time to learn at high levels, and students do not all learn in the same way. As teachers get to know their students and look at assessment evidence, clearer strategies emerge to help students learn by truly meeting them where they are and responding to where they need to go in order to learn essential grade-level standards.

Intentionally, teams assess at grade level—this ensures access to grade-level standards. Sometimes, students who are far behind receive a lot of instruction below grade level, which means those students have little possibility of reaching grade-level standards. Teams assess at grade level to keep standards high, and then respond in their instruction and intervention to support and ensure student learning. When the guiding coalition builds Tier 2 time into the master schedule, and teacher teams analyze student work and data from common end-of-unit assessments to plan instruction, they create the conditions that ensure time and below-grade-level expectations won't be reasons students do not achieve.

Designing Tier 2 interventions does not mean teachers are sending students who did not learn essential standards to supplemental staff (often an interventionist) to be "fixed"; rather, the teachers lead the interventions themselves. Supplemental staff might be part of Tier 2 interventions, but they are not solely responsible. Despite teachers' differentiating and responding to common formative assessment data using a flex day or stations during a unit (see chapter 3, action 5, page 138), some students still need additional time and support to learn the essential standards taught while teams begin to address the next unit's Tier 1 instruction (as shown in the upper-left part of the team teaching-assessing-learning cycle in figure 3.2, page 83).

Students who have not yet learned the essential standards from the previous unit by the common end-of-unit assessment date will most likely have different targeted needs to learn them. Hence, the teacher team must identify the students needing targeted support and plan for each Tier 2 intervention to grow student learning. Intentionally planning and implementing Tier 2 interventions leads to higher achievement.

Here's How

Collaborative teams design Tier 2 interventions based on results from common formative and end-of-unit assessments. As we have emphasized throughout this book, the more targeted an intervention is, the more likely it will work. This means Tier 2 interventions most often drill down from the full essential standard to the target level. Which parts of the standard are causing students to struggle? We call this focusing on causes (targets), not symptoms (mastery of the entire standard not demonstrated—or failure).

As we pointed out in chapter 3, some essential standards at the primary level are discrete and don't have many learning targets (for example, students will count to 100). However, beginning in grade 2 and beyond, most academic content standards are composed of many different targets, as shown in the "Sample Grade 3 Mathematics Unit Assessment Plan" (page 107) and "Sample Grade 9

ELA Unit Assessment Plan" (page 110). To help students who are struggling to master essential standards, we need to know which part or parts are problematic for each student.

The collaborative teacher team's discussion about the common assessment results (both formative and end-of-unit) includes recognizing how all the team's students collectively did as well as how teachers compare (which teacher or teachers on the team seem to have had greater success with certain learning targets). This leads to a discussion of which strategies and materials might have the greatest impact on student achievement, not who the best teacher is. Our colleague Jon Yost often says, "Data [are] for learning, not for judging" (J. Yost, personal communication, February 7, 2022).

What can we learn about student thinking and teacher instruction from the data? This information is important in two ways. First, the team might assign students struggling with certain learning targets to the teacher who had the strongest results on those same targets. Keep in mind sometimes one teacher does not have significantly better results than another, in which case the teacher team decides which teacher should work with each group of students. This is not about evaluating a teacher's effectiveness, as all educators have strengths and areas of growth. As a team, teachers lean into their strengths. This is about collectively understanding how to best serve the students' needs and taking action to do so. Second, the team records this discussion so the following year, when it is teaching these same essential standards, the entire team can utilize the most powerful strategies as part of its Tier 1 instruction.

Once teacher teams meet to both identify which students need a little more time and support to master essential standards and to discuss which teacher might work best with each group based on assessment results, the guiding coalition must establish a schedule ensuring students receive this help without missing instruction in new essential standards. This is commonly referred to as *flexible time* built into the school timetable. We suggest scheduling this flexible time at least two days per week, for about thirty minutes.

We recommend the following six-step process to help teacher teams design Tier 2 interventions.

1. **Identify concerns:** The teacher team uses the common end-of-unit assessment data to discuss team members' concerns about some of the students who were not successful. The team looks for common patterns affecting groups of students and digs down to discover what may be preventing individual students from having success. It also discusses concerns about the assessment itself and whether it is constructed to yield valid and reliable information about the students.

2. **Determine the cause:** The teacher team should consider the various formative assessment information it gathers during Tier 1 instruction, as well as the end-of-unit assessment results, to more specifically diagnose the causes leading some students not to master essential standards. Typically, this discussion results in forming three to five different intervention groupings at a grade level or within a particular course. Each grouping reflects different causes leading to students' struggles.

3. **Target the desired outcome:** The teacher team now discusses exactly what desired outcome each grouping of students must achieve as a result of the supplemental Tier 2 interventions. Rather than discussing what students have not been able to do, the team states exactly what it wants them to be able to do. For example, a third-grade mathematics intervention group might desire that students will be able to find the unknown number (variable) in a multiplication equation.

4. **Design intervention steps:** Next, the teacher team brainstorms potential intervention strategies for each targeted group and shares any available resources with the staff assigned to particular groups. This is where teachers get creative and tap into additional

research-based instructional strategies they did not use during Tier 1 instruction. Sometimes, these strategies emerge as team members compare their scores with one another. When one teacher records results that are significantly better than those of their teammates, the teachers collectively inquire about how that teacher produced those results. What strategies, materials, and techniques did they use?

In the primary grades, especially in reading, these strategies might be part of a scientific, research-based intervention program. Many excellent programs exist to help primary teachers with students who need assistance with phonological awareness, decoding, fluency, and comprehension. However, beginning in third grade, Tier 2 interventions more often deal with academic content standards in which knowledge and reasoning must be applied to demonstrate mastery of a standard.

Prepackaged Tier 2 intervention programs are rarely available for students requiring additional time and support with academic content standards. For example, we do not know of a program one can purchase that is designed to help students struggling with mitosis and meiosis. However, if your team has access to a computer program designed for Tier 2 interventions, often in mathematics or reading, the team, not the program, must strategically choose the modules used for intervention based on student need, and simultaneously work with small groups using live instruction for Tier 2 interventions.

Once students move beyond the primary grades, support with foundational reading skills should be part of a school's Tier 3 program. Students struggling with mitosis and meiosis, for example, need targeted instructional strategies at Tier 2 to help them master these important concepts, and some also require ongoing Tier 3 intensive reinforcement to learn universal skills (reading comprehension) and knowledge they should have mastered in prior grades. We call that *core (Tier 1)*; *core (Tier 1) and more (Tier 2)*; and *core (Tier 1) and more (Tier 2), and more (Tier 3)*. Some students require all three.

5. **Monitor progress:** The team now decides what tools to use to monitor the progress of students receiving the supplemental Tier 2 interventions. Again, unless we are dealing with primary students who are struggling with reading skills, the common end-of-unit assessment questions provide much, if not all, of what we need to know about whether a student has achieved mastery of a learning target (or targets) underpinning an essential standard. (We dig deeper into this step in action 3, page 219.)

6. **Assign lead responsibility:** Next, the teacher team discusses which staff members are most highly qualified to help which students. During this important step, the team should consider the following.

   - Which staff have specialized training in a particular area (for example, phonemic awareness)?

   - Which staff recorded stronger results on particular targets from the end-of-unit assessment than other teachers on the team?

   - Which additional staff (administrators, counselors, or instructional aides) might be trained and able to assist certain groups of students?

   - How will additional staff providing interventions gain understanding of the essential standards assessed, the learning targets supporting the standards, and the exact causes impacting student achievement?

We capture this six-step process in the reproducible "RTI at Work Pro-Solve Intervention Targeting Process: Tier 1 and Tier 2" (page 209), which separates academic skills from behavioral issues. The collaborative teacher team focuses its attention on academic issues first because it has lead responsibility for this part of the split pyramid supporting students' academic learning.

With all the pressures from the various accountability programs at the district and state or provincial levels, it is imperative that teams have a focused approach to supplemental Tier 2 interventions. These interventions should represent a little more help with the essential standards the teacher teams prioritized, not with everything on a state or provincial test. Schools that try to intervene on everything in the curriculum quickly become exhausted and frustrated.

It's important to note that Tier 2 help should not be reduced to a purchased program. Unless the essential standards directly relate to specific skills on the reading spectrum, Tier 2 interventions probably won't come from such a program. Because we want these interventions to go beyond "more of what didn't work the first time—louder and slower," teams use professional protocols, like the one previously described, to determine which teacher or teachers are best equipped to help a particular group of students.

Additionally, teams should not refer to students as *Tier 2 kids*; there simply are some students who might need Tier 2 interventions. Supplemental Tier 2 interventions should be fluid and flexible. Students should be released as soon as they demonstrate mastery and should never be "trapped" in a Tier 2 intervention for a predetermined amount of time. It is ridiculous to assume that all students in a school or district require precisely the same amount of additional time and support to master essential standards.

Helpful Tools

The following tools will help you accomplish the work for this essential action.

- ▶ **"RTI at Work Pro-Solve Intervention Targeting Process: Tier 1 and Tier 2" (page 209):** Teams can use this form to separate academic skills from behavioral issues and target each student's particular needs for intervention.

- ▶ **"Team Protocol for Reviewing Student Work to Plan Tier 1 or Tier 2 Responses" (see chapter 3, action 5, page 149):** Teacher teams use this protocol to plan Tier 1 or Tier 2 responses by reviewing student work from common formative or end-of-unit assessments.

- ▶ **"KASAB Chart" (for the guiding coalition, page 210):** Teams can use this chart to define the knowledge, attitudes, skills, aspirations, and behaviors needed for intended learning and changes to positively impact student success.

- ▶ **Chapter 8 of *Learning by Doing, Fourth Edition* (DuFour et al., 2024), "Responding When Some Students Don't Learn":** This chapter provides foundational content knowledge as well as tools that can help schools accomplish the action steps outlined in this section.

- ▶ *It's About Time: Planning Interventions and Extensions in Elementary School* **(Buffum & Mattos, 2015) and** *It's About Time: Planning Interventions and Extensions in Secondary School* **(Mattos & Buffum, 2015):** These books are great resources for guiding coalitions to consult as they build in intentional time and understand how to design the best workflow for teacher teams in ensuring Tier 2 intervention effectiveness.

- ▶ *Best Practices at Tier 2: Supplemental Interventions for Additional Student Support, Elementary* **(Kramer, Sonju, Mattos, & Buffum, 2021) and** *Best Practices at Tier 2:*

***Supplemental Interventions for Additional Student Support, Secondary* (Sonju, Kramer, Mattos, & Buffum, 2019):** These resources dig deeper into specific, proven practices to guide Tier 2 academic interventions.

Coaching Tips

Implementing new ways of helping students learn is much more about building relationships and learning than it is about completing tasks and to-do lists. With that in mind, the most important work guiding coalition members do, as coaches, is inspire and support those they coach to become model learners. And what does it mean to be a model learner? A *model learner*, we propose, is an educator who engages in study and constant practice with a commitment to continuous improvement and improved results. This is the work of leading change!

In support of teacher teams as they design and implement Tier 2 interventions, it is incumbent on the guiding coalition to model, check for understanding, clarify, and celebrate progress teams make for each of the six steps. A helpful tool for coaches is a KASAB chart (Killion, 2008), which can help them define the essential knowledge, attitudes, skills, aspirations, and behaviors needed for the intended learning and changes to positively impact student success. As coaches work alongside teachers and teams, a KASAB chart helps clarify what to look for, listen for, and provide feedback on.

Figure 5.2 shows a completed KASAB chart that identifies teacher changes needed for designing and implementing Tier 2 interventions. (See page 210 for a blank reproducible version of this chart.) This chart may also be helpful as an assessment tool to determine current levels of implementation and, in turn, what type of coaching support is needed.

Types of Change	Teachers
Knowledge: Conceptual understanding of information, theories, principles, and research	Teachers understand the academic content of essential standards they have identified and the rationale for prioritizing their collaborative work on them.
Attitudes: Beliefs about the value of particular information or strategies	Teachers believe in the importance of mastery rather than coverage and in the efficacy of collaboration to ensure high levels of learning for all students.
Skills: Strategies or processes to apply knowledge	Teachers share and use evidence-based instructional strategies to assist all students in demonstrating mastery of essential standards.
Aspirations: Desire and internal motivation to engage in a certain practice	Teachers demonstrate a sincere desire for all to learn at high levels, and they take ownership for making it happen.
Behaviors: Consistent application of knowledge and skills	Teachers consistently use common formative and end-of-unit assessments to inform their instruction and to collaboratively design and implement Tier 2 interventions.

FIGURE 5.2: KASAB chart example.

Simply stated, pay attention to adult learners! They need and deserve differentiated amounts of time and levels of support just as much as the students they serve.

RTI at Work Pro-Solve Intervention Targeting Process: Tier 1 and Tier 2

Student: _____

Participant: _____

Meeting date: _____

Targeted Outcomes		1. Concern	2. Cause	3. Desired Outcomes	4. Intervention Steps	5. Who Takes Responsibility
Led by Teacher Teams	Essential Standards					
	Immediate Prerequisite Skills					
	English Language					
Led by Guiding Coalition	Academic Behaviors					
	Social Behaviors					
	Health and Home					

Next meeting date: _____

Source: Buffum, A., Mattos, M., Weber, C., & Hierck, T. (2015). Uniting academic and behavior interventions: Solving the skill or will dilemma. Bloomington, IN: Solution Tree Press.

KASAB Chart

Use the following chart to define the knowledge, attitudes, skills, aspirations, and behaviors needed for the intended learning and changes adults must embrace to positively impact student success.

Types of Change	Teachers
Knowledge:	
Attitudes:	
Skills:	
Aspirations:	
Behaviors:	

Action 2

Identify and Target Immediate Prerequisite Skills

There are two types of prerequisite academic skills students need to be successful at learning essential grade-level standards. *Immediate prerequisite skills* and vocabulary often precede current instruction by a few units, a few weeks, or, at most, the previous year. *Foundational prerequisite skills* come from instruction that should have been learned years ago, usually two or more years previous. Teams determine immediate prerequisite skills for possible Tier 2 intervention, while foundational prerequisite skills are learned in Tier 3 intensive reinforcement of universal skills.

For example, in third grade, students are expected to add and subtract multidigit numbers with regrouping using strategies based on place value. A foundational prerequisite skill might be the ability to add and subtract single-digit numbers, an essential kindergarten or first-grade standard. Students struggling with these kinds of learning gaps receive intensive reinforcement in Tier 3 (which we discuss in chapter 7, page 263). Other students might struggle with this essential grade 3 standard not because they are unable to add and subtract single-digit numbers, but because they are unable to recognize when regrouping is necessary with two-digit numbers, a second-grade skill.

While some students demonstrate mastery of this skill when taught, others need to re-engage in learning this essential immediate prerequisite skill to demonstrate mastery in adding and subtracting multidigit numbers. This team intervention might occur as part of supplemental Tier 2 interventions or as part of the teaching-assessing-learning cycle in Tier 1.

The third column of the "Essential Standards Chart" (see chapter 3, action 1, page 93) asks teacher teams to identify and discuss what immediate prerequisite skills and vocabulary students need to master a particular essential standard. Teams determine immediate prerequisite skills to use in Tier 1 or Tier 2 instruction, while universal foundational skills are part of Tier 3.

Teams should utilize the information from the essential standards chart, analyzing the causes of student struggles, as they consider how to design Tier 2 interventions. Some students don't just need more time to practice; instead, they need reinforcement of immediate prerequisite skills required to master the current essential standard.

If a team wants to improve its results, it should consider assessing for immediate prerequisite, or prior, skills as part of the Tier 1 team teaching-assessing-learning cycle, as shown in the top-right portion of figure 5.3 (page 212). This kind of assessment acts like a screener and is brief—done unit by unit, essential standard by essential standard—as opposed to universal screening, which is done as early as possible in a school year to proactively identify students for Tier 3 intensive reinforcement in universal foundational skills.

As part of their unit assessment plan, collaborative teacher teams consider how and when to assess prerequisites for the particular unit of instruction. For example, a team might decide to administer a brief assessment about two weeks before instruction begins on a new unit or essential standard. The information from this assessment might tell team members that many students have some gaps in immediate prerequisite skills and vocabulary, leading teachers, during the two weeks prior to introducing the new unit or standard, to start each lesson with a sponge activity directly related to these prerequisite skill gaps.

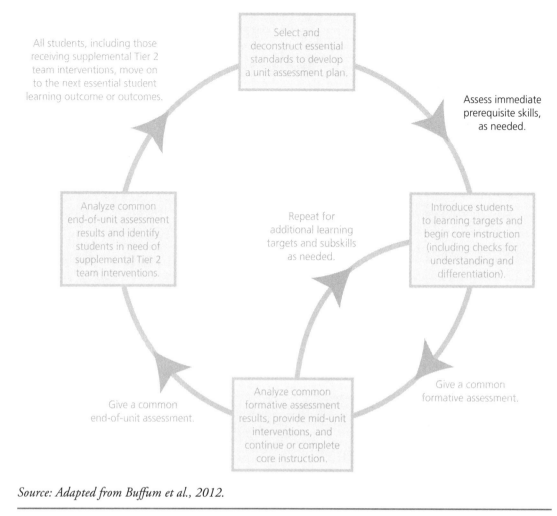

Source: Adapted from Buffum et al., 2012.

FIGURE 5.3: Team teaching-assessing-learning cycle—Assess immediate prerequisite skills.

It might also be the case that a team already knows which students need additional support with identified prerequisite skills from information gleaned when teaching previous essential standards. If the team already has the needed knowledge about prerequisite skills, a screener is unnecessary. This Tier 1 application of assessing prerequisite skills truly represents our proclamation that the best intervention is prevention.

Here's Why

Tier 2 interventions should target the causes of student struggles. It is important to ask questions such as the following about why a student was unable to demonstrate mastery of an essential standard.

- ▸ Does the student need more time to master the standard?
- ▸ Does the student lack motivation (an essential academic behavior), so they won't demonstrate the effort needed to learn the standard?
- ▸ Did the student not understand the way the standard was taught the first time?
- ▸ Does the student not have the foundational skills from prior years related to mastery of the standard?
- ▸ Does the student not have the immediate prerequisite skills to master the standard?

If, for example, the team's short assessment of prerequisite skills indicates a direct link between the student's inability to demonstrate mastery and a lack of immediate prerequisite skills, then Tier 2 interventions would focus first on strengthening these skills as the primary cause of the student's struggles. This is especially true of knowledge that is procedural in nature. *Procedural knowledge* (for example, analyzing the causes and effects of a historical event) involves knowing how to do something, and it often includes a step-by-step process, as opposed to *declarative knowledge*, which involves knowing that something is true (for example, knowing the stages of the water cycle).

Students struggling with declarative knowledge might need just a little more time to master knowing something, while students struggling with procedural knowledge might need to strengthen the immediate prerequisite skills that are part of the learning progression to achieve the standard. This difference demonstrates why screening for immediate prerequisite skills, or intentionally gathering the information from prior assessments, is so important in designing interventions for students struggling with essential procedural knowledge standards.

One of the lasting educational impacts of the COVID-19 pandemic is that more students are entering each school year with gaps in previous learning. Because it is impossible to reteach years of previous content, preteaching immediate prerequisite skills in a timely and targeted way is required as part of best first core instruction.

Here's How

Collaborative teacher teams use the information from the third column of the essential standards chart to build brief common assessments to use as screeners for students. For example, figure 5.4 (page 214) shows an essential standards chart for students in grade 5 mathematics. (See chapter 3, action 1, page 93, for a blank reproducible version of this figure.)

Teacher teams should create and administer a short preassessment, if needed, a week or two before teaching this standard to find out how many and which students do not know how to add and subtract fractions with like denominators or how to generate equivalent fractions.

As shown in figure 5.5 (page 215), team members then use this information to help plan their Tier 1 instruction. If most students fail to show mastery of the prerequisite skills on the preassessment, the team might decide to start the next unit with a reteaching of immediate prerequisite skills. If fewer students lack the immediate prerequisite skills, the team might discuss how it will review this information with targeted students prior to instruction on the essential standard; for example, the team might utilize small groups or Tier 2 intervention to provide additional instructional time before the next unit begins. The team can use this same information to inform the conversation about designing Tier 2 interventions after the end-of-unit assessment, which may reveal that some students have not mastered the essential standard. Ask, "To what extent is this the result of lacking immediate prerequisite skills? Or is another skill or misconception influencing students' current level of proficiency?"

It is highly likely that teams already have examples of actual prompts they would use to assemble a short common assessment for prerequisite skills, whether in their own materials or those of a prior grade or course. They could pull many of these items from existing assessments and assemble them into a quick screener. Assembling these brief assessment tools helps guarantee a good match between what teams are assessing and what they want all students to master. It also helps teams design better supplemental Tier 2 interventions because they selected or constructed the screener items.

What Do We Expect Students to Learn?

Grade: Fifth | Subject: Mathematics | Semester: First | Team Members: N. Dimich and S. Schuhl

Description of Standard	Example of Grade- or Course-Level Rigor	Immediate Prerequisite Skills	When Proficiency Is Expected	Common Formative and End-of-Unit Assessments	Extension
What is the essential standard to be learned? Describe it in student-friendly language, but avoid reducing the cognitive level of the standard.	What does proficient student work look like? Provide an example or description of the items and tasks to use to demonstrate proficiency.	What prior knowledge, skills, and vocabulary are needed for a student to master this standard?	When will this standard be taught, and when will proficiency be expected?	What common assessments will be used to measure student mastery?	What will we do when students have already learned this standard?
I can add and subtract fractions with unlike denominators.	$\frac{3}{5} + \frac{5}{6} = ?$ $2\frac{1}{2} - \frac{3}{5} = ?$	Add and subtract fractions with like denominators. Generate equivalent fractions.	February	Administer team CFAs during the unit and the team common end-of-unit assessment.	Create word problems that require adding and subtracting fractions with unlike denominators. Measure objects using a custom ruler, and simplify measurements. Compare the measurements collected for different-sized objects (for example, how much taller is the doorframe than it is wide?).

FIGURE 5.4: Fifth-grade mathematics sample essential standards chart.

Essential Standard

Add and subtract fractions with unlike denominators (including mixed numbers) by replacing given fractions with equivalent fractions to produce an equivalent sum or difference of fractions with like denominators.

Immediate Prerequisite Skill	Tier 1 Strategies *During Grade- or Course-Level Learning*	Tier 2 Strategies *Before Teaching the Essential Standard*
Add and subtract fractions with like denominators.	For the bell-ringer activity, give students fractions to add and subtract that have like denominators. Follow the learning progression used to teach the essential standard. 1. Add fractions and mixed numbers with like denominators. 2. Subtract fractions and mixed numbers with like denominators that do not require regrouping. 3. Subtract fractions and mixed numbers with like denominators that require regrouping.	• Use fraction tiles to add and subtract fractions with like denominators. • Use number lines to add and subtract fractions with like denominators.
Generate equivalent fractions.	On the first day of the unit, use part of the mathematics block to have student pairs generate equivalent fractions by giving the students problems with an initial fraction equal to another fraction with a different denominator and a missing numerator. Students find the missing numerator. Allow students to use fraction tiles, graph paper (draw the fraction), and number lines. Include second fractions whose denominators are multiples of the denominators in the initial fractions. Include mixed numbers.	• Use fraction tiles to generate equivalent fractions (for example, $\frac{1}{2} = \frac{?}{8}$). • Use double number lines to generate equivalent fractions. • Use graph paper or picture models to generate equivalent fractions.

FIGURE 5.5: Fifth-grade sample immediate prerequisite skill planning.

Some schools also employ computer programs to assist with Tier 2 interventions. It is important that teams not rely on a computer assessment to determine students' needs, because the initial computer assessment often serves as a universal screener and is not specific to essential standards. Instead, when a team identifies students in need of specific immediate prerequisite skills, it should assign the students computer program modules that match the prerequisite skills as one part of a Tier 2 intervention. Live instruction is also needed for effective Tier 2 learning experiences.

Teacher teams create Tier 2 experiences that will identify and support immediate prerequisite skills needed to achieve essential standards informed by the "Essential Standards Chart" reproducible. The teams can choose from several resources to support student learning of these prerequisite skills, whether before or after an essential standard is taught.

Helpful Tools

The following tools will help you accomplish the work for this essential action.

▶ **"Essential Standards Chart" (see chapter 3, action 1, page 93):** This powerful tool will assist teacher teams in identifying and creating a common understanding of their essential standards.

▶ **"Immediate Prerequisite Skills Planning Template" (page 218):** This discussion tool allows teams to record their plans to address prerequisite skills to an essential standard before or during a unit.

▶ **"Immediate Prerequisite Skills Plan: Grade 4 ELA Example":** This example illustrates how a grade 4 team focused on the essential standard *compare and contrast two texts on the same topic* and developed a plan for addressing the immediate prerequisite skills during Tier 1 and Tier 2 instruction. (Visit **go.SolutionTree.com/RTIatWork** to download this free reproducible.)

Coaching Tips

Coaches need to bring the concept of assessing for immediate prerequisite skills to the teams' attention as they explore avenues of improvement. For teams that are still in the process of learning, practicing, and gaining confidence in the team teaching-assessing-learning cycle, introducing assessments for prerequisite skills as a mandate may overwhelm them, frustrate them, or cause resistance. We recommend short common assessments for prerequisite skills as a way to improve results, rather than as an essential step in the process of building student success. However, connecting current knowledge to prior knowledge during instruction is integral to student learning, so as a coach, do discuss with teams how to make this connection while they are teaching the unit, whether or not an initial prerequisite common assessment has been done.

Once teams are ready to consider assessing for prerequisite skills, they have a perfect opportunity to practice shared decision making. Teacher team members gather research, consider all the pros and cons, explore assessment tools, advocate their positions, and, hopefully, reach consensus on next steps as a team. Coaches might provide several open-ended questions, such as the following, as a starting point to facilitate this process.

▶ What does research say about the possible advantages of assessment for prerequisite skills and formative assessment?

▶ How might students use prerequisite skill assessments for self-assessment and goal setting?

  ▶   How can we, as a team, share the work of developing assessment tools for prerequisite skills?

  ▶   How can we use assessment results for prerequisite skills to strengthen our instruction?

As teams navigate the potholes on the road to reaching consensus, the challenge for coaches is to stay in a guide-on-the-side role. Providing resources, protocols, and reflection questions supports teams in doing the work for themselves. When teams reach true consensus, they grow more skilled, cohesive, and collaborative—exactly what a coach wants to see happen!

Immediate Prerequisite Skills Planning Template

Identify each immediate prerequisite skill for an essential standard in your unit (see the "Essential Standards Chart," chapter 3, action 1, page 93). Determine how to review and connect the essential standard to each immediate prerequisite skill during Tier 1 instruction. Additionally, determine how to address the prerequisite skills before teaching the essential standard in Tier 2, if needed.

Essential Standard

Immediate Prerequisite Skill	Tier 1 Strategies *During* Grade- or Course-Level Learning	Tier 2 Strategies *Before* Teaching the Essential Standard

Action 3

Monitor the Progress of Students Receiving Tier 2 Academic Interventions

Imagine that on Tuesday, you take your child to the pediatrician because they have a sore throat and a fever. The pediatrician prescribes amoxicillin four times daily and asks you to bring your child again on Friday. The doctor wants to monitor your child's progress to see if they respond to the intervention prescribed. For the same reason, educators want to determine whether the treatment they prescribe for students receiving supplemental Tier 2 interventions is working. Are students responding to the interventions? If not, how should the team respond?

Progress monitoring is an essential component of RTI. Without it, there is no *R* (response) in what we are doing. Without progress monitoring, we simply intervene for a predetermined amount of time and then move on to the next set of essential standards not yet mastered. Monitoring progress is akin to shifting from a focus on teaching to a focus on learning. Here, the shift is from a focus on intervening to a focus on asking, "Are students responding?"

After teams identify students in need of extra time and support and determine the interventions targeted to the cause of students' struggles, they monitor how each student responds to the interventions. If an intervention is working, it confirms that the team's diagnosis targeted the right causes. If a student is not responding, it means that the intervention was not targeted properly (an incomplete or incorrect diagnosis), or the diagnosis was correct, but the team selected an ineffective treatment.

In most cases, teams can use different versions of the common end-of-unit assessment items measuring the essential standards to progress monitor, or check, if a Tier 2 intervention is working and if students who did not demonstrate mastery before this intervention have grown. Unless the underlying cause of students' struggles with academic content standards is reading comprehension difficulty, teams can logically monitor progress using a tool that measures mastery of the standards. If, for example, the students are reading at or above grade level but are unable to correctly explain and analyze the four layers of the Earth on the end-of-unit assessment, ask them to do so again after receiving targeted intervention using a different form of the original common assessment.

When monitoring the progress of students who struggle with reading, we would most often select a curriculum-based measure (CBM) such as oral reading fluency, or words read correctly per minute. Teams can use CBMs to monitor letter-naming fluency, letter-sound fluency, nonsense-word fluency, and phonemic-segmenting and phonemic-blending tasks. CBMs offer the added benefits of being standardized across large groups of students and helping to establish growth over time with words read correctly per minute (WRCM; for example, 120 WRCM to 148 WRCM). Accordingly, first-grade and second-grade teachers might use CBMs to progress monitor their supplemental Tier 2 interventions in reading because they represent skills currently taught and reinforced at their grade levels. Students in third grade and beyond would most likely experience CBM progress monitoring at Tier 3, since Tier 3 represents the reinforcement of foundational skills from prior school years.

Finally, it is important to remember that progress monitoring does not have to be a "test." The objective is to determine whether a student has met the goal of an intervention. This means progress monitoring could be achieved through teacher observation—"I know the student learned it because I watched them actually do it."

Because schools want to quickly understand whether students are responding to an intervention, we recommend applying some kind of progress-monitoring tool at least every three weeks, if not weekly or daily. If and when a collaborative teacher team discovers that a few students are still not responding, the team can discuss this at its next meeting and brainstorm possible solutions. We recommend that the team review these data as often as every three weeks to ensure students are able to apply and transfer their learning outside the Tier 2 intervention.

The team can potentially discuss students not yet learning in Tier 2 with the site intervention team (described in chapter 8, page 293), which is composed of staff with different training and perspectives—special education teachers, speech-language pathologists, psychologists, and so on. This discussion may uncover some previously undetermined deficits in foundational skills and knowledge from prior school years, which the school's universal screening tools did not detect. In these rare cases, students may then begin to receive Tier 3 intensive reinforcements in addition to receiving support with ongoing essential grade-level standards.

Here's Why

Progress monitoring provides teachers with information that can help students accelerate learning to grade level and beyond. It also helps teachers make better decisions about targeting the type of instruction that works with each student. Simply put, it helps teachers intervene more effectively and students master material more quickly. In their article "Progress Monitoring Within a Response-to-Intervention Model," Douglas D. Dexter and Charles Hughes (n.d.) quote the National Center on Student Progress Monitoring's stated benefits of monitoring progress:

> Progress monitoring has the following benefits when it is implemented correctly: (1) students learn more quickly because they are receiving more appropriate instruction; (2) teachers make more informed instructional decisions; (3) documentation of student progress is available for accountability purposes; (4) communication improves between families and professionals about student progress; (5) teachers have higher expectations for their students; and, in many cases, (6) there is a decrease in special education referrals. Overall, progress monitoring is relevant for classroom teachers, special educators, and school psychologists alike because the interpretation of the assessment data is vital when making decisions about the adequacy of student progress and formulating effective instructional programs. (Fuchs, Compton, Fuchs, Bryant, & Davis, 2008)

When RTI was first implemented across the United States, almost all examples of progress monitoring were through curriculum-based measures, such as oral reading fluency. Teams must determine what measures might be most appropriate to monitor student progress based on the nature of the essential standards on which students are receiving additional time and support.

Here's How

Teacher team members meet to discuss and analyze the results from their common end-of-unit assessment. As part of this discussion, they should take the following three steps.

1. Discuss teachers' concerns about specific students and identify underlying causes of student struggles at the learning target level.

2. Decide which teachers will work with which students and why, as described in Action 1: Design and Lead Tier 2 Interventions for Essential Academic Standards (page 203).

3. Identify what prompts teachers might use to monitor the progress of students receiving supplemental Tier 2 interventions. When dealing with academic content standards, teachers should take prompts from the common formative and end-of-unit assessments that comprised the team's unit plan.

Within three weeks, the team meets to review the progress-monitoring data to make further decisions about individual students. The team releases some students from the interventions because they have demonstrated mastery. Others may require continued time and support. A few may have underlying skill deficits that were revealed, so teachers might consider them for Tier 3 intensive reinforcements in addition to ongoing support with the essential standards at Tier 2.

While the team needs to capture and record the progress-monitoring data on each student, it is imperative to streamline this documentation process for teachers. Unfortunately, many schools and districts create paper-trail equivalents of IEPs, which place an undue burden on teachers. Again, technology use affords schools the opportunity to capture and store these data without placing too great a burden on teachers. We want teachers to focus on teaching and helping students, not on filling out byzantine forms.

Helpful Tools

The following tools will help you accomplish the work for this essential action.

▶ **Chapter 8 of *Learning by Doing, Fourth Edition* (DuFour et al., 2024), "Responding When Some Students Don't Learn":** This chapter provides foundational content knowledge as well as tools that can help schools accomplish the action steps outlined in this section.

▶ **"RTI at Work Pro-Solve Intervention Monitoring Plan: Tier 1 and Tier 2" (page 222):** Teams can use this form to separate academic skills from behavioral issues and target each student's particular needs for intervention.

Coaching Tips

The implementation tips we offer at this point are simply reminders of tips we provided previously. Because teachers are sharing, analyzing, and responding to data, it is important to remember that collective ownership for the process is the goal. Involving teachers at every step and clearly communicating with them creates ownership along the way. If teacher teams are clearly balking at monitoring progress, it may indicate a need to pause and back up. It may signal a need to clarify expectations, processes, or tools, or have teachers be more involved in developing the tools and processes they use.

RTI at Work Pro-Solve Intervention Monitoring Plan: Tier 1 and Tier 2

Student: _____

Participant: _____

Meeting date: _____

	Targeted Outcomes	Desired Outcomes	Intervention and Action Steps	Who Takes Responsibility	Data Point 1	Data Point 2	Data Point 3	Data Point 4	Data Point 5
Led by Teacher Teams	Essential Standards								
	Immediate Prerequisite Skills								
	English Language								
Led by Guiding Coalition	Academic Behaviors								
	Social Behaviors								
	Health and Home								

Next meeting date: _____

Note that the teacher team completes the Desired Outcomes, Intervention and Action Steps, and Who Takes Responsibility columns of this chart as part of the design of supplemental Tier 2 interventions. In the team's follow-up progress-monitoring meeting, team members collect a series of data points to document an individual student's progress. Depending on the nature of the essential standard, data points might include things such as results from a curriculum-based measure (grades 1 and 2), three out of four correct on selected-response items, and a rubric score of four out of five, representing the team's definition of mastery.

Source: Buffum, A., Mattos, M., Weber, C., & Hierck, T. (2015). Uniting academic and behavior interventions: Solving the skill or will dilemma. Bloomington, IN: Solution Tree Press.

Action 4

Extend Student Learning

As teachers gather information about how students are responding to their Tier 1 instruction and intervention, they will inevitably discover that some students have already learned the skills and knowledge that collaborative teacher teams prioritized as essential. The ongoing use of formative assessments, both common and individual, helps reveal students who have already learned. Teachers must provide opportunities for these students to extend their learning. This outcome is captured in the fourth critical question of the PLC at Work process: "How will we extend the learning for students who are already proficient?" (DuFour et al., 2024, p. 44).

It is important here to review the difference between extension and enrichment.

- *Extension* means students are stretched beyond essential grade-level curriculum or levels of proficiency.

- *Enrichment* means students have access to the subjects that specials or electives teachers traditionally teach, such as music, art, drama, applied technology, and physical education.

All students should have access to enrichment. When schools offer enrichment opportunities to high-achieving students during intervention time, their peers who are receiving targeted academic interventions usually miss these opportunities. Tier 2 is learning time for *all* students to meet *and* exceed essential grade-level standards. This is why we advocate extension for students during Tier 2 time. As Guskey (2010) writes:

> Students engaged in [extension] activities gain valuable learning experiences without necessarily moving ahead in the instructional sequence. This makes it easier for other students who have been doing corrective work (or Tier 2 intervention in an RTI model) to resume their place in the regular instructional sequence when they are done. (p. 56)

Access to extension should not be limited to a handful of predetermined students who have been deemed gifted, talented, or advanced. Like any other Tier 2 targeted outcomes, extension groups should be fluid and flexible based on student progress related to each essential standard. When students have shown mastery on all essential standards, extension becomes their next step in growing and achieving at high levels.

The challenge for teachers in designing and implementing extension activities is ensuring that these activities provide students with meaningful learning experiences, rather than saddling them with more work or busy work. Guskey (2010) writes, "[Extension] activities must provide students with opportunities to pursue their interests, extend their understanding, and broaden their learning experiences" (p. 56).

Here's Why

MTSS should never provide help to students still working to learn essential standards at the expense of our highest-achieving students. Schools should use their intervention process as a way of optimizing student learning by raising the floor of student achievement while raising the ceiling at the same time. We can best capture this thinking with the saying, "A rising tide lifts all boats."

Unfortunately, extension is too often regarded as something extra, something more—a nonessential "nice-to-have" thing if we can squeeze it in somehow. This viewpoint ignores the importance of student engagement and motivation to learn. Engaging students by letting them make choices related to their own learning enhances their achievement (Reis & Fogarty, 2006; Roberts, 2020a; Siegle & McCoach, 2005).

In *Visible Learning and the Science of How We Learn*, John Hattie and Gregory Yates (2014) point out that feedback helps students on their personal journeys, and that the type of feedback required depends on students' achievement outcomes. While students struggling to learn need corrective feedback, highly competent learners require sincere efforts to extend and apply knowledge even further.

Within the context of essential standards and outcomes, each student is on a personal journey. While some students need Tier 2 interventions that include personalized corrective feedback, others need personalized feedback that further engages them in their own journey—extending and enriching their knowledge and their ability to apply that knowledge to solve problems in new and challenging ways.

Here's How

Just as teachers must plan to provide Tier 2 interventions to students who need help learning their essential standards, they also should plan to provide extensions for students who have already mastered the standards. Extension planning is best done before a team begins a unit of study that includes new essential curriculum. This preplanning is captured in the final column of the essential standards chart, as shown in figure 5.6. (See chapter 3, action 1, page 93, for a blank reproducible version of this figure.)

Every time a teacher team plans a unit of study that contains new essential curriculum, it knows that some students will not demonstrate proficiency on its common end-of-unit assessment. This is why team members collectively create a teaching-assessing-learning-cycle plan so they are prepared to collectively respond to intervene at Tier 2. Likewise, the team also knows that many students *will* show they have learned the essential curriculum on the team's end-of-unit assessment, so student extension will undoubtedly be needed. Plan ahead for it.

Teacher teams can create meaningful extension opportunities in multiple ways. Some potential outcomes include the following.

 ▶ Ask students to demonstrate mastery of essential standards at a level beyond what is deemed grade-level proficient. They can achieve this in several ways. Teachers can make the content more rigorous; make the process or activities in which students engage more rigorous; or make the culminating product, which applies what students have learned, more rigorous (Tomlinson, 2000).

 ▶ Give students access to more of the required grade-level or course-specific curriculum that is deemed important but not essential. Teachers often express the concern that there is not enough time to teach all the state or provincial standards. While teachers should never introduce new essential curriculum while students receive Tier 2 interventions and Tier 3 reinforcements, it is acceptable to introduce important—but nonessential—supporting standards (often nice-to-know standards) from the state or provincial standards.

 ▶ Have students engage in personalized learning opportunities. The authors of *Personalized Learning in a PLC at Work: Student Agency Through the Four Critical Questions* (Stuart, Heckmann, Mattos, & Buffum, 2018) define personalization in two ways.

What Do We Expect Students to Learn?

Grade: Subject: Semester: Team Members:

Description of Standard	Example of Grade- or Course-Level Rigor	Immediate Prerequisite Skills	When Proficiency Is Expected	Common Formative and End-of-Unit Assessments	Extension
What is the essential standard to be learned? Describe it in student-friendly language, but avoid reducing the cognitive level of the standard.	What does proficient student work look like? Provide an example or a description of the items and tasks to use to demonstrate proficiency.	What prior knowledge, skills, and vocabulary from earlier this year or last year are needed for a student to master this standard?	When will this standard be taught, and when will proficiency be expected with part, or all, of the standard?	What common assessment will be used to measure student mastery?	What will we do when students have already learned this standard?

Source: Adapted from Buffum, A., Mattos, M., & Weber, C. (2012). Simplifying response to intervention: Four essential guiding principles. Bloomington, IN: Solution Tree Press.

FIGURE 5.6: Essential standards chart with extensions emphasized.

1. **Learning progressions:** Students can progress through targeted curricular outcomes by accelerating or decelerating their rate of learning based on their learning needs.

2. **Learning pathways:** Schools can provide opportunities for students to pursue their interests and passions.

Providing personalized learning opportunities also develops *student agency*—a student's ability to take specific and purposeful action to impact their level of success (Stuart et al., 2018). Students with high levels of agency do not respond passively to their circumstances; they tend to seek meaning and act with purpose to achieve the conditions they desire in their own and others' lives.

Helpful Tools

The following tools will help you accomplish the work for this essential action.

▸ **"Essential Standards Chart" (see chapter 3, action 1, page 93):** This powerful tool will assist teacher teams in preplanning for extension standards.

▸ **"Creating a Tiered Task Card to Extend Student Learning" (page 227):** This outstanding tool, from *The Big Book of Tools for RTI at Work* (Ferriter et al., 2025), is designed to help a team prepare extension activities.

▸ *Enriching the Learning: Meaningful Extensions for Proficient Students in a PLC at Work* **(Roberts, 2020a):** This book provides practical examples and tools to plan for meaningful extensions at all grade levels.

Coaching Tips

Again, the implementation tips we offer at this point are reminders of tips previously offered. That said, the great challenge here is time. With all the time demands that they face, teachers might view building a bank of resources for extending learning as time consuming and low priority. Often, teachers simply don't realize how many ideas and resources they already have within their own teams. Creating a virtual folder or some other location for extension ideas can ease the workflow that can accompany meeting the needs of all learners.

To help address this challenge, the guiding coalition might consider designating an entire faculty meeting, early in the school year, to explore extension activities. Teams will need to know the faculty meeting's focus ahead of time so they can come prepared with ideas and resources to share. Designating the time, adhering to a single focus for the meeting, and providing structured facilitation help the guiding coalition send a clear message that extension is both essential and expected.

Creating a Tiered Task Card to Extend Student Learning

To create a tiered task card to extend student learning, review the following key, which outlines Norman L. Webb's (2002) Depth of Knowledge (DOK) levels. Then, use those descriptions to create four leveled tasks connected to your current grade-level essentials. Record those tasks on the Tiered Task Card template (page 228). When you finish, you will have a tiered task card to engage students ready for extensions.

Depth of Knowledge Key

DOK Level 1	DOK Level 2	DOK Level 3	DOK Level 4
Recall and Reproduction	**Skills and Concepts**	**Strategic Thinking**	**Extended Thinking**
DOK 1 tasks involve the simple recall of information. Answers to DOK 1 tasks are either right or wrong. No reasoning is required to complete DOK 1 tasks. Instead, students gather facts and information or apply simple formulas.	DOK 2 tasks involve the application of knowledge. Students explain, describe, categorize, or interpret acquired information. DOK 2 tasks always require students to decide how to approach the problem.	DOK 3 tasks involve higher levels of reasoning than the two previous task types. Students develop logical arguments based on evidence, draw conclusions based on data, or provide justifications and reasoning to defend their positions.	DOK 4 tasks involve the highest level of cognitive demand. Students make connections within or between content areas, evaluate several possible solutions, or explain alternative perspectives from multiple sources. DOK 4 tasks may also ask students to apply what they learn to real-life contexts.
Sample task: *Can you list the four primary pathogens that cause human diseases?*	**Sample task:** *What are the similarities and differences between the two main types of pathogens that cause human diseases: viruses and bacteria?*	**Sample task:** *Rank the four main types of pathogens that cause human diseases in order from most dangerous to least dangerous. Defend your rankings with reasoning.*	**Sample task:** *Find an example of a disease outbreak in the world. Research the reasons for the outbreak, and offer recommendations about how the outbreak should have been treated.*

page 1 of 3

Tiered Task Card

Name: _____ Unit of study: _____

Directions: When you have demonstrated mastery of essential grade-level standards through our classroom assessments or work products, you are ready for extension tasks that push your thinking beyond grade-level mastery. This card includes the extension activities for our current unit of study. To complete your task card, follow these steps.

1. Unless your teacher gives you different instructions, start with the activity labeled DOK Level 1.

2. When you have completed the first activity, move to the tasks labeled DOK Level 2, DOK Level 3, and DOK Level 4.

3. Choose any work product from the list at the bottom of the task card to demonstrate mastery of each task.

4. Your teacher will use the work you complete as additional evidence showing your current level of mastery for the essential standards.

Tasks to Complete

DOK Level 1	DOK Level 2	DOK Level 3	DOK Level 4
Recall and Reproduction	**Skills and Concepts**	**Strategic Thinking**	**Extended Thinking**
Task:	Task:	Task:	Task:

You may choose to demonstrate what you know in any of the following ways.

Write a paragraph.	Create a set of Google slides.	Record a video.	Make a podcast or audio recording.
Develop a Venn diagram.	Make a graphic organizer.	Create a cartoon.	Have a debate with a friend.

Taking Action © 2018, 2025 Solution Tree Press • SolutionTree.com
Visit **go.SolutionTree.com/RTIatWork** to download this free reproducible.

Sample Tiered Task Card: Middle-Grade Science (Fossils)

Over the past two weeks, we have been studying fossils in class. Specifically, we have been looking at:

- The differences between the main types of fossils
- What index fossils are and why they are important
- How scientists use fossils to better understand the development of life on Earth

Interestingly, a major fossil discovery was made in Northern Canada in 2020!

Read more about that discovery in the *Newsweek* article "Our Hands Originated in Earth's Oceans at Least 380 Million Years Ago, 'Missing Link' Fossil Fish Reveals" by Aristos Georgiou (2020; https://tinyurl.com/dmj2h659).

See if you can complete the following tasks related to this fossil discovery.

Tasks to Complete

DOK Level 1	DOK Level 2	DOK Level 3	DOK Level 4
Recall and Reproduction	**Skills and Concepts**	**Strategic Thinking**	**Extended Thinking**
Task: Summarize the fossil discovery made in Northern Canada.	**Task:** Name the type of fossil discovered in Northern Canada. Defend your decision with reasoning. Remember: We have been studying mold fossils, cast fossils, petrified fossils, preserved fossils, carbonized fossils, and trace fossils.	**Task:** Rate the fossil discovery made in Northern Canada on a scale of 1–5, in which 1 represents "not very important" and 5 represents "most important fossil discovery ever." Defend your rating with reasoning.	**Task:** Find an example of another significant fossil discovery in the last one hundred years. Then, explain why that fossil discovery was even *more* important than the discovery made in Northern Canada.

You may choose to demonstrate what you know in any of the following ways.			
Write a paragraph.	Create a set of Google slides.	Record a video.	Make a podcast or audio recording.
Develop a Venn diagram.	Make a graphic organizer.	Create a cartoon.	Have a debate with a friend.

Source: Webb, N. L. (2002, March 28). Depth-of-Knowledge levels for four content areas. Accessed at http://ossucurr.pbworks.com /w/file/fetch/49691156/Norm%20web%20dok%20by%20subject%20area.pdf on January 12, 2024.

Conclusion

In this chapter, we described the critical work of collaborative teacher teams in providing additional time and support to students who, at the end of a unit, have not mastered essential standards the teams prioritized. This additional time focuses like a laser beam on the underlying causes of students' struggles, not on the symptoms, such as a letter grade or percentage score.

While some students receive this additional time and support to master essential standards, it is equally important for teacher teams to plan and deliver meaningful and engaging extension activities for students who have demonstrated mastery. All of this focuses on academic skills. In the next chapter, we discuss the guiding coalition's responsibilities at Tier 2, including scheduling Tier 2 time in the master schedule and leading behavior interventions.

CHAPTER 6

Tier 2 Guiding Coalition Essential Actions

Intelligence plus character—that is the goal of true education.

—Martin Luther King Jr.

In this chapter, we focus on the Tier 2 middle-left portion of the RTI at Work pyramid (see figure 6.1, page 232). Let's consider what this portion of the pyramid visually represents.

- ▶ The primary purpose of Tier 2 is to systematically provide interventions to ensure every student learns the knowledge, skills, and behaviors deemed essential to success in the next grade or course.

- ▶ The left side of the pyramid represents outcomes that must be coordinated across the school, so the school's guiding coalition takes lead responsibility for these outcomes.

- ▶ While teacher teams take primary responsibility to lead interventions and extensions for essential academic standards at Tier 2, the guiding coalition leads schoolwide processes for intervening with students who need support in learning essential social and academic behaviors.

- ▶ Behavior interventions are often provided by schoolwide support staff such as administrators, counselors, the school psychologist, special education teachers, and instructional aides. The guiding coalition determines who is best trained and available to provide each type of behavior intervention.

In the previous chapter, we described why and how teacher teams should take lead responsibility for reteaching essential grade-level academic standards at Tier 2. In this chapter, we describe how the school's guiding coalition can leverage schoolwide staff to lead interventions for students who require additional time and support to consistently demonstrate the essential behaviors needed for future success. The guiding coalition's essential actions at Tier 2 are the following.

1. Schedule time for Tier 2 interventions and extensions.
2. Establish a process to identify students who require Tier 2 behavior interventions.

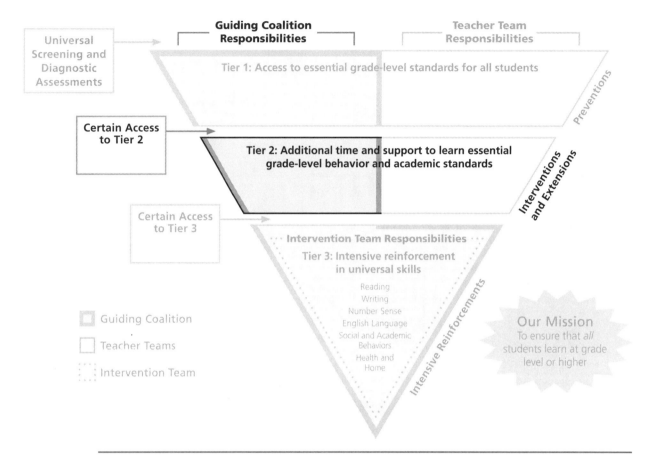

FIGURE 6.1: Focus on Tier 2 guiding coalition essential actions.

3. Plan and implement Tier 2 interventions for essential social and academic behaviors.

4. Coordinate interventions for students needing academic *and* behavior supports.

We begin with one of the most important jobs of the guiding coalition—scheduling time for Tier 2 interventions and extensions.

Action 1

Schedule Time for Tier 2 Interventions and Extensions

We have repeatedly stressed that interventions must be provided in addition to all students' access to new essential grade-level curriculum at Tier 1, not in place of it. So, when some students fail to learn essential grade-level academic or behavior standards by the end of a unit at Tier 1, the school must create dedicated Tier 2 time in the master schedule for these students to continue to work on those standards, while not missing the next essential standards taught during core instruction.

Some educators claim that their school doesn't need to create Tier 2 time in their master schedule because individual teachers provide interventions in their own classrooms. This is a "one-room schoolhouse" model—an approach that has historically failed to achieve the goal of high levels of learning for all students. It's unrealistic to expect teachers to simultaneously reteach essential grade-level curriculum to some students while introducing new essential standards to the entire class. We have collectively worked with thousands of schools across the world, and we have not identified a single school that has created a highly effective system of interventions *without* embedded intervention time in its master schedule. Not one. There *must* be dedicated time in a school's master schedule to provide Tier 2 interventions and extensions, and the staff must take collective responsibility for each student's success.

Creating a master schedule that ensures students access to both Tier 1 essential curriculum *and* Tier 2 interventions requires schoolwide coordination. For this reason, the school's guiding coalition should take primary responsibility for this essential action. While the actual schedule will look different from school to school, consider the following essential characteristics.

- ▸ **Frequency:** Tier 2 intervention time should be embedded in the master schedule at least two days a week, and up to five days a week, if needed. (A school can also achieve this minimum outcome by offering two intervention sessions on the same day.) The reason why once a week is insufficient is because some students will need help in multiple subjects. For example, suppose a high school provides Tier 2 support once a week, but a particular student needs help in algebra 1, English language arts, world history, and physical education. It would take almost a month to get help once in each class. Some students will undoubtedly need more frequent support.

  Due to fiscal, contractual, or transportation needs, a school will unlikely be able to lengthen its school day to create Tier 2 time. Instead, this time comes from Tier 1. In other words, some of the time teachers currently use to introduce new curriculum should be repurposed to reteach essential standards.

- ▸ **Duration:** Each session should be about thirty minutes. Consider for a moment how long the "new teaching" part of a regular class period at Tier 1 is. How much time does a teacher need to effectively teach a new learning target? Most teachers say around fifteen to thirty minutes, depending on the age of the student and the complexity of the learning target. Because the priority of Tier 2 is reteaching essential grade-level standards, we suggest about thirty-minute blocks of time for Tier 2 interventions and extensions.

- ▸ **Availability to all students:** If a school's mission is to ensure all students learn at high levels, then Tier 2 time must be scheduled when all students can attend. This means it must be during the school's instructional day. There are two significant drawbacks to providing interventions before or after school or during lunchtime. First, some students will not be able to attend before or after school due to transportation or family needs. Second, these times are usually outside the faculty's contractual teaching time. If teacher teams are the best-trained staff to provide Tier 2 academic interventions and extensions, but they are not available during a school's Tier 2 time, then the interventions will be much less effective. When a school carves out Tier 2 time within its current instructional day, it ensures the faculty are contractually available to teach students, and by law, the students must be at school.

  Because we advocate intervention time to be embedded within the school day, we are often asked if it is acceptable to provide any interventions before school, after school, or during off-track times (like summer school). We are not against utilizing these times, but the school must assume that some students will be unable to attend. So, these additional times could be leveraged in addition to embedded Tier 2 time in the master schedule, but not in place of it.

- ▸ **Fluid and flexible placement:** Tier 2 interventions work best when they are targeted by student, by standard, and by learning target. Because Tier 2 intervention groups, sessions, or offerings all focus on very specific learning outcomes, students should transition out of a session once they have met the targeted outcome.

▶ **No introduction to new essential curriculum:** The faculty must commit to never introducing new essential curriculum during Tier 2 time. This time is to reteach essentials, so if new essential standards are introduced at the same time, the students receiving reteaching will fall behind. Teachers can introduce nonessential curriculum during Tier 2.

It is critical to remember that if the tiers are value added in MTSS, then a school cannot provide Tier 2 *and* Tier 3 supports during this time, because some students will need both interventions in grade-level curriculum (Tier 2) and reinforcement in foundational prerequisite skills (Tier 3).

Here's Why

No research supports the idea that all students learn at the exact same speed, so why should the time allotted to learn specific content be the same for all students? Regardless of this fact, time-restricting practices are prevalent in many schools—from rigid pacing guides that predetermine how many days a teacher can spend teaching each standard to the traditional secondary master schedule that provides every student with the same number of instructional minutes for every class. These practices were designed to cover material and rank student achievement instead of ensuring all students succeed.

If we condense what it takes to have all students learn into a simple formula, the equation looks like this (Bloom, 1968; Buffum et al., 2012; Guskey & Pigott, 1988):

$$\text{Targeted Instruction} + \text{Time} = \text{Learning}$$

A school that makes both teaching and time variables in this equation and targets them to meet each student's individual learning and developmental needs is more likely to achieve high levels of learning for every student. Applying this formula in practice requires creating flexible time in the school's master schedule, such as dedicated Tier 2 time.

Schools often tell us that transitioning to a block schedule has provided more time for their teachers to differentiate in class. While we are not opposed to block scheduling, we do not consider having larger blocks of Tier 1 class time the same as creating flexible time. Whether a high school has a traditional six-period day, or it has a block schedule in which students take four classes every other day for longer blocks of time, each student is still getting the same number of minutes as other students following the same schedule. The premise of flexible time is that some students need more time to learn the curriculum and some require less. So, the school must create a flexible block of time in which some students receive more time on an essential standard, while others extend learning because they have already mastered the curriculum.

Here's How

The specific schedule used to create Tier 2 intervention and extension time is likely to look different from school to school. Elementary and secondary master schedules work quite differently. State or provincial regulations, district policies, contractual agreements, site resources, and student needs all impact the specific design of a school's master schedule. So, while we can't provide a universal, generic, all-purpose Tier 2 master schedule, we can recommend the following seven steps for the guiding coalition to create the right schedule for its school.

1. Learn together.

2. Look beyond the bell schedule.

3. Determine the frequency and duration needed for Tier 2 interventions.

4. Create a draft plan.

5. Solicit staff input and build consensus.

6. Teach students the purpose of the new schedule and the specific steps of how it works.

7. Predetermine how to monitor and revise the process.

Learn Together

Many schools, differing in size and demographics, have successfully embedded intervention and extension time during their existing school day. *Why reinvent the wheel?* The guiding coalition should study how to schedule Tier 2 time during the school day. To support this learning, we recommend the following resources.

▶ See *It's About Time: Planning Interventions and Extensions in Elementary School* (Buffum & Mattos, 2015) and *It's About Time: Planning Interventions and Extensions in Secondary School* (Mattos & Buffum, 2015) to learn how other elementary and secondary schools create intervention time in their school day. The featured schools significantly increased student achievement and created their new schedule within their existing conditions—they did not lengthen their school day nor receive additional funding to make the intervention time possible.

▶ Visit AllThingsPLC (https://allthingsplc.info) to locate and contact hundreds of model schools that have successfully created intervention time during the school day. Each school has submitted a written narrative as well as contact information.

▶ Contact your local regional, state, or provincial office of education and inquire about model schools in your area that would be worth visiting. Because these offices support many area schools and districts, they often have a good idea of which schools are further along on the journey.

While it is unlikely you will find a school with the perfect bell schedule for you, seeing different examples can provide options that you can tailor to best meet your school's needs.

Look Beyond the Bell Schedule

Most schools assume that the biggest obstacle to creating dedicated Tier 2 time is manipulating the minutes in the master schedule to create the time. Yet schools regularly revise their bell schedules throughout the year for events like school assemblies, pep rallies, testing schedules, and poor weather. An alternative schedule that a school has already created for an assembly usually can be easily modified into a Tier 2 intervention and extension bell schedule.

The real obstacles begin when a school considers the logistics of having potentially hundreds of students transition to specific interventions. Critical questions arise, such as the following.

▶ How do we successfully use this time to support student learning?

▶ How do we determine what interventions to offer?

▶ How do we identify students?

- ▶ How do we assign staff?

- ▶ How do we transition students to the right sessions?

- ▶ How do we hold students accountable to attend?

- ▶ How do we efficiently monitor student progress?

- ▶ What do we do with students who don't need extra help?

- ▶ What if students need help in multiple academic areas?

- ▶ How do we keep the process from becoming a paperwork nightmare?

- ▶ How can we achieve these outcomes within our current resources and without asking teachers to work beyond their contractual obligations?

These are all legitimate and difficult logistical questions that can stall a school's efforts to provide additional time for learning. When contacting model schools, the guiding coalition should dig deeper than just asking to see the schools' bell schedules. More than learning how to schedule the time, it is important to learn how to use the time once it is scheduled.

Determine the Frequency and Duration Needed for Tier 2 Interventions

We noted that Tier 2 interventions and extensions should take place at least twice per week, around thirty minutes per session. Within these general guidelines, there is flexibility for schools to tailor the time to fit students' needs. When Mike Mattos was principal of Marjorie Veeh Elementary in Tustin, California, a school that served mostly students at risk, the staff dedicated time every day to providing Tier 2 help because these students had many academic gaps to fill. The primary grades' Tier 2 time each day was slightly shorter because younger students are not developmentally ready for large blocks of direct instruction. Upper-grade students could focus for longer, and often their essential learning targets were more complex, requiring longer blocks of time to effectively teach.

When Mike later became principal of Pioneer Middle School (also in Tustin, California), the staff dedicated two time slots per week to providing Tier 2 interventions and extensions because most of the students entered the school at grade level. These periods occurred at the same time for all grades. This was because developmental needs are similar for the middle school grades and also because a secondary master schedule is structured very differently than an elementary one. At the elementary level, grade levels can all run different daily schedules and not disrupt the other grades. At the secondary level, the entire school runs on the same bell schedule.

Based on the school's unique needs, the guiding coalition should determine the desired frequency and duration of Tier 2 time needed to meet its students' needs.

Create a Draft Plan

After learning about the process and determining specific school needs, the guiding coalition is then ready to create a proposal for how its school can provide dedicated Tier 2 time during the school day. This plan should address not only how to create time within the school day but also the logistics of how to use that time. (See the reproducible "Creating Flexible Time Worksheet: Critical Considerations," page 240, to assist with this process.)

Solicit Staff Input and Build Consensus

The draft plan is just that—a draft. The guiding coalition should consider how it will share the plan with faculty, provide the rationale and research behind the design, and solicit staff feedback. Our experience is that some staff members resist *any* change to the master schedule and will use this opportunity only to point out potential problems. When allowed, these naysayers often dominate the conversation. This is why the guiding coalition must plan how to solicit feedback from everyone, not just the most vocal staff.

Also, when teachers raise potential concerns, it is important to press for potential solutions. Remind the faculty that if their current schedule were meeting the mission of all students learning at high levels, then there would be no need to improve it. While you cannot guarantee that the proposed new schedule will work perfectly, there is no doubt that the current schedule does not.

Teach Students the Purpose of the New Schedule and the Specific Steps of How It Works

When flexible time is well targeted, students transition to different locations, staff members, and activities on any given day. Transitional times in a school day can trigger student misbehaviors, so it is critical to teach students specific actions, processes, and behaviors that they must demonstrate during these times.

Before Mike Mattos and the staff at Pioneer Middle School started their Tier 2 period—which they called *Tutorial*—they taught students the reasoning behind the schedule change, the goals of their new tutorial period, and the specific steps in the process. They had a dry run, in which students just practiced the transition from their last class to their tutorial location. Teachers carefully taught students the routine before they asked them to participate in a flexible period in which 1,500 middle school students were expected to transition to different interventions and extension opportunities across the entire campus. They shared the rationale and design with parents and families as well.

Predetermine How to Monitor and Revise the Process

Regardless of how well you complete the previous steps, it is highly unlikely you will come up with a perfect plan. There are bound to be unexpected bumps. School faculty find it easier to commit to trying a new schedule if they know there will be opportunities to tweak the process when it's not working well. For example, the leadership at Pioneer Middle School pledged that it would survey the entire staff after three months of trying the new schedule, and it would make revisions as needed. Additionally, every faculty member and student completed a survey at the end of the year.

Having worked with hundreds of schools on how to create Tier 2 time, we share the following advice on potential pitfalls to avoid when designing this time.

- **Intervention time should not be "fun and games" for some students:** We have seen schools decide that students who do not need Tier 2 interventions receive privileges, such as—

  - Extra lunch and social time

  - The opportunity to leave campus early

  - Enrichment activities, like learning how to play guitar or participating in an intramural dodgeball tournament

There are two problems with this approach. First, most schools create their Tier 2 time from existing Tier 1 instructional time. So, when you offer some students "free time," they lose instructional time. Tier 2 time should not come at the cost of students who learn essential standards during core instruction. The second problem is that when you offer some students these privileges, it makes the students assigned to required reteaching feel punished. Students should not perceive interventions as punitive actions. This is why in chapter 3 (page 81), we recommended that teacher teams consider how to extend student learning during unit planning. This time is for interventions and extensions.

- **Tier 2 interventions should not be in place of electives or specials:** As discussed in chapter 1 (page 11), there is a difference between extension and enrichment. All students deserve access to enrichment subjects, such as music, drama, computer technology, and art. Most schools offer these through specials time (elementary) or elective classes (secondary). Tier 2 reteaching should not be scheduled in place of these opportunities.

- **Student assignments must be flexible and fluid:** We have seen many schools create an intervention period and then assign a group of students to each teacher for weeks at a time. When Tier 2 is targeted well—by student, standard, and learning target—students should move fluidly from group to group, based on their individual needs. More often, schools that assign students to the same intervention for weeks at a time do so because of the inconvenience of regrouping students frequently.

And we cannot stress this point enough: *the primary purpose of this time is the reteaching of essential grade-level standards.* Too often, schools create Tier 2 time but then use it like a glorified study hall—students with markedly different needs are in a room with a single teacher monitoring them. Not much teaching takes place, nor targeted practice. Students just work—or act like they are working—on something.

Helpful Tools

The following tools will help you accomplish the work for this essential action.

- **"Creating Flexible Time Worksheet: Critical Considerations" (page 240):** This tool provides teams with a list of questions they can consider when creating effective flexible time in their schedules to provide intervention and enrichment.

- **"Using Flexible Time Well" (page 241):** Teams can use these critical questions to help them draft a plan for using flexible time well.

Coaching Tips

To ensure successful implementation of flexible time, a guiding coalition must consider and address one additional challenge to changing the schedule: How will the guiding coalition involve teachers, students, and parents throughout all steps of the process, including researching, drafting a plan, trying it out, and revising? The following are several suggestions for addressing this challenge.

- Each member of the guiding coalition takes on the role of communication liaison for designated groups of stakeholders. For example, the team should assign members to communicate with teachers in specific grade levels or departments, specific student leadership groups, or specific parent groups.

▸ As communication liaison, each guiding coalition member is responsible for sharing information, gathering input as necessary, and reporting on guiding coalition decisions to the faculty.

▸ Guiding coalition members might also form and coordinate the work of topic-specific committees to research, brainstorm, and propose solutions to critical considerations.

Take note! To keep stakeholders informed and involved, the guiding coalition needs to be patient and allow enough time for all voices to be heard as staff complete the work. Rushing the process usually creates a lack of clarity, poor follow-through, and, ultimately, resistance. On the other hand, taking the time needed to bring everyone along on the journey means each team member will understand and support the final plan, thus leading to greater outcomes for student learning.

Creating Flexible Time Worksheet: Critical Considerations

Discuss and address the following considerations.

1. Do we have frequent time during the school day to reteach and extend students?

2. Is there a process to require or monitor student attendance?

3. Are there at least two times per week for Tier 2 interventions and extensions?

4. How often are students assigned or reassigned for targeted support?

5. How targeted is each offering? Is the time used to reteach specific essential standards?

6. Is the time used to extend learning for students who have already mastered essential standards?

Using Flexible Time Well

As you draft your plan for using flexible time well, discuss and address the following critical considerations.

1. How will we successfully use this time to support and extend student learning?

2. How will we determine which interventions to offer?

3. How will we determine which staff member should lead each intervention?

4. How will students transition to the correct help sessions?

5. How will we hold students accountable?

6. How will we monitor student progress efficiently?

7. How will this time serve students who don't need extra help? How will we extend student learning?

8. How will this time serve students who need help in multiple academic areas?

9. How will we avoid a process that becomes a paperwork nightmare?

10. How will we use only current resources and not ask teachers to work beyond their contractual obligations to achieve our desired outcomes?

Action 2

Establish a Process to Identify Students Who Require Tier 2 Behavior Interventions

In chapter 5 (page 201), we discussed how teacher teams can use their common formative assessments to identify students for Tier 2 academic interventions. For example, if a mathematics team identifies *order of operations* as an essential standard and then administers an assessment on this topic, the information provided would be an outstanding way to identify students in need of additional instruction and practice to learn order of operations. And if a specific student's only current need is a little extra support to learn order of operations—assistance that the teacher team can provide—then the mathematics team probably has no need to formally request additional resources to support this student.

But some students need academic help in multiple subjects at Tier 2, and some students struggle to learn new essential grade-level curriculum because they still lack essential behaviors. These students may exhibit behaviors or needs such as the following.

- ▸ Demonstrating aggressive behavior toward peers

- ▸ Lacking the academic behavior of motivation

- ▸ Being consistently absent

- ▸ Facing a medical condition that impacts their education

- ▸ Having trouble making friends

- ▸ Dealing with a difficult home situation

These problems are a reality in every classroom and can impact students' academic success. Any school dedicated to ensuring the success of every student must be prepared to support students who need additional help with essential behaviors, trauma, or problems outside of school that impact their learning. Teachers do not measure these potential obstacles to student success through team common assessments—they usually observe them.

This is why, in addition to using common assessments to identify students in need of Tier 2 academic interventions, a school must have a schoolwide staff recommendation process to identify students who need behavior interventions, and students whose academic interventions must be coordinated across multiple teacher teams. Because the very purpose of the guiding coalition is to lead schoolwide support processes at each tier, this team will lead this action step at Tier 2.

Here's Why

As discussed in chapter 1 (page 11), one defining characteristic of a multitiered system of supports is that a school's interventions are systematic—the school can guarantee that every student in need of help will receive it, regardless of the teacher to whom they are assigned. A systematic response is composed of five steps.

1. Identify students who need help.

2. Determine the right intervention to meet students' learning needs.

3. Monitor each student's progress to determine whether the intervention is working.

4. Revise if the student is not responding to the intervention.

5. Extend once the student has mastered essential curriculum.

Of these five steps, there is one step a school must do perfectly—identify the students who need help. If the school does not initially determine the best interventions for these identified students, it will realize this problem as it monitors each student's progress. But a school cannot perform any of these steps unless it identifies these students in the first place. A system of interventions is useless for any student who slips through the cracks. Creating a systematic, timely staff recommendation process to identify students who need behavior interventions is critical to a highly effective system of interventions.

Here's How

Because the goal is to identify students across the entire school for additional help, designing and implementing this process is a guiding coalition responsibility. While specific identification procedures vary from school to school, we recommend aligning the process to the following criteria.

- ▶ **Timely:** An effective staff recommendation process must be timely. We recommend soliciting teacher input at least once every three weeks.

- ▶ **Mandatory:** Participation from all site educators must be mandatory. If even one faculty member is allowed to disengage from the process, then this teacher's students are much less likely to receive additional time and support. Consequently, the school can't tell parents it doesn't matter which teacher their child has—it does matter.

- ▶ **Deliberate:** All staff members should start the year knowing when the identification process takes place, how they will gather the information, and what criteria they are to use for identifying students in need.

- ▶ **Efficient:** The process should not require an unreasonable amount of time for teachers to complete.

We have seen Model PLC schools dedicate a portion of their teacher team meetings to systematically identifying students for extra help. At least once each month, staff members who work with students from the designated grade level (including administrators, special education teachers, and support staff) attend the meeting. Each attending staff member comes to the meeting with a list of students who need to be considered for schoolwide Tier 2 interventions, especially for behavior. The members discuss students collectively and determine appropriate interventions.

Having in attendance all staff members who work with a particular grade level or student group means the school can more effectively solve each student's needs. The staff get a 360-degree view of the student's entire school day. Figure 6.2 (page 244) shows an elementary view and figure 6.3 (page 244) shows a secondary view.

So, for example, if teachers have behavior concerns, the group can determine if these behaviors are being demonstrated all day (during class time, recess, specialist time, and so on) or just in particular settings. Also, because all teacher team and schoolwide team members participate, they can coordinate interventions based on whether a student needs support that falls under the lead responsibility of the teacher team or interventions the schoolwide team leads.

Using a set meeting time to identify students for additional help might not work well at a larger school, where there are hundreds of students at each grade level. For example, at a large comprehensive high school, it would not be practical to have all staff members who work with freshmen meet and discuss the individual needs of every ninth grader in need of help. The meeting could potentially take hours.

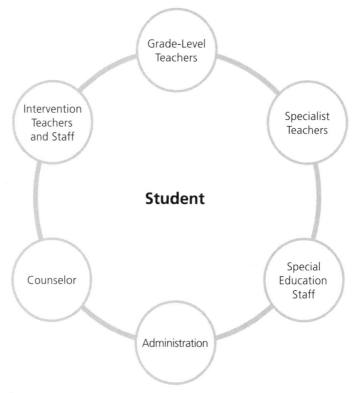

Source: Buffum et al., 2012.

FIGURE 6.2: Elementary 360-degree view.

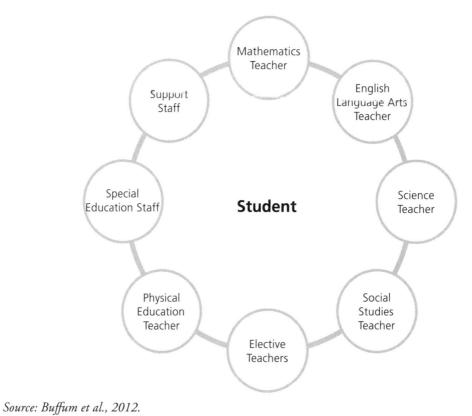

Source: Buffum et al., 2012.

FIGURE 6.3: Secondary 360-degree view.

Instead of holding a meeting, the school could solicit staff input through a recommendation process. The guiding coalition could develop a process to have all teachers refer students in need of schoolwide Tier 2 support approximately every three weeks. These recommendations can be submitted in writing or electronically. A school might use its current progress-reporting process, usually done through the school's student data management software, to collect this information from each teacher.

It is important that teachers provide more than a letter grade for each student; they should also use targeted comment codes as to why the students are struggling. For example, a mathematics teacher may refer three students from their first-period class who are currently failing. Along with the letter grade, the teacher may add a comment for each student to indicate poor attendance or missing work. Administrative or counseling staff can serve as intervention coordinators, using this combined student information to get the 360-degree view of each student's needs, meet with each student, determine what schoolwide supports might be needed, and take primary responsibility to ensure that these interventions take place.

Helpful Tool

The following tool will help you accomplish the work for this essential action.

▶ **"Establishing a Process for Schoolwide Student Intervention Identification" (page 246):** Using a three-point scale, teams can assess whether their school's intervention identification process is not in place, partially in place, or 100 percent in place.

Coaching Tips

As previously discussed, the guiding coalition is responsible for designing and implementing an effective process to identify students for intervention support. That said, the process never works effectively unless all stakeholders understand the process and, therefore, actively support that process. The guiding coalition must *communicate, communicate, communicate* to build shared understanding.

In his article "Leading Change: Why Transformation Efforts Fail," Kotter (2007) points out that a key reason change efforts fail is because the vision is undercommunicated by a factor of ten. In other words, leaders provide ten times less communication of the vision than is actually needed. All the criteria we recommend in the Here's How section (page 243) are related to effective communication. Stakeholders must understand *why* their participation in a student intervention identification process is necessary. Once that understanding is in place, they have a much greater likelihood of also supporting all steps in the process.

Guiding coalition members can use the reproducible "Establishing a Process for Schoolwide Student Intervention Identification" (page 246) to align their work with the recommended criteria. First, they collaboratively self-assess the current reality and then identify challenges or obstacles. They can then identify action steps to overcome each obstacle. Kotter (2007), again, sums up the importance of communication: "Without credible communication, and a lot of it, the hearts and minds of the troops are never captured."

Establishing a Process for Schoolwide Student Intervention Identification

To assess your current reality, use the following three-point scale: 1 point = Not in place, 2 points = Partially in place, 3 points = 100 percent in place

Critical Criterion to Consider	Current Reality	Challenges or Obstacles	Next Steps to Effectively Meet This Criterion
Timely ☐ Minimum of once every three weeks			
Mandatory ☐ All teachers participate.			
Deliberate ☐ All staff know when the identification process takes place. ☐ All staff know how information is gathered. ☐ All staff know what criteria to use for identifying students in need.			
Efficient ☐ Minimal time needed ☐ Minimal paperwork ☐ No student allowed to fall through the cracks			

Action 3

Plan and Implement Tier 2 Interventions for Essential Social and Academic Behaviors

In chapter 4 (page 153), we discussed how a school's guiding coalition should oversee a process to identify and teach schoolwide essential academic and social behaviors. Just as one would not expect every student to learn essential *academic* standards by the end of initial instruction, a school must not assume every student will consistently demonstrate essential behaviors merely because they were taught at the beginning of the year. Some students will need additional time and support to consistently demonstrate essential behaviors.

The guiding coalition is responsible for planning and implementing Tier 2 behavior interventions. These interventions should target both essential academic and social behaviors. Refer to table 4.1 (page 166).

Additionally, some students might struggle at school due to difficulties happening in their personal lives. These students might not lack critical behaviors needed for success in school, but instead be dealing with emotions related to trauma, grief, neglect, or personal conflict outside of school. Teams should consider supports needed for all types of situations.

Here's Why

While the academic and social behaviors listed in table 4.1 (page 166) do not represent all the behavioral needs that can impact a student's success in school, they do capture prevalent concerns that exist in most classrooms. Unfortunately, many schools fail to effectively address these needs because they leave it up to each teacher to intervene when students show repeated minor misbehaviors. We are not suggesting that teachers should abdicate responsibility for addressing classroom behaviors, but there are significant pitfalls to this individualistic approach.

First, we find that teacher preparation programs usually teach classroom management techniques but rarely train teachers in assessing and targeting systemic behavior concerns. There is a big difference between managing student behavior and using functional behavioral assessment information to target the cause of a student's misbehaviors. A school psychologist or counselor often has this type of training, but schoolwide coordination is required to systematically include them in providing Tier 2 behavior supports.

Second, making each teacher responsible for classroom behavior creates inconsistency and inequity for students. For example, when a student fails to complete homework, one teacher might require them to come in at lunch to make up the assignment; another teacher might call home and expect the student's parents to fix the problem; and another might just give the student an F and be done with it. A systematic intervention process ensures that students receive additional time and support *regardless* of which teacher they are assigned to. This promise must apply to behavior interventions too.

A third drawback to individual teacher responses for behavior interventions is that they restrict the ability to provide coordinated behavior interventions for students. When a student lacks an essential behavior—such as staying on task in class—the student usually demonstrates this behavior in other classroom settings. Having each of the student's teachers individually address this behavior can create disjointed or contradictory expectations. When a student demonstrates misbehavior throughout the school day, the best way to respond is with a coordinated schoolwide intervention plan. This is difficult to achieve when the school has an individualistic approach to Tier 2 interventions.

Finally, even if every teacher is a behavior intervention expert, it is unrealistic to expect them to have the time to provide behavior interventions. When students can do their homework but just lack the motivation and effort to get the work done, the school must require the students to complete the work—but how? If every teacher is responsible for this, when will they provide this help? In class? The teacher provides instruction to all students. At lunch or after school? Contractual obligations rarely compensate teachers for helping students at these times. At the students' homes? Of course not. The school might be able to have schoolwide staff oversee students who need to complete work, but individual teachers rarely have the authority to allocate and assign these staff members. It takes a schoolwide, systematic effort, which is why the guiding coalition must coordinate Tier 2 behavior interventions.

Here's How

Tier 2 behavior interventions should start by directly targeting the schoolwide essential social and academic behaviors the school identifies at Tier 1. To effectively respond when students need additional support to learn an essential behavior, the school's guiding coalition should consider the following six steps.

1. Regularly review schoolwide behavior information.

2. Target the cause, not the symptom.

3. Learn together.

4. Allocate time and resources to target specific behavior interventions.

5. Reteach!

6. Monitor each intervention's effectiveness and revise as needed.

Regularly Review Schoolwide Behavior Information

While Tier 2 interventions should target the individual needs of each student identified for behavioral help, getting an overall view of the school's behavioral needs is equally important. The guiding coalition should regularly analyze trends in schoolwide behavior data, including office behavior referrals, absence and tardy data, and teacher recommendations for interventions.

Reviewing this information means the guiding coalition might determine that certain behavioral needs are still in Tier 1. For example, when teachers at Pioneer Middle School referred students for schoolwide behavior interventions for the first time, staff identified more than seven hundred students in need of help with missing assignments—almost 40 percent of the student body. Obviously, a large portion of students did not learn the academic behaviors necessary to consistently complete their homework or were lacking the academic skills needed to independently complete the work. When that many students have the same need, it signals a Tier 1 problem. Readdressing these behaviors at Tier 1 would be the most effective way to help these students.

Additionally, reviewing this big-picture information helps the guiding coalition prioritize its efforts and resources. We find that some schools have many students with behavioral needs, but they begin the MTSS process with very few schoolwide behavior interventions. Under the weight of so many needs, the task of providing behavior supports can seem overwhelming. The guiding coalition looks at the bigger picture to identify the school's most pressing needs and where immediate action steps will be most effective.

Target the Cause, Not the Symptom

When schools begin to consider behavior interventions, they often ask us questions like:

- What intervention is best for students who won't do their work?

- What is the intervention for students who are absent too much?

Our answer is this: there is no single intervention that will effectively address these needs for each student. Do all students fail to turn in homework assignments for the same reason? Missing assignments are a symptom of a larger need. Absences are a symptom of a problem, not the cause. To effectively intervene, a school must identify what causes each student's problem. It must ask, "*Why* isn't this student completing homework?" and "*Why* is this student absent from school?" This is why we recommend that schools target interventions not only by student and by standard but also by cause. Eliminate what causes the problem, and you fix the problem.

To prove this point and to model a process a guiding coalition can use to target Tier 2 behavior interventions, let's dig deeper into a behavioral need that many schools have—getting students to complete their homework. The guiding coalition can use the reproducible "Reasons Why Students Might Fail to Complete Homework" (page 254) to help identify causes for missing homework. To begin, the guiding coalition should brainstorm reasons why a student might fail to bring in a completed homework assignment, recording each answer down the first column. Possible answers might include that the student:

- Chooses not to do the assignment

- Has after-school responsibilities (such as watching their younger siblings while their parents work) and is unable to get the assignment done

- Does not know how to do the work

- Forgets to write down the assignment

- Lacks the supplies at home to complete the work

- Does the assignment but leaves it at home

- Knows how to do the work and does not understand why the teacher is requiring them to practice (seems like busywork)

After brainstorming likely reasons, the guiding coalition can list across each row the current interventions the school provides to address missing assignments. Our experience is that most schools can only list about three traditional responses.

1. Contact the parents and ask them to monitor their child to be sure they do the work.

2. Assign the student to some form of detention as a punishment.

3. Give the student a failing grade, with the expectation that the mark will persuade the student to be more motivated in the future.

Now, the guiding coalition should identify which of these interventions effectively addresses each cause, which would potentially be counterproductive, and which causes are not addressed by the school's current interventions. For example, contacting the parents may not help the student who is watching their younger siblings because their parents are working. And assigning an F grade does not help the student who left class without the ability to do the assignment. After completing this step, many schools realize one-size-fits-all, punitive consequences are insufficient for addressing all needs, and can actually prevent students from wanting to apply effort at school.

With this information, guiding coalition members can now begin to design interventions that target each specific cause. They may ponder the following questions.

▶ How can we support a student who is disorganized and fails to bring completed assignments to class?

▶ How can we require students to complete the work when they just don't want to?

The team can use this same process to brainstorm solutions to other behavior concerns, such as poor attendance or disruptive classroom behavior.

Learn Together

A constant theme in this book is applying a cornerstone practice of the PLC at Work process—collective inquiry. If a school's staff want to get better at something that impacts student learning, they must start by studying the topic and identifying better practices. Most schools approach behavior interventions with what we call the *bigger hammer* philosophy. When students demonstrate misbehavior, educators implement punitive consequences. If those do not work, and the students continue to demonstrate the misbehavior, then there needs to be even more severe consequences—a bigger hammer. We challenge educators to find any research that suggests students best learn proper behaviors through fear, intimidation, and exclusively punitive responses from adults. For our profession, there is more definitive research on how to effectively intervene for behavioral needs than there is for academic needs. The research is clear that using punitive consequences is generally ineffective as a behavior modifier (Horner, Sugai, & Lewis, 2015). Instead, the characteristics of effective behavior interventions include the following.

▶ Building positive relationships with students

▶ Teaching or reteaching specific behaviors needed for success

▶ Targeting specific behaviors on which the student needs to focus

▶ Identifying the causes or triggers of counterproductive behaviors and working to address and eliminate these causes

▶ Providing frequent, short-cycle opportunities for self-assessment and feedback

▶ Awarding targeted positive recognitions and privileges earned for demonstrating desired behaviors

▶ Coordinating efforts across the student's school day and between school and home

It is difficult to achieve these goals if a hammer is the only tool in your behavior intervention toolbox. When all you have is a hammer, every misbehaving student looks like a nail.

Allocate Time and Resources to Target Specific Behavior Interventions

While classroom teachers certainly play a role in providing behavior interventions, schoolwide staff should take lead responsibility. Schoolwide staff include administrators, counselors, the school psychologist, special education staff, health services staff, instructional aides, and other classified staff. The guiding coalition will determine how to best utilize these schoolwide personnel.

Because the goal is to target the cause of each behavioral need, staff should be assigned to lead specific interventions based on their expertise. The guiding coalition should aim to:

- Assemble the right team of people to lead each behavior intervention

- Schedule frequent, dedicated times for each team to meet

- Allocate the resources needed to provide targeted help for each identified student

As a concrete example, consider how a school could create a Tier 2 attendance team to lead Tier 2 interventions in this area. The guiding coalition should first ask, "Who on our staff has knowledge or expertise that would help identify, diagnose, coordinate, and monitor interventions for students who have emerging attendance problems?" The guiding coalition might decide that the school's attendance secretary would be valuable to such a team, as this person keeps the daily attendance records and speaks with students and parents regarding each absence.

Because some students are late to school due to factors beyond their control—such as a parent who consistently drops them off late—the attendance team should include someone trained in counseling parents and family. A school counselor might be perfect for this task. Finally, some students fully understand the school's attendance and tardy policies and choose not to meet these expectations. In this case, interventions that hold students accountable to meeting the expectations could be necessary. A school administrator would be best for these. So, the guiding coalition could form a Tier 2 attendance team composed of the attendance secretary, a counselor, and a site administrator.

Next, the guiding coalition would want to schedule frequent, regular meetings for this team, in which members could take these five steps.

1. Review recent school attendance information to identify students who might need attendance support.

2. Discuss each identified student to determine what causes the student's attendance problems.

3. Design a course of action for each student.

4. Determine if other staff members should be included in a student's plan.

5. Monitor whether each plan is working and revise as needed.

Notice that this example represents an ongoing problem-solving process to systematically target and implement Tier 2 attendance interventions. The key is not trying to find a perfect, universal, one-size-fits-all attendance intervention, but instead identifying the best-trained staff to lead specific interventions and creating dedicated time for them to solve problems together.

Reteach!

We cannot stress this point strongly enough: behavior interventions are no different from effective academic interventions—both require effective reteaching and targeted practice to ensure students learn an essential outcome. Suppose a student is struggling with learning the Pythagorean theorem in geometry. Would the following steps comprise an effective set of interventions?

1. The student does not learn how to apply the Pythagorean theorem by the end of initial instruction, so the teacher removes the student from class for a few minutes, then has them come back in and try to now demonstrate the skill.

2. That does not work, so the teacher assigns the student to lunchtime detention, where they can sit in silence. Afterward, the teacher asks the student to demonstrate the skill.

3. The student still can't independently apply the Pythagorean theorem, so they are assigned after-school detention. The student sits in silence and reflects on their actions. Then the next day in class, the teacher asks the student to demonstrate the skill.

4. Now the student is being defiant to the school's demands by appearing to refuse to learn the Pythagorean theorem. The student is suspended for a day at home. Then the next day, the teacher again asks them to demonstrate the skill.

Most educators would never respond to an academic need with such a misguided approach. Yet our experience is that most schools respond to student misbehaviors this way. The biggest problem with this approach is it assumes the student knows how to self-address their behavior and is willfully choosing to misbehave instead. Our experience is that almost all students *want* to succeed in school, *want* to please others, and *want* positive interactions with adults and peers. Most misbehavior is not driven by defiance or a deep-rooted desire to fail—the students misbehave because they don't know how to succeed.

Instead of an overreliance on punishment, effective *reteaching* is required. Utilize the same types of best teaching practices used for academic instruction.

1. Clearly identify the specific skill you want targeted students to learn.

2. Provide students with context regarding why the skill is important to learn.

3. Explicitly reteach—step by step—how to do the skill.

4. Have students practice or role-play the skill.

5. Assess each student's proficiency with the skill.

6. Provide targeted feedback and support.

Because students should not miss Tier 1 class time for behavior interventions, some schools use time during lunch and after school to provide behavior support. The key is to move from detention time to reteaching and reflection time. Organizing the time and staff needed for reteaching is why the guiding coalition must lead this process.

Monitor Each Intervention's Effectiveness and Revise as Needed

Many schools perpetuate interventions that are not very effective. For example, we have worked with schools whose intervention for students who have tardiness problems is to suspend them. Let's think about this—a student is missing valuable class time, so the intervention to get the student to class on time is to prevent them from attending class. If a school wants to continue such a practice, the guiding coalition should monitor the intervention's effectiveness. How many targeted students, after being removed from class as a consequence for missing class, improve their timeliness? Does the intervention achieve the goal? If so, then keep the practice in the school's intervention toolbox. But if most students do not improve, why continue a practice with little evidence that it works?

We do *not* intend for the preceding recommendations and examples to suggest that behavior interventions must only be positive experiences for students. Some interventions require students to do things that are not fun or enjoyable. What we are suggesting is the intent of any intervention should be not to punish students for mistakes or misbehavior but to teach students the right actions. In the end, we find that the adults in the building respond much better to positive supports from their supervisors than to punitive, fear-based policies. Why would students be any different?

Helpful Tools

The following tools will help you accomplish the work for this essential action.

▸ **"Reasons Why Students Might Fail to Complete Homework" (page 254):** This tool helps teams determine possible reasons why a student might fail to complete a homework assignment and the interventions they could use to most effectively address these concerns. Educators can use this same process to brainstorm and target other types of Tier 2 behavior interventions.

▸ **"Tier 2 Interventions for Essential Social and Academic Behaviors: Critical Questions" (page 255):** This tool provides four critical questions teams must consider when developing an effective supplemental intervention system to help students with essential academic and social behaviors.

▸ **"Tier 2 Menu of Response Options":** This tool from the book *Behavior Solutions* (Hannigan et al., 2021) is an example of how a school can develop a list of options to target specific behaviors at Tier 2. We highly recommend this book for digging deeper into each option. (Visit **go.SolutionTree.com/RTIatWork** to download this free reproducible.)

Coaching Tips

Everything a guiding coalition needs to know to effectively plan and implement Tier 2 interventions for essential academic and social behaviors is explained in detail in the previous sections. The question guiding coalition members must ask themselves is, "Do we have the skill and the will to follow through?" Most school staff have the skills needed to develop and implement an effective supplemental intervention process. Together, they can research, collectively work on, and address whatever skills might be missing.

The more challenging part of the question is, "Do we have the *will*?" Changing an education system historically built to categorize and weed out students who are unsuccessful, and to depend on individual teachers' autonomy for addressing any needs students might demonstrate, is a significant cultural change and an even greater challenge. This is the reason we recommend spending extensive and consistent time and effort building a culture of collective responsibility for high levels of student learning. Within such a culture, stakeholders readily accept the challenge of learning together to build any needed skills and holding each other accountable for embracing and demonstrating the will to make changes for students.

Reasons Why Students Might Fail to Complete Homework

In the first column, list logical reasons why a student might fail to complete a homework assignment. Across each row, list the responses and interventions currently applied to the reason you listed for why students fail to complete a homework assignment. Next to each potential cause, draw a plus sign for each response and intervention that likely would help the student improve. Draw a minus sign for each response and intervention that likely would not help the student improve. Finally, circle each logical cause for which your school has no response and intervention to help the student improve.

Logical Reasons Why Students Might Fail to Complete Homework	Current Site Responses and Interventions for Missing Homework						

Tier 2 Interventions for Essential Social and Academic Behaviors: Critical Questions

To ensure the development of an effective Tier 2 intervention system to help students with essential academic and social behaviors, carefully and collaboratively think through the following four questions.

1. How will we regularly review schoolwide behavior information?

    a. How often and when will we meet?

    b. What information do we need to review?

2. How will we target the cause of student misbehavior, not just the symptoms?

    a. Which behaviors happening across our school need our attention?

    b. Who has expertise in assisting with this challenge?

    c. What are appropriate intervention strategies?

3. What do we need to learn together?

    a. What research do we need?

    b. Who, beyond this team, needs to be involved?

4. How will we allocate time and resources?

    a. What focus team or teams do we need? Who needs to be on each team?

    b. How often and when will these teams meet?

    c. What will be the process for requesting and allocating resources to support the focus team or teams?

Action 4

Coordinate Interventions for Students Needing Academic *and* Behavior Supports

We know that some students struggle in school for academic reasons—that is, they lack essential academic skills and knowledge needed to succeed in core curriculum. Other students' struggles are due to an inability to consistently demonstrate the behaviors and motivation necessary for academic success.

However, often the students most at risk demonstrate both needs. To successfully intervene when students demonstrate academic and behavioral difficulties, a school must have a process to coordinate these supports. Because this requires coordination between classroom teachers and schoolwide support staff, the school's guiding coalition should take lead responsibility for this outcome.

Here's Why

Sometimes, it can be difficult to determine whether students' behavior is causing their academic struggles or if the academic struggles are prompting negative behaviors. (Which came first, the chicken or the egg?) Many schools struggle with targeting interventions for these students because they endlessly debate whether they should first target their behavior or their academic needs. As Austin Buffum, Mike Mattos, Chris Weber, and Tom Hierck (2015) write in their book *Uniting Academic and Behavior Interventions: Solving the Skill or Will Dilemma*:

> The reason we struggle with the skill-or-will dilemma is because we are asking the wrong question. It is not a "chicken or egg" question, but rather a "chicken and egg" solution. If you were a farmer, and your goal was to successfully raise a flock of healthy chickens, you would not need chickens or eggs—you would need chickens and eggs. Likewise, if our job as educators is to raise healthy, productive, successful adults, our students will not need either the academic skills or the behaviors and dispositions needed to succeed as an adult, but both the skill and the will. (p. 12)

Creating a systematic, collaborative process to coordinate academic and behavior interventions for targeted students is the key to achieving this outcome.

Here's How

We offer the following four steps for the guiding coalition to create a targeted, comprehensive Tier 2 intervention plan for students who need academic and behavior supports.

1. Systematically identify students who could potentially benefit from both academic and behavior interventions.

2. Schedule meeting time to plan and coordinate academic and behavior interventions.

3. Utilize the pro-solve process.

4. Monitor and revise.

Systematically Identify Students Who Could Potentially Benefit From Both Academic and Behavior Interventions

As discussed earlier in this chapter, we recommend that a school have a systematic process for identifying students who might need schoolwide Tier 2 support approximately every three weeks. Because this process is designed to create a 360-degree view of a student's entire school day, it helps identify students who might need both academic and behavior supports.

Schedule Meeting Time to Plan and Coordinate Academic and Behavior Interventions

Because the goal is to coordinate academic and behavior interventions, the process must include the teachers who are responsible for meeting the targeted student's academic needs and the school-wide staff who lead Tier 2 behavior supports.

Utilize the Pro-Solve Process

Determining the appropriate academic and behavior interventions for an individual student requires a highly effective problem-solving process. This process must identify not only the obstacles hindering the student's success but also the causes of these obstacles, the best interventions to address these needs, the desired outcomes, and the lead person or team responsible for carrying out each intervention. These goals are captured in the reproducible "RTI at Work Pro-Solve Intervention Targeting Process: Tier 1 and Tier 2" (page 209; Buffum et al., 2015).

At the heart of the protocol is a sequence of five critical questions that help with determining the causes and potential solutions for a student in need of academic and behavior interventions.

1. **What is the concern?** Obviously, a student is unlikely to be referred for schoolwide interventions unless there are concerns regarding the student's current level of achievement. Specific academic and behavior concerns should be listed. Try not to spend more than a few minutes on this step.

2. **What is the cause of the concern?** Many struggling students demonstrate the same academic and behavioral concerns, such as low test scores, poor grades, inconsistent attendance, missing assignments, and disruptive behavior. It is critical to remember that these concerns represent similar symptoms, but the underlying causes can vary from student to student. For example, numerous students may demonstrate poor attendance, but this does not mean the cause of each student's absences is the same. The key is to determine *why* each student is missing school. Eliminate the cause and solve the problem.

3. **What is the desired outcome?** Many schools fall into the trap of focusing on eliminating the negative concern instead of targeting the desired positive outcomes. For example, the concern might be that a student inappropriately blurts out answers during whole-group instruction, thus demonstrating disruptive behavior. Instead of discussing what steps the staff can take to stop the disruptive behavior, a better discussion would be to determine the appropriate academic behaviors the student must learn to successfully participate in whole-group learning opportunities.

4. **What steps should the school take to best achieve the desired outcome?** By moving beyond assigning students to interventions based on common symptoms, and instead diagnosing the cause of each student's struggles and then determining the desired

positive outcomes, the school is now ready to identify the interventions and action steps necessary to meet each student's specific needs. How will teams effectively teach each of the desired outcomes for this student?

5. **Who is going to take lead responsibility to ensure each intervention is implemented?** The best-laid plans are useless if they are not effectively implemented. Yet when everyone is responsible for an intervention, no one is responsible. At some point, the buck must stop with specific staff members who take the lead for each intervention for this student.

Notice that we divided the rows of the "RTI at Work Pro-Solve Intervention Targeting Process: Tier 1 and Tier 2" tool (page 209) into broad sections: teacher team responsibilities and guiding coalition responsibilities. Teacher teams should take lead responsibility for reteaching the following.

- ▶ **Essential grade-level standards:** These are the academic skills and knowledge the teacher team identifies as essential for every student to master to be adequately prepared for success in the next course or grade level.

- ▶ **Immediate prerequisite skills:** These are the specific academic skills and knowledge that represent the immediate building blocks to essential grade-level standards. They were most likely taught in either a previous unit, a previous school year, or the previous course within a subject-based sequence of coursework.

- ▶ **English language:** At Tier 2, students who need support in English language have already learned basic conversational English but might still need assistance with subject-specific academic vocabulary and the written structures of English.

The guiding coalition should take the lead for the following.

- ▶ **Academic behaviors:** School support staff can help students who need assistance in academic behaviors, such as completing assignments, studying and organizing, staying focused and on task, and participating in classroom activities.

- ▶ **Social behaviors:** Interventions in social behaviors can include assistance with school attendance, positive peer relationships, good conduct in competitive activities, and appropriate school language.

- ▶ **Health and home:** Sometimes, specific health concerns and home factors can negatively affect student achievement in school. For example, a student might miss class time due to a mild bout of asthma caused by a windy day, or they might be upset at school because their parent is being deployed for military duty. The school's health and counseling staff could provide supplemental support, thus helping the student attend class and stay focused.

Monitor and Revise

Once you develop an intervention plan, team members must monitor student progress to determine whether students are achieving the desired outcomes. While we designed the pro-solve targeting process to determine a student's needs, identify effective interventions, and assign responsibilities for carrying out the intervention plan, it is unlikely that initial results will reflect a perfectly implemented intervention plan. Expect to revise the intervention plan based on the results collected.

Because the pro-solve process forces the team to determine the specific desired outcomes for the targeted student, this process should guide what data the team collects to monitor student progress and who will be responsible. Included for the pro-solve activity is a complementary monitoring tool, "RTI at Work Pro-Solve Intervention Monitoring Plan: Tier 1 and Tier 2" (page 222; Buffum et al., 2015).

We aligned this tool to the outcomes determined through asking pro-solve questions and designed it to simplify the paperwork associated with the monitoring process. Because staff refer students for additional help every three weeks, it seems logical to complete and review this monitoring form about every three weeks. The team can use this information to revise a student's plan, discontinue services as the student achieves goals, and prompt celebration when the student is succeeding.

Helpful Tools

The following tools will help you accomplish the work for this essential action.

▶ **"RTI at Work Pro-Solve Intervention Targeting Process: Tier 1 and Tier 2"** **(see chapter 5, action 1, page 209):** This activity is designed to help identify, diagnose, target, and monitor Tier 2 academic and behavior interventions.

▶ **"RTI at Work Pro-Solve Intervention Monitoring Plan: Tier 1 and Tier 2"** **(see chapter 5, action 3, page 222):** Teams should use this tool in coordination with the "RTI at Work Pro-Solve Intervention Targeting Process: Tier 1 and Tier 2" reproducible. Members can record a student's progress in meeting their academic and behavior goals.

Coaching Tips

Use the same strategy to successfully coordinate interventions for students with multiple needs—communicate, communicate, communicate! Within that communication, the guiding coalition must ensure that all stakeholders:

▶ Understand why a coordinated system is necessary

▶ Have opportunities to provide input

▶ Understand their role in making any needed decisions

▶ Can articulate how and when they need to participate

▶ Actively support the system once it is in place

Meeting these communication needs requires multiple ongoing forms of communication—print, digital, verbal, and collaborative. In other words, use every possible channel, especially those used for nonessential information (for example, newsletters, blogs, and faculty meetings).

Perhaps even more important, every guiding coalition member must walk the talk. For example, requesting staff members' participation in other activities when they're needed in a pro-solve meeting sends a mixed message. Casual conversations over lunch must consistently communicate the same message that formal forms of communication send. Fundamentally, communication depends on both words and deeds, and often, day-to-day conversations and behaviors are the most powerful vehicles for sharing important information.

Conclusion

The goal of Tier 2 is to approach and solve problems when they are small. When a student first begins to struggle with a new essential academic standard, or fails to demonstrate the behaviors necessary to succeed, the school should be ready to respond quickly and effectively. We don't allow students to fall too far behind when we systematically identify students through common assessments and frequent teacher recommendation procedures. Assigning lead responsibility for academic and behavior interventions across the school—and based on expertise—makes responding effectively realistic, even when school resources are limited. Over time, the school should have fewer and fewer students in need of Tier 3 intensive reinforcements because of this proactive approach.

But regardless of how well a school implements Tier 1 and Tier 2, there undoubtedly will be students who need more. Some students might have significant gaps in essential skills that they should have mastered years ago. These foundational prerequisite skills are not the focus of Tier 1 or Tier 2—they are the purpose of Tier 3. The next two chapters (part three) focus on how to provide these intensive reinforcements.

PART THREE

TIER 3 ESSENTIAL ACTIONS

CHAPTER 7

Tier 3 Guiding Coalition Essential Actions

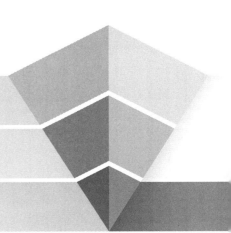

All students can be successful given the right environment. By supporting them both inside and outside the classroom, we can ensure they gain the skills they need to excel in adulthood.

—Jasper Fox

In this chapter, we focus on Tier 3 of the RTI at Work pyramid (see figure 7.1, page 264). Visually, this portion of the pyramid represents the following.

▶ Tier 3 is not regular education or special education—it must be available for *any* student who demonstrates the need.

▶ Tier 3 is provided collaboratively, leveraging the experts on campus who are best trained to meet the outcomes of each intervention. Most often, intensive reinforcements are led not by classroom teachers but by specialized support staff.

▶ Tier 3 reinforcements should be embedded into a student's schedule nearly every day.

▶ This intensive support must be in addition to Tier 1 and Tier 2, not in place of them.

▶ Reinforcements must be targeted to individual student needs.

We have previously identified supports that students receive at Tier 2 as *interventions* (extra support to learn essential grade-level standards and immediate prerequisite skills) and at Tier 3 as *reinforcements* (intensive support with foundational prerequisite skills that should have been mastered in prior years).

If a school provides students with access to essential grade-level curriculum and effective initial teaching during Tier 1 core instruction, and targeted academic and behavior interventions in meeting those standards at Tier 2, then most students should succeed. But there inevitably will be some students who still struggle because they lack the critical foundational prerequisite skills needed to learn—skills that span all subject areas and grade levels.

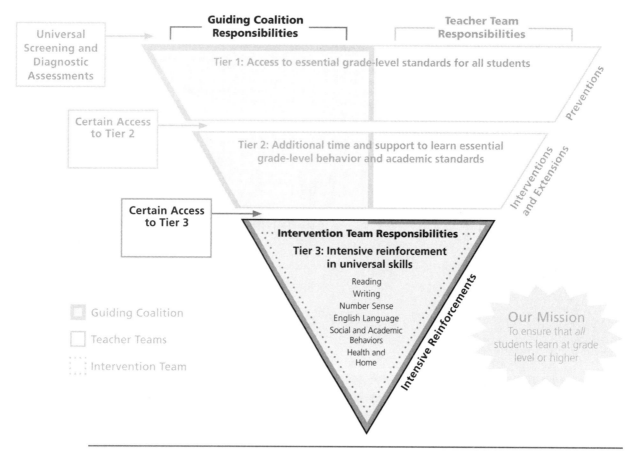

FIGURE 7.1: Focus on Tier 3 guiding coalition essential actions.

Notice that six universal skills of learning are listed at Tier 3 of our RTI at Work pyramid.

1. **Reading:** The ability to decode and comprehend grade-level text

2. **Writing:** The ability to effectively communicate grade-level thinking through writing

3. **Number sense:** The ability to understand and apply basic mathematical reasoning

4. **English language:** The ability to communicate in English (or the school's primary language)

5. **Social and academic behaviors:** The ability to regularly demonstrate foundational, age-appropriate behaviors at school

6. **Health and home:** The ability to overcome complications due to health or factors outside of school

These universal skills represent much more than a student's need for help in a specific learning standard. Instead, they represent a series of skills that enable a student to comprehend instruction, access information, demonstrate understanding, communicate effectively, and function behaviorally in a school setting. Universal skills are foundational competencies that support a student's ability to learn. If a student is significantly behind in just one of these universal skills, they will struggle in virtually every grade level, course, and subject, and usually a school's most at-risk students are behind in more than one. When students lack foundational prerequisite skills, their education is like a house being built on a faulty foundation. This is why we call Tier 3 supports *reinforcement*. If your house's foundation were unstable, you would call in specialists to *reinforce* it.

Elementary schools do not assume that students entering kindergarten possess basic literacy, numeracy, and self-monitoring skills, so these universal skills comprise most of the essential grade-level standards in the primary grades. Due to this schoolwide focus in the early years of school, most students enter the upper grades with at least an adequate level of mastery in these foundational prerequisite skills.

Beyond the primary grades, schools generally assume that students entering upper-elementary, middle, and high school already possess these universal skills, and so does the state or provincial grade-level curriculum. Students who have not learned these skills need intensive instruction to catch up, as these skills are no longer part of grade-level core instruction.

Determining the individual students in need of Tier 3 help, creating a master schedule that provides multiple tiers of support, and allocating the resources necessary to achieve these outcomes require a schoolwide effort. For this reason, we recommend that two schoolwide teams take lead responsibility for Tier 3 reinforcements: (1) the guiding coalition and (2) the site intervention team. The guiding coalition takes lead responsibility for allocating and coordinating time and resources to support students in need of intensive support, while the school intervention team takes primary responsibility for diagnosing, planning, and monitoring the interventions provided for each student at Tier 3.

In this chapter, we discuss the responsibilities of the guiding coalition at Tier 3. Its essential actions include the following.

1. Create a dynamic, problem-solving site intervention team.
2. Identify students needing intensive reinforcements.
3. Prioritize resources based on the greatest student needs.
4. Create a systematic and timely process to refer students to the site intervention team.
5. Assess intervention and reinforcement effectiveness.

Let's explore each of these essential actions.

Action 1

Create a Dynamic, Problem-Solving Site Intervention Team

When determining who should serve on the site intervention team, the guiding coalition must consider the key responsibilities of the intervention team at Tier 3.

- Diagnose the specific needs of each student requiring intensive reinforcements.
- Determine and prioritize targeted supports.
- Monitor the progress of students receiving Tier 3 reinforcements.
- Revise student reinforcements as needed.
- Recommend if consideration for special education identification is needed and justified.

It is unlikely that an individual teacher or teacher team has the diverse expertise needed to take lead responsibility for these outcomes, or that a teacher or teacher team has the authority to assign the schoolwide resources (for example, the school psychologist, speech-language pathologist, counselor, and special education teachers) needed to potentially provide these intensive supports. This is why the guiding coalition must create a team whose purpose is to take lead responsibility for these outcomes—the site intervention team.

Here's Why

When patients experience vexing, persistent medical problems, doctors often refer them to a specialist, or even more than one specialist, to receive a second or third opinion regarding a course of treatment. In much the same way, education specialists, working with classroom teachers, should address vexing, persistent academic or behavioral problems to best serve individual students. This in no way minimizes the importance of classroom teachers but instead recognizes the overwhelming tasks we expect them to undertake every day.

Elementary teachers are responsible for somewhere between twenty and forty students, and we expect them to prepare and deliver instruction in reading, writing, mathematics, science, social studies, and so on. Secondary teachers see literally hundreds of students each day, each one a unique individual with specific learning needs. How can we possibly expect classroom teachers to diagnose and prescribe interventions to solve complex problems without consulting and working with education specialists such as the school psychologist, speech-language pathologist, counselor, content specialists, and special education teachers?

Again, the site intervention team must solve students' complex problems, not merely label students or refer them for special education testing, although that may indeed be the best course of action for some. A team of educators with specialized training and perspective, working with the classroom teachers, is best to conduct this lifesaving work.

Here's How

The needs of students requiring Tier 3 reinforcements are usually quite daunting. These students rarely have a single deficit but, instead, a tangled knot of academic and behavioral challenges. Effective problem solving is key to finding the right solutions.

What is the best team structure to brainstorm solutions to a tough problem—a team of people who all possess the same expertise, or a team of people who possess diverse expertise? The logical answer, of course, is a team with diverse expertise. If a student struggles in a specific essential academic skill—like the ability to solve a linear mathematics equation—then the similarly trained algebra team would be perfectly designed to identify effective interventions for the singular need. But if a student has significant gaps in foundational reading, number sense, and behavior, the algebra team would not be the most effective problem solver for this student. A team composed of people with expertise in all the students' areas of need would be best. Because the site intervention team should purposely have highly trained educators in the universal skills focused on at Tier 3, this diverse team has the best chance to diagnose, target, prioritize, and monitor the intervention needs of students who face daunting problems.

When creating the site intervention team, the guiding coalition must consider the six universal skills listed at Tier 3: (1) reading, (2) writing, (3) number sense, (4) English language, (5) academic and social behaviors, and (6) health and home. Now answer this question: Who that your school has access to has the greatest level of expertise in each of these areas? If your school has a designated reading specialist, then this faculty member will be an excellent candidate to serve on the intervention team to brainstorm solutions for identified students needing intensive reading support. If your school does not have a reading specialist, then which educator on your faculty is best trained in the subject of reading? The "Building a Site Intervention Team" reproducible (page 269) can help the guiding coalition with assembling this team.

When a school lacks expertise in a specific area, the guiding coalition should creatively consider these needs during the hiring process. For example, consider a high school principal who has an opening to fill in social studies and also has a vacancy for a varsity girls' basketball coach. For years, high school principals have been mindful to look for teaching applicants who also have backgrounds in coaching. To apply this same thinking, we find that many secondary schools are not staffed with a reading specialist position. And while the schools have credentialed ELA teachers, secondary ELA teachers usually do not have a deep level of experience teaching foundational reading skills. But what if, when hiring for a subject-specific opening, a secondary school has applicants with previous primary-grade experience? Or an applicant with a special education background? Hiring one of these professionals could potentially add much-needed expertise to the school, without requiring additional staffing resource approval from district administration. Remaining mindful of the specific roles needed on a site intervention team should be part of hiring decisions for K–12 schools.

We highly recommend that the principal serve on the intervention team. Tier 3 help should be embedded in a student's daily schedule; this means determining the right interventions for a student at Tier 3 depends on the school's available instructional time and resources. And in the end, the principal usually has final say on staffing and the master schedule. If the principal is not part of the planning conversation, it is harder to finalize student supports.

Finally, the guiding coalition is responsible for scheduling time for the intervention team to meet. We recommend the intervention team meet weekly for at least thirty minutes. If this is not possible, then twice-monthly meetings should be the minimum.

Helpful Tools

The following tools will help you accomplish the work for this essential action.

- **"Building a Site Intervention Team" (page 269):** This template helps the guiding coalition determine who is most highly trained to fill a particular role; this is especially helpful when someone with the exact title listed is not available.

- **"Dimensions of Success" (page 270):** This form helps the guiding coalition determine its effectiveness across three dimensions: (1) results, (2) process, and (3) relationship.

Coaching Tips

Writer and critic Marcel Proust (1923) claims that the real voyage in discovery consists not in seeking new landscapes but in having new eyes. How, you might wonder, does this statement apply to the establishment of a site intervention team and its potential impact? Consider the following.

- The site intervention team's power results from not only seeking new intervention strategies but also seeing each student with new eyes. This is why diverse team membership is so important. Each member brings a different expertise and a unique perspective to understanding students and brainstorming ways to best support student success.

▶ A voyage of discovery is one that requires thoughtful reflection. Questions such as the following may help team members think about the students' view of their world and school: "How does my school respond when I am struggling? What message do I get from my teachers and peers? What is important to me?"

▶ Additionally, the site intervention team must establish a meeting culture of open dialogue and respect for all voices.

To accomplish a culture of open dialogue and respect, Interaction Associates (Harris, n.d.) suggests that leaders who are tasked with facilitating team meetings attend equally to three dimensions of success—(1) results, (2) process, and (3) relationship (the RPR model)—to build strategic, self-aware, and highly collaborative teams.

1. *Results* refers to achievement of a goal and accomplishment of a task.

2. *Process* refers to how a team does the work, how it designs and manages the work, and how it measures and evaluates the work.

3. *Relationship* refers to the quality of team members' experiences, their relationships with each other and with the organization as a whole, and the level of trust and respect team members show each other.

To maximize success, leaders—and in turn, teams—consider all three dimensions and build and maintain a balanced view of what success really is. Clearly understood goals, tasks, meeting roles, and team norms are essential to this balanced view of success. Equally important, teams must consistently take advantage of facilitative protocols that ensure effective use of time and maximum participation.

Building a Site Intervention Team

Team members: _____

Use the following tool to build a site intervention team. Remember, when you don't have access to someone with the title in the second column, ask yourself, "Which staff member is best trained to meet this need?"

Essential Role	Recommended Title	Staff Members Best Trained to Meet This Need
Administration	Principal	
Reading	Reading specialist	
Writing	English language arts specialist	
Mathematics	Mathematics specialist	
English language	English learner specialist	
Language	Speech-language pathologist	
Teaching differentiation	Special education teacher	
Behavior	Psychologist or counselor	
Social or family needs	Counselor	
Instructional resources	Librarian	
Community resources	Community resource officer, social worker, or counselor	

When will this team meet? (Determine a weekly meeting time and location.)

- Time: _____

- Location: _____

What are the team norms?

_____

_____

_____

_____

_____

Source: Adapted from Buffum, A., & Mattos, M. (2014, May). Criteria for selecting essential standards [Presentation]. Simplifying Response to Intervention Workshop, Prince George, British Columbia, Canada.

Dimensions of Success

Effective teams, like effective leaders, balance their focus across three dimensions: (1) results, (2) process, and (3) relationship.

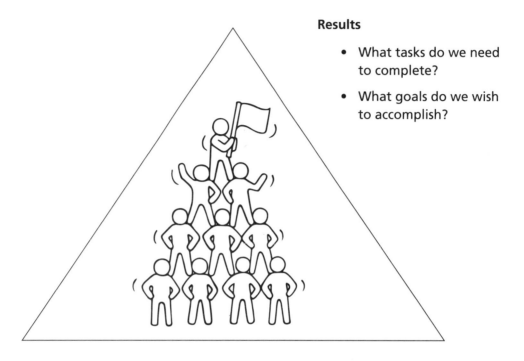

Results

- What tasks do we need to complete?

- What goals do we wish to accomplish?

Process

- How do we do our work?

- How do we design and manage our work?

- How do we monitor and evaluate our work?

Relationship

- How do people experience each other on our team?

- How do we relate to our whole school?

- How do we feel about our involvement and contributions?

Source: Adapted from Harris, J. (n.d.). Facilitative leadership: Balancing the dimensions of success [Blog post]. Accessed at http://interactionassociates.com/insights/blog/facilitative-leadership-balancing-dimensions-success#.WVFGhjOZPUo on June 25, 2017.

Action 2

Identify Students Needing Intensive Reinforcements

Because the best intervention is prevention, schools must create a timely process to identify students who need Tier 3 reinforcements. When schools and districts view RTI as a potential pathway to special education identification, they mistakenly move students from tier to tier. As a result, the following sequence plays out.

- ▶ All students start each year at Tier 1.

- ▶ When students start to struggle, move them to Tier 2 for some extra help.

- ▶ When Tier 2 is not working, move students to Tier 3 for intensive help.

- ▶ When students continue to fail in Tier 3, recommend them for special education.

In this misguided approach, students must fail at Tier 1 and Tier 2—and be properly documented—before they can receive Tier 3 support. If the faculty already know (or quickly determine) that a student has significant gaps in foundational prerequisite skills upon entering a new school year, why delay starting Tier 3 support? The student is academically drowning; why let them sink deeper before providing a life preserver?

In RTI research, the process for proactively identifying students for Tier 3 reinforcements is known as *universal screening*. Rather than waiting weeks into the school year for students to demonstrate the need, schools should identify these students as early as possible and place them into Tier 3 intensive reinforcements.

When done well, Tier 3 supports can be planned prior to the start of school, so intensive help can begin the first week. Unless these students are new to the school or school district, you probably already know enough about them to avoid waiting for them to fail once again before referring them to the most intensive reinforcements. This kind of universal screening relies not on a series of tests but on data and knowledge already accumulated relating to students who are most in need of support.

Here's Why

Honestly, how many times have you witnessed the following scenario? A student who has a reading comprehension level several grades below their current grade level, and who lacks fluency with key arithmetic operations, goes home for the summer. When school resumes in the fall, this student returns reading at or above their current grade level and having reliable fluency with all arithmetic operations. Probably zero!

Why would we wait to see if some kind of miracle occurs over summer break? If we are concerned about false positives (students placed into Tier 3 who don't actually need that level of support), frequent progress monitoring will soon reveal if something significant happened to the student academically (Fuchs & Fuchs, 2007) and we can remove them from Tier 3 reinforcements. This thinking should apply to behavior interventions as well. Students with extreme deficits in social and academic behaviors seldom, if ever, completely heal over summer break.

Administering nationally normed universal screening instruments at the start of a new school year can consume many precious days, if not weeks, of instructional time. At the end of each year, schools usually have achievement data on students that clearly identify those who will enter next year in need of intensive help. Except for newly enrolled students, schools already know who these students are, and they can plan and schedule intensive support in their master schedule and begin providing targeted Tier 3 help beginning the first day of school.

This is not to say that schools should not administer diagnostic assessments at the beginning of the year to better target exactly what interventions would best benefit students who are struggling. This idea is like the vision screening that many elementary schools do—students come to the nurse's office and read from the Snellen eye chart. The school refers those students who can't accurately read line six, E D F C Z P, to an ophthalmologist to receive a more diagnostic evaluation. This is an example of screening followed by a more diagnostic assessment. Notice that the school doesn't have every student take an ophthalmologist exam.

Using end-of-year data to proactively identify students allows schools to place those with the greatest need in Tier 3 intensive reinforcements the very first week of school. Schools then follow up with just these students using a highly diagnostic assessment that helps target the Tier 3 interventions on *causes* rather than symptoms.

Here's How

For students returning to a school from the previous year—or transitioning from a feeder school within the district—the leadership team should use the information they have already gathered to identify students in need of Tier 3 intensive reinforcements. For academic interventions, this information could include state or provincial tests, end-of-course exams, common summative and formative assessments, diagnostic assessments, running records, and informal assessment data. For behavior interventions, schools should use information, such as functional behavioral analyses and other behavior screening scales, to initially place students into Tier 3 intensive reinforcements at the beginning of the school year.

For transfer students new to the school, the guiding coalition should have a plan to administer short, targeted universal screening assessments to get a quick baseline for the students in the universal skills (for example, the Northwest Evaluation Association's [NWEA's] Measures of Academic Progress). We have seen schools administer these screening assessments during students' registration process so the data are immediately available when creating the students' schedules.

It is possible that a student will not show up on the school's radar at the beginning of the year but at some point in the year will need Tier 3 support. Perhaps the student disengages and becomes depressed because some tragic event has befallen them and their family. This is but one example of how a student might draw concern later in the year. In this instance, the site intervention team becomes involved (see chapter 8, page 293).

Systematic, timely, and targeted identification of students in greatest need is the one area of RTI at Work in which schools must be near perfect. If they don't identify the students who are failing academically or behaviorally, it may be too late to help.

Helpful Tool

The following tool will help you accomplish the work for this essential action.

▶ **"Universal Screening Planning Guide" (page 274):** This tool helps the guiding coalition determine which criteria, personnel, and processes to use to screen students needing intervention support in universal skills of reading, writing, number sense, English language, social and academic behaviors, and health and home.

Coaching Tips

To accurately identify students needing intensive support, keep in mind that the concept of universal screening needs to apply to every teacher and, as a result, every student. Educators must identify students who are failing in art and business education classes as well as in English language arts and mathematics.

That said, once again, communicate, communicate, communicate! In a staff meeting devoted to the singular topic of universal screening, provide all teachers and support staff members with background information to facilitate a shared understanding of *what* universal screening means and *why* it is imperative. To ensure understanding, staff members must see examples of universal screening tools, dialogue with each other, raise questions, and challenge each other's thinking. A short survey can provide an overview of both their understanding of the concepts and their level of support for implementation. If the survey shows either is lacking, it is essential to spend additional time strengthening these key outcomes.

Finally, the guiding coalition must establish a clearly articulated schoolwide expectation for developing and using universal screening tools before moving to implementation. This expectation must include all teachers and all subject areas, as well as support staff who focus on student behavior. Include a deadline and accountability for developing screening tools. Additionally, teachers must know the expectations for using their universal screeners, collecting the data, and communicating to the guiding coalition their results and recommendations for students in need of Tier 3 reinforcements.

As with all decisions and actions, once the process for referring students for Tier 3 support is up and running, the guiding coalition must revisit and re-evaluate its effectiveness on a regular basis. Staff input, as well as student learning results, must be part of evaluation.

As a final note, it is important to remember that RTI at Work is based on a fundamental commitment to *all* students learning at high levels. Creating a systematic and timely process for referring students to Tier 3 support is critical to making that commitment a reality.

Universal Screening Planning Guide

Use the following guide to screen students needing intensive reinforcements.

Universal Skill	At-Risk Criteria *What criteria will be used to determine whether a student needs intensive support?*	Screening Process *What screening assessment, process, or both will be used to identify students who need intensive support?*	When *When will the screening process take place?*	Who *Who will administer the screening?*	Intensive Reinforcements Available *What intensive reinforcement or reinforcements will be used to accelerate student learning and support the identified students?*
Reading					
Writing					
Number Sense					
English Language					
Social and Academic Behaviors					
Health and Home					

Universal Screening Planning Guide Protocol

This activity is designed to help a guiding coalition plan for universal screening by creating a process to identify students who need intensive reinforcements *before* they fail. Because the purpose is to provide preventive support, this activity is best completed prior to the start of the school year.

For each universal skill, answer the question for each column.

1. **At-risk criteria:** At each grade level, what criteria will be used to determine whether a student needs intensive reinforcements? For example, an elementary school may determine that any student entering first grade without the ability to properly recognize all twenty-six letters (uppercase and lowercase) is extremely at risk in reading and will be considered for immediate intensive support. At a high school, any student whose reading ability is two or more years below grade level (grade-level equivalent) could be considered for immediate intensive support.

2. **Screening process:** What screening assessment, process, or both will be used to identify students who need intensive reinforcements? The guiding coalition should identify the most effective, efficient, and timely process to gather the at-risk criteria data for each student.

3. **When:** When will the screening process take place? Obviously, if the purpose of universal screening is to provide preventive support, then these data should be collected either prior to the start of the school year or as early in the school year as possible. Finally, as new students enroll in school throughout the year, it is important to consider how they can be screened during the enrollment process.

4. **Who:** Who will administer the screening? Because the guiding coalition has representation from every teacher team, as well as responsibility for coordinating school support staff, this team is best positioned to organize the necessary resources.

5. **Intensive reinforcements available:** What intensive reinforcements will be used to accelerate student learning and support the identified students? There is no point to universal screening if the school has no plan to provide these students with extra support in their area or areas of need.

One final consideration: For a school new to universal screening, it may be overwhelming to begin screening in all six universal skills, at all grade levels, immediately. In this case, we recommend that the guiding coalition identify the universal skill (reading, writing, number sense, English language, social and academic behaviors, or health and home) that is currently the greatest area of need in its school. Start by focusing on this one. As the school builds skill and competence in this area, others can be added.

Source: Adapted from Buffum, A., Mattos, M., & Weber, C. (2012). Simplifying response to intervention: Four essential guiding principles. *Bloomington, IN: Solution Tree Press.*

Action 3

Prioritize Resources Based on the Greatest Student Needs

Students requiring Tier 3 reinforcements are the students most at risk in schools. Schools must utilize their very best available resources and think outside the box as they prioritize how best to use what they have on hand to meet these students' needs.

An example of this kind of thinking occurs in a scene from the movie *Apollo 13* (Howard, 1995). Having discovered that the flight crew will die from increasing levels of carbon dioxide, the flight director tells staff at the Johnson Space Center to fit a square peg into a round hole, and quickly, to find a way to solve the problem. Next, a flight engineer dumps an assortment of every available thing on the lunar and command modules and says to a group of engineers, "We've got to find a way to make this [the square peg] fit into the hole for this [the round peg], using nothing but that [the assorted objects]" (Howard, 1995).

This metaphor relates to what we ask schools to do: take a system of schooling designed to sift and sort students into a rank order based on their perceived ability and turn it into a system that ensures high levels of learning for all students. The catch is that most schools must make this fundamental change using only their current resources. To perform this lifesaving work, schools need to prioritize using resources in new ways as part of the past paradigm, just as the flight engineers cobbled together what was available to them into an unconventional device that saved the lives of three astronauts.

Here's Why

In the medical field, patients are assigned the help of medical professionals based on the severity of their illness and the expertise needed to address the problem. For example, someone suffering from the flu usually sees a nurse practitioner or family physician, while a cancer patient visits an oncologist. Effective learning interventions should apply this same guiding principle. Reeves's research (2009a, 2009b) concludes that one of a school's most effective learning strategies is to have highly trained teachers work with the students most at risk.

The reason why the cancer patient receives more specialized help is because the impact of their illness and the potential consequences of failed medical treatment are so much greater. As discussed in the introduction (page 1), students who fail in the K–12 system are much more likely to be unemployed (U.S. Bureau of Labor Statistics, 2019), live in poverty (Statista, 2023), be incarcerated (Camera, 2021), and die prematurely (Lee-St. John et al., 2018). This is why the leadership team, when allocating its limited time and resources in its master schedule, must prioritize the needs of students who require Tier 3 reinforcements.

Here's How

The saying that best captures the how of prioritizing a school's resources for students with the greatest needs is *all hands on deck*! The key to providing intensive reinforcements is to utilize the staff most highly trained in the specific area of need. Consider that a family doctor or general practitioner is well versed in a broad range of maladies that impact their patients. They are, in fact, a generalist, as described in the term *general practitioner*. Within the medical profession, there are other doctors who have board certification and highly specialized training in a particular area of medicine.

Similarly, in education, there are classroom teachers with training and certification in a broad domain of learning, such as mathematics, science, or English language arts. Elementary teachers have even broader training in many domains of learning. In schools, there are also personnel with highly specialized training in more targeted areas of learning—speech-language pathologists, occupational therapists, special education teachers, psychologists, counselors, and behavior specialists, to name a few.

Unfortunately, in too many schools, the silo mentality culture that has developed over time isolates these highly specialized educators. The fact that these specialists must comply with a series of laws, regulations, and guidelines that reinforce this feeling of isolation and autonomy partly drives this mentality. Too often, we hear elementary school speech-language pathologists say things like, "I'm too busy serving the students in my caseload. I don't have time to collaborate with classroom teachers, although I probably have a lot of ideas and materials that would help their struggling students."

Another exacerbating factor is that many of these specialists are itinerant employees who move between several schools each week. This makes it difficult for them to interact with and serve as resources to classroom teachers. Sometimes, the school or district culture discourages interaction between specialists and classroom teachers. These itinerant employees often report to someone other than the school principal and are evaluated on how well they comply with the regulations under which they operate, not on how well they support school efforts to help all students learn at high levels.

All hands on deck recognizes the fact that classroom teachers (generalists) alone can never be successful in helping *all* students learn at high levels. The only way schools can succeed in this mission is to better utilize their specialists' specific skills and training in consulting with classroom teachers as well as working with their students most in need (much the same way that general practitioners utilize the skills and training of medical specialists when their patients require a more intensive level of support).

Specialists can serve as resources in one of two main ways.

1. **Specialists can and should be seen as resources to classroom teachers:** Regular education teachers should have ongoing access to a school's speech-language pathologist, special education teachers, content specialists or coaches, and occupational therapists so they can better support students who are struggling and prevent them from falling so far behind that they eventually end up in the specialists' caseloads. School psychologists and counselors should also be readily available to support classroom teachers dealing with extreme behavioral issues.

2. **Many schools find creative ways of having specialists actually deliver Tier 3 intensive reinforcements to students who are not part of their official caseloads:** These schools pry their specialists away from exclusively working with students in their caseloads to help nonidentified students who need exactly the same interventions as the students they regularly serve. Section 613(a)(4) of the Individuals With Disabilities Education Act (IDEA) of 2004 and its implementing regulations at 34 CFR §300.208(a)(1) permit using special education–funded personnel for this purpose (IDEA, 2004).

Melody Musgrove (2013), director of the Office of Special Education Programs for the U.S. Department of Education, writes (as cited in Pierce, 2015):

Pursuant to 34 CFR §300.208(a), special education teachers fully funded by Part B (non-CEIS) funds may perform duties for children without disabilities if they would already be performing these same duties in order to provide special education and related services to children with disabilities. For example, a special education teacher is assigned to provide five hours of reading instruction per week to three students with disabilities consistent with those students' IEPs. The IEPs provide that the students need specialized reading instruction that is at grade level but handled at a slower pace because of auditory processing issues. The school decides that, although they are not children with disabilities, there are two general education children who would benefit from this instruction. The special education teacher must prepare lesson plans for each of these classes regardless of the number of children in the class. She may do so and conduct the class for all five children because she is only providing special education and related services for the three children with disabilities and the two children without disabilities are benefiting from that work. (p. 2)

Another practical strategy in prioritizing resources, beyond the use of specialists, is to consider which classroom teachers are best prepared and trained to work with the students most in need. The guiding coalition should consider the following questions in a more thoughtful approach to prioritizing teacher resources.

▶ Does one of our teachers have specialized training in what these students need? Is one of our classroom teachers credentialed or experienced in a specialized area?

▶ Has one or more of our teachers demonstrated greater success on common assessments during our comparison of scores, teacher to teacher?

▶ Is one of our teachers currently pursuing an advanced degree with a special emphasis on a specific area of need, such as phonemic awareness or decoding?

▶ Is one of our teachers currently researching a specific area of need as part of their thesis or dissertation?

These are the questions to ask and answer in completing the Who Takes Responsibility column of the reproducible "RTI at Work Pro-Solve Reinforcement Targeting Process: Tier 3" (page 280). Remember, this does not mean that others do not bear some responsibility in delivering Tier 3 intensive reinforcements—the guiding coalition identifies which staff take the lead or have primary responsibility for designing and delivering this lifesaving help. The guiding coalition must ensure that powerful resources existing at the school are available to students who require this help. This might mean that the school needs to adjust schedules and re-examine normal routines and protocols, all of which are within the guiding coalition's control.

The guiding coalition must also remember the effectiveness of direct instruction. While many digital programs are designed to provide intensive support in reading and mathematics, a computer alone can seldom solve a student's learning difficulties. Many of these programs are designed to be delivered in conjunction with close progress monitoring by a highly trained individual familiar with the programs' design, and not by an instructional aide—or even worse, by no one at all.

All hands on deck means precisely what we described. Instead of *my* room, *my* class, and *my* students, successful RTI at Work schools take collective responsibility so that *we*, as an entire school, utilize and prioritize all the resources available to meet the goal of high levels of learning for all students.

Helpful Tool

The following tool will help you accomplish the work for this essential action.

▶ **"RTI at Work Pro-Solve Reinforcement Targeting Process: Tier 3" (page 280):** The intervention team, the guiding coalition, or both can use this form to separate academic skills from behavioral issues and target each student's particular needs for intensive reinforcements.

Coaching Tips

Building a deep shared understanding of what Tier 3 is all about and why it is essential increases the likelihood that teachers will support the steps needed to implement Tier 3, including prioritizing resources.

Each of the steps for prioritizing resources, as well as the rationale for taking them, must be shared and discussed with the staff. To maximize teachers' engagement, place students they know personally at the center of the work to personalize the discussion.

A full-staff meeting might look like this: teachers sit in assigned mixed groups (cross-grade-level or cross-content). The groups each receive a description of a student with Tier 3 needs. The descriptions can be based on real students in the school, but if they are, change the names to protect their confidentiality. Each group then determines what the student needs and how and when to provide support for addressing those needs, including who might best provide support. Following at least twenty to thirty minutes of discussion, each group charts and shares its recommendations.

Once each group presents its recommendations, the guiding coalition clarifies how to use those recommendations, how to make relevant decisions, and when teachers can expect to hear about next steps. Clear communication is key! To summarize, clear, ongoing communication and appropriate staff involvement in decision making continue to strengthen the cultural norm of taking collective responsibility for *all* students learning at high levels.

RTI at Work Pro-Solve Reinforcement Targeting Process: Tier 3

Student: _____

Participant: _____ Meeting date: _____

Targeted Outcomes	Desired Outcomes	Reinforcement and Action Steps	Who Takes Responsibility	Data Point 1	Data Point 2	Data Point 3	Data Point 4	Data Point 5
Led by Intervention Team								
Foundational Reading								
Foundational Writing								
Foundational Number Sense								
Foundational Language								
Academic Behaviors								
Social Behaviors								
Health and Home								

Next meeting date: _____

Source: Buffum, A., Mattos, M., Weber, C., & Hierck, T. (2015). Uniting academic and behavior interventions: Solving the skill or will dilemma. Bloomington, IN: Solution Tree Press.

Action 4

Create a Systematic and Timely Process to Refer Students to the Site Intervention Team

As we discussed in action 2 of this chapter (page 271), a school can proactively identify most students for Tier 3 reinforcements through existing information and universal screening practices. Yet it is possible that some students might not begin the year needing intensive support but develop the need at a later point. This need could develop over time, such as when a student continues to fail in Tier 1 and Tier 2 supports—or it could happen suddenly, like when a student's parent dies unexpectedly, causing tremendous upheaval in the student's life. When this happens, the guiding coalition must have a systematic and timely process to refer these students to the site intervention team.

Here's Why

The goal of Tier 3 is to close sizable learning gaps in foundational prerequisite skills. To do this, students must demonstrate multiple years of academic growth in a single school year. If a student enters fifth grade reading at a third-grade level, and demonstrates one year of reading growth by the end of the year, they will end the year still two years below grade level in reading, as the student is now a rising sixth grader reading at a fourth-grade level. *The goal of Tier 3 intensive reinforcements should be at least two years of academic growth per school year.*

To achieve at least two years of academic growth, targeted students must demonstrate at least one year's growth by the end of the first semester. And this rate of improvement would require a half year of growth by the end of the first quarter of the year, which means the student should show a quarter year of growth within the first month or so of school.

Our point is this: for students who need Tier 3 reinforcements, every week of effective help makes a big difference! The sooner a school can systematically identify a student who needs intensive reinforcements, the better its chances of closing the gap. If schools wait until the end of grading periods—quarters or semesters—to identify students who are severely struggling, they lose precious time.

Here's How

How do schools identify students for Tier 3 reinforcements if they did not demonstrate the need based on prior-year information, universal screening data, or both at the start of the year? Schools can answer this question with two more questions.

1. Who best knows the academic and behavioral needs of students throughout the year?

2. Who might notice if a student has an unexpected severe need?

Classroom educators usually know their students best. They see their students almost every day. They know their academic needs and often have insight into emotional needs and problems that might be happening outside of school. For this reason, it is important that the guiding coalition create a schoolwide, systematic process for school staff to refer students to the school intervention team.

Over the years, we have seen schools design such a process in creative ways. For example, the school's intervention team can hold regularly scheduled meetings, at least every three weeks, during which each teacher can refer students for consideration. Similarly, some schools designate one weekly teacher team meeting each month to discuss and coordinate interventions across Tier 2 and Tier 3. At this designated meeting, representatives from the guiding coalition and intervention team can join each teacher team to identify students needing Tier 3 reinforcements and consider how students are responding to Tier 2 interventions. Especially at larger schools, with many students to consider, they might create an electronic process for staff to refer students for Tier 3 support. (See chapter 6, action 2, page 242, for more details on a schoolwide identification process.)

It is imperative that classroom teachers and interventionists have a process for regularly referring students to the site intervention team in a timely fashion for placement in Tier 3 reinforcements. We recommend that the site intervention team hold time slots open in its regularly scheduled meetings to discuss students with these emerging needs. We recommend using the reproducible "RTI at Work Pro-Solve Reinforcement Monitoring Plan: Tier 3" (page 283) to guide conversations around these students.

It is not enough to develop systems of Tier 3 support for students and then allow them to languish and fail as they wait for a cumbersome process to provide access. If you have ever dealt with a sick child, spouse, parent, or friend, you know how frustrating it can be to know that help exists inside the hospital, but accessing that help might take days, weeks, or even months. We must create a process that is both systematic and timely so students don't wait so long for help that it might be too late to save them.

Helpful Tool

The following tool will help you accomplish the work for this essential action.

▶ **"RTI at Work Pro-Solve Reinforcement Monitoring Plan: Tier 3" (page 283):** Teams should use this activity in coordination with the "RTI at Work Pro-Solve Reinforcement Targeting Process: Tier 3" reproducible (page 280). Members can record a student's progress in meeting their academic and behavior goals at Tier 3.

Coaching Tips

For any process to be systematic and timely, every person on campus must understand the rationale for the system, the logistics of the system, and the role they play in ensuring the system works effectively. The guiding coalition might create and offer a Tier 3 referral process handbook that explains the rationale for the process and outlines, step by step, how the process works.

Additionally, the guiding coalition should hold at least one faculty meeting each year to focus on the importance of the referral process. One strategy for engaging staff members in this process might be to role-play an actual site intervention team meeting. The guiding coalition assigns seats for the meeting to create teams with diverse perspectives and then gives each team several profiles of students (which the site intervention team creates) who require Tier 3 services. These profiles include students who have fallen further behind due to attending a school that does not have a systematic and timely referral process.

To conclude the meeting, the guiding coalition asks staff members to share any insights they have gained as to *why* a systematic and timely referral process is important, *how* the process works, and *what* role they play in its success. Only when every adult on campus clearly understands and supports the referral process will the school have the potential to ensure no students fall through the cracks.

RTI at Work Pro-Solve Reinforcement Monitoring Plan: Tier 3

Student: _____

Participant: _____

Meeting date: _____

Targeted Outcomes	Desired Outcomes	Reinforcement and Action Steps	Who Takes Responsibility	Data Point 1	Data Point 2	Data Point 3	Data Point 4	Data Point 5
Led by Intervention Team								
Foundational Reading								
Foundational Writing								
Foundational Number Sense								
Foundational Language								
Academic Behaviors								
Social Behaviors								
Health and Home								

Next meeting date: _____

Source: Buffum, A., Mattos, M., Weber, C., & Hierck, T. (2015). Uniting academic and behavior interventions: Solving the skill or will dilemma. Bloomington, IN: Solution Tree Press.

Action 5

Assess Intervention and Reinforcement Effectiveness

A multitiered system of supports is only as effective as each individual support—intervention or reinforcement—that comprises it. Some schools devote significant time and effort to identify students for additional help and create scheduled time to provide the help, but then place students into supports that are ineffective. If a school builds an MTSS process on ineffective instructional programs and practices, then all it has done is guarantee students access to support that won't offer much help.

No single intervention or reinforcement works perfectly for every targeted student, but each support should achieve its purpose most of the time. When this is not the case, either the school is not targeting students well—meaning the support works, but the assigned students don't have the specific needs of the targeted help—or students are targeted correctly, but the support is just ineffective at achieving its goal. Additional help that is ineffective not only underserves the targeted students, but also uses valuable resources that could be repurposed for better results. Because the guiding coalition is responsible for allocating school resources—both fiscal and personnel—it's important that it regularly assesses each intervention's effectiveness.

Here's Why

Unfortunately, many schools continue to build their interventions with practices that don't work, have never worked, and have no promise of getting better results the following year (Buffum et al., 2012). The numerous examples discussed throughout this book include traditional special education practices, retention, and punitive actions mistakenly intended to motivate better behavior. Let's explore another example—summer school.

Each year, thousands of schools offer abbreviated summer classes. While some students use this option to accelerate learning, such as by taking a required class to open up their schedule for an additional class next school year, most summer school students are required to take it due to failure during the school year. The goal is for students to make up a class or receive reinforcement over the summer to get them back on track and ready for the next year. While the intention is good, the way most schools provide summer school makes achieving this goal nearly impossible. Consider how summer school is commonly designed.

- ▶ **Broad indicators:** The school identifies students for summer school using broad indicators, such as a student failed a class or scored well below grade level on end-of-year assessments, or the services are included in a special education student's IEP. Students can fail on these indicators for markedly different reasons. Yet typically, students don't receive deeper diagnostic assessments to identify their wide range of needs, and they are all placed in the same summer school course.

- ▶ **Shortened time span:** For example, the school assigns a student to summer school because they failed a semester of freshman English—a class required for graduation. During the school year, the course met every day for about eighteen weeks. In summer school, the makeup class is typically about six weeks long. To make up for the shortened time span, the student attends class for three hours each day. But how realistic is it to fit an entire semester's worth of reading, discussion, and writing into those compacted weeks? Add to the timing difficulty the fact that some students are enrolled because they are reluctant readers, have difficulty writing, or lack motivation.

- ▶ **Teacher assignment:** Mike Mattos taught summer school every year that he was a classroom teacher, and often, he was assigned to teach at a different school than his school-year assignment. In the new classroom, he had limited teaching materials. He knew nothing about the students except that they failed the class during the school year. The summer school term was just about over by the time he began to build a rapport with and understanding of each student.

Looking at these factors, what is the likelihood that students assigned to summer school are going to master the essential skills and knowledge they failed to learn during the previous school year and return the following fall ready to succeed? Students might make up credits needed to graduate, but it is highly unlikely that they will actually learn the essential content.

Unsurprisingly, in his meta-analysis of the research on summer school's effectiveness, Hattie (2023) finds it not to be a high-impact practice. When asked if going to summer school makes a difference, he answers, "In general, not much" (Hattie, 2023, p. 163). Yet, despite what research and common sense prove, thousands of schools across the United States assign summer school every year. This seasonal intervention program is expensive, costing tens of thousands of dollars to extend the school year for some students.

Here is the critical point: we are not suggesting that summer school is inherently bad. The problem rests in how schools have traditionally implemented summer school—it is not designed to align with the traits of effective interventions. In the next section, we explore how the guiding coalition can assess the effectiveness of its existing site interventions as well as make these interventions more effective.

Here's How

There are six essential characteristics of an effective intervention.

1. **Targeted:** The more targeted the intervention, the more likely it will work. An effective intervention identifies the specific standard(s), learning target(s), or behavior(s) to be retaught. All the students assigned to the intervention should have the same need.

2. **Systematic:** There must be a systematic process to identify every student who needs a specific intervention. Even if the intervention is effective, a student will not benefit from it if the school is ignorant of the student's needs.

3. **Research based:** Research and evidence should support the instructional practice so it has a high likelihood of working. This means the school can reference research that the practice works or cite evidence that the intervention is working.

4. **Administered by a trained professional:** An intervention is only as effective as the person administering it. If the practice is proven to work, but the staff member implementing it is untrained or incompetent, then the intervention is unlikely to work.

5. **Timely:** Schools should not allow students to fail for long before receiving an intervention. When this happens, they can fall too far behind to fully benefit from the intervention.

6. **Directive:** Intervention must be a directive, meaning students must be required to attend if they have the need. When interventions are optional, the students who need help most often choose not to attend. If the students most at risk in the school were already actively seeking extra help, they would probably not be at risk. Even when an intervention is effective, students do not benefit if they do not attend.

All six characteristics are essential, meaning for an intervention to be effective, it must align with all six traits.

We created the reproducible "Intervention or Reinforcement Evaluation and Alignment Chart" (page 289) to help schools evaluate their current site interventions and align them to the six characteristics. The site intervention team and teacher teams can also use it to plan and assess specific interventions they might lead.

1. **Targeted:** What exactly is the purpose of the intervention or reinforcement? What specific skill, content, or behavior should students learn by the end of the intervention or reinforcement? If you can't specify this, that's a clear indication the support is not targeted enough. To remedy this problem, make the help more focused.

2. **Systematic:** Is there a systematic process to identify every student who needs help in the intervention or reinforcement's targeted area? Once identified, can all the students who need this help actually receive it? If the team answers no to either of these questions, what steps can you take to make the support more systematic?

3. **Research based:** What research or evidence validates that the intervention has a high likelihood of working? If you can't cite any, then discontinue the practice and study better practices to reteach the targeted outcome.

4. **Administered by a trained professional:** Who is currently administering the intervention or reinforcement? Are they properly trained and competent at this task? If not, does the school have staff who are better trained, or can the school provide the staff member with additional training and support to become more effective?

5. **Timely:** How long does it take to identify students for and place them in the intervention or reinforcement? We suggest it should not take longer than three weeks.

6. **Directive:** Are targeted students required to attend? If not, what steps can you take to ensure students needing help are present?

After determining the current reality of an intervention or reinforcement in relation to the six criteria, teachers, the site intervention team, or the guiding coalition should identify where the intervention is out of alignment and determine steps to fix it.

Referring to the summer-school example, suppose that a middle school guiding coalition wants to improve the effectiveness of its summer school mathematics offerings, specifically for students who failed seventh-grade pre-algebra. Here is what the six characteristics might look like at the middle school.

1. **Targeted:** Students are placed in a summer school mathematics program because they failed pre-algebra. Instead of trying to reteach all the pre-algebra curriculum, the team decides to have the mathematics department identify the specific skills students must learn to master the essential algebra 1 standards taught during the first semester of the following year.

2. **Systematic:** The seventh-grade pre-algebra teachers receive a list of the prerequisite skills to be taught in the summer session. At the end of the year, these teachers identify pre-algebra students who could benefit from extra teaching and practice on these specific skills.

3. **Research based:** The pre-algebra team discusses instructional practices that proved effective and ineffective while teaching these standards during the regular school year and gives this information to teachers who are teaching the summer school course.

4. **Administered by a trained professional:** The school identifies the teachers who are best trained to reteach this content and encourages them to apply for this extended learning opportunity.

5. **Timely:** Traditional summer school is usually offered right after the regular school year ends. This often means that at the end of summer school, students are home for about one month before school starts. Because the targeted mathematics outcomes of this course relate to the first units of study the following fall, the school decides to move summer school closer to the start of school. This new jump-start approach prepares students for immediate success in their new grade-level mathematics class.

6. **Directive:** Teachers notify and highly encourage parents of identified students to have their children attend this targeted summer school class. If a parent is unable or unwilling to have their child attend, the school creates an alternative way to intervene. The school assigns students who do not attend this summer school class to a two-period block mathematics class at the start of the school year. This class provides the teacher with the time to both reteach the pre-algebra skills needed for success in algebra 1 (the same skills taught during summer school) and teach the new mathematics curriculum. Because the second option is offered during the regular school year, the school can require the student to receive the help without needing parental consent.

For the guiding coalition, we recommend allotting time so it can evaluate all the school's Tier 2 and Tier 3 supports at least twice per year.

1. **At the midpoint of the year:** At this point in the year, there has been sufficient time for the school's interventions to work.

2. **At the end of the year:** With this information, the school can reconsider revising and reallocating resources for the coming year.

We know that most schools have very limited resources. The beauty of the evaluation and alignment process is that it is designed to help a school get better results with the resources it has, instead of trying to secure more resources to get better results. We used this process at our schools, so we can say with confidence that it works!

Finally, it is important to note that these six essential characteristics of effective supports are applicable to any type of additional intervention or reinforcement—academic or behavioral. In fact, these six characteristics work for Tier 1 preventions too. This means educators can use the process and tools in this section to evaluate and improve additional help at any tier.

Helpful Tools

The following tools will help you accomplish the work for this essential action.

▸ **"Intervention or Reinforcement Evaluation and Alignment Chart" (page 289):** Teachers, the site intervention team, or the guiding coalition can use this tool to evaluate and improve the effectiveness of a specific intervention.

▸ **"Intervention or Reinforcement Evaluation and Alignment Chart Protocol" (page 290):** This protocol guides team discussions as members complete the "Intervention or Reinforcement Evaluation and Alignment Chart."

Coaching Tips

Research consistently and continuously points out the value of formative assessment and the positive impact it has on student learning when done well (Chappuis, Stiggins, Chappuis, & Arter, 2012; Hattie, 2023; Wiliam, 2018). Given the fact that assessing interventions for effectiveness is a form of formative assessment, it is no surprise that doing so is essential to the overall success of RTI at Work. When assessing interventions for effectiveness, schools should consider the following underlying formative assessment questions.

- ▶ How well are our current actions achieving our desired outcomes?
- ▶ What strategies can we use to increase our effectiveness?
- ▶ What goals for improvement do we need to commit to?

Keeping in mind that teams of teachers are routinely implementing interventions in their classrooms during Tier 1 instruction and collaboratively implementing Tier 2 interventions in response to common formative assessments, it is important to not only recommend but also facilitate opportunities for teachers to experience the process for assessing intervention effectiveness. The same criteria described in the previous sections are equally applicable to Tier 1 and 2 interventions, and the conversations among teams as they consider each criterion are foundational to making improvements.

Though this may seem like preaching to the choir, remember the power of formative assessment lies in its focus on improvement rather than judgment or evaluation. When all participants approach the process of assessing intervention effectiveness with the dual lenses of identifying and celebrating what is working well and identifying and solving what is not, the dialogue remains open and productive. If, however, the approach becomes one of judgment or evaluation, the conversations often become stilted and defensive, thus hampering creative thinking and yielding few solutions or improvements.

To ensure the dialogue during the process of assessing interventions for effectiveness maintains a positive focus, the guiding coalition should apply the same formative assessment questions to themselves and their work. Questions to consider might include these.

- ▶ How well are our current actions achieving our desired outcomes? What evidence do we have that our school culture is becoming one of collective responsibility for high levels of student learning?
- ▶ To what degree do team meetings and staff meetings utilize norms and protocols to strengthen collaboration and teamwork?
- ▶ What strategies that we, as a guiding coalition, are using are working well? How do we know?
- ▶ What areas need improvement? How do we know?
- ▶ What goals and timelines do we need to agree on to enhance the development of systematic support for all students?
- ▶ What actions do we need to take to increase our effectiveness as a guiding coalition? How will we monitor our progress?

In summary, formative assessment, in all its forms and uses, is critical to moving forward. Robert Garmston says it best: "Anyone too busy to reflect on one's practice is also too busy to improve" (Garmston & Wellman, 2009, p. 144). Reflection is an essential part of formative assessment. By reflecting on our errors and successes, we gain the knowledge and confidence we need to improve.

Intervention or Reinforcement Evaluation and Alignment Chart

First, identify the intervention or reinforcement you want to evaluate. Write it in the far-left column. Be as specific as possible. Then, working from left to right, evaluate the intervention or reinforcement against each of the six essential characteristics.

Current Site Interventions or Reinforcements	Targeted	Systematic	Research Based	Administered by a Trained Professional	Timely	Directive	Alignment Steps

Intervention or Reinforcement Evaluation and Alignment Chart Protocol

Use the following protocol to guide team discussions as team members complete the "Intervention or Reinforcement Evaluation and Alignment Chart" (page 289).

The guiding coalition or site intervention team can use this activity to evaluate schoolwide interventions and reinforcements, or the teacher team can use it to evaluate teacher-led interventions. We recommend completing this activity twice per year—prior to the start of the school year and at the midpoint of the school year.

1. Brainstorm your current site interventions and reinforcements in the far-left column—one intervention or reinforcement per box. When evaluating each characteristic, it can be helpful to use these symbols:

   + Highly aligned

   ✓ Somewhat aligned

   × Not aligned

   For each, ask the following questions.

   a. **Targeted:** What exactly is the purpose of the intervention or reinforcement? What specific skill, content, or behavior should students learn by the end of the intervention or reinforcement? If you can't specify this, that's a clear indication the support is not targeted enough. To remedy this problem, make the help more focused.

   b. **Systematic:** Is there a systematic process to identify every student who needs help in the intervention or reinforcement's targeted area? Once identified, can all the students who need this help actually receive it? If the team answers no to either of these questions, what steps can you take to make the support more systematic?

   c. **Research based:** What research or evidence validates that the intervention has a high likelihood of working? If you can't cite any, then discontinue the practice and study better practices to reteach the targeted outcome.

   d. **Administered by a trained professional:** Who is currently administering the intervention or reinforcement? Are they properly trained and competent at this task? If not, does the school have staff who are better trained, or can the school provide the staff member with additional training and support to become more effective?

   e. **Timely:** How long does it take to identify students for and place them in the intervention or reinforcement? We suggest it should not take longer than three weeks.

   f. **Directive:** Are targeted students required to attend? If not, what steps can you take to ensure students needing help are present?

2. Address any Xs in the chart. *This is the most important step!* Because all the characteristics are essential to support's effectiveness, you must address any X on the chart. For example, if a particular intervention has an X under Directive, then the team should discuss and determine how the staff will require students to attend. Fix the X, and the intervention or reinforcement becomes more effective.

Conclusion

Successfully completing the five essential actions in this chapter enables the guiding coalition to create the time, resources, and collaborative structures necessary to provide intensive reinforcements. The next step is to make sure each student in need of Tier 3 reinforcement receives interventions that target their individual needs. The site intervention team, which is the focus of the next chapter, will lead this process.

CHAPTER 8

Tier 3 Intervention Team Essential Actions

In this chapter, we once again focus on Tier 3 of the RTI at Work pyramid. However, while chapter 7 focused on the role of the guiding coalition in relation to Tier 3, this chapter focuses on the contributions of the site intervention team to the same section of the pyramid.

Whereas the guiding coalition is responsible for the systematic processes of Tier 3, including the scheduling and allocation of resources, the site intervention team is responsible for determining the specific needs of each student requiring intensive support. See figure 8.1.

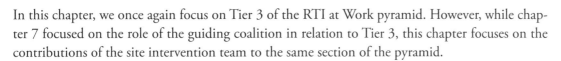

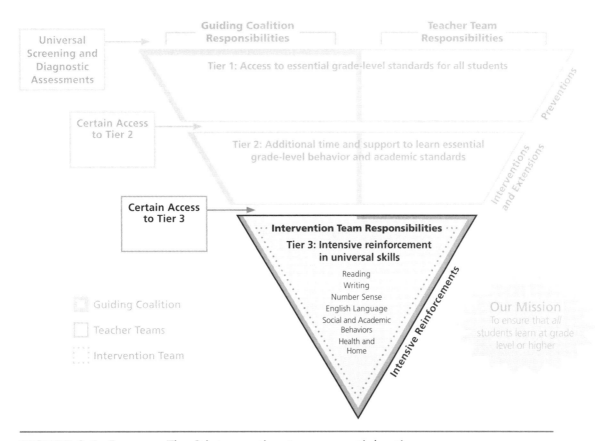

FIGURE 8.1: Focus on Tier 3 intervention team essential actions.

The site intervention team's essential responsibilities at Tier 3 are as follows.

1. Diagnose, target, prioritize, and monitor Tier 3 reinforcements.

2. Ensure proper instructional intensity.

3. Determine whether special education is needed and justifiable.

Of these three actions, the first is paramount to providing effective Tier 3 supports.

Action 1

Diagnose, Target, Prioritize, and Monitor Tier 3 Reinforcements

Consider for a moment the characteristics that define students who need intensive reinforcements. These students are multiple years below grade level in the foundational prerequisite skills that are indispensable to success in school, including the following five.

1. The ability to decode and comprehend text

2. The ability to convey ideas through the written word

3. An understanding of numbers, sequencing, and basic mathematical functions

4. The ability to comprehend and speak the native tongue of the school

5. The demonstration of basic social and academic behaviors

Students with these characteristics often come from home environments that cannot provide academic support, and in some cases, actually contribute to the students' struggles in school. Some of these students have identified learning disabilities, but most do not (Brooks-Gunn & Duncan, 1997; O'Connor & Fernandez, 2006).

While these students often need intensive supports in the same foundational prerequisite skills, they do not all struggle for the same reasons. Some students could be reading below grade level because they can't decode text, while others have decoding skills but poor fluency and comprehension. So, targeting each student's specific needs is critical to responding effectively. And finally, these students must receive intensive support in addition to Tier 1 and Tier 2, not in place of them. Asking individual teachers to diagnose, target, prioritize, and monitor this level of help is unreasonable and unrealistic. The site intervention team, collectively experienced in all the foundational prerequisite skills that must be retaught at Tier 3, is a school's best hope to achieve these outcomes.

Students needing Tier 3 help must improve multiple grade levels (at least two) in a single school year. If a fifth grader who is reading at a third-grade level improves one year's growth in reading by the end of the year, then this student is now a sixth grader reading at a fourth-grade level—still two years below grade level. So, Tier 3 reinforcements must be highly effective for these students to have any realistic chance of reaching high levels of learning.

Here's Why

In almost every case, students in need of Tier 3 supports have been attending school for years. Dedicated professional educators have provided core instruction and most likely additional help, when possible; yet these students are still *years* below grade level. A school must assume that finding solutions for these students is going to be very difficult.

Faced with this challenge, a school would be best served by using a team approach to brainstorm and identify potential solutions. However, unlike in Tier 2, where we advocate that teacher teams lead the intervention process, we recommend that an intervention team with diverse expertise lead Tier 3. When students struggle to master specific essential academic standards, teachers who teach the same grade or course can brainstorm together to identify better ways to teach the standards.

Some might assume that their school already has such a process—their student study team (SST) meetings. The origin of holding SST meetings was to gather a diverse team—administration, classroom teachers, specialist staff, and home representatives—to dig deeply into the needs of a specific student and create a comprehensive plan of support. Sadly, we find that most schools use the SST process merely as a mandatory step in referring a student for special education testing. Meetings are usually held infrequently or as needed, are driven by documentation, and require little to no subsequent follow-up to revise the plan when it fails to work. What we are advocating is a systematic process in which a diverse team of experts—the site intervention team—meet frequently to diagnose, determine, monitor, assess, and revise the interventions for students needing Tier 3 support. An SST-type meeting that includes home representatives and other involved individuals might be part of this process. But we find that most schools' current SST process does not align with these recommendations.

Here's How

Like any other team on campus, the intervention team should develop norms. Our experience is that this team will discuss very sensitive information about both students and staff. Team members must be honest, which requires an environment of trust and confidentiality. Also, meeting time for this team will likely be limited, so protocols to keep the conversations focused and on task are critical.

Regarding protocols, we introduced our RTI at Work pro-solve process—a series of five critical questions designed to diagnose and target interventions—in chapter 5 (page 201). We apply these five questions to the universal skills taught at Tier 3, creating the "RTI at Work Pro-Solve Reinforcement Targeting Process: Tier 3" (page 280) and "RTI at Work Pro-Solve Reinforcement Monitoring Plan: Tier 3" (page 283) reproducibles.

The RTI at Work pro-solve reinforcement targeting process helps the team focus on a particular student's areas of need. It is likely that students at risk need intensive supports in more than one of the six universal skills, as shown in figure 8.1 (page 293): (1) reading, (2) writing, (3) number sense, (4) English language (or the primary language spoken in the school), (5) academic and social behaviors, and (6) health and home. Providing intensive reinforcements all at once—and still guaranteeing the student access to Tier 1 and Tier 2—might not be possible. When this is the case, the site intervention team must also prioritize the student's needs, determining the best sequence of supports.

While the guiding coalition and intervention team focus on different essential actions at Tier 3, coordination between the teams is critical. As the site intervention team determines a specific student's needs, it might realize that the current schedule prohibits the recommended reinforcements. At this point, the guiding coalition would consider if it can adjust the school's scheduling and resources to meet the student's needs. Likewise, it is difficult for the guiding coalition to allocate resources unless it knows each student's specific needs.

We recommend the principal serve on both the guiding coalition and the intervention team to help with coordination. While additional people might serve on both teams, the principal has more direct control over schoolwide resources. When the principal defers site intervention team responsibilities to another site administrator, the intervention team will likely find it difficult to make immediate decisions because the decisions might require the principal's approval. This just adds an extra unnecessary step. In the end, we cannot think of a more important use of the principal's time than to help the students most at risk to succeed.

There are two last critical points. First, the site intervention team should assume that its initial plan will *not* work perfectly. The identified students have been failing for years and their problems are complex, so the team should not expect easy solutions. This is why the site intervention team meets frequently. These students are moving targets, and so are their reinforcements.

Second, and more important, Tier 3 is for *any* student who needs intensive reinforcement in foundational prerequisite skills. This includes both regular education students and students who have qualified for special education. For a student referred for Tier 3 who doesn't have a defined disability, the intervention team must not assume the student probably has a learning disability and needs to be referred for testing. Later in this chapter, we detail how this team makes the final recommendation if a student should receive special education identification and services. But here is what we know—if the site intervention team begins a student's Tier 3 supports by assuming the student probably has a disability, the odds are good the RTI process will lead to that outcome.

The site intervention team must assume that students are capable of learning at high levels if they receive effective targeted instruction at Tier 1, Tier 2, and Tier 3. And equally important, if students *have* qualified for special education services and need Tier 3 support, the intervention team must assume that they are capable of learning at high levels if they receive effective targeted instruction at Tier 1, Tier 2, and Tier 3. The students' disability is not an excuse to lower expectations or defer responsibility for their support to special education staff alone.

Helpful Tools

The following tools will help you accomplish the work for this essential action.

▶ **"RTI at Work Pro-Solve Reinforcement Targeting Process: Tier 3" (see chapter 7, action 3, page 280):** This activity is designed to help the site intervention team identify, diagnose, target, and monitor Tier 3 academic and behavior supports.

▶ **"RTI at Work Pro-Solve Reinforcement Monitoring Plan: Tier 3" (see chapter 7, action 4, page 283):** Teams should use this tool in coordination with the "RTI at Work Pro-Solve Reinforcement Targeting Process: Tier 3" reproducible. Members can record a student's progress in meeting their academic and behavior goals at Tier 3.

Coaching Tips

The site intervention team must create a team culture built on trust, honesty, and respect. When working with teams that are struggling to achieve this culture, we often hear the mistaken beliefs, "We don't need team norms, because we get along just fine," and "We don't have time for protocols; we can get this done by talking to each other."

Becoming a highly productive, true site intervention team requires much more than getting along. It requires a shared understanding of the goals the team is seeking to achieve, and the tasks required to reach those goals. Norms define the playing field for accomplishing that work. Not only must site intervention team members agree on the ground rules for their dialogue, but they also must agree on how to monitor themselves and respond when a team member does not adhere to the team's agreed-on norms.

Using protocols is equally important. As Joseph P. McDonald, Nancy Mohr, Alan Dichter, and Elizabeth C. McDonald (2003) state in *The Power of Protocols: An Educator's Guide to Better Practice*, "The kind of talking needed to educate ourselves cannot rise spontaneously and unaided from just talking. It needs to be carefully planned and scaffolded" (p. 4). Site intervention team discussions require careful planning and scaffolding so team members can learn from each other as well as improve learning for the school's students most in need. Protocols are just that. They are tools and strategies that create conversations in which:

- All members get time to speak and time to listen, thus ensuring all voices are heard

- Dialogue proves to be optimally honest and respectful

- Members are open to others' perspectives

- Members maintain balance among presenting information, examining data, questioning the current reality, and responding to the information and data

- Members achieve positive outcomes

The helpful tools for this action include two critical protocols to assist the site intervention team's work. We included additional resources in the References and Resources (page 315), and you can find more protocols available online on the National School Reform Faculty's website (https://nsrfharmony.org), on the School Reform Initiative's website (www.schoolreforminitiative.org), and in Teachers College Press's (n.d.) "Protocols" (http://bit.ly/2vFMR46). You can adjust these protocols to meet your needs or make up some of your own—but be sure to use them! (Visit **go.SolutionTree .com/RTIatWork** to access live links to the websites mentioned in this book.)

Action 2

Ensure Proper Instructional Intensity

Imagine that you discover your child has a temperature of 103.5 degrees Fahrenheit. You rush your child to the pediatrician, who discovers that they are suffering from streptococcal pharyngitis (strep throat). Your doctor prescribes four hundred milligrams of amoxicillin, which you must give your child four times per day. As a conscientious parent, you dutifully carry out these instructions with fidelity, but your child's condition does not improve. Unbeknownst to you, the pharmacist misread the doctor's prescription and filled each capsule with only forty milligrams of amoxicillin rather than four hundred. Right medicine, wrong intensity.

Similarly, students requiring Tier 3 reinforcements are failing academically or behaviorally and need our strongest possible "medicine"—the level of support that can accelerate their learning. They are often years behind in terms of academic skills and frequently experience social behaviors and academic behaviors that make it impossible for them to improve. Students requiring intensive reinforcements often have more than one area of concern, and their struggles often impact multiple subjects as well as their motivation, attendance, and mindset. At Tier 3, students need intensive instruction designed to meet their individual needs *and* provide the proper intensity. These "instructional intensity" decisions at the heart of Tier 3 reinforcements are best made, monitored, and revised by the site intervention team.

Here's Why

Almost every school provides Tier 3 reinforcements, especially for students who qualify for special education. But most schools do not have effective intensive supports, in which students close their achievement gaps so they no longer need this level of help. Without these supports, Tier 3 becomes an educational prison, and the Tier 3 identification process an unintended life sentence.

There are many reasons why a school's Tier 3 efforts fail to work effectively, including the following.

1. A student's intensive supports are not targeted to their individual needs.

2. A student's intensive supports are targeted to their individual needs, but the school uses ineffective or mismatched instructional practices.

3. A student's intensive supports are targeted to their needs, and effective instructional practices are applied, but the student needs this help more often and with more intensity.

4. A student's intensive supports are targeted to their needs, and effective instructional practices are applied at the right intensity, but the staff member leading the help is not properly trained.

5. A student's intensive supports are targeted to their needs, and effective instructional practices are applied at the right intensity and administered by a highly trained staff member. However, the student misses Tier 1 essential curriculum to receive this help. One step forward, one step back.

These are five common reasons why Tier 3 supports might be ineffective—and why the diverse expertise on the school's intervention team is best positioned to lead Tier 3 reinforcements.

Here's How

Tier 3 reinforcements must be directive, not invitational. Many students who are far behind in school may have become so disengaged with learning that they decline invitations for help. For this reason, Tier 3 supports should be part of the regular school day, and teams must carve out time for these students to receive help without missing Tier 1 and Tier 2. See Buffum and Mattos (2015) and Mattos and Buffum (2015) for multiple examples of how real elementary and middle schools have modified their timetables to accomplish this.

It is also important to consider how to make Tier 3 interventions so intensive and effective that both students and teachers can see the achievement gap closing. Sharon Vaughn and Greg Roberts (2007) of the University of Texas at Austin's Meadows Center for Preventing Educational Risk note that Tier 3 supports should:

> Be intensive enough to provide students with a reasonable opportunity to "catch up" to grade-level expectations. Students should not be "locked into" the intervention for long periods of time without ongoing progress monitoring and consideration of their trajectory for meeting grade-level expectations. (p. 44)

So, how do schools ensure these supports are of sufficient intensity? First, consider the frequency with which they are delivered. Based on our experience as practitioners in schools, Tier 3 reinforcements are best delivered daily. Psychologists Rachel Brown-Chidsey, Louise Bronaugh, and Kelly McGraw (2009) also support this viewpoint.

Next, consider the interventions' duration. While schools might successfully deliver Tier 2 interventions (a little more help with essential grade-level standards) twice per week for approximately thirty minutes, we found that schools should deliver Tier 3 interventions five days per week for around thirty to fifty minutes—enough time for targeted direct instruction and guided practice on specific learning targets in each session.

For secondary schools, this works out nicely because most class periods range from forty to sixty minutes. Students needing Tier 3 support can then receive daily intensive help during one regularly scheduled period without being removed from their required grade-level coursework. Students in kindergarten and grade 1 should not receive thirty to fifty straight minutes of instruction, but instead have these minutes dispersed throughout the day. The combination of daily reinforcements totaling around thirty to fifty minutes gives students the support necessary to make significant progress. But duration and frequency alone are not enough.

Group size is another consideration for Tier 3 reinforcements. Historically, RTI researchers have recommended group sizes as small as three-to-one or even one-to-one (Haager, Klingner, & Vaughn, 2007; Simmons et al., 2007; Vaughn, Linan-Thompson, & Hickman, 2003). As practitioners, we recognize these ratios are extremely daunting for many schools. For that reason, we present the following two factors, which make more of a difference than group size alone: (1) targeting Tier 3 support and (2) training staff for delivering Tier 3 reinforcements.

Targeting Tier 3 Support

While focusing on causes rather than symptoms is important for Tier 2 interventions, it is critical at Tier 3. It is not enough to know students are "low readers," "far below basic," or "red" (the color teachers often use to represent students who are struggling). Schools must target Tier 3 help like a laser beam on the cause of the student's struggles. Is the student struggling with phonological awareness, phonemic awareness, decoding, fluency, comprehension, or some combination thereof? Accurate targeting can overcome the fact that staff may deliver some Tier 3 support to larger groups of students.

Think about it this way: As a teacher, would you prefer to have a Tier 3 group consisting of three students with three different needs—one struggling with phonemic awareness, one struggling with fluency, and the third struggling with comprehension (all far below basic or red)—or a group of ten students who all need the same help?

Training Staff for Delivering Tier 3 Reinforcements

The final consideration in organizing Tier 3 reinforcements is the level of training of those delivering the supports. When you consider assigning the most highly trained teachers to the students most in need of Tier 3 help, do not forget the wonderful special education teachers, speech-language pathologists, occupational therapists, and other itinerant teachers who come to a school, service their caseload, but are too seldom involved in preventing students with Tier 3 needs from falling even further behind. Increasingly, schools use these kinds of specialists to inform their Tier 3 reinforcements if not actually deliver them.

How do schools ensure that Tier 3 reinforcements are sufficiently intense—that they do indeed represent four hundred milligrams of amoxicillin and not forty milligrams?

1. Increase the frequency to five days per week.

2. Increase the duration to thirty to fifty minutes daily.

3. Decrease the group size as much as possible and feasible.

4. Target the causes and not the symptoms, and group students with identical needs.

5. Leverage the collective expertise of the intervention team to determine the supports for each student, and utilize the best-trained staff available to provide these daily supports.

These five traits increase the intensity of Tier 3 reinforcements, which enables students to close their learning gaps faster.

Helpful Tool

The following tool will help you accomplish the work for this essential action.

▶ **"Ensuring Proper Intensity for Tier 3 Reinforcements" (page 302):** Teams can use this tool to determine whether their Tier 3 supports have the proper intensity for struggling students by assessing their current reality, obstacles, and next steps.

Coaching Tips

Because establishing Tier 3 interventions is primarily the site intervention team's responsibility, the most important tip to keep in mind, once again, is to communicate! Teachers and staff members who are not directly involved in Tier 3 still must be fully informed and share a deep understanding of the rationale and process for providing Tier 3 support. Even if a teacher does not have a student in need of Tier 3 reinforcements, they still share responsibility for ensuring high levels of learning for *all* students and must be informed, committed, and able to articulate the process. Why? Because that same teacher may be called on to deliver an intervention or receive a new student who needs Tier 3 support.

Equally important, parents must understand the RTI at Work process's rationale and structure. Proactive, consistent communication is often the site intervention team's most valuable strategy for building understanding and minimizing resistance. It is only when all stakeholders understand the system as a whole that teachers, support staff, and parents alike can advocate for every student.

Former classroom teacher James A. Beane (1995) says it this way: "None of the pieces means anything taken alone; only when the pieces are put together do they mean something" (p. 1). These "pieces" are essential in making sure all students achieve success.

Ensuring Proper Intensity for Tier 3 Reinforcements

To assess your current reality, use the following three-point scale:

1 point = Not in place   2 points = Partially in place   3 points = 100 percent in place

Critical Criteria to Consider	Current Reality	Challenges or Obstacles	Next Steps to Effectively Meet These Criteria
Frequency ☐ Daily: Five times per week			
Duration ☐ Fifty minutes per day			
Group Size ☐ The group is as small as possible. ☐ All students require the same intervention for the same cause.			
Targeting ☐ Focused on cause, not symptoms			
Training ☐ The staff member with the best training provides the support matched to their training.			

Action 3

Determine Whether Special Education Is Needed and Justifiable

The premise of RTI is that schools should not delay providing help for struggling students until they fall far enough behind to qualify for special education. Instead, we should provide timely, targeted help to all students in need.

RTI does have a secondary benefit—schools can use it as a process to identify students with learning disabilities and potentially qualify them for special education services. But a school must be sure the student's lack of response to previous interventions and reinforcements is due to a potential learning disability and not a failure on the school's part to provide highly effective core instruction and supports that meet the student's individual needs. It would be both unprofessional and unethical to convince a parent that their child has a learning disability when, in fact, the school has not done its due diligence to help the child.

Here's Why

Prior to the reauthorization of IDEA (2004), the only legally required systematic intervention process to provide students additional time and support was special education. To qualify students for special education services prior to 2004, schools traditionally used the discrepancy model— also known as the wait-to-fail model. Utilizing a combination of IQ and achievement testing, this model required students to demonstrate a discrepancy of at least two standard deviations between their perceived ability and their current level of achievement to qualify for special education. Standard deviations are used to determine whether scores are significantly above or below average—or in this case, significantly below what might be expected of students of similar IQ. Two standard deviations would indicate a very significant difference.

As mentioned previously, research confirms that once students fall this far behind (two or more standard deviations), it is extremely difficult for them to catch up (Fuchs & Young, 2006; Vellutino, Scanlon, Zhang, & Schatschneider, 2008). In many cases, a student's struggles are not due to a disability. However, the school waits so long to systematically respond that the student drops significantly behind, and this achievement gap becomes their qualifying disability. In other words, the student is not born with a disability—the school's neglect creates it.

This is why the RTI process is a superior way to identify students with true disabilities. Because the process is timely and proactive, students do not have to fall too far behind to receive help. And because the site intervention team is the most diverse team—expertise-wise—on campus and has coordinated the most intensive reinforcements for students it considers for special education, it is in the best position to determine whether a student's continuing struggles are evidence of a learning disability. This decision has profound implications for students, so the site intervention team must have clearly defined criteria and processes for making these decisions.

Here's How

As previously discussed, when RTI focuses on identifying students for special education, the process often becomes driven by rigid timelines, a predetermined sequence of interventions, and laborious documentation. We acknowledge that schools must consider laws and regulations, especially when special education is a possibility. A school must be confident, beyond a reasonable doubt, that a student truly has special learning needs. To achieve this goal, the site intervention team should answer the following questions at each tier when considering identifying a student for special education. (See "Special Education Identification: Critical Questions" on page 306.)

- ▸ **Tier 1**

  - ▪ Did the student have ready access to essential grade-level curriculum as part of their core instruction?

  - ▪ Did the student receive effective supports, accommodations, or differentiation to reinforce their success in learning essential grade-level standards? What were these supports?

  - ▪ Is there evidence that the school's core instructional practices are working for a large majority of students, including similar students?

- ▸ **Tier 2**

  - ▪ Did the school identify the student for Tier 2 interventions in a timely manner?

  - ▪ What were the student's specific learning needs at Tier 2? (The team should be able to list exact standards, learning targets, and behaviors.)

  - ▪ What caused the student not to learn these essential learning outcomes?

  - ▪ What research- or evidence-based interventions did teacher teams use to address the student's specific learning needs?

  - ▪ Did the school provide these interventions in addition to Tier 1?

  - ▪ Is there evidence that these interventions were effective for similar students?

- ▸ **Tier 3**

  - ▪ Did the school identify the student for Tier 3 supports in a timely, proactive manner?

  - ▪ What quality problem-solving process did the school use to better identify the student's specific learning needs and the causes of the student's struggles?

  - ▪ What were the student's specific learning needs at Tier 3? (The team should be able to list exact standards, learning targets, and behaviors.)

  - ▪ What research- or evidence-based instructional practices did the school use to address the student's specific learning needs?

  - ▪ Did highly trained professionals in the student's areas of need provide this help?

  - ▪ Did the school provide these reinforcements in addition to Tier 1 and Tier 2?

  - ▪ How often did the school monitor the student's progress for each Tier 3 support? What revisions or modifications did the school make based on this information?

  - ▪ Is there evidence that these Tier 3 reinforcements were effective for similar students?

  - ▪ Are there any other supports the school should try before considering special education placement?

  - ▪ What will qualifying this student for special education make available—in terms of supports—that the school cannot already provide without qualification?

- Does the site intervention team unanimously feel that special education identification is necessary and appropriate for this student? What benefits will the student receive due to this recommendation that they could not receive without it?

- Would team members make the same recommendation if the student in question was their child?

If the site intervention team can't successfully and affirmatively answer each question, then it should not be recommending the student for special education. Student assessment data undoubtedly play a critical role in answering these questions. The decision should not rest on whether a school satisfactorily completes all the necessary paperwork and protocols. Instead, special education eligibility should measure the school's confidence that it has served the student well and they truly have unique learning needs that the school's general education and RTI resources cannot meet or maintain (Buffum et al., 2012). Qualifying for special education is not in itself the solution to a student's learning needs, but it creates opportunities for them to receive even more highly specialized, targeted, and personalized support.

Helpful Tool

The following tool will help you accomplish the work for this essential action.

▸ **"Special Education Identification: Critical Questions" (page 306):** This form offers questions for the site intervention team when considering identifying a student for special education.

Coaching Tips

The most important tip the site intervention team should consider as it determines whether special education is needed and justifiable is to keep an open mind. That may sound simple, but it is, in reality, very difficult. Given the fact that special education has historically been the only intervention available to struggling students, many educators still approach support for their students with a singular focus—get them into special education! Shifting that mindset is what this entire book is all about, from working to establish a culture of collective responsibility to implementing a multitiered system of supports.

With that in mind, the guiding coalition and the site intervention team must be prepared and proactive about countering the rush to identify students for special education. Conversation about the history, pros, and cons of special education needs to happen on a consistent basis. The challenge is never to diminish the special educators' work, while simultaneously highlighting the reasons why special education has not been the best solution for many students.

There are no shortcuts for keeping minds open or for shifting people's mindsets. Rather, it is part of a school's never-ending mission to ensure high levels of learning for all students. Reeves (2009b) reminds us, "Failure in change strategies need not be inevitable. In fact, it is avoidable if change leaders will balance their sense of urgency with a more thoughtful approach to implementing change" (p. 7). That said, it has never been more important for members of the leadership and intervention teams to walk the talk.

Special Education Identification: Critical Questions

The site intervention team must ask the following questions when considering a student for special education placement.

Tier 1

- Did the student have ready access to essential grade-level curriculum as part of their core instruction?

- Did the student receive effective supports, accommodations, or differentiation to reinforce their success in learning essential grade-level standards? What were these supports?

- Is there evidence that the school's core instructional practices are working for a large majority of students, including similar students?

Tier 2

- Did the school identify the student for Tier 2 interventions in a timely manner?

- What were the student's specific learning needs at Tier 2? (The team should be able to list exact standards, learning targets, and behaviors.)

- What caused the student not to learn these essential learning outcomes?

- What research- or evidence-based interventions did teacher teams use to address the student's specific learning needs?

- Did the school provide these interventions in addition to Tier 1?

- Is there evidence that these interventions were effective for similar students?

Tier 3

- Did the school identify the student for Tier 3 supports in a timely, proactive manner?

- What quality problem solving process did the school use to better identify the student's specific learning needs and the causes of the student's struggles?

- What were the student's specific learning needs at Tier 3? (The team should be able to list exact standards, learning targets, and behaviors.)

- What research- or evidence-based instructional practices did the school use to address the student's specific learning needs?

- Did highly trained professionals in the student's areas of need provide this help?

- Did the school provide these reinforcements in addition to Tier 1 and Tier 2?

- How often did the school monitor the student's progress for each Tier 3 support? What revisions or modifications did the school make based on this information?

- Is there evidence that these Tier 3 reinforcements were effective for similar students?

- Are there any other supports the school should try before considering special education placement?

- What will qualifying this student for special education make available—in terms of supports—that the school cannot already provide without qualification?

- Does the site intervention team unanimously feel that special education identification is necessary and appropriate for this student? What benefits will the student receive due to this recommendation that they could not receive without it?

- Would team members make the same recommendation if the student in question was their child?

Conclusion

The students most at risk in a school face complex problems. A student might be below grade level in reading *and* have weak number-sense skills *and* be an English learner *and* consistently demonstrate impulsive behaviors in class. Schools often ask us what intervention program to provide for a student like this. Our initial answer is, "We don't know what the right intervention is—there is no effective reading, mathematics, English language program you can buy."

What we can offer, instead of a program recommendation, is the right problem-solving *process*. We can't promise that the recommendations described in this chapter guarantee that a site intervention team will always find the right solution for each student in need of intensive supports—we never achieved perfection at our schools. But we know that these ongoing essential actions give your school the best chance to successfully help your students who are most at risk.

Get Started . . .
Then Get Better

> Not I, nor anyone else can travel that road for you. You must travel it by yourself. It is not far. It is within reach.
>
> **—Walt Whitman**

Within the eight chapters of this book, we outlined the essential actions a school must take to create a highly effective multitiered system of supports to ensure every student learns at high levels. (We provide a cumulative list of these actions at the end of this epilogue: "RTI at Work Essential Actions for Tiers 1, 2, and 3," page 313.) For each action, we provided specific steps and proven tools to help achieve each outcome. Our goal in writing an MTSS handbook was to make the work understandable, logical, and achievable.

Nevertheless, as you reflect on what you read, the totality of the PLC and RTI processes might seem daunting. It *should* feel that way. It would be naive to think that guaranteeing every student's success in school is a trivial, easy-to-achieve endeavor, especially after a historic global pandemic. Radically rethinking and restructuring an education system that successfully served the United States for more than two hundred years is monumental work. We acknowledge this point not to dissuade you from the journey but to honestly confirm that the challenges in your path are formidable. This is not a sprint, but a marathon.

Facing this reality, educators often ask us, "Our school has almost none of these practices in place. It all seems so overwhelming. Where do we start?" Every journey begins with a first step. Seriously—even the longest journey starts with a first step in the right direction. The key is to get started, and then get better.

We know that successful PLC at Work implementation does not happen by accident or through random individual efforts. This is why the first essential action in this book is to build a guiding coalition—the right team of people to lead the process. After this team is established, its first job is to build consensus on the school's fundamental purpose—to ensure high levels of learning for *all* students. Achieving this mission takes a collaborative effort, so forming teacher teams and scheduling time for frequent collaboration is the logical next step. *Learning by Doing* (DuFour et al., 2024) and *Taking Action* were written to provide that step-by-step pathway—one step at a time.

Another question educators ask us is how long it should take to build an effective system of interventions within a PLC school. To this, we offer three answers: (1) one year, (2) three years, and (3) forever. As Fullan (2019) states, "Research has shown that leaders armed with practical knowledge and partnering within their communities can achieve remarkable changes within a year or two" (p. xiii). With effective leadership, the essential foundational elements can be in place in one year. These steps would include the following.

1. Create a guiding coalition.

2. Build consensus on the school's mission.

3. Create teacher teams and a site intervention team.

4. Schedule weekly collaboration time.

5. Prepare for rational and irrational forms of staff resistance.

6. Identify a limited number of essential standards (academic and behavior).

7. Ensure all students have access to this essential curriculum.

8. Create and use common assessments on your limited list of essential standards.

9. Create a schoolwide teacher recommendation process for Tier 2 interventions.

10. Schedule time for Tier 2 interventions, and begin by focusing on your limited number of essential standards.

11. Select a Tier 3 universal skill—such as reading, number sense, or English language—to begin to focus your schoolwide efforts.

12. Identify students who need Tier 3 intensive reinforcements in this one universal skill.

13. Leveraging the expertise of the intervention team, begin Tier 3 reinforcements in this one universal skill.

14. Evaluate what is working and what is not . . . and get better.

Note that the preceding list has some critical qualifiers, such as focusing on a *limited number* of essential standards and beginning Tier 3 reinforcements in *one* subject area. When Mike Mattos served as principal of Marjorie Veeh Elementary School, which predominantly served students at risk, the staff focused on one subject—reading—to begin the PLC journey. Each grade-level team selected a limited number of essential reading standards for its collaborative focus. The school modified its schedule to ensure students were not pulled from class while these essential standards were taught at Tier 1 or retaught during each team's daily supplemental intervention time. Tier 3 resources focused on students who needed intensive reading support. While students had needs in other subjects, the school was not ready to address them all.

For the first year, it made more sense to do a few things well rather than many things poorly. As one might expect, the school saw increases in its end-of-year reading assessments. But to the staff's surprise, the school also saw growth in its end-of-year assessments in mathematics, science, and social studies. The staff concluded that because more students could read and comprehend grade-level texts, this universal skill helped students across the curriculum. The second year, the staff continued their focus on reading, but because they had some parts in place in that subject, they began to identify essential standards in writing. They included mathematics in the third year—one step at a time.

While it is possible to get the foundational pieces in place for at least one subject per year, a school will probably not be very efficient or effective at these new steps. A school should expect it to take closer to three years of focused efforts to get good at the work. The first year, many of the initial steps create the conditions to begin to do the work. Because the second year begins with those structures already in place, the staff can then hit the ground running, identify what isn't working, and make refinements. By the third year, the school can begin to reap the benefits of its efforts, confirming that the steps work. This reinforces the staff's commitment to the process. As time progresses, the faculty will stop talking about implementing the PLC process and RTI, and instead will start being a true professional learning community.

Because the school's reason for implementing the PLC process is to achieve its mission of ensuring high levels of learning for all students, the work does not stop until it achieves this mission. As long as there is at least one student who is not succeeding, the staff must commit to continuously seeking better ways to serve their students, making the implementation timeline forever.

While we suggest that schools implement MTSS one step at a time, we would *not* suggest the following approach: "Let's just focus on Tier 1 this year. We will form teams and begin to identify essential standards. In the second year, we will have teams start to create and administer common assessments while exploring ways to create intervention time during the school day. In the third year, we will begin providing systematic interventions."

There are two significant drawbacks to that approach. First, students can't wait two years to start getting extra time and support. As mentioned in the introduction (page 1), there is great urgency to this work. Every day a student is not succeeding means they are probably falling further behind. Second, the key to creating staff commitment to the MTSS process is having teachers see it work—seeing students who are failing start to succeed. If it takes two years to begin systematic interventions, then it is unlikely that teachers will start to see more of their struggling students succeed before then. Momentum is often lost in drawn-out implementation. It is better to start with a small number of essential standards and begin to assess and intervene on these during the first year. This provides opportunities for short-term wins. For teachers, the most rewarding part of their job is when they see students succeed.

Finally, as you begin your journey, we offer a few cautionary suggestions.

- **There are no shortcuts:** It can be tempting to have a district committee identify essential standards, removing most teachers from the process. Yet, when teacher teams roll up their sleeves and dig deeply into the curriculum, they become students of the standards. They gain deeper understanding of the essential curriculum and ownership of the process that creates deep levels of commitment.

  It can also be tempting to simply buy packaged assessment systems and intervention programs instead of committing to the process necessary to target interventions to the unique needs of each student. These shortcuts are seductive. But in the end, the educators in the building are the school's greatest resource. The foundational assumption of the PLC process is that the best way to improve student learning is through the job-embedded, collaborative learning of the adults. The people doing the work are doing the learning (DuFour et al., 2024). Avoid the work, and the learning stops.

- ▶ **There is never going to be a perfect time to begin:** All the stars in the education universe—district, state or provincial, and federal leadership—are unlikely to align. Regardless, we know of no existing laws or regulations that would prohibit a school from working in teams, identifying essential curriculum, giving common assessments, and providing targeted students with extra help.

- ▶ **There are sufficient resources to get started:** Having worked with schools around the world, we can confidently say that no school ever has enough resources. For every school that claims a lack of resources for its inability to start, we can provide model schools that have done it with less. We are not suggesting it is easy, but it is being done.

- ▶ **There is a difference between uncomfortable and unreasonable:** Unreasonable demands are unjust, but change sometimes requires discomfort.

Undoubtedly, the work will be hard. That is the nature of our work as educators. If there is one thing for certain at the start of every school year, it is this: educators are going to work hard. The question is whether we will work hard and succeed or work hard and fail.

And without question, you are going to make missteps. Mistakes are not only inevitable but indispensable to learning and growing. Extend some grace to your students, your colleagues, and yourself. Just surviving a historic pandemic was a monumental accomplishment, and the scars of that difficult time are still present. Flowers grow best when provided warmth and care. So do our students, as do the adults.

In our profession, we do not build widgets, nor do we measure our success in profit margins. We deal in futures—the futures of our students. Every day that we collectively get better at doing the right work right, it is measured in the life of a student. Gaining an essential academic skill or behavior can open doors of opportunity for a student over their lifetime. Achieving this outcome for every student takes more than proven research and good intentions; it requires *action*. Get started . . . then get better!

RTI at Work Essential Actions for Tiers 1, 2, and 3

A Culture of Collective Responsibility
ACTION 1: Establish a Guiding Coalition
ACTION 2: Build a Culture of Collective Responsibility
ACTION 3: Form Collaborative Teacher Teams
ACTION 4: Commit to Team Norms
ACTION 5: Prepare for Staff Resistance

Tier 1	
Guiding Coalition Essential Actions	**Teacher Team Essential Actions**
ACTION 1: Ensure Access to Essential Grade-Level Curriculum	ACTION 1: Identify Essential Standards
	ACTION 2: Design a Unit Assessment Plan
ACTION 2: Identify and Teach Essential Academic and Social Behaviors	ACTION 3: Create Common Assessments and Begin Instruction
ACTION 3: Create a Balanced Assessment Approach	ACTION 4: Foster Student Investment
ACTION 4: Co-Create Schoolwide Grading Practices	ACTION 5: Analyze and Respond to Common Assessment Data
ACTION 5: Provide Preventions to Proactively Support Student Success	

Tier 2	
Guiding Coalition Essential Actions	**Teacher Team Essential Actions**
ACTION 1: Schedule Time for Tier 2 Interventions and Extensions	ACTION 1: Design and Lead Tier 2 Interventions for Essential Academic Standards
ACTION 2: Establish a Process to Identify Students Who Require Tier 2 Behavior Interventions	ACTION 2: Identify and Target Immediate Prerequisite Skills
ACTION 3: Plan and Implement Tier 2 Interventions for Essential Social and Academic Behaviors	ACTION 3: Monitor the Progress of Students Receiving Tier 2 Academic Interventions
ACTION 4: Coordinate Interventions for Students Needing Academic *and* Behavior Supports	ACTION 4: Extend Student Learning

Tier 3	
Guiding Coalition Essential Actions	**Intervention Team Essential Actions**
ACTION 1: Create a Dynamic, Problem-Solving Site Intervention Team	ACTION 1: Diagnose, Target, Prioritize, and Monitor Tier 3 Reinforcements
ACTION 2: Identify Students Needing Intensive Reinforcements	ACTION 2: Ensure Proper Instructional Intensity
ACTION 3: Prioritize Resources Based on the Greatest Student Needs	ACTION 3: Determine Whether Special Education Is Needed and Justifiable
ACTION 4: Create a Systematic and Timely Process to Refer Students to the Site Intervention Team	
ACTION 5: Assess Intervention and Reinforcement Effectiveness	

REFERENCES AND RESOURCES

Accelerate Student Learning. (n.d.). *Self-reported grades/student expectations (d = 1.33)*. Accessed at https://sites.google.com/view/acceleratestudentlearning/es3-self-reported-grades on January 12, 2024.

Ainsworth, L. (2013). *Prioritizing the Common Core: Identifying specific standards to emphasize the most*. Englewood, CO: Lead + Learn Press.

American Diploma Project. (2004). *Ready or not: Creating a high school diploma that counts*. Washington, DC: Achieve. Accessed at www.achieve.org/publications/ready-or-not-creating -high-school-diploma-counts on January 11, 2024.

Andrade, H. L., & Cizek, G. J. (Eds.). (2009). *Handbook of formative assessment*. New York: Routledge.

AZ Quotes. (n.d.). *Margot Fonteyn quotes*. Accessed at www.azquotes.com/author/4969-Margot _Fonteyn on February 20, 2017.

Bailey, M. J., & Dynarski, S. M. (2011, December). *Gains and gaps: Changing inequality in U.S. college entry and completion* (NBER Working Paper No. 17633). Cambridge, MA: National Bureau of Economic Research.

Balu, R., Zhu, P., Doolittle, F., Schiller, E., Jenkins, J., & Gersten, R. (2015, November). *Evaluation of response to intervention practices for elementary school reading* (NCEE 2016-4000). Washington, DC: National Center for Education Evaluation and Regional Assistance. Accessed at https://ies.ed.gov/ncee/pubs/20164000/pdf/20164000.pdf on July 23, 2024.

Barber, M., & Mourshed, M. (2007, September). *How the world's best-performing school systems come out on top*. Chicago: McKinsey & Company. Accessed at www.mckinsey.com /industries/education/our-insights/how-the-worlds-best-performing-school-systems-come -out-on-top on July 23, 2024.

Beane, J. A. (Ed.). (1995). *Toward a coherent curriculum: The 1995 ASCD yearbook*. Arlington, VA: ASCD.

Bloom, B. S. (1968). Learning for mastery. *Evaluation Comment, 1*(2), 1–12.

Bloom, B. S. (1971). Mastery learning. In J. H. Block (Ed.), *Mastery learning: Theory and practice* (pp. 47–63). New York: Holt, Rinehart & Winston.

Boudett, K. P., & Lockwood, M. (2019). The power of team norms. *Educational Leadership, 76*(9). Accessed at www.ascd.org/el/articles/the-power-of-team-norms on April 12, 2024.

BrainyQuote. (n.d.). *Mahatma Gandhi quotes*. Accessed at https://brainyquote.com/quotes /quotes/m/mahatmagan109075.html on May 27, 2017.

Brantlinger, E. A. (Ed.). (2006). *Who benefits from special education? Remediating (fixing) other people's children.* Mahwah, NJ: Erlbaum.

Breslow, J. M. (2012, September 21). *By the numbers: Dropping out of high school.* Accessed at www.pbs.org/wgbh/frontline/article/by-the-numbers-dropping-out-of-high-school on July 23, 2024.

Brookhart, S. M. (2011). *Grading and learning: Practices that support student achievement.* Bloomington, IN: Solution Tree Press.

Brookhart, S. M. (2020). Feedback and measurement. In S. M. Brookhart & J. H. McMillan (Eds.), *Classroom assessment and educational measurement* (pp. 63–78). New York: Routledge.

Brookhart, S. M., & McMillan, J. H. (Eds.). (2020). *Classroom assessment and educational measurement.* New York: Routledge.

Brooks-Gunn, J., & Duncan, G. J. (1997). The effects of poverty on children. *The Future of Children, 7*(2), 55–71.

Brown, T., & Ferriter, W. M. (2021). *You can learn! Building student ownership, motivation, and efficacy with the PLC at Work process.* Bloomington, IN: Solution Tree Press.

Brown-Chidsey, R., Bronaugh, L., & McGraw, K. (2009). *RTI in the classroom: Guidelines and recipes for success.* New York: Guilford Press.

Brown-Chidsey, R., & Steege, M. W. (2010). *Response to intervention: Principles and strategies for effective practice* (2nd ed.). New York: Guilford Press.

Buffum, A., & Mattos, M. (2014, May). *Criteria for selecting essential standards* [Presentation]. Simplifying Response to Intervention Workshop, Prince George, British Columbia, Canada.

Buffum, A., & Mattos, M. (Eds.). (2015). *It's about time: Planning interventions and extensions in elementary school.* Bloomington, IN: Solution Tree Press.

Buffum, A., Mattos, M., & Malone, J. (2018). *Taking action: A handbook for RTI at Work.* Bloomington, IN: Solution Tree Press.

Buffum, A., Mattos, M., & Weber, C. (2009). *Pyramid response to intervention: RTI, professional learning communities, and how to respond when kids don't learn.* Bloomington, IN: Solution Tree Press.

Buffum, A., Mattos, M., & Weber, C. (2012). *Simplifying response to intervention: Four essential guiding principles.* Bloomington, IN: Solution Tree Press.

Buffum, A., Mattos, M., Weber, C., & Hierck, T. (2015). *Uniting academic and behavior interventions: Solving the skill or will dilemma.* Bloomington, IN: Solution Tree Press.

Burrus, J., & Roberts, R. D. (2012). Dropping out of high school: Prevalence, risk factors, and remediation strategies. *R&D Connections, 18,* 1–9. Accessed at www.ets.org/Media/Research/pdf/RD_Connections18.pdf on July 23, 2024.

Camera, L. (2021, July 27). Study confirms school-to-prison pipeline. *U.S. News & World Report.* Accessed at www.usnews.com/news/education-news/articles/2021-07-27/study-confirms-school-to-prison-pipeline on January 26, 2024.

Chang, H. (2023, October 12). *Rising tide of chronic absence challenges schools* [Blog post]. Accessed at www.attendanceworks.org/rising-tide-of-chronic-absence-challenges-schools/?preview=true on January 11, 2024.

Chappuis, J., & Stiggins, R. (2020). *Classroom assessment for student learning: Doing it right—Using it well* (3rd ed.). New York: Pearson.

Chappuis, J., Stiggins, R., Chappuis, S., & Arter, J. (2012). *Classroom assessment for student learning: Doing it right—Using it well* (2nd ed.). Boston: Pearson.

Collins, J. (2001). *Good to great: Why some companies make the leap . . . and others don't.* New York: HarperBusiness.

Collins, J. (2017). *Confront the brutal facts (Stockdale paradox)* [Video transcript]. Accessed at www.jimcollins.com/media_topics/Confront-the-Brutal-Facts.html on January 11, 2024.

Conley, D. T. (2007, March). *Redefining college readiness.* Eugene, OR: Educational Policy Improvement Center.

Conzemius, A. E., & O'Neill, J. (2014). *The handbook for SMART school teams: Revitalizing best practices for collaboration* (2nd ed.). Bloomington, IN: Solution Tree Press.

Cooper, H., Charlton, K., Valentine, J. C., Muhlenbruck, L., & Borman, G. D. (2000). Making the most of summer school: A meta-analytic and narrative review. *Monographs of the Society for Research in Child Development, 65*(1), i–v, 1–127.

Corwin Visible Learning Plus. (2023). *Teacher estimates of achievement.* Accessed at www.visiblelearningmetax.com/influences/view/teacher_estimates_of_achievement_ on April 25, 2024.

Covey, S. R. (1989). *The 7 habits of highly effective people: Powerful lessons in personal change.* New York: Fireside.

Cruz, L. F., & Pilar, C. (2023, October 11). *The leadership action plan* [Professional development presentation]. California Principals' Support Network, Sun Valley, CA.

Daly, E., Glover, T., & McCurdy, M. (2006). *Response to intervention: Technical assistance document.* Lincoln: Nebraska Department of Education.

Darling-Hammond, L., Hyler, M. E., & Gardner, M. (2017, June). *Effective teacher professional development.* Palo Alto, CA: Learning Policy Institute. Accessed at https://learningpolicyinstitute.org/product/teacher-prof-dev on April 12, 2024.

Deal, T. E., & Peterson, K. D. (1999). *Shaping school culture: The heart of leadership.* San Francisco: Jossey-Bass.

Deno, E. (1970). Special education as developmental capital. *Exceptional Children, 37*(3), 229–237.

Dexter, D. D., & Hughes, C. (n.d.). *Progress monitoring within a response-to-intervention model.* Accessed at http://rtinetwork.org/component/content/article/10/22-progress-monitoring-within-a-response on July 23, 2024.

Diament, M. (2014, April 29). Graduation rates fall short for students with disabilities. *Disability Scoop.* Accessed at www.disabilityscoop.com/2014/04/29/graduation-rates-disabilities/19317 on July 23, 2024.

Dill, K. (2022, June 20). School's out for summer and many teachers are calling it quits. *The Wall Street Journal.* Accessed at www.wsj.com/articles/schools-out-for-summer-and-many-teachers-are-calling-it-quits-11655732689 on January 11, 2024.

Dimich, N. (2015). *Design in five: Essential phases to create engaging assessment practice.* Bloomington, IN: Solution Tree Press.

Dimich, N. (2024). *Design in five: Essential phases to create engaging assessment practice* (2nd ed.). Bloomington, IN: Solution Tree Press.

Dimich, N., Erkens, C., & Schimmer, T. (2023). *Jackpot! Nurturing student investment through assessment.* Bloomington, IN: Solution Tree Press.

Donovan, M. S., & Cross, C. T. (Eds.). (2002). *Minority students in special and gifted education.* Washington, DC: National Academies Press.

Dorn, S. (1996). *Creating the dropout: An institutional and social history of school failure.* Westport, CT: Praeger.

Drucker, P. F. (1992). *Managing for the future: The 1990s and beyond.* New York: Plume.

DuFour, R. (2015). *In praise of American educators: And how they can become even better.* Bloomington, IN: Solution Tree Press.

DuFour, R. (2016). *Advocates for professional learning communities: Finding common ground in education reform.* Bloomington, IN: Solution Tree Press. Accessed at https://allthingsplc.info/wp-content/uploads/2024/04/AdvocatesforPLCs-Updated11-9-15.pdf on May 1, 2024.

DuFour, R., DuFour, R., Eaker, R., & Many, T. W. (2006). *Learning by doing: A handbook for Professional Learning Communities at Work* (1st ed.). Bloomington, IN: Solution Tree Press.

DuFour, R., DuFour, R., Eaker, R., & Many, T. W. (2010). *Learning by doing: A handbook for Professional Learning Communities at Work* (2nd ed.). Bloomington, IN: Solution Tree Press.

DuFour, R., DuFour, R., Eaker, R., Many, T. W., & Mattos, M. (2016). *Learning by doing: A handbook for Professional Learning Communities at Work* (3rd ed.). Bloomington, IN: Solution Tree Press.

DuFour, R., DuFour, R., Eaker, R., Many, T. W., Mattos, M., & Muhammad, A. (2024). *Learning by doing: A handbook for Professional Learning Communities at Work* (4th ed.). Bloomington, IN: Solution Tree Press.

DuFour, R., DuFour, R., Eaker, R., Mattos, M., & Muhammad, A. (2021). *Revisiting Professional Learning Communities at Work: Proven insights for sustained, substantive school improvement* (2nd ed.). Bloomington, IN: Solution Tree Press.

DuFour, R., & Eaker, R. (1998). *Professional Learning Communities at Work: Best practices for enhancing student achievement.* Bloomington, IN: Solution Tree Press.

DuFour, R., Eaker, R., & DuFour, R. (2007). *The power of Professional Learning Communities at Work: Bringing the big ideas to life* [DVD]. Bloomington, IN: Solution Tree Press.

Dweck, C. S. (2006). *Mindset: The new psychology of success.* New York: Random House.

Dweck, C. S. (2017). *Mindset: Changing the way you think to fulfil your potential* (Updated ed.). New York: Random House.

Education for All Handicapped Children Act of 1975, Pub. L. No. 94-142, 20 U.S.C. § 1401 (1975).

Education Week. (2020, May 6). *Map: Coronavirus and school closures in 2019–2020.* Accessed at www.edweek.org/ew/section/multimedia/map-coronavirus-and-school-closures.html on April 24, 2024.

Education Week. (2024). *The state of teaching.* Accessed at www.edweek.org/the-state-of-teaching on April 12, 2024.

Effective schools. (n.d.). In *Wikipedia*. Accessed at https://en.wikipedia.org/wiki/Effective _schools on March 1, 2017.

Eller, J. (2004). *Effective group facilitation in education: How to energize meetings and manage difficult groups.* Thousand Oaks, CA: Corwin.

Erkens, C., Jakicic, C., Jessie, L. G., King, D., Kramer, S. V., Many T. W., et al. (2008). *The collaborative teacher: Working together as a professional learning community.* Bloomington, IN: Solution Tree Press.

Fendler, L., & Muzaffar, I. (2008). The history of the bell curve: Sorting and the idea of normal. *Educational Theory, 58*(1), 63–82.

Ferri, B. A., & Connor, D. J. (2006). *Reading resistance: Discourses of exclusion in desegregation and inclusion debates.* New York: Peter Lang.

Ferriter, W. M., Mattos, M., & Meyer, R. J. (2025). *The big book of tools for RTI at Work.* Bloomington, IN: Solution Tree Press.

Fischhoff, B. (1992). Risk taking: A developmental perspective. In J. F. Yates (Ed.), *Risk-taking behavior* (pp. 133–162). New York: Wiley.

Fischhoff, B., Crowell, N. A., & Kipke, M. (Eds.). (1999). *Adolescent decision making: Implications for prevention programs—Summary of a workshop.* Washington, DC: National Academies Press.

Fish, R. E. (2019). Teacher race and racial disparities in special education. *Remedial and Special Education, 40*(4), 213–224.

Fisher, D., & Frey, N. (2014). *Checking for understanding: Formative assessment techniques for your classroom* (2nd ed.). Arlington, VA: ASCD.

Fleming, C. B., Harachi, T. W., Cortes, R. C., Abbott, R. D., & Catalano, R. F. (2004). Level and change in reading scores and attention problems during elementary school as predictors of problem behavior in middle school. *Journal of Emotional and Behavioral Disorders, 12*(3), 130–144.

Fuchs, D., Compton, D. L., Fuchs, L. S., Bryant, J., & Davis, G. N. (2008). Making "secondary intervention" work in a three-tier responsiveness-to-intervention model: Findings from the first-grade longitudinal reading study of the National Research Center on Learning Disabilities. *Reading and Writing, 21*(4), 413–436.

Fuchs, D., & Young, C. L. (2006). On the irrelevance of intelligence in predicting responsiveness to reading instruction. *Exceptional Children, 73*(1), 8–30.

Fuchs, L. S., & Fuchs, D. (2007). A model for implementing responsiveness to intervention. *Teaching Exceptional Children, 39*(5), 14–20.

Fullan, M. (1993). *Change forces: Probing the depths of educational reform.* London: Falmer Press.

Fullan, M. (1994, May 5–7). *Keynote address.* Symposium sponsored by the California Center for School Restructuring, Anaheim, California.

Fullan, M. (2003). *The moral imperative of school leadership.* Thousand Oaks, CA: Corwin.

Fullan, M. (2019). Foreword. In D. Reeves & R. Eaker, *100-day leaders: Turning short-term wins into long-term success in schools* (pp. xiii–xiv). Bloomington, IN: Solution Tree Press.

Gallimore, R., Ermeling, B. A., Saunders, W. M., & Goldenberg, C. (2009). Moving the learning of teaching closer to practice: Teacher education implications of school-based inquiry teams. *Elementary School Journal, 109*(5), 537–553.

Garmston, R. J., & Wellman, B. M. (2009). *The adaptive school: A sourcebook for developing collaborative groups* (2nd ed.). Norwood, MA: Christopher-Gordon.

Garmston, R. J., & Wellman, B. M. (2016). *The adaptive school: A sourcebook for developing collaborative groups* (3rd ed.). Lanham, MD: Rowman & Littlefield.

Georgiou, A. (2020, March 18). Our hands originated in Earth's oceans at least 380 million years ago, "missing link" fossil fish reveals. *Newsweek*. Accessed at www.newsweek.com/human-hands-earth-oceans-fish-fossil-1493033 on January 12, 2024.

Gerstner, L. V., Jr. (1995). *Reinventing education: Entrepreneurship in America's public schools.* New York: Penguin.

Goldhaber, D., & Holden, K. (2020). *Understanding the early teacher pipeline: What we can (and, importantly, can't) learn from national data* (CALDER Policy Brief No. 21-1120). Washington, DC: National Center for Analysis of Longitudinal Data in Education Research.

Goldhaber, D., Kane, T. J., McEachin, A., Morton, E., Patterson, T., & Staiger, D. O. (2022, May). *The consequences of remote and hybrid instruction during the pandemic* (NBER Working Paper No. 30010). Cambridge, MA: National Bureau of Economic Research. Accessed at www.nber.org/system/files/working_papers/w30010/w30010.pdf on January 26, 2024.

Goodreads. (n.d). *Tom Landry quotes.* Accessed at www.goodreads.com/quotes/58284-a-coach-is-someone-who-tells-you-what-you-don-t on July 23, 2024.

Goodwin, B., & Rouleau, K. (2022). *The new classroom instruction that works: The best research-based strategies for increasing student achievement.* Arlington, VA: ASCD.

Gopalan, M., & Lewis, M. M. (2022). K–12 civil rights complaints: A nationwide analysis. *Educational Researcher, 51*(9), 584–587.

Graham, P., & Ferriter, W. M. (2010). *Building a Professional Learning Community at Work: A guide to the first year.* Bloomington, IN: Solution Tree Press.

Guskey, T. R. (2010). Lessons of mastery learning. *Educational Leadership, 68*(2), 52–57.

Guskey, T. R. (2015a). Mastery learning. In J. D. Wright (Ed.), *International encyclopedia of the social and behavioral sciences* (2nd ed., Vol. 14, pp. 752–759). Oxford, United Kingdom: Elsevier.

Guskey, T. R. (2015b). *On your mark: Challenging the conventions of grading and reporting.* Bloomington, IN: Solution Tree Press.

Guskey, T. R. (2018). Does pre-assessment work? *Educational Leadership, 75*(5), 52–57.

Guskey, T. R. (2022). Can grades be an effective form of feedback? *Kappan, 104*(3), 36–41. Accessed at https://kappanonline.org/grades-feedback-guskey on September 23, 2023.

Guskey, T. R., & Pigott, T. D. (1988). Research on group-based mastery learning programs: A meta-analysis. *Journal of Educational Research, 81*(4), 197–216.

Haager, D., Klingner, J., & Vaughn, S. (Eds.). (2007). *Evidence-based reading practices for response to intervention.* Baltimore: Brookes.

Hannigan, J., Hannigan, J. D., Mattos, M., & Buffum, A. (2021). *Behavior solutions: Teaching academic and social skills through RTI at Work.* Bloomington, IN: Solution Tree Press.

Hanson, M. (2023, October 29). *College dropout rates.* Education Data Initiative. Accessed at https://educationdata.org/college-dropout-rates on April 12, 2024.

Harlen, W., & James, M. (1996, April). *Creating a positive impact of assessment on learning* [Paper presentation]. Annual conference of the American Educational Research Association, New York.

Harris, J. (n.d.). *Facilitative leadership: Balancing the dimensions of success* [Blog post]. Accessed at http://interactionassociates.com/insights/blog/facilitative-leadership-balancing-dimensions -success#.WVFGhjOZPUo on June 25, 2017.

Hattie, J. A. C. (2012). *Visible learning for teachers: Maximizing impact on learning.* New York: Routledge.

Hattie, J. A. C. (2023). *Visible learning: The sequel—A synthesis of over 2,100 meta-analyses related to achievement.* New York: Routledge.

Hattie, J. A. C., & Yates, G. (2014). *Visible learning and the science of how we learn.* New York: Routledge.

Hess, K. (2018). *A local assessment toolkit to promote deeper learning: Transforming research into practice.* Thousand Oaks, CA: Corwin.

Hierck, T., Coleman, C., & Weber, C. (2011). *Pyramid of behavior interventions: Seven keys to a positive learning environment.* Bloomington, IN: Solution Tree Press.

Hord, S. M. (1997). *Professional learning communities: Communities of continuous inquiry and improvement.* Austin, TX: Southwest Educational Development Laboratory. Accessed at https://sedl.org/pubs/change34/plc-cha34.pdf on January 12, 2024.

Horner, R. H., Sugai, G., & Lewis, T. (2015, April). *Is school-wide positive behavior support an evidence-based practice?* Accessed at https://assets-global.website-files.com/5d3725188825e07 1f1670246/5d79730226acc65b8ce8a9a6_2014%2007-07%20evidence%20base%20for%20 swpbs.pdf on January 11, 2024.

Howard, R. (Director). (1995). *Apollo 13* [Film]. Universal Pictures.

Individuals With Disabilities Education Improvement Act of 2004, Pub. L. No. 108-446 § 300.115 (2004).

Interaction Associates. (1997). *Facilitative leadership: Tapping the power of participation.* San Francisco: Author.

Jacobs, H. H. (2001). New trends in curriculum: An interview with Heidi Hayes Jacobs. *Independent School, 61*(1), 18–24.

Jerald, C. D. (2009). *Defining a 21st century education.* Alexandria, VA: Center for Public Education.

Jimenez, K. (2022, October 24). *Reading and math test scores fell across US during the pandemic. How did your state fare?* Accessed at www.usatoday.com/story/news/2022/10/24/naep-report -card-test-scores-reading-math/10552407002 on January 26, 2024.

Kallick, B., & Colosimo, J. (2009). *Using curriculum mapping and assessment data to improve learning.* Thousand Oaks, CA: Corwin.

Killion, J. (2008). *Assessing impact: Evaluating staff development* (2nd ed.). Thousand Oaks, CA: Corwin.

Killion, J., & Roy, P. (2009). *Becoming a learning school.* Oxford, OH: Learning Forward.

Kotter, J. P. (1996). *Leading change.* Boston: Harvard Business School Press.

Kotter, J. P. (2007, January). Leading change: Why transformation efforts fail. *Harvard Business Review*. Accessed at https://hbr.org/2007/01/leading-change-why-transformation-efforts-fail on July 23, 2024.

Kotter, J. P., & Whitehead, L. A. (2010). *Buy-in: Saving your good idea from getting shot down.* Boston: Harvard Business Review Press.

Kramer, S. V., & Schuhl, S. (2023). *Acceleration for all: A how-to guide for overcoming learning gaps.* Bloomington, IN: Solution Tree Press.

Kramer, S. V., Sonju, B., Mattos, M., & Buffum, A. (2021). *Best practices at Tier 2: Supplemental interventions for additional student support, elementary.* Bloomington, IN: Solution Tree Press.

Langston University. (n.d.). *Transformational leadership.* Accessed at www.langston.edu/sites /default/files/basic-content-files/TransformationalLeadership.pdf on January 12, 2024.

Lee-St. John, T. J., Walsh, M. E., Raczek, A. E., Vuilleumier, C. E., Foley, C., Heberle, A., et al. (2018). The long-term impact of systemic student support in elementary school: Reducing high school dropout. *AERA Open, 4*(4), 1–16.

Leighton, J. P. (2020). Cognitive diagnosis is not enough: The challenge of measuring learning with classroom assessments. In S. M. Brookhart & J. H. McMillan (Eds.), *Classroom assessment and educational measurement* (pp. 27–45). New York: Routledge.

Lencioni, P. (2002). *The five dysfunctions of a team: A leadership fable.* San Francisco: Jossey-Bass.

Lencioni, P. (2005). *Overcoming the five dysfunctions of a team: A field guide for leaders, managers, and facilitators.* San Francisco: Jossey-Bass.

Lezotte, L. W. (2005). More effective schools: Professional learning communities in action. In R. DuFour, R. Eaker, & R. DuFour (Eds.), *On common ground: The power of professional learning communities* (pp. 177–192). Bloomington, IN: Solution Tree Press.

Lortie, D. C. (2002). *Schoolteacher: A sociological study* (2nd ed.). Chicago: University of Chicago Press.

Mader, J., & Butrymowicz, S. (2014, October 29). *For many with disabilities, special education leads to jail.* Accessed at www.disabilityscoop.com/2014/10/29/for-sped-leads-jail/19800 on July 23, 2024.

Malone, J. (2006, August 17). *Are we a group or a team? 2006 Getting Results Conference— The impact of one, the power of many* [Handout]. Accessed at http://results.ocde.us/downloads /JMalone-Group_Team_Handout.pdf on April 17, 2017.

Many, T. W., Maffoni, M. J., Sparks, S. K., Thomas, T. F., & Greeney, B. (2022). *Energize your teams: Powerful tools for coaching collaborative teams in PLCs at Work.* Bloomington, IN: Solution Tree Press.

Marr, B. (2022). *Future skills: The 20 skills and competencies everyone needs to succeed in a digital world.* Hoboken, NJ: Wiley.

Marzano, R. J. (2003). *What works in schools: Translating research into action.* Arlington, VA: ASCD.

Marzano, R. J. (2010). *Formative assessment and standards-based grading.* Bloomington, IN: Marzano Resources.

Marzano, R. J. (2017). *The new art and science of teaching.* Bloomington, IN: Solution Tree Press.

Marzano, R. J., Heflebower, T., Hoegh, J. K., Warrick, P. B., & Grift, G. (2016). *Collaborative teams that transform schools: The next step in PLCs.* Bloomington, IN: Marzano Resources.

Marzano, R. J., Warrick, P. B., & Acosta, M. I. (2024). *Five big ideas for leading a high reliability school*. Bloomington, IN: Marzano Resources.

Marzano, R. J., Warrick, P. B., Rains, C. L., & DuFour, R. (2018). *Leading a high reliability school*. Bloomington, IN: Solution Tree Press.

MathGives YouPower. (2014, January 3). *Slope dude* [Video file]. Accessed at www.youtube.com /watch?v=ZcSrJPiQvHQ on January 12, 2024.

Mattos, M. (2015). *Making time at Tier 2: Creating a supplemental intervention period in secondary schools* [DVD]. Bloomington, IN: Solution Tree Press.

Mattos, M. (2017). *Timebomb: The cost of dropping out* [DVD]. Bloomington, IN: Solution Tree Press.

Mattos, M., & Buffum, A. (Eds.). (2015). *It's about time: Planning interventions and extensions in secondary school*. Bloomington, IN: Solution Tree Press.

Mattos, M., DuFour, R., DuFour, R., Eaker, R., & Many, T. W. (2016). *Concise answers to frequently asked questions about Professional Learning Communities at Work*. Bloomington, IN: Solution Tree Press.

Mayer, D. P., Mullens, J. E., & Moore, M. T. (2000, December). *Monitoring school quality: An indicators report* (NCES 2001-030). Washington, DC: National Center for Education Statistics. Accessed at https://nces.ed.gov/pubs2001/2001030.pdf on July 23, 2024.

McDonald, J. P., Mohr, N., Dichter, A., & McDonald, E. C. (2003). *The power of protocols: An educator's guide to better practice*. New York: Teachers College Press.

McMillan, J. H. (2020). Discussion of part I: Assessment information in context. In S. M. Brookhart & J. H. McMillan (Eds.), *Classroom assessment and educational measurement* (pp. 79–94). New York: Routledge.

Mehta, J. (2013). Why American education fails: And how lessons from abroad could improve it. *Foreign Affairs, 92*(3). Accessed at www.foreignaffairs.com/articles/united-states/2013-04-03 /why-american-education-fails on December 30, 2015.

Morrison, G. M., Anthony, S., Storino, M., & Dillon, C. (2001). An examination of the disciplinary histories and the individual and educational characteristics of students who participate in an in-school suspension program. *Education and Treatment of Children, 24*(3), 276–293.

Mourshed, M., Chijioke, C., & Barber, M. (2010, November). *How the world's most improved school systems keep getting better*. Chicago: McKinsey & Company. Accessed at www.mckinsey. com/industries/social-sector/our-insights/how-the-worlds-most-improved-school-systems -keep-getting-better on July 23, 2024.

Muhammad, A. (2018). *Transforming school culture: How to overcome staff division* (2nd ed.). Bloomington, IN: Solution Tree Press.

Muhammad, A. (2024). *The way forward: PLC at Work and the bright future of education*. Bloomington, IN: Solution Tree Press.

Muhammad, A., & Cruz, L. F. (2019). *Time for change: Four essential skills for transformational school and district leaders*. Bloomington, IN: Solution Tree Press.

Musgrove, M. (2013, March 7). *Response to Troy Couillard* [Memorandum]. Accessed at https:// sites.ed.gov/idea/files/policy_speced_guid_idea_memosdcltrs_12-011637r-wi-couillard-rti3 -8-13.doc on January 11, 2024.

National Governors Association Center for Best Practices & Council of Chief State School Officers. (2010a). *Common Core State Standards for English language arts and literacy in history/ social studies, science, and technical subjects.* Washington, DC: Authors. Accessed at https:// learning.ccsso.org/wp-content/uploads/2022/11/ELA_Standards1.pdf on April 30, 2024.

National Governors Association Center for Best Practices & Council of Chief State School Officers. (2010b). *Common Core State Standards for mathematics.* Washington, DC: Authors. Accessed at https://learning.ccsso.org/wp-content/uploads/2022/11/ADA-Compliant-Math -Standards.pdf on January 11, 2024.

National Partnership for Teaching in At-Risk Schools. (2005). *Qualified teachers for at-risk schools: A national imperative.* Washington, DC: Author. Accessed at www.ecs.org/clearinghouse/57 /96/5796.pdf on January 11, 2024.

National Working Group on Advanced Education. (2023, June). *Building a wider, more diverse pipeline of advanced learners: Final report of the National Working Group on Advanced Education.* Washington, DC: Thomas B. Fordham Institute. Accessed at https://fordhaminstitute.org /sites/default/files/publication/pdfs/wider-more-diverse-pipeline-advanced-learners-final -report-national-working-group-advanced-education.pdf on April 12, 2024.

Nelson, J. R., Benner, G. J., Lane, K., & Smith, B. W. (2004). Academic achievement of K 12 students with emotional and behavioral disorders. *Exceptional Children, 71*(1), 59–73.

No Child Left Behind (NCLB) Act of 2001, Pub. L. No. 107-110, § 115, Stat. 1425 (2002).

Oakes, J. (2005). *Keeping track: How schools structure inequality* (2nd ed.). New Haven, CT: Yale University Press.

O'Connor, C., & Fernandez, S. D. (2006). Race, class, and disproportionality: Reevaluating the relationship between poverty and special education placement. *Educational Researcher, 35*(6), 6–11.

Organisation for Economic Co-operation and Development. (2014). *Education at a glance 2014: OECD indicators.* Accessed at www.oecd.org/education/education at a glance-2014.pdf on May 28, 2024.

Peterson, D. B., & Hicks, M. D. (1996). *Leader as coach: Strategies for coaching and developing others.* Minneapolis, MN: Personnel Decisions International.

Pierce, C. (2015). *Revised RTI² implementation guide July 2014—State of Tennessee.* Nashville, TN: Tennessee Department of Education. Accessed at www.noexperiencenecessarybook.com /W85Wa/revised-rti2-implementation-guide-july-2014-state-of-tennessee.html on May 8, 2017.

Pink, D. H. (2009). *Drive: The surprising truth about what motivates us.* New York: Riverhead Books.

Powers, K. M., Hagans-Murillo, K. S., & Restori, A. F. (2004). Twenty-five years after Larry P.: The California response to overrepresentation of African Americans in special education. *California School Psychologist, 9*(1), 145–158.

Prasse, D. P. (n.d.). *Why adopt an RTI model?* Accessed at www.rtinetwork.org/learn/what/whyrti on July 23, 2024.

Profession. (n.d.). In *Merriam-Webster's online dictionary.* Accessed at www.merriam-webster.com /dictionary/profession on July 23, 2024.

Proust, M. (1923). *The prisoner* (Vol. 5 of *Remembrance of things past*). Paris: Gallimard.

Reardon, S. F. (2011). The widening academic achievement gap between the rich and the poor: New evidence and possible explanations. In G. J. Duncan & R. J. Murnane (Eds.), *Whither opportunity? Rising inequality, schools, and children's life chances* (pp. 91–116). New York: Russell Sage Foundation.

Reeves, D. B. (2002). *The leader's guide to standards: A blueprint for educational equity and excellence*. San Francisco: Jossey-Bass.

Reeves, D. B. (Ed.). (2008). *Ahead of the curve: The power of assessment to transform teaching and learning*. Bloomington, IN: Solution Tree Press.

Reeves, D. B. (2009a, July 13). In education, standards aren't enough. *The Hill*. Accessed at https://thehill.com/opinion/op-ed/50089-in-education-standards-arent-enough on July 23, 2024.

Reeves, D. B. (2009b). *Leading change in your school: How to conquer myths, build commitment, and get results*. Arlington, VA: ASCD.

Reis, S. M., & Fogarty, E. A. (2006). Savoring reading schoolwide. *Educational Leadership, 64*(2), 32–36.

Roberts, M. (2020a). *Enriching the learning: Meaningful extensions for proficient students in a PLC at Work*. Bloomington, IN: Solution Tree Press.

Roberts, M. (2020b, March 4). Finding your team's foundation with fundamentals [Blog post]. *AllThingsPLC Blog*. Accessed at https://allthingsplc.info/finding-your-teams-foundation-with-fundamentals on April 12, 2024.

Rouse, C. E. (2005, October 24–26). *The labor market consequences of an inadequate education* [Paper presentation]. Teachers College Symposium on Educational Equity, Columbia University, New York.

Ruiz-Primo, M. A., & Brookhart, S. M. (2018). *Using feedback to improve learning*. New York: Routledge.

Ryan, C. S. (n.d.). *Empathy: A critical skill for effective leadership*. Accessed at https://bouncebackhigher.com/articles/empathy-a-critical-skill-for-effective-leadership on January 11, 2024.

Sadler, D. R. (1989). Formative assessment and the design of instructional systems. *Instructional Science, 18*(2), 119–144.

Samuels, C. A. (2010, September 8). *Learning-disabled enrollment dips after long climb*. Accessed at www.edweek.org/teaching-learning/learning-disabled-enrollment-dips-after-long-climb/2010/09 on January 11, 2024.

Santos, J. L., & Haycock, K. (2016). Higher education's critical role in increasing opportunity in America: What boards should know and 10 questions they should ask. *Trusteeship Magazine, 24*(1), 14–20.

Saphier, J. (2005). *John Adams' promise: How to have good schools for all our children, not just for some*. Acton, MA: Research for Better Teaching.

Schermele, Z. (2023, October 17). *Teacher shortages continue to plague US: 86% of public schools struggle to hire educators*. Accessed at www.usatoday.com/story/news/education/2023/10/17/teacher-shortage-2023-us-schools-struggle-hiring/71208579007 on January 11, 2024.

Schimmer, T. (2016). *Grading from the inside out: Bringing accuracy to student assessment through a standards-based mindset*. Bloomington, IN: Solution Tree Press.

Schimmer, T. (2023). *Redefining student accountability: A proactive approach to teaching behavior outside the gradebook.* Bloomington, IN: Solution Tree Press.

Schimmer, T., Knight, M., & Townsley, M. (2024). *Grading reform that lasts: Eight steps to transform your school's assessment culture.* Bloomington, IN: Solution Tree Press.

Schmoker, M. (2011). *Focus: Elevating the essentials to radically improve student learning.* Arlington, VA: ASCD.

Schneider, M. C., Egan, K. L., & Julian, M. W. (2013). Classroom assessment in the context of high-stakes testing. In J. H. McMillan (Ed.), *SAGE handbook of research on classroom assessment* (pp. 55–70). Thousand Oaks, CA: SAGE.

Senge, P. M. (1990). *The fifth discipline: The art and practice of the learning organization.* New York: Doubleday/Currency.

Sergiovanni, T. J. (1996). *Leadership for the schoolhouse: How is it different? Why is it important?* San Francisco: Jossey-Bass.

Sickbert-Bennett, E. E., DiBiase, L. M., Willis, T. M. S., Wolak, E. S., Weber, D. J., & Rutala, W. A. (2016). Reduction of healthcare-associated infections by exceeding high compliance with hand hygiene practices. *Emerging Infectious Diseases, 22*(9), 1628–1630.

Siegle, D., & McCoach, D. B. (2005). Making a difference: Motivating gifted students who are not achieving. *Teaching Exceptional Children, 38*(1), 22–27.

Simmons, D. C., Kame'enui, E. J., Harn, B., Coyne, M. D., Stoolmiller, M., Santoro, L. E., et al. (2007). Attributes of effective and efficient kindergarten reading intervention: An examination of instructional time and design specificity. *Journal of Learning Disabilities, 40*(4), 331–347.

Simms, J. A. (2024). *The Marzano synthesis: A collected guide to what works in K–12 education.* Bloomington, IN: Marzano Resources.

Simonsen, B., Sugai, G., & Negron, M. (2008). Schoolwide positive behavior supports: Primary systems and practices. *Teaching Exceptional Children, 40*(6), 32–40.

Skiba, R. J., Poloni-Staudinger, L., Gallini, S., Simmons, A. B., & Feggins-Azziz, R. (2006). Disparate access: The disproportionality of African American students with disabilities across educational environments. *Exceptional Children, 72*(4), 411–424.

Skiba, R. J., Simmons, A. B., Ritter, S., Gibb, A. C., Rausch, M. K., Cuadrado, J., et al. (2008). Achieving equity in special education: History, status, and current challenges. *Exceptional Children, 74*(3), 264–288.

Smith, M. (2022, November 22). *"It killed my spirit": How 3 teachers are navigating the burnout crisis in education.* Accessed at www.cnbc.com/2022/11/22/teachers-are-in-the-midst-of-a -burnout-crisis-it-became-intolerable.html on January 11, 2024.

Sonju, B., Kramer, S. V., Mattos, M., & Buffum, A. (2019). *Best practices at Tier 2: Supplemental interventions for additional student support, secondary.* Bloomington, IN: Solution Tree Press.

Sparks, D. (2005a). *Leading for results: Transforming teaching, learning, and relationships in schools.* Thousand Oaks, CA: Corwin.

Sparks, D. (2005b). Leading for transformation in teaching, learning, and relationships. In R. DuFour, R. Eaker, & R. DuFour (Eds.), *On common ground: The power of professional learning communities* (pp. 155–176). Bloomington, IN: Solution Tree Press.

Sparks, S. D. (2015, November 6). *Study: RTI practice falls short of promise.* Accessed at www .edweek.org/teaching-learning/study-rti-practice-falls-short-of-promise/2015/11 on January 11, 2024.

Sparks, S. D. (2022a, October 24). *Explaining that steep drop in math scores on NAEP: 5 takeaways.* Accessed at www.edweek.org/teaching-learning/explaining-that-steep-drop-in-math-scores-on -naep-5-takeaways/2022/10 on April 25, 2024.

Sparks, S. D. (2022b, October 24). *5 things to know about the slide in reading achievement.* Accessed at www.edweek.org/teaching-learning/5-things-to-know-about-the-slide-in-reading -achievement-on-naep/2022/10 on May 6, 2024.

Sparks, S. K. (2008). Creating intentional collaboration. In C. Erkens, C. Jakicic, L. G. Jessie, D. King, S. V. Kramer, T. W. Many, et al., *The collaborative teacher: Working together as a professional learning community* (pp. 31–55). Bloomington, IN: Solution Tree Press.

Spring, J. (2001). *The American school, 1642–2000* (5th ed.). New York: McGraw-Hill.

Stanford, L. (2023, October 6). *Students are missing school because they're too anxious to show up.* Accessed at www.edweek.org/leadership/students-are-missing-school-because-theyre-too -anxious-to-show-up/2023/10 on January 11, 2024.

Statista. (2023, November 3). *U.S. poverty rate 2022, by education level.* Accessed at www.statista .com/statistics/233162/us-poverty-rate-by-education on January 26, 2024.

Stiggins, R. (2007). Assessment through the student's eyes. *Educational Leadership, 64*(8). Accessed at www.ascd.org/el/articles/assessment-through-the-students-eyes on January 11, 2024.

Stuart, T. S., Heckmann, S., Mattos, M., & Buffum, A. (2018). *Personalized learning in a PLC at Work: Student agency through the four critical questions.* Bloomington, IN: Solution Tree Press.

Tavernise, S. (2012, February 9). *Education gap grows between rich and poor, studies say.* Accessed at www.nytimes.com/2012/02/10/education/education-gap-grows-between-rich-and-poor -studies-show.html on July 23, 2024.

Teachers College Press. (n.d.). *Protocols.* Accessed at www.tcpress.com/filebin/PDFs/mcdonaldprot .pdf on July 25, 2024.

Tomlinson, C. A. (2000). *Differentiation of instruction in the elementary grades.* Accessed at https://files.eric.ed.gov/fulltext/ED443572.pdf on January 11, 2024.

Tomlinson, C. A., & McTighe, J. (2006). *Integrating differentiated instruction and understanding by design: Connecting content and kids.* Arlington, VA: ASCD.

UNESCO. (2022, February 8). *COVID-19 educational disruption and response.* Accessed at www .iiep.unesco.org/en/covid-19-educational-disruption-and-response-13363 on May 6, 2024.

U.S. Bureau of Labor Statistics. (2019, September 11). *44.6 percent of high school dropouts and 72.3 percent of college graduates employed in August 2019.* Accessed at www.bls.gov/opub /ted/2019/44-6-percent-of-high-school-dropouts-and-72-3-percent-of-college-graduates -employed-in-august-2019.htm on January 29, 2024.

Vagle, N. (2009). Finding the meaning in numbers. In T. Guskey (Ed.), *The principal as assessment leader* (Reissue ed.; pp. 149–173). Bloomington, IN: Solution Tree.

Vaughn, S., Linan-Thompson, S., & Hickman, P. (2003). Response to instruction as a means of identifying students with reading/learning disabilities. *Exceptional Children, 69*(4), 391–409.

Vaughn, S., & Roberts, G. (2007). Secondary interventions in reading: Providing additional instruction for students at risk. *Teaching Exceptional Children, 39*(5), 40–46.

Vellutino, F. R., Scanlon, D. M., Zhang, H., & Schatschneider, C. (2008). Using response to kindergarten and first grade intervention to identify children at-risk for long-term reading difficulties. *Reading and Writing, 21*(4), 437–480.

Webb, N. L. (2002, March 28). *Depth-of-knowledge levels for four content areas.* Accessed at http://ossucurr.pbworks.com/w/file/fetch/49691156/Norm%20web%20dok%20by%20 subject%20area.pdf on January 12, 2024.

White, K. (2017). *Softening the edges: Assessment practices that honor K–12 teachers and learners.* Bloomington, IN: Solution Tree Press.

White, S. H. (2011). *Beyond the numbers: Making data work for teachers and school leaders* (2nd ed.). Englewood, CO: Lead + Learn Press.

Wikiquote. (n.d.). *W. Edwards Deming.* Accessed at https://en.wikiquote.org/wiki/W._Edwards _Deming on April 12, 2024.

Wiliam, D. (2009). An integrative summary of the research literature and implications for a new theory of formative assessment. In H. L. Andrade & G. J. Cizek (Eds.), *Handbook of formative assessment* (pp. 18–40). New York: Routledge.

Wiliam, D. (2018). *Embedded formative assessment* (2nd ed.). Bloomington, IN: Solution Tree Press.

Wiliam, D., & Leahy, S. (2015). *Embedding formative assessment: Practical techniques for K–12 classrooms.* West Palm Beach, FL: Learning Sciences International.

Will, M. (2022, December 16). *The teaching profession in 2022 (in charts).* Accessed at www .edweek.org/teaching-learning/the-teaching-profession-in-2022-in-charts/2022/12 on January 11, 2024.

Willis, J., Adie, L., Addison, B., & Kimber, M. (2023). Students drawing conclusions about assessment to inform school change. *Cambridge Journal of Education, 53*(6), 779–801.

Wyner, J. S., Bridgeland, J. M., & Dilulio, J. J., Jr. (2007, September). *Achievement trap: How America is failing millions of high-achieving students from lower-income families.* Lansdowne, VA: Jack Kent Cooke Foundation. Accessed at www.jkcf.org/assets/1/7/Achievement_Trap .pdf on July 23, 2024.

YouthTruth. (2022, Fall). *Insights from the student experience, part I: Emotional and mental health.* Cambridge, MA: Center for Effective Philanthropy. Accessed at https://youthtruthsurvey .org/wp-content/uploads/2023/07/EMH_2022.pdf on January 26, 2024.

Zimmerman, B. J., & Schunk, D. H. (Eds.). (2003). *Educational psychology: A century of contributions.* New York: Routledge.

INDEX

The Big Book of Tools for RTI at Work™
William M. Ferriter, Mike Mattos, and Rob J. Meyer

In *The Big Book of Tools for RTI at Work™*, William M. Ferriter, Mike Mattos, and Rob J. Meyer deliver a robust set of tools for teachers and leaders to employ on their journey to implementing effective additional support for struggling students. Practical and full of resources, this book supplies educators with the means to transform their school response to intervention process and create a highly effective multitiered system of supports.
BKG132

Behavior Academies
Jessica Djabrayan Hannigan and John Hannigan

With student behavioral problems and teacher turnover at all-time highs, educators need behavioral interventions that work. With its practical behavior intervention method, this book replaces problematic behaviors with essential life skills for school and beyond. Educators can implement effective targeted interventions in twenty-five minutes or less using eight predefined behavior academies and a process to create their own.
BKG114

Behavior Solutions
John Hannigan, Jessica Djabrayan Hannigan, Mike Mattos, and Austin Buffum

When students' behavioral, emotional, and social needs are met, they excel in school and in life. Take strategic action to begin closing the systemic behavior gap with the guidance of *Behavior Solutions*. This user-friendly resource outlines how to utilize the PLC at Work® and RTI at Work™ processes to create a three-tiered system of supports that is collaborative, research-based, and practical.
BKF891

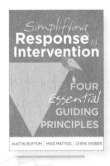

Simplifying Response to Intervention
Austin Buffum, Mike Mattos, and Chris Weber

The follow-up to *Pyramid Response to Intervention* advocates that a successful RTI model begins by asking the right questions to create a fundamentally effective learning environment for every student. RTI is not a series of implementation steps, but rather a way of thinking. Understand why bureaucratic, paperwork-heavy, compliance-oriented, test-score-driven approaches fail. Then learn how to create a focused RTI model that works.
BKF506

Best Practices at Tier 1, 2, 3 Series
The research is conclusive: response to intervention (RTI) is the best way to respond when students don't learn. With the support of this essential series, you'll discover how to implement a multitiered system of interventions strong enough to help every learner succeed. Together, the books deliver a complete toolkit of practices and strategies for providing essential K–12 support at all three tiers of the RTI at Work™ process.
BKF650, BKF651, BKF714, BKF715, BKF747, BKF748

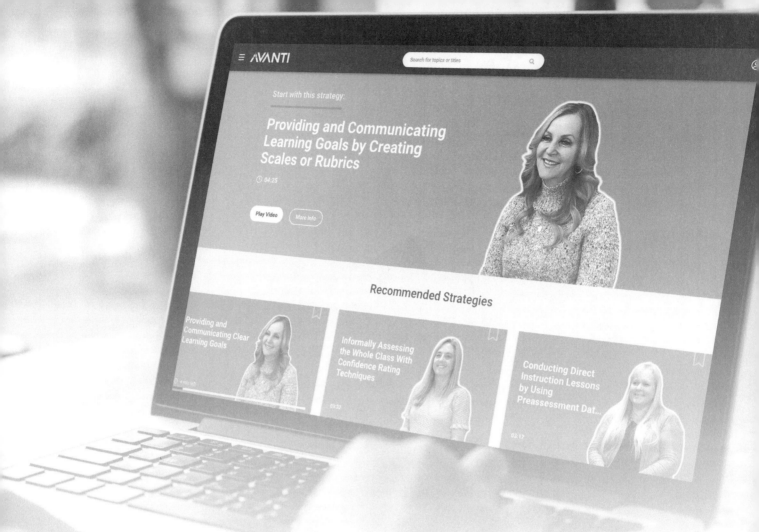